MW01127650

WHY CONFEDER★TES FOUGHT

CIVIL WAR AMERICA

Gary W. Gallagher, editor

WHY CONFEDER★TES FOUGHT

Family and Nation in Civil War Virginia

Aaron Sheehan-Dean

The University of
North Carolina Press
Chapel Hill

© 2007 The University of North Carolina Press
All rights reserved
Designed by Kimberly Bryant
Set in Scala by Keystone Typesetting, Inc.
Manufactured in the United States of America

This book was published with the assistance of the Fred W. Morrison
Fund for Southern Studies of the University of North Carolina Press.

Library of Congress Cataloging-in-Publication Data
Sheehan-Dean, Aaron Charles.
Why confederates fought : family and nation in Civil War Virginia /
Aaron Sheehan-Dean.
p. cm. — (Civil War America)
Includes bibliographical references and index.
ISBN 978-0-8078-3158-8 (cloth : alk. paper)
1. Virginia—History—Civil War, 1861–1865—Social aspects. 2. Soldiers—Virginia—
Social conditions—19th century. 3. Soldiers—Virginia—Family relationships—
History—19th century. 4. Family—Virginia—History—19th century. 5. Nationalism—
Virginia—History—19th century. 6. Social classes—Virginia—History—19th century.
7. War and society—Virginia—History—19th century. 8. Virginia—Social
conditions—19th century. 9. Nationalism—Confederate States of America—History.
10. United States—History—Civil War, 1861–1865—Social aspects. I. Title.
E581.S54 2007
975.5'03—dc22   2007019498

Portions of this work appeared earlier, in somewhat different form, as
"Everyman's War: Confederate Enlistment in Civil War Virginia," *Civil War
History* 50 (March 2004); " 'It Is Old Virginia and We Must Have It': Overcoming
Regionalism in Civil War Virginia," in *Crucible of the Civil War: Virginia from Secession
to Commemoration*, ed. Edward L. Ayers, Gary W. Gallagher, and Andrew Torget
(Charlottesville: University of Virginia Press, 2006); "Justice Has Something to Do
with It: Class Relations and the Confederate Army," *Virginia Magazine of History and
Biography* 113 (December 2005); and "Success Is So Blended with Defeat: Virginia
Soldiers in the Shenandoah Valley," *The Shenandoah Valley Campaign of 1864*, ed.
Gary W. Gallagher (Chapel Hill: University of North Carolina Press, 2006), and are
reprinted here with permission.

11 10 09 08 07   5 4 3 2 1

THIS BOOK WAS DIGITALLY PRINTED.

For My Mother & the Memory of My Father

CONTENTS

ILLUSTRATIONS, MAPS, TABLES, & FIGURES

ACKNOWLEDGMENTS

History is often said to be a solitary pursuit—so much time sitting in archives and writing alone. I am happy that my experience has been otherwise. From the beginning of graduate school through to my current position at the University of North Florida, collegiality and camaraderie have defined my development as a historian. Accordingly, it is with profound gratitude that I take this opportunity to thank those people who helped me complete this project. I would like to express my appreciation to the staffs of the special collections departments at the following institutions: the University of Virginia, the Virginia Military Institute, Duke University, the Library of Virginia, the Henry E. Huntington Library, the U.S. Army Military History Institute at Carlisle Barracks, the Southern Historical Collection at the University of North Carolina, Chapel Hill, and, most of all, the Virginia Historical Society. I would also like to thank Mary Roy Edwards, who graciously arranged for me to include the images of John and Mary Jones.

The Virginia Historical Society granted me a Mellon Fellowship to support my research in its massive and remarkably well-documented holdings on Civil War Virginia. Frances Pollard and Nelson Lankford ensured that the week was productive and enjoyable. Charles Bryan organized an opportunity for me to share my research with the knowledgeable staff there in what proved to be a timely incentive for me to organize my thoughts. My thanks to them all. A Fletcher Jones fellowship from the Henry E. Huntington Library provided a month of research and writing time in Pasadena. Susi Krasnoo expertly facilitated my visit. John Rhodehamel guided me through the Huntington's trove of resources. My thanks to them and to Robert Ritchie for the financial support and for creating such a dynamic and inspiring program for scholars. I received financial support from a variety of sources at the University of Virginia, including travel money from the Corcoran Department of History and the Graduate School. Most importantly, a Dissertation Year Teaching Fellowship awarded by the Faculty Senate made the last year of writing possible. I would also like to thank Mary Jane Barnwell, Elizabeth Bradley, and the staff at the Island Bookstore in Mackinaw City, Michigan, where a good part of this book was composed.

The Office of Academic Affairs at the University of North Florida provided important financial support that helped me finish revisions on the manuscript. I am grateful to the current provost, Mark Workman, and to my former and current chairs—Dale Clifford and Dan Schafer—all of whom have supported my work at UNF. As chair for my first three years at UNF, Dale has read much of my work and helped me learn how to be a historian, in all senses of the word. I have benefited from her criticism of my writing and especially from her willingness to explain the vagaries of our institution and the profession of history. It would be hard to imagine a more supportive group of colleagues than those I have been fortunate to join at UNF. They have encouraged me to write, tutored me in teaching, and generally provided the guidance that every novice academic should receive. My deep thanks to Dan Schafer, David Courtwright, Tom Leonard, Theo Prousis, Betty Furdell, Carolyn Williams, Michael Francis, Phil Kaplan, Harry Rothschild, Charles Closmann, and David Sheffler.

At the University of Virginia, Mark Thomas tutored me in quantitative methodology and Stephen Cushman encouraged me to always question the narrative. At UVa's Geospatial and Statistical Data Center, Mike Furlough and Blair Tinker provided patient instruction in the use of geographic information systems. My friends at the Virginia Center for Digital History provided continual support. Will Thomas served as a tireless advocate, generous critic, and good friend. Kim Tryka offered technical support on a range of topics and moral support whenever needed. Bill Wilson of the University of North Florida provided timely assistance in the construction of my sample, particularly in the arcane science of determining sample sizes. In the early years of this project, Barb Guglielmo fielded what felt like weekly panicked phone calls with naive questions about statistical methodology. I am grateful for her patient and always helpful advice.

I was fortunate to enter UVa with a remarkable group of people intent on studying U.S. history in the friendliest and most supportive atmosphere possible, and Megan and I have cherished the lasting friendships formed in Charlottesville. In particular, Charles Irons, Brian Schoen, Susanna Lee, Watson Jennison, Johann Neem, Carl Bon Tempo, and Kristin Celello provided support, encouragement, spirited discussions, and plenty of good food. Amy Feely Morsman deserves special praise for responding to endless queries about southern history. Johann and Kate hosted me on several return trips to Charlottesville, where their companionship and insights proved more valuable assets than even their spare bedroom. The Horn Family—Jolee, Doug, Emily, and Callie—opened their home to our family for several summers and allowed me to finish research while our kids played in the pool. Even with this book completed, they will remain a special part of our summers.

Michael Holt guided me through a master's essay on Reconstruction and generously continued to read and critique my work long after I had switched to studying the war years. Ed Ayers provided astute advice since I first arrived at UVa. He instructed me in the art of writing history and in the practice of digital humanities, all the while providing a probably unattainable model of scholarly achievement and teaching prowess. Joe Miller inspired a vision for how and why to study history that informs all of my work. He has proved to be my toughest critic, a valued adviser, and a good friend. Gary Gallagher offered everything that a graduate student could ask of an adviser. He has given encouragement without pressure, sage advice on the practice and profession of history, and patient instruction in the pursuit of graceful prose. His humor leavened the seriousness of graduate school, and his seriousness has helped me learn to be a historian. I am profoundly grateful for the good fortune to have worked with him and for the friendship that has developed out of that work.

A number of historians commented on parts of this work at conferences. Although they may not recognize the finished work, their insights helped me shape the project. Thanks to Joe Glatthaar, Lesley Gordon, Michael Parrish, John Willis, LeeAnn Whites, Jim Marten, and John Neff. Peter Carmichael has read this manuscript more times than he would have preferred, but each time it emerged stronger as a result of his ideas and questions. I value both his insights and his friendship. I am grateful for the close reading that the manuscript received from George Rable. He challenged the logic where it was flawed and helped me clarify the writing throughout. Late in the process, Jennifer Trueman Resek bravely volunteered to read the whole manuscript. I sincerely appreciate her useful comments and generous encouragement. Every writer should be so lucky to have readers who take their work as seriously as mine did. At the UNC Press, my thanks to Brian MacDonald, whose expert eye strengthened the manuscript considerably. My deep thanks to Zach Read, Ron Maner, and most of all David Perry, who helped make this book a reality.

Most important of all has been the support I received from my family. The various members of the Sheehan clan have continued to feign interest in the Civil War for many years longer than necessary and provided welcome breaks from work with visits and vacations. The rest of my family has read conference papers and listened to lectures and loved me anyway. Thanks to

Ruthie, Jake, Jon, Anand, and Kimberley for all they have done. Megan has supported me through all of our adventures together. She has taught me how to teach, how to parent, and helped me live every moment of life to its fullest. Liam and Annie have added to the joy in my life and have reminded me, often hourly, of the necessity of balancing my family time with the my professional pursuits. I owe my love of learning, and the skills to satisfy that desire, to my parents. It is to my mother and the memory of my father that I dedicate this work.

WHY CONFEDER★TES FOUGHT

Introduction ✶ CHOOSING WAR

Despite the massive volume of writing on the American Civil War, one of the fundamental questions about it continues to bedevil us. Why did nonslaveholders sacrifice so much to build a slave republic? Nonslaveholders' commitment was not marginal; they formed the vast majority of soldiers who fought on behalf of the Confederacy. Nor was slavery a tangential concern to the conflict; the political debate over slavery and its expansion drove the North and South to arms, and the shift to emancipation by the North ensured a desolating war. Though relatively brief in comparison to other nineteenth-century wars, the Civil War generated catastrophic losses for both sides. What facilitated the level of division and destruction witnessed in this war? In what follows, I answer this question by exploring the inspirations that compelled Confederate soldiers into the war and sustained them in the face of horrific losses. Inspirations is not too strong or romantic a word; southern white men felt moved to enlist by a host of personal, familial, communal, religious, and national obligations. Similarly, the decision to reenlist or remain in service was not undertaken lightly. Southern men drew on a variety of motivations when they considered why they needed to resist the North's efforts to recreate the Union. Understanding how those motivations developed offers insight into what leads human beings to support a war and fight in it.

Despite the increasing cost of the war to southern civilians and soldiers, white Virginians grew increasingly committed to the Confederacy and to the Confederate war goals of establishing independence and maintaining slavery. This study explains that seemingly contrary interpretation. It focuses on soldiers and their families, tracing the evolving motivations that inspired the war and prolonged the fighting. My goal has been to analyze how men understood the purpose of the war and how those understandings changed over time.

White Virginians did not enter the war out of a sense of deference to the slaveholding elite who composed the state's political leadership. Instead, Virginia Confederates entered the war with a host of overlapping motivations, including a defense of home, a belief in state rights, and a desire to protect slavery. An independent Confederacy promised the perpetuation of all that white Virginians found rewarding about their antebellum world. During the war, Virginians refined their explanations of why they fought. Virginia soldiers developed a genuine attachment to the Confederate nation, and this inspired their service. Likewise, the Union's hard-war policy, because it exposed soldiers' families to hardships and occupation, strengthened the commitment to keep fighting. Emancipation, in particular, clarified the consequences of defeat for Confederates and demanded a vigorous defense of slavery.

As the war's toll on both soldiers and civilians rose, men placed increasing importance on their emotional ties with family members, even as the violence of the war alienated them from the values of home. Over time, Virginia soldiers issued clearer and stronger justifications for staying in service in terms of their families and their interests. This perspective ensured that the longer the war lasted, the less likely men were to consider rejoining the Union. Instead, they vigorously defended southern society, especially slavery and racial hierarchy, in order to protect their families. Because Confederate soldiers participated fully in both the battlefront and the home front, they did not distinguish the political nation from the domestic nation. At times, the obligations of family and nation conflicted with one another, but Virginians increasingly saw a harmony of interests between their dual responsibilities, and this perception inspired a determined pursuit of Confederate independence.

This study began as an attempt to answer the question of which Virginians fought for the Confederacy, hoping that would provide an answer to the debate among Civil War historians about whether class grievances encouraged people to abandon the Confederate cause. I anticipated that social conflict, especially between slaveholders and nonslaveholders, played a signal role in Confederate defeat, but the evidence led in another direction. In the case of Virginia, the Confederate military drew wide support, from rich and poor men, from urban and rural men, from Democrats and Whigs, from slaveholders and nonslaveholders. Recognizing this, I focused my attention on explaining why so many Virginians supported independence. Because almost all of the men who fought the Civil War volunteered, and because they functioned as the most tangible link between the home front and battlefronts, soldiers compose one of the most useful groups to study in order to understand the changes people wrought on their worlds through the waging of war. The men who filled the Confederate armies were soldier citizens. Their new military habits and responsibilities modified but never supplanted their base identities as citizens, fathers, husbands, and sons. Setting soldiers' wartime experiences within the context of their family, community, and military networks to explore how they accommodated the changing fortunes of the Confederacy demands a dynamic model of inspiration and commitment.[1] Such an approach helps explain why the war lasted as long as it did and why it took such a high human toll. It also reveals that Virginia Confederates sustained the war for different reasons than the ones for which they began it.

One important index of the willingness of Virginians to support the Confederacy can be seen in the massive mobilization of men to serve in Confederate armed forces; nearly 90 percent of military-age men in those parts of Virginia controlled by the Confederacy served in the army.[2] This figure does not indicate a unanimous endorsement of all the Confederate war aims or all the policies pursued by the state and national governments during the conflict. Neither does it prove that all Virginians believed uniformly in Confederate victory at all moments during the war. However, the enlistment rate in the state does reveal a broad commitment to the cause of Confederate independence. Equally important, in terms of evaluating the effort Virginians made to achieve Confederate independence, is the evidence on desertion patterns in the state. Among Virginia soldiers, desertion peaked in 1862, in response to anger over the Draft Act, and declined thereafter.[3] The longer the conflict extended in time, the less likely Virginia men were to leave the Confederate army. Virginians came slowly and reluctantly to secession, but once they left the Union, most white citizens desired and sought permanent separation from the North.

The argument that white Virginians strengthened their attachments to the Confederacy over time runs counter to a current perception that white southerners, especially lower- and middle-class civilians, eventually abandoned their decision to separate from the North.[4] In considering why Virginians initiated the war, three elements of antebellum Virginia form an especially important backdrop for understanding the decisions of soldiers and their families during the war. The first is the one that historians typically focus on: southern white men lived within a liberal, rights-based democracy that granted them wide autonomy in political decision making.[5] In the decade before the war, Virginians removed the last property-holding restrictions on voting and officeholding, made more positions elected rather than appointed, and established greater parity between the eastern and western sections of the state. These changes empowered white men by increasing their influence within the political system. While the expansion of political liberties in prewar Virginia hampered the ability of the Confederate government to coerce men's participation in the defense of the nation, that same expansion stimulated those men to preserve their hard-won rights. The extension of democracy gave white men a language with which they could define the war as a principled defense of individual liberty.

The second element plays a prominent role in the literature on antebellum Virginia but rarely figures in wartime explanations: the late antebellum period was economically productive for many Virginians. The prosperity of the 1850s convinced white southerners that their society was both dynamic and competitive and ensured among them a strong commitment to sustaining the status quo.[6] The success of the late antebellum era rested on the sophisticated management of the human resources of Virginia. In particular, the sale or employment of slaves in a wide variety of occupations facilitated much of the economic growth in the Old Dominion in the years before the war.[7] In spite of the ways that war exacerbated class divisions within the South, nonslaveholding whites supported the Confederacy because it protected both their racial privileges and economic interests.

The third context crucial for understanding Virginians' decisions to support the Confederacy was the rise of companionate marriage in the late eighteenth and early nineteenth centuries. In contrast to the older patriarchal conception of marriage where loyalty to the father was assumed as an expression of the natural order, love and respect formed the basis for companionate marriages. The shift from older, more authoritarian models of parenting to the newer, more egalitarian approaches was not uniform across all levels of society or even within individual families. Many fathers adopted patriarchal and loving practices without regard for the contradictions they entailed. Nevertheless, historians have demonstrated that during this period men came to value intimate family relations as the highest goal of life, or at least as worthy a goal as participation in the political and economic spheres.[8] Emotional connections made life rewarding on a daily basis. Evangelical churches increased the psychological reward and social support for this shift by strongly sanctioning domestic families. From within these families, soldiers made their decisions to enlist, serve, or desert. In Virginia, the pressures of military service encouraged men to identify their families' immediate and future well-being as the most important reason to participate in the war.

Once the war began, unpredictable events interacted with one another, leading Virginians to develop new understandings of the purpose of the war. Despite the considerable difficulties the conflict imposed upon both soldiers and their families, the war drove most white Virginians away from the Union and toward the Confederacy. The sequence of military encounters in Virginia and their outcomes emboldened Confederates. The victory at Bull Run, the repulse of McClellan's army outside Richmond in 1862, and the successive invasions of the North launched by Robert E. Lee convinced Confederates that southern independence was assured. Not until the middle of 1864 did northern forces achieve anything like a clear victory over Confederates in Virginia and even after the Overland campaign, Grant's army seemed immobile outside Petersburg. The pattern of military encounters in the state impressed upon white residents the capability and integrity of Confederate soldiers and their cause.

Conversely, Virginia Confederates saw in the destruction and violence wrought upon the state's places and people by the northern army clear evidence of Yankees' barbarism. Residents and soldiers watched as roving armies destroyed farms, fields, factories, and railroads. Each building destroyed by northern forces alienated another community of Virginians. Union troops occupied villages, towns, cities, and whole regions, invading and taking possession of private homes and, eventually, waging a hard war that included the destruction of any resources that could sustain an army in the field. A hard war may have successfully starved the Confederate armies, but it nourished Confederate hatred of the North.[9]

The most egregious aspect of the North's hard war, from the perspective of white southerners, was emancipation. From the first weeks of the war, enslaved southerners began seeking their freedom by flight or took advantage of the chaotic conditions on the home front to attain greater autonomy. White southerners resisted this process vigorously. Civilians determinedly maintained slavery as well as they could, continuing to own, rent, sell, and buy slaves throughout the whole of the war. Lee's army transformed itself into a giant slave patrol during its campaigns into Maryland and Pennsylvania in 1862 and 1863. Quite unintentionally, Lincoln's Emancipation Proclamation redefined the terms of the war for the South every bit as much as it did for the North. Although most Confederates assumed that Lincoln longed to end slavery, the enactment of his policy still shocked many white southerners. With the North publicly fighting to end slavery after January 1, 1863, the South automatically became its defender. The northern pursuit of emancipation precipitated a full-fledged defense of slavery by all classes of white Confederates, something that would have been impossible just a decade before when white Virginians argued among themselves about the appropriate place for the institution within the state.

The hardships imposed by emancipation, invasion, and occupation generated a sense of shared sacrifice among white Virginians. Soldiers began conceptualizing their military service and the deaths of their comrades as evidence of their devotion to the nation in early 1862. From this point on, the language of civic pride and patriotic devotion figured prominently in both public and private discussions of death. When civilians experienced hardships attributable to Union military action, they joined the pantheon of Confederate heroes. The most famous instance of this process was at Fredericksburg, where thousands of residents fled the city in advance of the Union occupation in December 1862. The resulting devastation practiced by Federal troops generated intense sympathy for Fredericksburg civilians all across the South. Communities across Virginia suffered through similar experiences, and residents around the state joined what one historian has called a "democracy of devastation."[10]

This is not to argue that white Virginians expressed a perfect solidarity. Far from it. The strains and necessities of war exacerbated the fault lines already present in antebellum Virginia society and created new ones. In particular, the privation experienced by civilians and the imposition of tight restrictions on soldiers inflamed class antagonisms. At a number of times during the war, social and political tensions within the state threatened to substantially impede the ability of the Confederacy to function. In late 1861 and early 1862 soldiers protested vigorously over the imposition of a national draft. In late 1862 deprivation and suffering on the home front inspired serious criticism of state and Confederate leaders. In the spring of 1863 Richmond became the focal point for public anger over food shortages. By late 1864 soldiers and civilians expressed an increasing frustration with the course of the war. At each of these points, soldiers and their families conveyed deep reservations about the process of the war, but events convinced most white Virginians that supporting the Confederacy remained the best strategy. Although class tensions were omnipresent through the conflict, in Virginia they did not fatally disrupt people's support for the Confederacy.

The ability of Virginia's Confederates to manage the strains of wartime life depended partly on how soldiers and their families understood and explained the purpose of the conflict. As men refined their inspirations for fighting over time, they created a new language to express their commitment to Confederate independence. In place of the political conceptualizations common early in the conflict, Virginians developed an explanation for fighting that expressed itself most clearly through the men's involvement in their families. Over the course of the 1830s, 1840s, and 1850s, white men had come to identify the interests and beliefs of their families as a strong determinant on their behavior, equal in many cases to the interests of state or nation.

The Confederacy generated wide support because, at the individual level, Virginians understood their family interests and the goals of the new nation as being in harmony. The Union's hard war reinforced this synthesis. Though it ultimately made Union victory possible, hard-war tactics also inspired greater devotion among Confederate soldiers, who sought revenge for the hardship and destruction experienced by Confederate noncombatants. Men who enlisted as soldiers envisioned the Confederate armies as protectors of their families. They were not alone in this belief. Family members at home, even many of those living in occupied areas, felt the same way and so supported the decision of men to join and fight in the armies.[11]

Explaining why men fought the Civil War requires attention to three elements of the historians' craft that are easy to lose track of in a war. The first challenge requires that we remember the context within which people at the time experienced the event. This task is particularly demanding in the case of the Civil War because the general story and, more importantly, the outcome are known to most Americans. Hindsight hinders our ability to conceptualize the flow of events and their meaning as participants in history lived it. This historical distance makes it doubly difficult to appreciate the ways that people at the time understood and explained their own actions. While it is certainly true that simple answers to the question of why men fought, such as "for their way of life" or "for freedom," or even "for independence," conceal the reality of slavery, hierarchy, and inequality in the southern social order, it is equally true that people at the time incorporated the oppressive elements of the antebellum South within abstract frameworks such as democracy, self-determination, and cultural autonomy. The fact that we value these abstractions but not the uses to which Confederates put them complicates matters still more.

An accurate picture of how participants experienced the Civil War also demands close attention to chronology. As the conflict developed, people on both sides changed their conceptions of what the war meant and how it should be fought. Historians today can demonstrate quite clearly that midway through the war the North added emancipation to its existing war goal of reunion. For Virginia Confederates, the change was a gradual one, as they developed an increasingly clear sense of their new country and the responsibilities they owed to it as citizens.

The importance of both time and place in crafting an explanation for southerners' participation in the Confederacy demands a chronological and geographic focus. Several elements suggest the relevance of the Virginia experience. Situated along the border with the Union and containing a large number of diehard Unionists, Virginia offers an ideal place to examine questions of loyalty. Second, Virginia was subject to repeated invasions and occupations by the Union army throughout the war, thus making it an excellent place to analyze how soldiers and civilians responded to a hard war.[12] Third, the vast majority of Virginia soldiers served in armies in the state, although many of them fought in places quite removed from their homes. Virginia thus provides the opportunity to explore both the overlap between defense of home and nation and those occasions when soldiers fighting in one section had to rely on other men to repel a Union invasion of their homes.

The characteristics of Virginia's Civil War experience suggest that the state was both unique and typical of the larger Confederate experience. As the site of the Confederate capital, as the place where much of the Civil War was fought, and as the state that sent the most men to fight for the Confederacy, Virginia merits attention on its own. In addition, the example of Virginia is valuable because the features of the war upon which this story focuses occurred elsewhere. The Union invasion and occupation of Tennessee mirrors that of Virginia, and that state, like Virginia, sent high numbers of men to fight. It may well be that an investigation of Tennessee soldiers would yield findings similar to those reached here.[13] Some parts of the Deep South—especially Georgia and South Carolina in 1864–65—experienced comparable hardships. Recent studies of these regions indicate that civilians there reacted much like the pro-Confederate Virginians chronicled here.[14] Any study based on a single state possesses limitations, and this study is no exception. Nonetheles, an investigation of soldiers and their families rooted in the soil of the Old Dominion enriches our understanding of an important theater of war and suggests new ways of thinking about the experiences of people in similar situations.

The last element that structures this study is a focus on those people who strove to make the South independent. War, perhaps more than any other human activity, invites explanations that ignore individuals. Even the best histories often treat wars as animate objects with drives, sensibilities, and intentions.[15] This study proceeds from the assumption that people and their decisions change history, and, consequently, the focus throughout is on the people who made war.[16] This study shows the changes in how Virginia Confederates experienced the war. Much of the writing on Civil War soldiers has tended to flatten out the extent to which soldiers' beliefs and actions changed over time.[17] Soldiers' physical investment in the creation of the Confederacy requires that we understand their perspectives on the war. This is not to deny the important role played by civilians, both men and women, black and white, in facilitating or inhibiting the development of the Confederacy. On the contrary, because most soldiers were volunteers, rather than professional military men, they remained intimately connected to their home communities. Thus, any study of soldiers must be rooted in the places from which they came and must elaborate the connections soldiers sustained with those places through the duration of the war. The Confederate experience of war was defined by the tension between competing forces. In Virginia, soldiers and their families sought balance between home front demands and military operations, between emotions and ideology, and between personal loyalties and state and national allegiance.

One of the central problems that historians have struggled with over the past two decades has been the extent to which the Confederacy existed as an independent nation. Its brief existence—just four years and two months— weighs against it, as do the considerable cleavages that existed among its citizens, divided as they were by race, region, class, gender, and culture. Substantial evidence reveals that serious conflict existed in the wartime South, but anger over state policies or dissatisfaction with state leaders does not prove that Confederates disavowed the struggle for autonomy. Important too is the skepticism of current historians that white southerners, especially nonslaveholders, would fully invest themselves in a slaveholding republic, although there is less concern about the extent to which northern soldiers did the same thing when they enlisted in U.S. forces in 1861. Nonetheless, historians in recent years have generally concluded that the Confederacy itself was a viable nation, although they disagree on the question of how nationalistic its citizens were.[18]

At the beginning of the war and periodically throughout it, Virginia soldiers expressed their motivation for fighting in purely nationalistic terms. Over time, they described their motivation in terms of the specific interests that Confederate independence would protect. Soldiers' refinement of the purposes of fighting grew out of the experience of the war and demonstrated the flexibility of Confederate nationalism over time. Within the context of the Confederacy, nationalism encompassed different claims and needs at different times for different people. Some people advocated a racial or ethnic identity for the nation, some pursued a new mode of political organization, some envisioned the chance to build a nation founded on God's will, while still others identified an opportunity to create a southern style of economic development unhindered by attachment to the North. Recent studies of northern nationalism have emphasized its capaciousness; the same seems true for the Confederacy.[19] The Confederacy derived support from most white southerners because it protected a wide array of their cherished values. Primarily, Confederates wanted to retain those aspects of the antebellum South, including slavery and local autonomy, that afforded them comfortable and rewarding lives.

Virginia Confederates constructed a nationalism built up out of nested loyalties to families, religion, communities, regions, the state, and finally the country.[20] Samuel Moore, a soldier in the 2nd Virginia Infantry, explained this convergence succinctly. "That my duty to my Country, my family, my neighbors, myself, all unite in requiring me to be just where I am," he wrote his wife, "a soldier in our noble army, ready to do and die in the cause of liberty."[21] Because of the state's position on the border and the extensive fighting within it, in most cases the demands of local, state, and national identity blurred together in Virginia. The language used to describe this system rarely reflected its constituent parts. Instead, Virginians spoke and wrote about family and state loyalty even as they practiced a vigorous nationalism. During most of the Civil War, the demands and responsibilities of all their different loyalties required the same action from Virginia's white men—to fight in the Confederate army. In their writings, speeches, and, above all, their actions, Virginia Confederates expressed a passion for their new country. They did not do so blindly or impulsively. Instead, Virginians chose the Confederacy and, consequently, chose war.

Part I ★ CONFLICT & COLLABORATION

I ★ BUILDING THE PLAIN PEOPLE'S CONFEDERACY JANUARY–JUNE 1861

It goes right hard for me to leave but I intend to hold to my company and defend my Country and our consolation is if I have to be killed it will be in defending my Country.
    —Robert Hooke, 1st Virginia Cavalry, April 20, 1861

B etween 1861 and 1865, almost 70 percent of Virginia's white men between the ages of fifteen and fifty served in Confederate forces. Calculating the figure using only those sections of Virginia controlled by the Confederacy, and thus reachable by enlistment and conscription agents, boosts the level to nearly 90 percent of eligible men.[1] Virginia mobilized more than twice as many men as the northern average of 35 percent and exceeded the rates for many other Confederate states as well.[2] The high rate of enlistment in Virginia was achieved across a diverse array of communities in spite of regional divisions that had prevailed in the antebellum period. The support white Virginians gave to the Confederacy reflected the considerable interest that they held in the social and economic institutions of antebellum southern life.

The broad pattern of mobilization in the state reveals that most white Virginians understood that they benefited from living in a slave society. Men from the mountains and the coast, rich and poor, slaveholders and non-slaveholders, urbanites and rural residents all pledged their lives to defend the antebellum South. Confederates successfully mobilized a very high proportion of eligible white men by drawing on those communities that profited from the economic development or the democratic politics of the late antebellum era. Residents who benefited from the slave economy, Virginia's dynamic regional and national markets, or the political networks of antebellum Virginia proved willing to defend that world in its Confederate form. This included a large community of nonslaveholders, who perceived the advantages of living in a slave society. A deep commitment to preserving the social, political, and economic status quo of antebellum Virginia compelled men to support secession and enlist in Confederate armies.

From our current perspective, it is clear that conflicts over slavery caused the war. But this, most historians also admit, is not the same as explaining what motivated men to enlist and fight. Causes reflect the deep social forces that generate historical change whereas motivations operate on the individual level. Typically, motivations are explained away with reference to hot-blooded, honor-bound southern men or submerged beneath a laundry list of all the possible elements that could inspire military service. In Virginia, some causes—protecting slavery, defending white southerners' conception of freedom, and repulsing the northern invasion of the region—were also motivations. Conversely, elements that previous historians have identified as motivations—defense of home and the emotional instinct to preserve southern virtue—functioned as causes of the conflict as well. Politicians may have initiated hostilities, but with only a token standing army in early 1861, the willingness of ordinary men to volunteer and fight made the war possible. If we regard the Civil War as a truly popular conflict, then understanding the relationship between causes and motivations becomes crucial. In what follows, I explore the structural and institutional conditions that facilitated war and how those elements were filtered through individual perceptions and orientations. The longevity of the Confederacy lay partly in the confluence of forces, both national and personal, that compelled white southerners to bear arms against the Union.

O n November 8, 1860, Virginians gave a narrow plurality of their presidential votes to the Whiggish compromise candidate John Bell. Five months later, on April 17, 1861, a majority of state delegates voted to approve the secession of Virginia from the United States. Two and a half months after that, on July 1, 1861, 150 artillery, cavalry, and infantry companies from Virginia, comprising 42,000 men, entered the military service of the newly established Confederate States of America. In retrospect, the eight months separating Lincoln's election and Virginia's commitment to defend the new Confederate States of America with military force look like a natural pause. Indeed, the sheer familiarity of the story of secession and war makes the decisions of Virginians over the winter, spring, and summer of 1860–61 appear inevitable. But to participants at the time, the future looked much less certain.[3]

Virginia Unionists controlled the state secession convention from its opening in February into the early days of April. On April 4, 1861, delegates considered and rejected secession, but news of the fight at Fort Sumter, South Carolina, on April 12 galvanized immediate secessionists. Opinion began to tilt in their direction. The decisive shift occurred on April 15, when Lincoln called for 75,000 ninety-day volunteers from the states to help put down the "insurrection" in the Lower South. Virginia Unionists interpreted Lincoln's actions as betrayal. All spring, they had negotiated in good faith with Republican officeholders and party leaders and had received assurances that Sumter would be given up and the Lower South slowly drawn back into the Union. Instead, Lincoln's call for troops confirmed the worst fears of the immediate secessionists, whom the Unionists had been denouncing as irresponsible for the previous three months. Now, the Unionists looked irresponsible, blind to the treachery of which a Republican administration was capable.

Demonstrating the common experience of the Upper South, a North Carolina Unionist made the case plainly, " 'We have greater reasons to fall out with Lincoln than you cecessionist. While we were watching and waiting he was undermining for our subjugation, but now we are for separation and against all sorts of compromise. Death or victory is our motto.' "[4] Worse still, Lincoln planned to raise an army to march south through Virginia. If he had deceived Virginians about his intentions on Sumter, perhaps he was lying about the purposes of the army. In many cases, former Unionists became the most immediate and ardent Confederates in response to what they perceived as Lincoln's duplicity. The anger of betrayal, the sting of honor insulted, and the fear of northern intentions transformed many reluctant secessionists into eager rebels.[5]

The *Lynchburg Daily Virginian*, a pro-Union paper until after the fall of Fort Sumter, characterized the anger of Unionists across the state. On April 16, 1861, the paper's editor resigned himself to joining the Confederacy and defending the state. Under the wistful headline "The Feeling Yesterday," he noted that "Those who have fought valiantly for the Union admitted that they had been outraged and deceived by the Administration; whilst professions of peace and compromise were on their lips, they were taking active measures to conquer and perhaps subjugate the South."[6] Throughout the state, men who had put their faith in Lincoln endorsed secession with passion. James B. Dorman, a Unionist delegate to the Secession Convention from Rockbridge County in the upper Shenandoah Valley, wrote to his cousin on the same day: " 'I have no idea that our people will tamely submit to Lincoln's arrogant and infamous usurpation of power, and to his diabolical purpose of waging war with a force of 50,000 Northern men against the Southern states. The issue is presented of a *fight*, and the question is simply 'which side will you take?' "[7] The response was immediate. A New Yorker, working as a clerk in Richmond described the atmosphere on the day following the convention's passage of the Secession Ordinance: "The ordinance of secession was passed yesterday afternoon and was made public today at 12. The excitement is intense. The wildest joy seems to prevail. All is war and bloodshed in the way of talk."[8]

The speed and scope of the state's shift toward secession surprised even some ardent pro-secessionists. Dorman's cousin, James D. Davidson, another Unionist Whig, noted the effect of Lincoln's proclamation on political alignments in the state: "Rockbridge was revolutionized at once; and now our secession friends say, they are true conservatives now, and that we are the fire eaters." The diversity of places that now supported secession revealed the complex nature of Confederate support in Virginia. Confederate and state leaders read in the broad support for secession a clear mandate for the new nation—the endorsement of secession confirmed for them the organic unity of the state. At the same time, the very diversity that signaled strength for Confederate leaders also meant the new nation would face the same challenge as prewar Virginians: reconciling the frequently antagonistic interests of different people and places across the state.[9]

A broad spectrum of Virginians supported secession because most white people in the state had shared in the successes of the antebellum period. Southerners explained secession most frequently as a political act, and in Virginia the structure and language of the state's political system made secession seem like an appropriate response. In Virginia, white yeomen had earned their rights with great difficulty and were reluctant to lose them. In 1830 a state constitutional convention had convened to discuss the deep inequalities in political rights between elites and yeomen. Despite a membership that included former presidents and eminent political philosophers, the delegates rejected most liberalizing measures.[10]

Only at a second convention, assembled in 1850, did all white men achieve political equality within the state. Westerners continued to complain about what they regarded as the state's unequal tax system, but even they recognized the profound expansion of political rights in late antebellum Virginia. During the 1850s, white men exercised those rights actively, participating in politics in larger and larger numbers. As a result of this new responsibility and authority, yeomen in the state thought of themselves as independent men. The old eastern slaveholding oligarchs who controlled the state in the late eighteenth and early nineteenth centuries had watched their political power and social prestige slip as economic supremacy within the state moved westward into the Piedmont. The new elites who came to power in the 1830s, 1840s, and 1850s demanded the allegiance of the middle classes, but they did so within a radically different political and economic system.[11]

released themselves from the shackles of monarchy only eighty years before, concerns about freedom were not solely the preserve of philosophers or theorists. Americans followed global independence struggles, in faraway eastern Europe or in nearby South America, with deep respect for the aspirations of freedom everywhere. Daily political struggles in the United States were waged in the language of liberty. In the South, proslavery politicians had built into the foundation of freedom the necessity of slavery. In this view, black slavery made white liberty possible, so any threat to the former attacked the latter. By 1860 many nonslaveholding whites strongly defended slavery because they understood an infringement on the institution as a threat to their rights as well.[19]

Virginia's economy in the 1840s and 1850s also gave residents cause to support secession. During these decades, agricultural reformers, urban boosters, and industrial developers all worked to transform Virginia's economy. By the 1850s these agents of change and the hundreds of thousands of Virginia families who adjusted their economic practices or changed occupations had substantially diversified the state's economic base. Combined with a general upswing in prices for agricultural goods in the 1850s, Virginians enjoyed a new period of prosperity and success.[20] Even those parts of the state that had been firmly committed to staple production added new cereal grains or learned to complement farming with successful animal husbandry.[21] Underneath the profitable agricultural sector of the economy lay a rapidly growing transportation network. Over the decade and a half following the Mexican-American War, Virginia laid more miles of railroad track than any state in the Union and could boast more total miles than any state except New York and Pennsylvania. Virginians of all classes and backgrounds made substantial investments in turnpikes, canals, and expanded ocean ports as well as the new technology of the railroad. Along these new channels to national and global markets flowed agricultural goods from all around the state, iron from forges in the Shenandoah Valley and the enormous Tredegar Iron Works in Richmond, salt from the mines in the southwestern part of the state, and glass from the factories in the Northwest.[22]

Virginia's economic success in the 1840s and 1850s, and especially the fact that a broad middle class shared in that prosperity, ensured that most white residents spurned alternative models of development. The free-labor scheme of northern Republicans stood in stark contrast to Virginia's mixed system of free and slave labor. As sectional agitators predicted the South's downfall if and when free labor was forced upon their section, residents could see evidence of their system's success all around. To most Virginians, preserving that success seemed most feasible from inside the Union, an attitude that helped delay secession.

All the latent fears and hatreds of northerners blossomed in the weeks before secession as southerners convinced themselves that the two sections were hostile and incompatible civilizations. The political system of the mid-nineteenth century thrived on difference, and the key difference between the two regions was the nature and logic of their social and economic systems. Northern Republicans and southern Democrats created aggressive political movements that appealed to large numbers of white male citizens by championing their regionally distinct visions of appropriate economic and social strategies and by obscuring the complementary nature of the northern and southern economic approaches. When faced with the choice of separating from the Union or abandoning the economic and social systems that had served them so well for so long, a choice seemingly imposed by Abraham Lincoln's militia call, Virginians had little difficulty choosing.[23]

All of the reasons that encouraged Virginians to sanction secession compelled them to physically support the Confederacy. In addition, the material concerns and ideological expressions that drove secession bonded with a public celebration of southern independence. The convention delegates who voted for secession on April 17 understood that the Ordinance of Secession committed them to war, and the convention reconvened that evening to instruct the governor to prepare for the state's defense. The delegates portrayed Virginia as a defender rather than an aggressor, a crucial rhetorical move designed to reassure conservative white southerners about the radical implications of the act of secession. Their resolution advised Governor Letcher that "he is hereby authorized and required to call into the service of the State, such portions of the military force of the Commonwealth as may be necessary to repel invasion and to protect the citizens of the State in the present emergency."[24] The resolution also called upon all those Virginians serving in the United States armed forces to resign and enroll with state units. For the several hundred Virginians who served in the U.S. Army, this was the first and clearest test of their national loyalties.

Elite politicians masterminded Virginia's secession, but once the state had officially left the Union, ordinary Virginians supported that decision by pledging their lives to defend its sovereignty. On July 1, 1861, 41,885 Virginia men mustered into Confederate service en masse.[25] One-third again as many men enlisted over the next six months, so that by February 1862 Confederate enlistment agents could count 54,950 Virginians in Confederate forces.[26] According to Confederate officials, this figure was now 85 percent of the total that Virginia would be expected to supply for the whole state if the state raised its full share of regiments.[27] On the ground at the start of the war, these figures seemed perfectly appropriate. One soldier wrote to a friend in mid-May from Loudoun County, "I believe Virginia has now nearly as many men in the field as she needs."[28] As with so many other expectations at the start of the war, this one proved to be wholly inaccurate. By the end of the Civil War, Virginia would raise another 100,000 troops beyond those in service in early 1862.

The drama of mobilization provided one way to undo the damage that had been done by the months of rancorous debate between secessionists and Unionists. Elites seized the opportunity presented in the process of organizing military companies and regiments to shore up the class structure. The pageants and parades that accompanied regimental organizations demonstrated the status and control of a community's great men. Speeches, flowers, marching bands, and waving flags all testified to the ability of local elites to organize and lead their people in times of crisis. The men who joined those companies pledged their allegiance to their nation, their state, and their new captains. Religious leaders added their sanction to the Confederate cause, describing the pursuit of southern independence as a duty of the faithful. One soldier described his inspiration in exactly these terms: "I feel proud that I have the health and energy to be useful in this war. I go into it might and main, relying upon the justice of our cause and the guidance of an over-ruling Providence as guarantees for our success." Echoing the comments of most Virginia ministers, he stated, "I feel conscious that a people never had a better cause to fight for, and in fact it is our religious duty to buckle on our armour and fight unto the death, if necessary, for the defence of Virginia. And I think this is the duty of every Virginian."[29] Confederate leaders across the state encouraged all white men to identify with the duties articulated by this soldier.

Through late April and May, existing militia companies were called out, and their members frequently enlisted en masse. Enrollment usually occurred at the courthouse or some other public place. Community leaders recognized early on the power of peer pressure and social ostracism to entice and compel men into enlisting. The results of this effort were visible in the weeks immediately after Virginia seceded. A man who rode with the army from Lexington down the Valley to Harpers Ferry noted, "When I left home I wondered if other counties were as enthused as Rockbridge, for I thought we

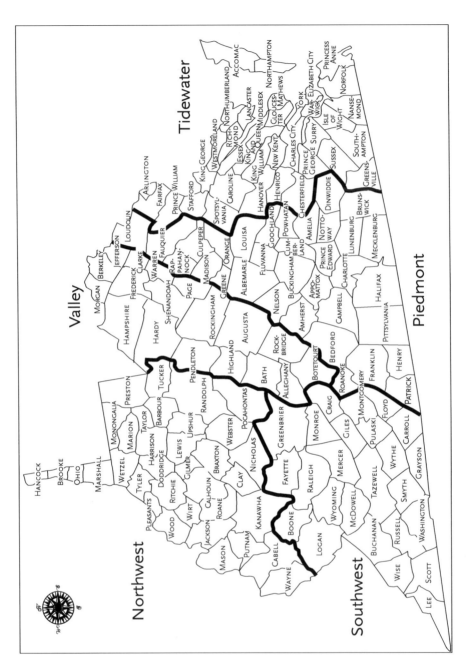

Virginia Counties and Regions, 1860

had been fired up almost to a conflagration. But I found, upon my 'winding way,' that Augusta, Albemarle, Orange, Culpeper, Prince William, Clark, Shenandoah, Jefferson, etc. were all like us—on fire."[30]

Everywhere, the first wave of recruits was feted by women of the town and usually presented with a flag. Men thus carried with them to their first camps and later into battle a physical token from those for whom they fought. These events, because of their ritualized nature, can appear trivial in retrospect, but at the time they helped fuse defense of home with defense of country and gave young men a very tangible reason to perform their service honorably. One young volunteer wrote his mother after arriving with his new company in Staunton, a regional recruitment and training center for the western side of the state. "I got three bunches of flowers before I left town," he reported. His letter to a sister the following day contained more salient details about the flower givers: "There are some of the best looking girls down here I ever saw."[31] The "girls" could also exert pressure is less benign ways, as one revealed to her cousin in a letter to him.

> I heard of the best thing on Nathan Price. He went to the blocks to wait on Miss *Nancy Miller Harvey* and she would not allow him thanked him that she didn't want *stay backs* to wait on her. Time afterwards her buggy and horse were in a rather critical condition. Nathan and Jimmie Thornton rode up and assisted her and said as they left, that 'the guessed she was glad to get *stay backs* now' and she announced 'No, I thank you sir, You volunteered your services. I didn't ask you.' Wasn't it a good thing?[32]

Women were not the only ones who identified service as the natural obligation of any true man. James Booker, who served with his twin brother in the 38th Infantry, wrote home to his cousin with a warning for "stay backs." "Tell them cowardly boys that lives in your neighborhood to look sharp," Booker wrote, "the drafted malitia is coming in dayley. I am sorry for the cowards they make them work so hard."[33]

With the exception of the upper northwestern corner of the state, the geographic pattern of enlistment over the course of the war reveals the evenly distributed and nearly total mobilization that Confederate Virginians accomplished during the crisis (see table 1). Antebellum leaders still feared the salience of the broad east-west division that had been so prominent as late as the early 1850s. What hindsight allows us to see is that regional animosities alone did not present a sufficient obstacle to organizing soldiers for the Confederacy. Throughout the Shenandoah Valley and the Southwest, both places where hostility to eastern elites ran deep, men enlisted in high numbers.

TABLE 1. Regional Enlistment as a Percentage of State Total

Region	Eligible Men	Actual Enlistees
Tidewater	21.2	25.7
Piedmont	23.6	32.3
Valley	15.6	16.3
Southwest	16.0	19.6
Northwest	23.5	6.3

Both contemporaries and subsequent historians have focused on the community debate among residents of the Valley about whether they should join with pro-secession counties from east of the Blue Ridge or follow their more conservative neighbors to the north and west who feared the destruction that war would bring to the places bordering the North. The early 1861 arguments over secession and its consequences undoubtedly reflected and generated tensions in the region, but once the war began, Valley men, like most others around the state, enlisted in high numbers.[34]

Because of the transformative nature of secession, the enlistment pattern during the war bore no relation to the patterns of votes in the 1860 election and little relation to the voting in the secession convention itself. Strongly pro-Union counties did form the majority of those places that organized no companies for the Confederacy, but even among diehard Unionist places, over half sent men, and nearly a third sent more than 50 percent of their eligible men. Several Valley counties that had been resolutely pro-Union during the convention became strongholds of support for the Confederacy once Virginia seceded. Frederick, Augusta, and Rockingham counties all sent more than 50 percent of their eligible men to serve in Confederate armies. Perhaps not surprisingly, all of the strong secession communities sent men to fight, and two-thirds sent more than 75 percent of their eligible men.

The weakest support for the Confederacy came in the far northwestern corner of the state. People in the Northwest organized many fewer Confederate companies than any other part of the state because of their prewar economic, political, and social ties to the North as well as their low rates of slaveholding and wealth holding, and also because Francis Pierpont's government, with the aid of the Union army, controlled much of that region for most of the war. All of those counties that organized no companies for Confederate service were located in the upper Northwest, along the border with the North. It was the specific combination of low slaveholding, low wealth holding, political attachment to the Union, and location that explained the unique response of northwestern residents in comparison to their southwestern brethren. The reluctance of people from this region to support secession or the Confederacy in mid-1861 produced a solid triangle of Confederate country in Virginia that ran from the lower Shenandoah Valley counties of Berkeley and Jefferson southwest through the Kanawha River Valley, east along the North Carolina state line, and north up the Atlantic seaboard to Washington, D.C.[35]

Scholars of the war have observed that the local nature of enlistment and organization fostered unity and boosted morale among soldiers. At the same time, this process reinforced the notion among soldiers that they fought for their own interests, relying on the virtues and strength of their literal neighbors. This was especially true in Virginia, where most Virginia forces fought, because the effort to protect state and nation overlapped. An important early boost to this principle came in the loss of the northern half of western Virginia to Union forces. Even though Virginians across the state denounced the breakaway region and refused to admit its legal separation, many also felt a sense of relief that a suspect and presumably disloyal section had been excised from the state. Rather than weakening the state or nation, the early exit of Unionist territory allowed the Confederacy to consolidate itself and sustain a long war with less internal opposition.[36]

The networks that men maintained with their home communities and created within their new army communities provided an additional bulwark for Confederate persistence. The political nature of secession, channeled as it was through existing elites, and the local nature of mobilization strengthened the communal bonds among Virginians. The culture of individualism so commonly regarded today as being a defining aspect of American character since the Revolution was, in fact, only developing in the mid-nineteenth century. In the predominantly rural environment of the South, communities were cohesive places. The pattern of enlistment within Virginia reflects, at least partly, the powerful social pressure that members of a community exerted on one another. One indication of this force can be seen in the enlistment rate of Virginia's less populous counties, which often sent higher proportions of men than more populous places.

The uniform response of much of Virginia drew on several elements of antebellum experience. Among nearly all white men, the most visceral response to Lincoln's election, and especially to his militia call, was of honor aggrieved. The masculine cult of honor, as it developed in the antebellum South, was highly attuned to offense, and its adherents demanded immediate

Confederate Enlistment, 1861–1865

Legend:
- No enlistment
- 1–10% enlistment
- 11–25% enlistment
- 26–50% enlistment
- 50–75% enlistment
- 75%+ enlistment

and usually physical retribution for perceived slights. John Apperson, a young doctor in training with the 1st Virginia Brigade, displayed the sharp anger of a southern man insulted. "The hired mercenaries of Northern vituperation have approached our border, have crossed it, and are now upon Virginia's sacred soil," he wrote, "Her army has been ignored, her interests disregarded, her rights *trampled* under foot, the property of her citizens destroyed and themselves persecuted and abused."[37] Apperson, and thousands like him, took the mobilization of Federal forces as both an insult and a threat. By electing a strictly sectional candidate, northerners had essentially told southerners that they were irrelevant to the nation's administration and perhaps to its future. The special betrayal felt by Virginia Unionists added a personal element that helped fuse the demands of individual, family, state, and national honor. For John Lightner, a young soldier stationed near Martinsburg, the stakes and causes appeared clear to him. "This war is certainly a holy & just one, on our side," he asserted, "the other is none else than unconstitutional, brought on by wicked usurpation of power."[38]

An additional masculine imperative compelled secession, one rooted in the home, not the storefront, where the very public culture of honor was maintained. Virginia men, like most southerners in the antebellum era, had developed strong bonds of emotion within their families. These loving relationships spurred secession and helped maintain the war. Samuel J. C. Moore, a lawyer from Charlestown, offered a frank assessment of the reason for his participation in the war in a letter to his young son. "My Dear Little Boy," Moore wrote, "War is a dreadful thing, and I would rather do anything in the world than kill a man or help to kill one—but then if we were to let Lincoln's army pass here, they might go into the State of Virginia and burn our homes and kill the old men and the women and children, and do a great deal more harm—and I am sure I would rather see a thousand of them killed around me, than to know that they had done any harm to my wife and dear little boys."[39] Moore's use of family as his reference point reflected the changes occurring in American social life during the half century before the Civil War, when men and women began to value affectionate family bonds as a central part of their lives. Although historians recognize that love and emotion played an increasingly important role in private lives, they rarely incorporate these factors into the very public narratives of war and secession. But families, and the relations within them, were intrinsically related to secession and the decision to fight and to sustain that fight. As Moore explained to his son, love for his family, not hatred of Yankees, inspired him to enlist.

The idea of familial defense loomed so large precisely because most Virginians had a very real fear of the Federal army. As the *Lynchburg Daily Virginian* had noted on April 16, it now seemed that the North was intent on "subjugating" the South. The horrors that might entail lingered in the air, and many men decided that the best way to protect their families was to join the army. Many men anticipated a war in the classic European tradition, with two opposing armies fighting in clear sight of one another. For this reason, leaving home initially embodied the fulfillment, not the abandonment, of the duty of familial protection. As the war progressed to include military occupations, guerrilla conflicts, and even direct attacks on civilian property, most soldiers were forced to reevaluate where and how they could best serve both their family and their nation.

The public nature of honor provided the opportunities for communities to apply social pressure on men to enlist. Newspapers all over the state played an active role in helping encourage men to volunteer. The *Lexington Valley Star*, published in one of the larger towns in the upper Shenandoah Valley, included extensive reports on the organization of companies in the area. Throughout May, the paper, like others around Virginia, included full lists of the names of men who had joined local companies.[40] The message to those men whose names were not on the list would have been quite clear. State leaders sought to mitigate opposition to a large army by linking it explicitly to the Continental army and the American Revolution. Confederate leaders aggressively used the rhetoric of the American Revolution to channel prewar patriotism into support for the Confederacy. The use of American symbols such as George Washington and the appropriation of hallowed terms like "rebels" helped maintain useful continuities between the American past and the Confederate future.[41]

Only in the upper Northwest did newspaper editors and political leaders discourage support of the Confederacy in the early months of the war. Regionalism provided the easiest explanation for divergent enlistment patterns within the state, but location alone does not adequately explain the decisions of people in this region. Out of the 148 Virginia counties in 1860, only 11 raised no companies for Confederate service.[42] All of these counties lay in the extreme northwest, and nine bordered the Union.[43] The most common socioeconomic factor among these places was the absence of slavery. None of the eleven counties had more than 5 percent of their households classified as slaveholding; nine out of eleven had fewer than 2 percent. In terms of wealth, most of these anti-Confederate places held less personal and real estate wealth than was common for the state as a whole. Probably just as important as any of these demographic factors was the location of these counties along the edge of the Confederacy and their frequent occupation by Union troops. Political opposition in mid-1861 took a variety of forms. Opposition to the Confederacy, which grew much stronger over the course of the war, was rooted in a fundamentally different vision of the proper political economy for the growing nation. Still, it was only with the combination of low wealth, low slaveholding, and proximity to the North that Unionism could confidently prevail. Places that possessed only one of these characteristics did not behave in uniform ways.[44]

Political ideologies played a key role both in spurring loyalty to the Union in the Northwest and in promoting enlistment in the southwestern and eastern parts of the state. For those people who had advocated a commitment to secession beginning immediately after Lincoln's election, enlistment followed logically from their political commitment. Many of these men were ideologues who believed strongly in the need for an independent Confederacy. Most assumed that southern victory would come with relative ease and committed themselves to the physical struggle, just as they had to the intellectual and social struggle for secession.

Edmund Ruffin, the Virginia planter, agricultural expert, and ardent pro-secessionist, provides one of the best-known examples of this phenomenon. He fired the first shot on Fort Sumter to start the war, and all his sons enlisted in Confederate military units at the war's opening. Many ordinary men absorbed the transfer of authority from one national government to the next just as smoothly as intellectuals such as Ruffin. Robert Hooke, who joined the 1st Virginia Cavalry in April 1861, wrote a brief note home after enlisting. His first camp letter reads like many sent by young soldiers in the heady days of April: "When I will see you all if ever I trust in God for that and I hope if it should be his will that we would not meet on earth I hope we may meet where there will be no war neither parting it goes right hard for me to leave but I intend to hold to my company and defend my Country and our consolation is if I have to be killed it will be in defending my Country."[45]

The idea of limited government, advanced from Madison and Jefferson's Virginia and Kentucky Resolutions of 1798 through the late antebellum vagaries of "state rights," offered an important justification, if not explanation, for secession. White men in the nineteenth century treated politics and political ideology very seriously, and a desire to preserve a political ideology they imagined to be endangered by Lincoln's election may have stimulated Confederates to enlist or support the new nation. The paradoxes of state rights—many of its most fervent supporters also advocated Federal protection of slavery and denounced the "personal liberty laws" of those northern states that sought to nullify the Fugitive Slave Act—did not deter most southerners from adopting it as the cornerstone of their political ideology in the 1850s. By itself, the theory of state rights or limited government could not compel secession. Southern political leaders understood this and shaped their rhetoric accordingly. They argued, and most southerners perceived, Lincoln's election as a threat to their social and economic order—abolition, free love, and urban-industrial slums all loomed in the nightmare to come under a Republican administration. When bundled with the specter of these dangers, state rights provided an elegant philosophical justification and a familiar political language with which to understand secession.

Alongside political ideology, Virginians considered their economic interests. More than half of the counties that organized no volunteer companies were located in places with low-income households. Many of these places were in the Northwest, where low rates of slaveholding may also have contributed to a lack of enthusiasm for the Confederate cause. Quite possibly, nonslaveholding families in this region with lower than average household wealth had grown dissatisfied with their inability to compete with the larger farms, manned with slave labor, in the rest of the state. Their desire to remain in the Union could have stemmed from concern over their economic future rather than any ideological opposition to slavery. Poor households in the Southwest seem to have had the opposite reaction. There, and in the Shenandoah Valley, many Virginia counties with middle- or lower-income families sent high numbers of men to fight. In these places, surrounded in all directions by slaveholders, poor men could just as easily have interpreted the possibility of not having access to slaves as the most serious threat to their economic future. This response was not unique to the western side of the state. Poor men all over Virginia fought for the Confederacy.[46]

An equally plausible explanation for this evidence is that poorer places sent more men to fight for the Confederacy precisely because the men in those communities had fewer opportunities for economic advancement. Prospective volunteers may have seen in the army a steady paycheck and the chance to acquire skills and perhaps connections. If men expected a short war, which the vast majority of people on both sides did, then seizing the opportunity for paid work in the army made sense. Although later in the war pay dates became scarce and that pay was mostly made in rapidly depreciating Confederate scrip, the experience of Virginia soldiers early in the war suggests that men paid careful attention to the salary they were earning. In September 1861, John Hill Lyon recorded the actions of men in his unit when pay was distributed, "The pay master today put up his tent (office) and com- menced paying off the troops that enlisted in the service of *Virginia*. His office is well attended by the boys, who manifest a great desire to speedily get hold of 'the needful.' "[47]

Together, the pressure of necessity, which may have driven poor men into the ranks, and the defense of established institutions, which may have driven rich men into the ranks, brought a wide cross section of Virginians together in the army. Orange County, in the central Piedmont, offers a good case study for how this approach took shape. Like most places in antebellum Virginia, economic success in Orange was based upon local conditions; however, peo- ple understood the importance of connections with larger markets and trade routes that straddled the state's regions and the nation's sections. Following the attack on Sumter, Orange County men suspended prewar conflicts in the interests of unity in order to defend themselves and their community, not because of an abstract belief in the Confederate nation. Although men with- out full-time jobs entered the army first, the 1862 draft increased the number of men with jobs who served. Because of the intense and continuous pres- sure on the Confederacy for more soldiers, the proportions of rich and poor men who enlisted remained fairly constant through the war.[48]

More important than either location or wealth, in terms of its relationship to enlistment rates, was slaveholding. Slaveholders had an obvious interest in protecting the economic and social system upon which they built their prosperity, and most of those places with high rates of slaveholding sent very high proportions of their men to fight. This was also true for communities with low rates of slaveholding that were located in Virginia's interior. Even in the upper Northwest, some low slaveholding counties raised a number of regiments for the Confederacy. Families living in Gilmer, Roane, and Brax- ton counties, all located in the northwestern part of the state, held much less wealth than their neighbors and had smaller white populations than was common in the area. The households in these counties owned farms with values almost 50 percent lower than the average for northwestern Virginia. Perhaps these families supported the Confederacy because they were dissat- isfied with the prevailing economic trends in their home region. As everyone in the state knew, the Northwest had a weak commitment to slavery and businessmen in the region increasingly traded with northern markets. The people of Gilmer, Roane, and Braxton do not seem to have benefited from that approach, and perhaps they saw a better economic future as members of an independent Confederacy. Located in contested territory in the middle of

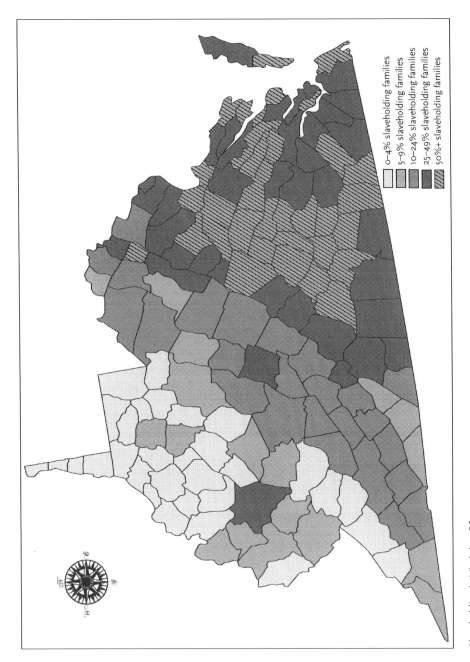

Slaveholding in Virginia, 1860

0–4% slaveholding families
5–9% slaveholding families
10–24% slaveholding families
25–49% slaveholding families
50%+ slaveholding families

northwestern Virginia, the families in this region had more autonomy to decide their loyalty than those counties along the border with the Union or deeper in the interior of the Confederacy.[49]

Like their northern counterparts, southwestern families maintained smaller-than-average farms and held less wealth than others in their region. They too could have been fighting for the Confederacy in an attempt to carve out a new economic future for themselves, albeit one based on slavery.[50] Throughout the 1850s, residents in this region deployed slave labor in a variety of agricultural and industrial settings to successfully expand the region's economy, and thus they had every reason to continue pursuing what had proved to be an effective economic strategy. The people in the Southwest advocated secession early in the year, at least partly because of the threat to slavery posed by the Lincoln administration. In March the *Abingdon Democrat*, published in a small town in the far southwest corner of the state, ran an article under the title "A Prospective Stampede," in which the editor noted "The *Richmond Enquirer* has private advices from different parts of the state, which inform it that a large number of the largest slaveholders in Virginia are already making preparations for an exodus." The *Democrat* bemoaned the loss to the state of those good men and noted that "they will carry away from us what is far more valuable to the state than property—thousands and tens of thousands of busy hands, which now constitute the productive labor of the state."[51] Men from the Southwest may have enlisted precisely because they held only a small stake in slavery. A new Confederacy that guaranteed their right to own slaves offered the only security that they could expand from their meager base in the coming years.[52]

Southwesterners' eager embrace of slavery reflected the overwhelming popular sanction of racial bondage in the state. Echoing the *Abingdon Democrat*'s orientation on the subject, the *Leesburg Democratic Mirror*, in the northern end of the relatively low-slaveholding Shenandoah Valley, reprinted an excerpt from Alexander Stephens's "Cornerstone" speech in its first issue after the attack on Fort Sumter. Stephens argued that the " 'CORNERSTONE [of the Confederate government] rests upon the great truth that the negro is not equal to the white man, that Slavery, subordination to the superior race, is his natural and moral condition.' "[53] Stephens made plain the centrality of slavery to the Confederacy, and the *Mirror's* editors made plain its centrality to Virginia.

In Virginia, as in most other southern states, the long history and pervasiveness of the system meant that few areas of life remained unaffected. Virginians' advocacy of and responses to slavery shaped their political and economic systems and even their personal relations within households and communities. Knowing this, it should come as no surprise that slavery played an important role in motivating men to enlist and serve in Confederate armies. At the most basic level, Confederates fought to retain the property they held and to protect their ability to pass that property on to their descendants. Edmund Ruffin himself recognized this relationship between protection of slavery and willingness to serve the Confederacy. As one of his biographers wrote, for Ruffin, "the cause involved no desire to preserve mastery over slaves for its own sake, nor to save some paternalistic rural lordship. Rather, it involved calculations of what he would lose materially if deprived of slave property and slave labor."[54]

This was true even for those who did not own slaves but who lived in communities with high numbers of enslaved black Virginians. During the antebellum era, the slaveholding elite sought to tie the interests and the ideologies of nonslaveholders to their own. Their success came not, as they supposed, because nonslaveholders deferred to slaveholding elites out of feudal gratitude, but rather because slavery offered valuable compensations to all white citizens. Evidence of their success surfaced in the rhetoric used to justify secession and war in those places where slaveholding played a relatively limited role in the economy, like the Shenandoah Valley. The *Winchester Republican*, for instance, rallied citizens to the Confederacy by announcing the "contempt we feel for those who would thus humbly bow the knee of servitude to the Baal of Northern Abolitionism."[55]

Slaveholders all over the state deployed slave labor to build the vibrant and flexible economy that provided many nonslaveholding families with a standard of living almost unmatched around the world. Though less tangible than the economic advantages, all nonslaveholders enjoyed the privilege of being white in a society built upon racial slavery. After John Brown's attempt to lead a slave rebellion in Virginia, the mere presence of enslaved black Virginians created anxieties among all whites about their personal safety. The threat of slave insurrection and the apocalyptic consequences that would flow from it spurred many to enlist. Whether fear outweighed opportunity as a motivating factor, or vice versa, those places with high numbers of slaves in a community sent the most men to Confederate armies (see table 2).[56]

From a current perspective, the paradoxical dimension of the Confederate experience in the Civil War was the claim to be fighting to defend freedom by preserving slavery. For Confederates no paradox existed. White liberty depended upon black slavery, as a generation of southern thinkers and propagandists had explained in intricate detail. Slavery shaped the ways that all

TABLE 2. Percentage of the Population Enslaved and Enlistment

Population Enslaved	Enlistment						
	0	1–10%	11–25%	26–50%	51–75%	75%+	Total
0–3%	10	6	5	6	6	1	34
3–10%	1	0	2	6	3	7	19
10–25%	0	0	1	3	10	11	25
25–50%	0	0	2	9	10	17	38
50%+	0	0	0	5	6	21	32
Total	11	6	10	29	35	57	148

Virginians related to one another: the types of employment they sought, returns on the investments of labor or capital that they made, the ways that race structured political exchanges and the growth of political rights for white yeomen, and the intimate details of family organization and daily life. Few soldiers discussed slavery in their letters precisely because the institution was so deeply embedded in their daily lives and historical memories. The scarcity of references to slavery as an explicit motivating factor should not mask the fact that fighting to defend Virginia meant fighting to defend slavery. The experience of the war did not convince soldiers that slavery was an inappropriate or inefficient institution. Instead, most became more committed to preserving slavery and expressed that through their eager capture of runaway slaves for return to masters around Virginia. What did change were attitudes on race itself, and not for the better. The efforts enslaved Virginians made to escape their bondage eroded the system of slavery and drove whites to resent blacks in a new and more aggressive way. By the conclusion of the war, many of those white Virginians who had formerly looked at black Virginians as docile brutes now saw them as active and conspiring enemies.[57]

Just as differences over slavery did not undermine mobilization, neither did differences in wealth. The anecdotal evidence of wealthy men who avoided service or poor men who were drafted into it has compelled some historians to emphasize the divisive nature of class relations within the Confederate South, in particular by arguing that poor men bore a disproportionate burden of the war effort. The experience of the war in Virginia does not bear out this argument. Despite periodic complaints about inequities, the middle and

TABLE 3. Enlistment and Wealth (in dollars)

Enlistment	Average Household Wealth	Average Farm Value
0	2,273.0	3,103.3
1–10%	2,447.2	4,109.8
11–25%	2,850.8	3,401.8
26–50%	4,431.2	3,908.7
51–75%	5,342.8	4,932.9
75%+	6,855.1	5,295.8

Note: Data are weighted by total free population.

lower classes of Virginia did not abandon their support for the Confederacy. The enlistment data buttress this argument. Places with higher than average household wealth tended to organize more companies than did the counties with mostly middle- and lower-income families. All of the state's wealthiest counties sent more than 25 percent of their men, and most sent more than one-half their eligible male population. When enlistment rates and wealth holdings are analyzed against each other, they reveal a positive linear relationship (see table 3). The more wealth a community held, the more likely that it would send high numbers of men to the army. Rich men fought this war.[58]

Despite all the martial work that both Union and Confederate men had accomplished by late June 1861, neither side knew what kind of a war they would create. Enlistment was in many ways a leap into the unknown. Some men recognized the uncertainty they faced. Rather than admit to loved ones how dim the future appeared, they offered jokes and confidence-boosting bromides. One young man wrote his sister in Gordonsville from his post at Harpers Ferry in May 1861. Facing an armed enemy just across the Potomac River, he asked his sister to forward those letters he received at home only if convenient; he was busy and would answer the letters as quickly as possible, "but tell them not to pester me when I am settling difficulties between Nations."[59]

Most of the men around this young private held similarly nonchalant views about the enterprise before them. They expected a short and successful war, if one came at all. Although some of this confidence came from prewar rhetoric that denigrated the manliness of northern clerks and factory laborers, many soldiers drew reassurance from the apparent solidarity of the new Confederacy. Men from all regions of the South had flocked to Virginia to defend the new nation. In their ethnic backgrounds, religious persuasions, occupations, socioeconomic position, and political views, they represented the rich diversity of antebellum America. Southern newspapers and political leaders celebrated that diversity, arguing that it revealed how serious an offense had been given by the North's actions. If all these different men had joined the military, the Confederacy's legitimacy was undeniable. Confederate officials saw in the initial wide support a permanent and uniform commitment by the men of the South to Confederate independence.

Indeed, the pattern of enlistment across Virginia reveals the Confederacy's widespread mobilization of men, including nonslaveholders, former Unionists, residents of wealthy and poor areas, and residents of both remote, mountainous communities and diverse urban ones. No single issue or characteristic created early Confederate loyalty. Those who supported the Confederacy did so by drawing on a wide variety of incentives. In 1861 the emotional inducements that men found in their families and communities, from love to honor to zeal to anxiety over proving one's manhood, tended to reinforce one another by encouraging secession and enlistment. Likewise, the intellectual justifications of a religious duty to preserve a biblically sanctioned social order and the political ideology of state rights initially blended with the material interests of most white Virginians. The security of slavery, the continuity of the robust economic order Virginians had built in the 1850s, and the privileges of being white in the antebellum South all depended upon defending the society as it was in 1861.

2 ✳ A NATION OF THEIR OWN
JULY 1861–MARCH 1862

Now is the time for every true & patriotic spirit to rally 'round the
Bonnie Blue Flag & fight & never cease to fight while there is an enemy
South of Mason's & Dixon's line.
  —James R. McCutchan, 14th Virginia Cavalry, March 19, 1862

Virginians had barely grasped the idea of secession and the prospect of building a new nation when they flung themselves into war. Tens of thousands of Virginia men volunteered in April, May, and June, and these new soldiers were joined by thousands more from other Confederate states sent to Virginia where everyone assumed the war, if it came, would be fought. It came soon, as Confederate soldiers battled Union troops in western and central Virginia from late May until late September. The fighting established the physical boundaries of Confederate Virginia, with much of the trans-Allegheny region controlled by Federal soldiers and their local Unionist allies, while central Virginia remained firmly within the orbit of the Richmond government. During late 1861 and early 1862, another fight occurred that helped establish the ideological boundaries of the Confederacy. The debate over conscription forced Confederates to spell out the terms of loyalty to the new nation and to clarify the penalties for those who did not follow them. Soldiers and their families played crucial roles in these exercises, resisting the Union advance in the West, driving Federals from the plains of Manassas, and accommodating themselves to the new rules of military service.

The experiences of 1861 and early 1862 forced Confederates to confront the prospect of a longer and more unpredictable war. Military defeats in South Carolina, Tennessee, and Virginia contradicted the narrative of inevitable victory. In northwestern Virginia, Confederates faced able U.S. troops and hostile Unionist civilians and suffered under ineffective leadership, illness, and dissension in their own ranks. The Confederacy's heavy-handed efforts to solve the manpower problems alienated many loyal citizens. Virginians debated the nature of military service and conscription more carefully than they had when they entered the war during the wave of martial celebrations that filled the state in April and May 1861. As a result, they entered a more articulate protest against what they felt were the unjust aspects of the draft. The combined effect of these problems created a crisis that severely tested the commitment of Virginians to form a new nation.

Nonetheless, Virginia men did accept the burden of reenlistment and continued service, as the war dragged on into a second year. In doing so, they drew upon several elements, some of which emerged out of their experience from the previous year, while others developed from the unpredictable pattern of the war itself. The resounding military success at Bull Run reversed the trend of defeats and confirmed Confederates' sense of their military superiority. Even as the Richmond government alienated prospective, and current, soldiers with its draft policy, the responsive rules and procedures within the army itself mollified tensions within the service. A strong emotional connection with their families at home and a growing belief in the new nation anchored the emerging sense of Confederate purpose.

The volunteers who enlisted in the spring of 1861 were eager to represent themselves, their families, and their communities in the face of the apparent threat from the North, but few were anxious to fight a real war. Their threats against Yankees and predictions of imminent victory were mostly the arrogance of youth. Outside of the Kansas Territory, very few Americans had practiced any organized sectional violence against one another. Many soldiers did not expect an actual war and most desired an honorable peace more than a military defeat of the North. One soldier enjoyed the privilege of shaking his new president's hand when Jefferson Davis visited his camp in late May. The serious demeanor of his commander in chief appropriately impressed the man, but zeal for the Confederacy did little to stimulate zeal for battle. He noted to his family "I hope that Peace will be made in a few weeks and we may all get home." Despite the rabid pronouncements filling southern papers, not all soldiers burned to actually fight the Yankees. A week later, in another letter home, he optimistically announced, "there is I think a good chance for Peace in a few weeks."[1]

Soldiers had initially imagined that a full war could be averted, but with troops massing in northern Virginia those same soldiers also needed to confirm for themselves that they would emerge victorious from any conflict. In a tangle of sentiments and wishes, one wrote home: "I think that Peace will be made in a few weeks after the fourth of July at the least and I hope to be at home safe by the first of august at least and if I do we can tell you all a story worth hearing." He then changed course, noting, "I do not doubt but we will have a fight hear first but I do not doubt for a moment but that we will whip them so badly that they will never forget it."[2] The alternating hesitancy and bluster expressed by this young man typify the nervous condition of most Virginia Confederates at this time. They could not foresee the outcome, and most earnestly desired some event that would settle the uncertainty.

That event appeared soon, as General George B. McClellan began organizing an invasion into northwest Virginia that he hoped would "secure [the region] . . . to the Union."[3] Like many conservative northerners, McClellan assumed a great latent Unionist majority in the South. With the proper support, he believed, these Americans would reassert their control of the region and return to the Union. Although the hopes of McClellan, Lincoln, and Secretary of State William H. Seward for a general Unionist uprising in the South failed, western Virginia did hold a sizable body of Unionists. It offered a prime place to begin a military campaign with clear political goals.

Confederate leaders in the area along the Potomac and Ohio Rivers watched this buildup nervously and petitioned Richmond for help. In response, Governor Letcher authorized the organization of men from the upper northwest counties in order to defend the region and the Baltimore & Ohio Railroad in particular. On May 23 the state's voters ratified the ordinance of secession. On May 26 McClellan entered western Virginia and his troops quickly drove a small Confederate force out of Grafton, where the Baltimore & Ohio and the Northwest Virginia Railroad intersected. Both armies targeted railroads, turnpikes, and rivers in order to take control of the sparsely settled region. Shortly after their entry into the state, Union troops tried to catch 800 Confederate recruits at Philippi, a small town along the Tygart River. Poor communication among the Federals, complicated by the foul weather that impeded military efforts on both sides all year, gave Confederates a chance to retreat still further into central western Virginia. Though the Confederates escaped mostly without harm, their hasty retreat was dubbed the "races at Philippi" in papers around the country, an ignominious start for the military forces of the Old Dominion.[4]

Confederates sent to western Virginia had to abandon most of what they expected about warfare, principally in the active role played by Unionist civilians in the region. One soldier described the depth of knowledge locals had of Confederate movements. Following the ambush of a Confederate scouting party, he wrote that "those prisoners that was brought informed us they were apprised of the attack as much as we ware." "So much for union men we cannot have a fare chance heare," he continued, "and western virginia are to be more dreaded than any other portion of the state on account of the union men. They have already done us great injury."[5] Soldiers encountered civilians

Headquarters, Va. Forces,
Staunton, June 6th, 1861.

To Arms! To Arms!!
BRAVE MEN OF
AUGUSTA, ROCKBRIDGE AND ROCKINGHAM.

Our forces under command of Col. PORTERFIELD, at Philippa, on Monday morning last, were attacked by superior forces with Artillery, and were compelled to retreat to Beverly. Our loss is reported to be SIX KILLED, with the loss of a quantity of Arms and Provisions. Among the killed, it is reported that the gallant

Capt. A. T. RICHARDS, of the Bath Cavalry,

is among the number. Immediately ORGANIZE VOLUNTEER COMPANIES, and report to me at once. Get Arms, and join our Brave Brothers in arms in the Northwest, and AVENGE HIS DEATH, and drive back these NORTHERN VANDALS AND TRAITORS from the soil of the Old Dominion, or very soon the whole of Western Virginia will be overrun. The Federal Forces are under the command of McClellan, aided by Traitors like Carlisle and others. This information is RELIABLE, as it was brought to me by two brave and gallant men from the Northwest, Messrs. SPALDING and COOK, who were in the engagement and rode through night and day to convey the news to our people. They are now in Staunton and can give full particulars, in detail, to all who desire it. It is proper to state that the reported loss of the enemy is SEVEN-TY KILLED. Let me again appeal to every man who has a

DOUBLE-BARRELLED SHOT GUN,

to bring it and loan it to the State, and take in lieu a good Musket, so that I may be enabled to arm two Companies of Cavalry who are now organizing and have no Arms. Let me again say

FLY TO ARMS!
and let us RAISE A LARGE FORCE AND REDEEM THE NORTHWEST FROM A
Ruthless Abolition and Fanatical Foe.
M. G. HARMAN, Major Commanding.

"To Arms! To Arms!" Confederates reacted to McClellan's invasion of northwestern Virginia with outrage and called upon locals to defend the "Old Dominion." The material shortages Confederates faced were already visible, as demonstrated by the recruiter's call for men to trade in their own weapons for military arms. This item is reproduced by permission of The Huntington Library, San Marino, California.

in this region with extreme trepidation, never knowing who would betray them, especially in those counties that formed the boundary between Union and Confederate territory in western Virginia. In Greenbrier County, according to one soldier, "Two of our picket guards were shot last week by a Union man and a very little boy. They rushed upon them and they ran upstairs and the pickets followed after them. They shot and killed one, wounded the other. The little boy shot one of the pickets. The pickets took them on to Staunton and placed them in prison." Despite the violence of this exchange, conditions would worsen considerably in 1862, when Union and Confederate civilians and soldiers commonly engaged in bushwhacking. In later cases, Unionists who surprised and shot Confederate pickets and were captured would be tried and executed as guerrillas.[6]

This was not the war that Virginia men had volunteered to fight. John Winfield, a junior officer with the 7th Virginia Cavalry wrote home to his wife from Winchester, at the lower end of the Shenandoah Valley, and a safe spot for Confederate forces to rest between attacks on Union forces in the northwestern part of the state. "You observe from the caption of this letter that I am again back in this miserable hole Winchester," wrote Winfield. "We were called here suddenly on yesterday from Sheppardstown—to prepare for another wild goose chase in the mountains of Hampshire—called away from the face of a foe—to seek one in the jungles and hills of a poverty stricken region."[7] Winfield's anger for both the enemy and the citizens of the region he was supposed to be defending typify the frustration among Confederates after several months of defeats in the mountainous and heavily Unionist Northwest. Many easterners who came west identified the enemy responsible for Confederate failures in the region—their fellow Virginians—and targeted them for destruction. "I believe we are surrounded by Unionists in this section," noted one man. "Though they are afraid to express their real sentiments—We have made but four arrests as yet. they have not had a trial— I hope to have the pleasure of shooting a few of them yet. . . . They are acting as guides to McClellans armey—& are responsible for our defeat."[8]

The conditions of service in western Virginia did little to inspire Confederates. The spread of diseases among men lacking the necessary immunities nearly wiped out whole regiments.[9] One soldier wrote to his sister with the news that several of his friends had died of typhoid fever: "I have always said that I feared disease in the army more than anything else; we have now in the mountains between Lewisburgh & this place not less than two thousand sick." More than most soldiers, this man recognized that he might very well share their fate. He remarked that his friends were "gone, yes gone where a great many of us will soon go."[10] Another soldier reported the numbers of sick and healthy men in his regiment stationed in Highland County in late 1861:"Times are very dull here in camp. The health is bad. We have 774 men in our regiment and there are only about 300 fit for duty."[11] The 46th Infantry, an all-eastern outfit stationed in the Alleghenies, fared little better. In late summer, its commander reported losing 25 men per day to measles, reducing the regiment to a mere 371 soldiers.[12] Death by disease seemed a poor reward for Confederates who fought hard battles against Union troops and Unionist civilians. Over the course of the war, 9 percent of Virginia soldiers died from illnesses, nearly twice as many as those killed in action.[13]

Aided by the Unionist majority in northwestern Virginia, the Federal advance under McClellan continued south and east. By July, Union troops under the command of General William S. Rosecrans pushed the Confederates out of Rich Mountain, capturing hundreds, including the commanding officer. Another Confederate commander, General Robert S. Garnett, was killed on July 13. His forces retreated thirty-five miles south to Monterey, along the Staunton and Parkersburg Railroad that led into the Shenandoah Valley. The combined effect of the loss at Rich Mountain and the barely successful retreat devastated the men involved. Many soldiers reacted by dismissing the region and its inhabitants. In a fit of anger, one volunteer wrote home from Pocahontas County in late July: "This is the meanest place that ever had a name and I wouldnt live here for anything in reason, and if it wasn't that the Yankees might get to Richmond through this way they are welcome to the whole country about here, as far as I am concerned." Another eastern soldier in the West calmly advocated giving up the whole region. "Although Western Virginia abounds in that grandest natural scenery," he remarked, "I am perfectly disgusted with the country and think we would be benefitted and not injured by a division of the state."[14] In the face of the embarrassingly poor leadership displayed by Confederate generals Henry A. Wise and John B. Floyd, Robert E. Lee arrived in late September and took command of the unified forces. Rosecrans, however, held firm control of the region and refused to engage with the Confederates. Lee returned to Richmond on October 30 without success, and his men returned to their mountain barracks.[15]

The challenges of battle against Union troops in the mountains of the West were matched by the political discomfort occasioned by the recognition that some Virginians really did prefer to stay in the Union. Confederate Virginians made a determined effort to hold the Old Dominion together, but the opposition of Unionist residents in the upper counties of the trans-Allegheny region compelled most soldiers to accept the division of the state. Ideology and the musket together marked the boundary between Confederate Virginia and the Union.

Confederate armies had substantially more success in central Virginia.

Like the fighting in the West, the late July battle at Bull Run helped determine the borders of the new nation. Responding to the pressure from northern civilians, anxious for a decisive end to the "rebellion," President Lincoln ordered General Irvin McDowell and his inexperienced army to take the offensive. The Federal army marched toward Manassas Junction, where the Orange & Alexandria Railroad met the Manassas Gap Railroad. Facing him was General P. G. T. Beauregard and 30,000 eager Confederate soldiers.

The commanding generals of each side struggled to direct armies bigger than any seen in North America since the American Revolution. Their men were untrained, and poor staffing complicated the execution of orders throughout the day. The morning's fighting brought what seemed to McDowell to be a Union victory, as his troops pushed Confederate soldiers back onto a rise known as Henry Hill. A delay in the Union offensive at midday gave the Confederates a chance to assemble a defensive line, cemented by the soon-to-be minted "Stonewall" Jackson. By late afternoon, the Confederates had repulsed the Union attack, and the disorganization of retreat multiplied itself as Union troops feared being caught by Confederate cavalry. As Confederate artillery batteries lobbed shells into the assembled spectators from Washington, D.C., the retreat turned into a rout. Northern soldiers abandoned guns, tents, haversacks, and all impediments that prevented flight back to the security of Washington's defenses.[16] An ignominious and chaotic retreat by Union troops at the end of the day spurred joy and celebration in the Confederacy.

Confederate confidence soared as news of the victory flashed along southern telegraph lines. Four days after the battle, Maurice Evans wrote home from Manassas. His unit had seen no action, and perhaps as a result he had a lopsided picture of the battle's outcome. As Evans told his mother, the Confederates had lost 400 men killed and 800 wounded, but the Federals had 6,000 killed and 1,500 prisoners: "They have lost all and we have won the most brilliant victory ever achieved by arms in America." This overrepresented Union deaths by a factor of thirteen but perfectly represented the sentiment prevailing among the victorious Confederates.[17] John Winfield concurred with his comrade. As he wrote his wife, "We have slaughtered them—it will take them two months to reorganize and supply the place up their lost ordinance and stores. *The war is ended* except for the enemy to skirmish a little while until they can decently get out of the difficulty they are in."[18] The outcome confirmed long-standing assumptions of southern martial superiority, and many Confederates assumed this one battle would compel the North to negotiate the South's peaceful exit from the Union. Southerners saw in the victory proof of the Confederacy's validity as a natural entity and a testament of God's favor. The victory offered retrospective confirmation of the wisdom of secession and fueled a stronger commitment to the Confederacy among both soldiers and civilians.

Even as citizens around the state and throughout the Confederacy celebrated the victory at Bull Run, soldiers on the battlefield recoiled from the horror of what they had seen and done. Philip Powers walked across the Manassas battlefield two evenings after the fight. "*Nothing—nothing* could lessen the horrors of the field by moonlight," he wrote, "Enough, I cannot I will not describe it—May God, in His infinite mercy avert a second such calamity."[19] Despite the thrill of victory, most of the soldiers present did not gloat over the Union dead. Only two months before, these dead men had been their business partners, brother Christians, and fellow Americans. The fire-eaters who preached destruction of the North were few and far between in antebellum Virginia. The majority of southerners harbored increasingly deep suspicions of northern intent toward slavery but favored a peaceful parting of the ways. After tallying the dead at Manassas, William L. Hill issued a prayer for peace: "May God slake any unnecessary shedding of blood and restore to us a speedy peace."[20] The scale and scope of violence at Bull Run surprised even the victors, who had not yet imagined the gravity and sorrow of real war. One man struggled to describe the scene to his wife, "O my God you never dreamed or read of such sights and such times Great God . . . I saw thousands of dead Yankees on the field killed and wounded in every shape every way there was . . ."[21]

The heavenly invocations offered by Powers and Hill after Manassas reveal one way that Confederates could reconcile the actions they were compelled to take. Most Confederates, even if they were not devout Christians, believed their cause was sanctioned by God. Although warfare and killing may have been repugnant, faith that they were following God's plan assuaged fear and guilt. One man, writing to his father after the death of several men in his company during a skirmish remarked that they must have been taken by God. "I have an abiding confidence that He will compel the right to right," he wrote, "and that ere long, all of the soldiers will be restored to their homes and friends, to spend the rest of their lives in prosperity and happiness. Our cause will triumph, so I must beg you to be hopeful and cheerful, and in due time the Great Ruler will bring all things right."[22] This faith, which increased in strength among Confederates through the conflict, did not reflect fatalism about man's incapacity before God's power. Rather, it confirmed the intentions and actions of Confederates as they sought to build a better world.

The next battle of 1861 was an internal war, a dispute among Confederates over the terms of military service and the definition of loyalty to the nation. Beginning in late 1861 and extending into early 1862, Confederate officials considered plans to avert the departure of the twelve-month enlistees in April and May 1862, just as the new military season would begin. The looming shortage of manpower hit Virginia especially hard. For the Confederacy as a whole, twelve-month men constituted 71 percent of the men in the field.[23] In Virginia, effectively all men were twelve-monthers.[24] Union successes in the western theater in early 1862 added to the pressure on the Confederate government to field larger and more effective armies. During the winter, debates over enlistment and conscription spilled out of the capitol and into parlors and camps across the state. The *Daily Richmond Examiner* reflected the logic of the times. After an accounting of the numbers of men available and the threat posed by the ever-growing Union forces, the paper issued a succinct judgment: "It is obvious from these facts that the safety of the South lies in the prompt and energetic adoption of such measures as will utilize the strong force of men that she has in reserve."[25] In mid-April 1862, the Conscription Act passed, making all white men between the ages of eighteen and thirty-five eligible for the draft.[26] The legislation included provisions that offered furloughs and pay bonuses to men who voluntarily reenlisted. Barring that, the act automatically re-enlisted all one-year volunteers as three-year enlistees.

The war's longevity and the fact that most early volunteers did serve until death or the war's end make it easy to assume that men enlisted with the foresight to imagine an extended conflict and the dedication to serve unconditionally, but the fervor of enlistment in April and May 1861 masked the fact that most men signed up for short terms of service. Volunteers perceived enlistment as a contract that obligated them to the Confederate military for a specified period of time. Further, they carefully monitored the execution of that agreement. Once in the army, volunteers became valuable soldiers to keep. The War Department, congress, and the president himself all sought remedies to the manpower crisis that would be acceptable to the men who had shown such early enthusiasm for the Confederate cause. Officers in the field reflected this concern for the rights and dignity of volunteers. They exercised considerable flexibility as they sought to refill the ranks before the implementation of an official draft act. In the face of high rates of absence in late 1861, commanders detailed junior officers to go home and retrieve absent men. Samuel Moore, a lieutenant serving in Stonewall Jackson's corps, led one such expedition in mid-October. Moore and eight enlisted men received instructions to "bring back or cause to return to duty all persons belonging to the Army of the Potomac whom you may find absent without leave or who may without lawful excuse have overstayed their 'leaves.'" The awkward euphemism "men who may without lawful excuse have overstayed their 'leaves,'" used instead of "deserter," revealed the necessity of dealing gingerly with men not at their posts of duty.[27]

Like most of the legislation passed by the Confederate Congress to meet the contingencies of war, the draft accomplished its stated purpose.[28] It enlarged the army but in the process generated foreseen and unforeseen conflicts among soldiers and within communities. Some objected on the simple grounds of class, knowing that wealthy or well-connected men could escape the draft. Others objected to the provision giving the opportunity for eligible men to hire substitutes to serve in their place. Littleton Robertson, with the 18th Virginia Infantry, wrote his wife that he was "not going to stay in the war eney longer untill I am forced to doe it as there is so meney men at home enjoying all the lugures of life and we are debard from all."[29] Others objected to the idea of coercion by the state. Still others saw in the draft and the requirement that they stay in service a mark of deep shame. They believed that military service was, and should remain, a voluntary act.

Robertson's sense of an unequally shared burden was acknowledged by other men in the service. As Edward Camden noted, "If the legislature adopts a tyrannical law, which they are trying to do they will disorganize the army and then we will be subject to yankee hirelings of the north for the volunteers came once to the defence of our honor and rights." He continued, "And now it seems that the object of the legislature is to make regulars of them by drafting them for two years more without even allowing them to go home." Like others, Camden believed that the volunteers had done their duty, fulfilled the terms of their contract, and should be relieved by fresh men. "There are a plenty of men in the state of Va who was able to bear arms, as the volunteers," Camden wrote, "and it is nothing but right and proper for them to relieve us after twelve months hard service." Camden then went on to raise the political objections common among libertarians in Richmond.

And when the volunteers came to the field there object was to put down a tyrannical laws which was then being hovered around our heads and in a war we have defeated that law with our faces turned northwards—and have broken and shaken it in its very walls and foundations. And now to think that the Legislature is coming in our rear and trying to put another obnoxious law on us. for us to live under for two years to come is too hard for us to submit to.[30]

The prospect of a draft also increased the caution among volunteers who often discouraged their relatives from joining the service. Although the physical danger and discomfort of camp life drove a great part of this advice, the number and specificity of letters encouraging siblings to avoid service picked up markedly after conscription passed. Few men saw a contradiction between serving faithfully themselves and giving advice to relatives about how to remain civilians. Robert Hooke corresponded with his brother at home in Rockingham County during his early months in the cavalry and was puzzled as to how his brother had avoided being called into service. Nonetheless, he advised, "if it is required I want you to do like a man but put it off as long as you can keep out of it honorably, for you will see the worst times that ever you experienced."[31]

Despite the objections raised to the idea and execution of the draft, most volunteers remained in the service because they had not yet achieved the goals for which they initially enlisted.[32] William Randolph Smith of the 17th Virginia Infantry confessed to his wife that some men grumbled about the draft but he approved of it as a measure for establishing a clear test of loyalty and manhood. "There is some dissatisfaction among the troops arising from the act of Congress keeping all in for ninety days," he noted, "and all between the ages of 18 and 55 for two years or the war. I am glad of it for the act cannot possibly take any effect upon the true Southerner, while those who have not enough respect or manhood about them to reenlist should be made to do their duty." In Smith's company, as in others, most men eventually reenlisted voluntarily. "There was not many, I am happy to say, in our company that had to be forced in, a majority of the company having previously reenlisted and received their Bounty," he reported. "Some twenty got their furlough of 30 days. I was among this number."[33] All soldiers craved time with their families, but most accepted the requirement that they remain in service in order to defend those very families. As Joseph Manson explained to his wife, "I came in it [the war] in a humble capacity and if I keep well intend to stay in it until it ends or some unforseen cause takes me out. I am willing to sacrifice everything for my children's independence & sacred rights & they are dearer to me than life itself."[34]

The threat of force that William Smith mentioned revealed how the process of enforcing service, begun by the state as a military necessity, redefined how soldiers understood and exercised their loyalty to the state. Just as those men who would be drafted and those who had already volunteered were classified as loyal, those who left the service or avoided the draft could be classified as disloyal. The language of desertion began to emerge more clearly in the period during and after passage of the Conscription Act. No longer would men missing from their posts for weeks at a time be listed as "absent" or as "probably being at home." The decision to remove oneself from military service for more than a few days now created the risk that a man would be classified as a "deserter." The *Lexington Gazette* addressed the problem forthrightly. "Those who are absent from the army 'without leave,' had better be getting back to their posts," the editors advised. "If they persist in remaining at home, until compelled to go back under the escort of a provost guard, they lay themselves liable to be treated as deserters; and the rules of military discipline inflict the penalty of being shot upon all who deliberately desert the army in time of war." Like most soldiers, however, the newspaper recognized an important distinction between types of absence and prescribed different treatments. "If on the other hand," they advised, "those who are absent on their own responsibility, return voluntarily, they will be liable to be treated only as delinquents, and be subjected to less severe penalty than that inflicted upon the real deserter."[35]

In the winter of 1861–62, some "real deserters" who opposed the war and supported reunion did absent themselves. But the vast majority who left the camps of northern Virginia that long fall and winter did so because they defined military service and duty differently than did the military planners in Richmond. Most who left during this period displayed no desire to rejoin the Union. Indeed, most returned to their camps and continued fighting in the spring.[36] But in making military service obligatory and in constructing a bureaucracy to enforce the new rules, the Confederacy created a clear standard of loyalty.

Civilian institutions also adopted the new definition, revealing that the government had the power to change the way civilians understood loyalty as well. The *Gazette*, after defining the problem in a way that assumed loyalty from most soldiers, carried ads listing deserters by name in an attempt to shame Lexington soldiers back into the ranks.[37] The *Daily Richmond Exam-*

iner went further still. An editorial on desertion condemned those men who abandoned the army without recognizing the varieties of absence that then existed within the service. "The man who deserts his colours and turns his back upon the sworn obligations of his country's service is beyond the reach of ordinary shame," the *Examiner* asserted; "he must be treated, without sentimental ado, as a criminal, not as a subject for moral suasion; he must be made an example to the army, and his crime must be expiated by the just vengeance of the laws."[38] Churches cooperated with this change, adding a spiritual dimension to the problem of desertion. More than one parish decided to excommunicate a member who left the army. For pious Christians, this may have been the most serious punishment of all. One case came before the members of Elon Baptist Church in Hanover County in early 1862 and the parishioners concluded: "'The man who is not willing to work for the freedom which God has given us, is a traitor to his country, a hypocrite in the church and unfit to die.'"[39]

Soldiers understood their enlistment as a contract between the state and themselves, one that created mutual rights and responsibilities. Because of this belief, few soldiers saw a contradiction in seeking a substitute after the expiration of their initial twelve-month enlistment. After being detailed to Richmond in early 1862 to catch and return some "runaways" from their units, William Kidd confessed to his wife, "I would give a thousand dollars if I had it if I could get clear and could get home to stay there, a person that never has been in the service can stay at home & do some big talking but if they had to take the fare that I have they would soon get tired of war."[40]

Others who sought a substitute did so less from a sense of justice and more from simple war weariness. George Harlow made this plain in his letters home. "I hope we will not have to fight any more soon for I am getting verry tired of it and intend to get out of it if I can," he wrote. Like many volunteers, Harlow found the marching and camp life unbearable. Accordingly, he sought an honorable way out of his service agreement: "I made arrangements to get a substitute and before he got here there was an act passed not to take any substitutes under 45 years old and the one I got was just 16 he was from Louisa by the name of harper I was to give him $600 and a suit of clothes but I had to send him back tell Henry to look around and see if he cannot find a man in passing about that I can get that is over 45 years old." Harlow's willingness to modify his plans to meet the letter of the law reflected both his concern to achieve a lawful release for himself and an acceptance of the legitimacy of the new terms of military service.[41]

The process of conscription and reorganization was hesitant, uncertain, and incomplete in many respects, but it resulted in the renewal of Virginia's military fortunes, albeit with an army composed of much more skeptical soldiers than the eager volunteers of 1861. The deliberations of James Old of Rockbridge County reveal this process in close detail. Old sensed that the war would be much worse than politicians and the press announced. Posted near Manassas in late June 1861, he wrote to his mother, "I hope and prey that I may bee spaired to met you all a gain but I will have to go through a hard time if ever I do get back I have already seen hard times but nothing to what I expect to see." By January 1862 he was nearing his breaking point as rumors of forced reenlistment swirled around the camps. "Dearest Mother," he wrote from Centerville, "I thought a while back the chance was tolably good to get a furlow but they have put a stop to all furlows except those that are sick and those that will reinlist in the army for the war I think I will try and tuff my time out. and perhaps mayby I can come then." Then he relayed the threat that hung over enlisted men that winter. "Captain saunders says he dont think there will bee any chance for ous to leave the field that wee will bee drafted as soon as our time is out." Old's response represented everything that Confederate leaders feared as they debated the conscription legislation: "They may do as they may but i am a counting when my time is out if I live I have not forgot how to walk yet I will desert if they do that way." Worse still, Old prophesied that a forced draft would alienate most soldiers, "and most of the army say they will fight against the south."[42]

Despite his dire predictions, Old underwent a change of heart early in the new year. He wrote home to the brother he had earlier counseled to stay out of the war. "I received your letter dated the 22," Old began, "and was very glad to here from you but was sorry to here that you exspected to bee drafted soon and I exspect you will have to come a bout the 10th of march that is what the papers says." Old's new perspective on military service now emerged. He wrote, "I am very sorry to here that you and Mr Sale will have to leave your Families but This war is going to bee a desperat one and A short one I think and wee will Need all the men that wee can get." Old gave no direct explanation for his change of heart, though he did remark that "they are whipping ous at all points and if wee dont do all that we can do they will whip ous and if they do what will be come of ous and our families they will all bee Taken from ous." Instead of the aggrieved and disaffected soldier he had been in late 1861, by early 1862 James Old recommitted himself to the preservation of the Confederacy. "So wee aught to do all that wee can and fight them untill the last drop of blood has gone," he wrote, "I Think the test will bee desided this somer John I think you had better Join some company and not bee drafted . . . I exspect to

Reaenlist before long." Old did reenlist and was even appointed color corporal for his unit before dying of disease in July 1862. His brother John enlisted in the same regiment in March 1862 and served for the duration of the war.[43]

Like all his fellow soldiers, James Olds's struggle with the question of reenlistment occurred within a new atmosphere of military camp life that followed the fighting in mid-1861. Confederates' experiences in those camps shaped their response to the new definition of loyalty created through fighting the Yankees and debating the draft. After the battle at Manassas and the campaign in western Virginia, Confederate troops returned to camps where they could train and rest for the spring campaigns. In western Virginia, they settled in Winchester and many of the smaller towns of the Shenandoah Valley and along the eastern edge of the Allegheny Mountains. In central Virginia, thousands settled around Orange Courthouse and at outposts along the Rapidan River. From these camps, officers and enlisted men met the challenge of maintaining discipline and resolving the class and regional tensions that emerged among volunteers by creating a surprisingly flexible and responsive system. Soldiers buttressed their commitment to the army by establishing a dense web of connections with families, through personal visits, regular correspondence, and fond recollection. Finally, soldiers drew upon the political nature of secession and the public nature of enlistment to formulate a new sense of national spirit that bolstered their resolve to accept the burdens of the draft, persevere despite the defeats in western Virginia, and prepare for future battles.

The development of a Confederate military that responded to soldiers' needs emerged, in many cases, before soldiers ever settled in their winter camps. Complaints over food, shelter, equipment, and leadership characterized the army from its earliest days, as did an almost continual contest for status and respect among soldiers and between enlisted men and officers. The Confederate victory at Manassas in July 1861 bolstered morale and helped subdue the frustration and tensions growing out of the volatile mix of eager, untrained volunteers and assertive and inexperienced officers that fermented in undersupplied training camps around the state that summer. As McClellan reorganized and reequipped Union troops in the fall of 1861, Confederate military leaders undertook the same effort. The drilling and discipline that company-level commanders imposed upon their men in the late summer and fall began to rankle many soldiers who were not, and had no ambition to be, professional warriors. Complaints about their treatment emerged quickly.

Samuel B. Blymon, just returned from picket duty on the evening of November 3, wrote to a friend from Centreville: "Soldiering is getting to be no fun now. I suppose the Confederate Authorities will never want any more volunteers after this war is over, from the manner in which they treat them now. And unless they change their treatment in a very great measure, it will be hard to force them back into service." Blymon's friend also served in the army, and Blymon stressed that his criticism of conditions and even leaders should not be interpreted as unpatriotic: "I love my country as dear as any man that breathes, and will take my rifle and march to meet its enemies as soon as any man. But when such upstarts get authority as we have amongst us, I feel no inclination to place my carcass at their disposal and shall be apt to look before I leap next time. As for Jeff Davis, & Stephens, Beauregard & Johnston, they are gentlemen but it is the petty officers who have the more immediate control over us that I complain of." Blymon's comments represent a fair estimate of the dissatisfaction that developed as the Confederate army began to organize its soldiers. His expression of support for the Confederacy was also typical.[44]

Similar complaints could be heard in other parts of the army. One soldier noted in a letter home, "Gen Longstreet remarked the other day that the 1st Virginia Regiment had become almost demoralized So I heard it reported one company was put under arrest for refusing to serve under a Lieutenant who had struck one of the men over the head with his sword. The men were sent to Manassas (that was company F Washington men)." Whatever the offense given to the men of company F it must have been grave, as was their reaction. The same month that the story circulated, Company F was detached from its service with the 1st Infantry and assigned to the 1st Virginia Artillery. The old Company F lasted in that position scarcely two months before being mustered out by special order. Though it was unusual for a whole company to disintegrate in the space of sixty days, the episode revealed the volatile nature of the Virginians who became soldiers and the need for circumspection when dealing with them.[45]

The problems that incompetent officers created held the potential to ruin what little discipline the effective officers had established in the fall and winter. The deterioration that could occur emerged clearly in the correspondence of James Langhorne with his family. In mid-June, Langhorne wrote to his mother with glowing remarks for his commanding officer: "Capt Trigg is one of the best and most impartial officers I ever saw but he is a rigid disciplinarian I being his Lieut. have to convey all his orders to the company and see that they are carried out, all the men in the company who have sense and know what discipline is like me, and think I do nothing more than discharge my duty." Langhorne continued, "those who are inattentive & negligent of duty all always receive the reproof or correction they deserve often complain, although the men complain of being strict on drill they say I have a kind heart." Langhorne's company fought at Bull Run, which he pronounced a "glorious victory." By late fall, however, a personnel change in the regiment had destroyed the positive morale and discipline established during the preceding five months. "Mr. John Wade is an excellent man," he reported, "but he makes a much worse Capt. than I had any idea he would, the men do not fear to violate his orders, and the company has lost more than I had any idea it would in discipline & morral since Capt Trigg left it, but in fact, our whole Reg has lost in discipline since the battle of 21st July."[46]

Military officials tried to solve the problems of leadership and discipline that emerged in 1861, but common soldiers often seized the initiative themselves. Most importantly, Confederate soldiers turned out unsatisfactory officers. Richard Waldrop wrote to his brother from Gaines Point in late May with news about his company commander, a respected Richmonder, who had written a book on military drill. Despite his captain's prominence, or perhaps because of it, Waldrop found him intolerable. In his letter, Waldrop promoted the man to Colonel, perhaps in an intentional jab at his pretensions. "Col. Cary has gone to R & it is said here that he has gone to try to have us kept here but he has made himself so obnoxious to us by his short & snappish way of speaking to us that I dont believe there are a dozen men in the co who will muster into service under him," Waldrop reported. In fact, Cary was transferred two weeks later to take command of the 30th Virginia Infantry. He lasted in that position until the regiment's reorganization in the spring of 1862, when elections were held. At that point he stepped down, noting an "unwillingness to hold position conferred by those subject to his control."[47] In other words, Cary refused to participate in the democratic structure established for selecting regimental-level officers in the Confederate army. The men of the 30th Virginia seem to have been untroubled. They elected a new colonel, just as Waldrop would have advised.[48] Virginia's soldiers obeyed the orders of officers they respected, men who gave them the respect that they earned and demanded as free white men in Virginia, and of those officers who displayed courage on the battlefield. They rarely abided aristocrats who presumed to lead by status alone.[49]

The power to select company-level officers was one of the most important rights granted to enlisted men. This power gave soldiers the ability to oust those commanders who treated their men with inadequate levels of respect or courtesy. William Boutwell Kidd, serving with the 30th Virginia Infantry observed in February 1862 that "Johnsons Co has refused to inlist under him positively." The blanket rejection of a company's commander was rare but almost always fatal. When Johnson's Company D reorganized in April, the men voted him out of office, and he spent the remainder of the war teaching at a military institute in Florida.[50] Men paid careful attention to the behavior of all their officers and replaced without much hesitation those who dissatisfied them. One soldier noted briefly: "Our company was organized the other day and we turned our first Lieutenant out and elected the second lieutenant who was Bagby for our first liet."[51] Although critics charged that electing officers elevated incompetent men to positions of leadership, the performance of Virginia troops through the war offers little evidence to support this charge. The high number of prewar elites who served in the military offered an important leadership advantage that also helped the Confederacy. Consequently, many officers already possessed skills at resolving class and ethnic tensions between other white men.[52]

The responsiveness of the Confederate military depended partly on those more astute officers facilitating an atmosphere of equality within their camps.[53] Captain James Jones White of the 4th Virginia Infantry wrote to his wife Mary from camp near Centreville in mid-August 1861 about a man in his company: "Coupland Page can take as good care of himself as any fellow in the services. He wanted me to take his bed made of barrel staves laid across poles but I wouldn't deprive him of it. He is a very generous & independent fellow—takes care of himself & allows nobody to interfere with his rights, which is very well understood." White wrote his wife about an episode where Page had trouble cooking dinner in the rain. One of Page's messmates began teasing him, and Page said he would "thrash" him if the man did not quiet down. As the commanding officer, White should have stepped in to prevent a fight, but instead he told Page he would not interfere and the messmate quickly departed. White concluded, "War is a firm business to develop character. I am surprised to make the discoveries that I do every day." Indeed, it seems more likely that Page's character did not "develop" in response to the war, but rather that Captain White had a previously unavailable opportunity to interact with men of Page's lower social standing, who possessed every bit as much pride and personal integrity as White's prewar associates. These types of opportunities probably came to officers and gentlemen with some frequency through the war. Those leaders who acted on their new knowledge, as White did, gained the confidence of their troops.[54]

Competent officers could, and did, help enlisted men suffer the strictures and indignities of military discipline by bending rules and making exceptions. William Fleming Harrison, a captain with the 23rd Virginia Infantry, explained the realities of his situation frankly to his men: "I have told them that I had to obey orders & I was carrying out the order of my superior officers & I had to obey & they should obey." Writing to his wife, Harrison confided that his men gave him "fits" in their efforts to assert their independence. Even as he was being pressured by his superiors to arrest and jail several of his men for breaches of discipline, he persevered in his attempts to persuade his company that a modicum of discipline was necessary. As the 1862 campaign season opened, regimental officers increased the pressure on Harrison to reclaim missing men and organize his company. Rather than report absent members of his company, he wrote to his wife and asked her to "tell Jno Wilson to see Wm Powell Charles Johnson Mo. N. Johnson & Wm. Ellis & tell them if they don't return forthwith they will be arrested as deserters & brought back which will be very disagreeable." Powell, a twenty-three-year-old farmer, had overstayed his sick leave but reported back for duty in time to avoid censure. He received a promotion to corporal in 1864 and lived to surrender at Appomattox. Ellis, on the other hand, did not return and regimental rolls listed him as absent without leave. At some point in 1863, he rejoined the company and a court-martial convened and acquitted him. Ellis died in action at the Wilderness in 1864. At least William Powell, and perhaps others, benefited from Harrison's efforts to deal gently with his men. Considering that the offenses that Powell and the others committed would soon warrant the death penalty, Harrison's sensitivity must have earned him plaudits from his men. His approach perhaps made the policies that he had to reluctantly enforce a little easier to manage.[55]

At the same time that soldiers worked out the strategies that would allow them to retain their dignity and autonomy while in military service, they also sought ways to satisfy their emotional needs. After the Confederate victory at Manassas, many soldiers who assumed they would return home were shocked to find rules and guards keeping them in camp. For most men, that fall was the longest period they had been apart from their families. The separation seemed unbearable. David Funsten, a private with the 11th Virginia Infantry, spent the winter in Centreville, near the Manassas battlefield. He wrote to his daughters regularly about daily life in the army but finally confessed to his wife, "For a long time, I kept you all out of my thoughts, as much as possible, but when I began to think of a furlough & you always the embodiment of every hope & desire connected with it I found myself often overwhelmed as day after day & week after week passed away without the

expected leave of absence." Funsten knew firsthand the danger of withdraw-
ing into one's emotions. He told his wife, "There was a young man from one
of the Southern states who applied a few days ago for a furlough & it was
refused. He was afterwards on guard . . . seeking an opportunity he stepped
into a tent & blew his brains out. The tragic is extensively carried on here."
Even without the drama of suicide, most Confederate soldiers would have
agreed that their separations from their families constituted one of the war's
central hardships.[56]

Without their families, soldiers struggled to recreate some sense of home
in the camps where they spent most of their time. This involved men assuming the values and performing the work often associated with women in the
antebellum South. In fact, soldiers were not adopting wholly foreign beliefs
or activities. During peacetime, most white men were active members of
their households who understood and internalized the values that made
them work. "The central values of the home," one historian has argued,
"were harmony, self-control, and moderation."[57] For families to function
successfully people had to suppress their individual needs, and the same was
true in camps. Men found familiar the tensions between domestic and public
space that they had also known at home, only now they enforced the femi-
nine rules as well. Battles demanded toughness, ambition, and aggression,
but in camp harmony, self-control, and moderation prevailed. Stable, home-
like camps offered the opportunity for soldiers to create or strengthen relationships among men that bolstered their psychological health.[58]

An important element of soldiers' efforts to recreate the parlor in the
camp lay in the domestic duties that they performed. Of necessity, most
Confederate soldiers had to do their own washing, cooking, and sewing.
More surprisingly, many seem to have enjoyed it. Typical of this group was
William Peek, who wrote his mother that, "As we lost our cook Steve and I
had to get supper ourselves. I made the bread & he did the meat & coffee. The
bread was pronounced the very best in the whole camp, and as good as any
body need have."[59] Food preparation in the camps seldom exceeded the
basic; most soldiers cooked meat (when there was any) in a skillet or roasted
over a fire, and vegetables surfaced infrequently. When ovens could be obtained from home or built in camps, baking seems to have attracted the most
interest. Confederate soldiers foraged rapaciously, and during the war they
denuded acres of Virginia's fruit trees and bushes. The apples, cherries, and
berries picked on these trips went into pies. As early as late 1861, Confederate
soldiers who had taken on these new duties began to surprise themselves
with their domestic abilities, and the accompanying sense of satisfaction.

Fletcher Moore, with the 12th Virginia Cavalry, boasted to his sister in mid-November, "we begin to understand cooking very well." His enthusiasm for cooking, probably not a frequent occurrence in prewar days, was not uncommon among Virginia's Confederate soldiers. Many men developed an affinity for assorted domestic duties and they openly proclaimed their new skills and the enjoyment they took from them.[60]

The ability to feed themselves was crucial, but the meaning of the new skills went well beyond mere relief at being self-sufficient. William Mordecai took such pride in his baking that he bragged to his mother and asserted his culinary superiority over his sister. "My Dear Mother," he wrote, "You seem to think we are all nakcd & starving. . . . Since we kicked a trifling cook we had in our mess, out, on account of his bad bread, we (six of us) take it by turns to cook, & have biscuits which, if I may use such a figure, would often put Sally to the blush."[61] Sally's first reaction might have been laughter rather than embarrassment, but like many Confederates, Mordecai was in earnest about his new skills. Daniel Hileman wrote to his brother from Fairfax Station in north-central Virginia, "Oh Philip I wish you could come down here to eat beefstake That oven you sent me is the very thing to fry beefstake in I flatter myself that I can cook beefstake as good as any woman and I can bake first rate bread too I am well pleased with the cooking instincts." Hileman frankly recognized that he hoped to reach a level of achievement already attained by most women. Further, his pride rested in developing his "cooking instincts," a skill few men would have bragged about before the war. The process of mastering domestic skills helped soldiers stay connected to the domestic worlds that they left behind when they joined the armies. Without a doubt, many soldiers learned to cook and clean because (like soldiers the world over) they had to, but soldiers' receptivity and interest in these tasks offers a valuable clue to the importance of domesticity in their lives.[62]

Efforts to recreate a sense of domestic intimacy partially helped offset the loneliness men felt at being separated from their families. A young captain admitted the difference between his real home and camp in a letter to his wife late in 1861. "We have been lying out for the past week on the ground without tents," he reported, "and as we started back to camp some one remarked that he was glad that we were going back home (meaning camp). I remarked that if I only was assured that I was on my way to my home, where my dear wife is, it would be the happiest moment of my life, except the meeting, but alas, it was not home that we were going to, but the tented field." To assuage the sense of loss at being separated, soldiers spent time establishing contacts with loved ones. Communication with families, rather than male bonding with other soldiers, satisfied most men's emotional needs during the war. One Confederate described the situation to his sister.

> It must have been a happy thought to you, if you knew, whilst you were writing the letter I received yesterday, how much real pleasure it would afford. I knew I was not forgotten. I knew that the affection you had always shown would increase rather than subside under existing circumstances. But letters are not intended merely to convey intelligence. They are more precious as a medium for carrying on a silent conversation between those who have thoughts and affections& sympathies & hopes alike. Such was your letter to me.[63]

Concern for families in the wake of Union invasion of the state, and the ensuing physical hardships, drove men to focus their emotional attention on their loved ones at home. Soldiers begged for descriptions of family members and activities, working to keep themselves connected to the domestic worlds they left. One soldier's plea to his wife is typical in this regard. "I want you to write me a long letter," he stated, "giving me a particular account of your own condition and telling me all about *our little daughter*. It is time she had a name—what do you want to call her?" The desperation felt by Virginia soldiers to stay involved in their families' lives emerges almost palpably from some letters. "Do write me soon," John Harrison pleaded with his wife. "It is cruel and unkind when I am so hampered with my duties to keep me so anxious about you all, when one little line might either set my mind at rest or call me to you—I am almost constrained that you do not care about my troubles or do not like to have me share yours." Many men maintained contact with their children through their spouses. A farmer from the Shenandoah Valley told his wife, "I want you to kiss the children once a day for me until I get home. Then I will get to take the job off your hands." When soldiers could not take furloughs to visit home, or read letters sent by relatives, they wrote letters themselves, or simply recollected the love and affection they enjoyed at home. All of this emotional work helped stabilize soldiers amid the uncertainty and violence of the war and served as a crucial counterpart to the institution building soldiers performed at the same time.[64]

The third element that emerged in late 1861 and early 1862 to help cement soldiers' dedication to Confederate victory was an emerging sense of Confederate nationalism. Most white Virginians transferred their national loyalties to the Confederacy with surprising ease. Letters at this time contain references to "our country," or "the country," or "the nation" in clear reference to the Confederacy, yet few correspondents betray any self-consciousness that this represented a shift of national loyalties. Rather, most Virginians seem to have adopted the perspective advocated by Confederate leaders, that the Confederacy represented the true intent of the Founding Fathers and should rightly be considered "America." One young soldier, who had joined the army without his parent's consent, revealed this perspective when he wrote home to explain his decision. Appropriately, he enlisted in the town of Liberty, Virginia. "Perhaps I have acted wrongly in acting without consulting you," he began, "but I could not stay here and see our lands overrun by those vile vagabonds of Black Republicanism I go with a brave heart and look to the Father of Battles for protection hoping that I may be spared to return and enjoy the freedom which was obtained by the blood of our forefathers." In the public atmosphere of secession and enlistment, dedication to nation as an end in itself emerged as a viable motivating factor.[65]

During 1861 and 1862, the new sense of national identity helped anchor soldiers' duty to remain in service despite hardships in camps or on campaigns, dissatisfaction with the draft, or simple loneliness. Benjamin F. Wade, with the 19th Virginia Infantry, explained the demands made on loyal men to his brother in early January 1862. "In these revolutionary times individual life is much less regarded than ordinarily," he instructed. "The issues are so momentous that the blood of the present generations must be the purchase money. And they involve a degree of self sacrifice that must often be stimulated to be preserved, rather than weakened by those to whom we temporarily entrust our lives and fortunes." Wade closed with a remarkably succinct expression of nationalism: "If we are to have a nation it matters little who he be."[66] Indeed, Virginia men took note of events around their new nation and redoubled their efforts in the face of defeats and setbacks in the western theater. A cadet at the Virginia Military Institute informed his sister that "since the great disaster to our arms at Roanoke Island and Fort Donalson the Cadets have all tendered their services to Gov. Letcher. I don't suppose he will accept us. We have not heard from him yet. I wish he would accept us. I think every one ought to be in the field."[67]

The eager young men at the institute were not the only Virginians who recognized in the losses of their new countrymen to the west a spur to action. James McCutchan of Augusta County drew from the western defeats a stronger sense of purpose. "This is the darkest hour the Confederacy has ever seen," he told his sister in March 1862. "Now is the time for every true & patriotic spirit to rally 'round the Bonnie Blue Flag & fight & never cease to fight while there is an enemy South of Mason's & Dixon's line."[68] Richard Waldrop expressed a similar sentiment to his mother, noting, "I think this is a bad time for men to be pushing forward their own interests when the country is in more imminent danger than it has been at any time yet & has need for every arm that can be raised in her defence."[69] The draft angered many soldiers, but the necessity of service overwhelmed individual concerns about the mechanism deployed to create the army. "I think it [automatic reenlistment] probably justifiable under the circumstances," Armistead Burwell wrote his brother, "for, it must be apparent to the most casual observer, that at least a large proportion of the twelve month volunteers must be kept in the field next Summer if we would meet the well drilled hordes of the North with any certainty of success." Burwell did not speak without consideration for what it meant for him. "As for myself," he wrote, "I expect to enlist again, and would like to make some arrangement with you, that we may both get into the same company."[70]

The commitment that Armistead Burwell made to the idea of a Confederate nation in the winter of 1861–62 came somewhat more easily than it may have for soldiers from the Lower South. Virginians recognized that the defense of the Confederate nation overlapped significantly with the defense of their own state. This understanding allowed soldiers like John Barrett Pendleton of Richmond to explain his duty as "the defense of our country, our liberty and the protection of our parents, wives, and children, and all that is dear to a man."[71] For Pendleton, as for most Virginia Confederates, there was little friction between the demands of home and the demands of nation. Samuel Moore grasped this idea as well. He criticized his company captain when the officer left the unit to care for his family. If his family could not survive without the captain's presence, Moore thought he should resign. "I rejoice that no such conflict exists in my case," he announced. "That my duty to my County, my family, my neighbors, myself, all unite in requiring me to be just where I am, a soldier in our noble army, ready to go and die in the cause of liberty."[72]

The Virginians who fought the Civil War, like all Americans who came of age in the antebellum era, were reared in a period when emotional celebrations of nationalism were the norm.[73] It seemed natural to them to identify closely with the Confederacy, because most had formed meaningful bonds with the United States before the war. That faith in the Confederacy would serve them well over the coming years. Although Virginians would not always agree with the policies of the Richmond government, or even continue to offer the paeans to nationhood that they did early in the war, the bedrock sense of national identity established by mid-1862 facilitated a deep commitment to southern independence.

Part II ★ THE CRUCIBLE OF WAR

3 ✻ THE ARDOR OF PATRIOTISM
APRIL–JULY 1862

*This war is a horrid thing, & though I shall devote my life & honor to the cause of
my country, still I would be very glad to see peace come . . . As it is I see only a
protracted struggle ahead, that many of us will not see the end of, & yet I try
always to think that I will live to see success crown our holy cause.*
   —John Meems, 11th Virginia Infantry, April 3, 1862

By late April 1862, the uncertainties and problems generated
by the enactment of the Draft Act receded as a new campaign season dawned. Virginia Confederates took solace
from the belief that this would be the last year of war, if indeed the war lasted
the whole year. Some men resigned themselves to a longer conflict, enlisting
for the unspecified term "for the war" but always with the expectation that
victory would come in one form or another. Many Confederates anticipated
foreign recognition, hoping that Britain and France would bestow the legitimacy upon Confederate nationhood that Abraham Lincoln refused to con-
cede. During 1862 Confederates gathered psychological sustenance from
their military victories even as their physical sustenance drained out of them.
With victories in battles around Richmond, in the Shenandoah Valley, on the
now-hallowed battleground at Manassas, and from the heights above Fredericksburg, morale soared among eager and resolute Confederates. But all
these battles, and those that did not go as planned, like the September invasion of Maryland, imposed massive casualties and consumed valuable resources upon which all Virginians depended.[1]

As the war grew longer and more intense, Confederate soldiers thought
more deeply about the purposes and goals of their new undertaking. The early
commitment of Virginia Confederates to fight through the bloody year of
1862 drew on several distinct but complementary sources of inspiration.
Institutional factors played an important role, with soldiers continuing to
favor a more democratic and responsive army, and with Confederate leaders
promoting a new nation that promised to serve the interests of all southerners. The sustained presence of Federal troops in the state, their increasingly
direct attack on slavery, and the rumors about the atrocities they committed
fueled a sense of revenge that sustained many soldiers. Soldiers' interest in

protecting their families' emerged as a key motivation as the scale and scope of the war expanded. Finally, Confederates built a new culture of sacrifice, displayed most publicly in the deaths of noble soldiers but also in the support given to the nation by civilians at home. These elements emerged among Virginians in different ways during the year; combined with the military victories in the region, they led Confederates to believe that permanent independence from the North was both the right course and a feasible one.

During a normal April, most Virginia men would have been preparing their tools, seeds, and work force for the planting season. The political excitement of secession and the ensuing martial celebrations after Virginia's exit from the Union had marked the preceding April as one of the most unusual in memory. April 1862 would be remembered as marking the shift to a new calendar ruled by the rhythms of the battlefield. After this year, Virginia men would look to the spring thaw not as a time of renewal but as the opening of a new season of warfare and violence.

The enactment of the conscription legislation in April followed several months of argument over the issue and in some ways served as an anticlimactic finish to the violent debate among soldiers and the public over the proper way to fill the ranks. As James Old's experience revealed, men often expended their energy denouncing the act in the early months of the year while still confined to camp. As the campaign season opened in April, and as Confederate officials sought to persuade men to reenlist, opposition to the draft within the army began to decline. Volunteers resented the notion that military service could, or would ever need to be, coerced from citizens, but in the face of the coming Union attack, most soldiers set aside their concerns with recruitment policy and prepared themselves for more war.

Most volunteers had entered the service with their neighbors and kin in the same company, and those who entered without contacts had formed bonds with the men in their units over the first twelve months of war. Consequently, most seized the opportunity granted by the Confederate Congress to keep their units together. Under the terms of the Draft Act, men were allowed to reenlist in their own companies as long as they achieved the minimum number of men necessary to qualify. The combination of incentives and penalties in the draft legislation, along with the desire of many volunteers to continue their service until they accomplished their war goals, ensured a fairly high reenlistment rate. A captain in the 9th Virginia Infantry reported to his father on his unit's progress, noting that, "nearly eighty of the old company has already reenlisted, & I expect to muster into service for two years one hundred & twenty five men." Though overly optimistic about his future prospects, the success this officer reported, about an 80 percent re-enlistment rate, was roughly average among Virginia units.[2]

Confederates built upon the effort by soldiers in 1861 to make the army a more flexible and responsive institution. Once volunteers had reorganized their units, they held elections for officers. From the perspective of the Confederate congressmen who wrote and passed the legislation, giving soldiers the opportunity to elect their commanders was the proper due they owed to volunteers. Officers complained continually about the process, asserting that soldiers rewarded those commanders who avoided enforcing discipline and granted excessive furloughs or liberal leave policies. As the 46th Infantry prepared to hold elections, Randolph Harrison (perhaps to soften the possible blow to his ego) ridiculed the behavior of soldiers who would replace their officers. "We are expecting to have a reorganization of our regiment," Harrison noted. "They have been playing sad havoc with company and field officers over the river generally turning out their best officers, so if we have the election you needn't be surprised to see me at home soon, if I should be defeated." Harrison's practice of referring to enlisted men as "they," rather than recognizing the unity of the army, revealed the distance between himself and his charges. "I think it possible," Harrison wondered, "though don't know at all, that my being home so long may go against me."[3] Despite his absence, Harrison's men retained their faith in him and he was reelected. Less fortunate officers in the 46th, including its colonel, were sent home.[4]

In other regiments across the state, soldiers did "turn out" officers who dodged the hardships of winter camps at home or in cities where they secured private housing. Many of the officers thus released may have been quite competent as drillmasters or on the battlefield, but their unwillingness to suffer the privations of camp with their men earned them short tenure as officers. The Confederacy's democratic process of electing officers earned the scorn of army leaders and subsequent historians. Members of the prewar regular army, in particular, found the idea that they were beholden to their charges abhorrent and blamed many of the problems of the spring upon the election process.[5]

The men who filled the army as enlisted men, however, possessed quite a different view of the matter. George Washington Peebles recorded the outcome of his regiment's reorganization with a nearly mutinous glee, "heard to day that this company will be reorganized and a complete new set of Officers elected with the exception of Capt. Let them rip. Sic Semper Tyrannis."[6] A captain who abandoned his men to the cold winds of "Camp Despair" in the

Allegheny Mountains to seek a warm room and home-cooked meals from a spouse or old friend lost the confidence of his men, usually permanently. The likelihood of that officer's being able to lead men effectively, especially in the pressure of battle, diminished immensely. In many cases, soldiers may have prevented worse disasters by expelling the officers before they were forced to rely upon them. Soldiers who discussed the process itself rarely commented upon the efficiency or inefficiency it supposedly produced. If pressed, most probably would have offered the performance of the army in battles in the Shenandoah Valley and on the Peninsula below Richmond as evidence that electing officers only strengthened the army. During the major battles of the spring, individual units responded quite well to orders; many of the errors that occurred during battle stemmed from miscommunications among senior officers.[7]

The pride that volunteers felt about their company identity formed the basis for the loyalty men felt toward the army. When regimental reorganizations worked properly, soldiers rewarded effective and impartial leadership and in the process welded their units together in a more permanent fashion. The military units created in early 1862, and reorganized periodically throughout the war, provided both structure for the process of loyalty building and a pole around which men could rally. An important part of this process was the fact that a significant majority—roughly 70 percent—of all the men who served in Virginia forces during the war enlisted before the Draft Act was passed (see figure 1). Although new enlistees, and a handful of draftees, would enter the service in each of the years of the war, most of the men who served counted themselves as early volunteers. They experienced the war together and bonded through the successes and failures they shared.

The local nature of enlistment meant that the companies and regiments into which men formed in 1861 would be of central value in keeping men in the ranks; the positive reinforcement of fighting alongside relatives and the more coercive knowledge that news of desertion, disobedience, or cowardice would quickly reach one's home and community served as twin pillars of support for men in the ranks. The support system that soldiers created can be thought of as a set of concentric circles, beginning at the tent or mess level and proceeding up through the company, regiment, brigade, division, corps, army, and finally nation. New identities organized around brigades and divisions strengthened men's resolve in early 1862. The possessive names attached to this level of organization—Winder's Brigade, Anderson's Brigade, Ewell's Division—revealed a personal dimension to the army that helped cement men's loyalties at higher levels. Once soldiers found a commander

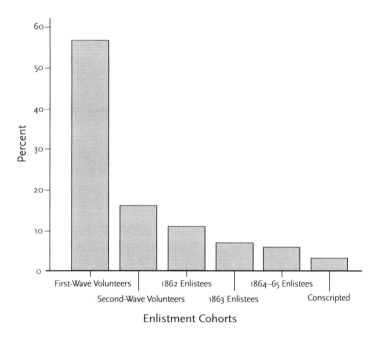

Figure 1. Aggregate Enlistment Patterns, 1861–1865. Note: *"First-Wave Volunteers"
are defined as those men who enlisted between April and the end of September 1861.
"Second-Wave Volunteers" enlisted between October and the passage of the Draft
Act on April 16, 1861.*

who treated them fairly and, most importantly, led them to victories, they
endorsed his leadership with pride.

As soldiers fought their way through the battles and negotiated their way
through the internal conflicts and challenges of 1862, the solidarity and
cohesion at the company level broadened to encompass the regiment, the
brigade, and eventually the whole Army of Northern Virginia. Through the
events of the year, Virginia soldiers developed a new and deep loyalty to the
corps commanders Stonewall Jackson and James Longstreet, who directed
their movement on the battlefields outside Richmond, Manassas, Sharpsburg, and Fredericksburg. Alongside and intertwined with this admiration
and respect for the generals at their head, Virginia soldiers developed a strong
faith in, and affection for, their commander, Robert E. Lee. Beginning with
the expulsion of McClellan from the gates of Richmond in July, Lee led the
Army of Northern Virginia to victories that reinforced the soldiers' confidence in themselves and in their army as an unit. From June 1862 until the
end of the war, most Virginians fought under Robert E. Lee, while many
northern soldiers operated under six different commanders over the same

period. The affection, and eventually reverence, with which most Confederate soldiers viewed Lee helped establish a remarkable solidarity and confidence within the Confederacy's main army. Although many northern soldiers developed great faith in George B. McClellan, Lee's repeated success on the battlefield helped forge a unique bond between him and his men. By the fall of 1862 much of this infrastructure was in place, and although men would shift regiments and sometimes receive new brigade or division commanders, they continued to take solace and support from all levels of their army.[8]

The process of building confidence and solidarity extended to the nation itself in 1862, as the Confederacy organized its permanent government and set about developing the culture and symbols of an independent nation. Alexander S. Pendleton, a young staff officer under Stonewall Jackson, wrote to his mother in Rockbridge County in the upper Shenandoah Valley in mid-February. Though far removed from the political heart of Virginia and the Confederacy, Pendleton followed the growth of his new national government in the newspapers. In one of his regular epistles, Pendleton encouraged his mother to let his sister make the long trip over the Blue Ridge Mountains to witness the inauguration of Jefferson Davis as president of the Confederacy. Davis had been elected by the Provisional Congress in February 1861 when the new nation consisted of only the seven Gulf States. A subsequent election by the full voting populace of the Confederacy confirmed Davis for one six-year term. "Really I don't see the slightest harm in innocent enjoyment," Pendleton wrote, "and remember, mother mine, a first Inauguration doesn't, if my arithmetic is right, take place but once in an ordinary lifetime."[9]

Pendleton's grandfather had probably been alive during George Washington's inauguration, so for the Pendletons, a new nation was a novelty but not a purely historic event. European nations had long prophesied the collapse of the American experiment in democracy, and Pendleton, probably like many Confederates, took the rise of their new nation in stride. The inauguration itself, and the broad historical perspective with which people like Pendleton engaged it, brought a new form of solidarity to the South that had not existed before the war began and was only faintly discernible outside official pronouncements or newspaper editorials through most of 1861.

The new nationalism connected soldiers to each other and to citizens, integrating the sacrifice of volunteering into a larger tapestry of national protection and growth. A soldier with Virginia's 41st Infantry observed the effect of the close of the first year of fighting on the army and the country as a whole. This man suggested that a shift had occurred and observed that the growing resolve of Confederates to secure their independence stemmed at least partly from the new national allegiance discussed by Pendleton. He relished the arrival of northern troops, knowing that "when they do come, it will afford us pleasure to teach them how dangerous & hazardous a thing it is to invade the shores of a great and high spirited country; & they will know the difference between the ardor of patriotism & the turbulency of a rebellion."[10]

In winter camps across the state, men identified new and more permanent reasons for their support of Confederate independence, meshing personal and public factors. Ironically, for a war ostensibly fought on the basis of state rights, it was during the war that most Virginia men finally saw their state. In letters home and diary entries, soldiers from all regions recounted the novelty of being in parts of the state about which they had only read. Detailed sociologies of hardy westerners or wealthy Tidewater plantations filled the journals of soldiers as they struggled to splice together their actual experiences of Virginia with their prewar assumptions. In many cases, men thrilled at the sight of mountains or basked in the grandeur of the statues of Washington, Jefferson, and Madison around the capitol building in Richmond. These experiences provided a new sense of state solidarity and added strength to the belief that Virginia was a place worth preserving.

Virginia Confederates could not necessarily assume that all men would rise to the defense of the Old Dominion. Some Virginians encountered one another with suspicion and, occasionally, hostility. The rough terrain of the Alleghenies spurred many easterners to accept the loss of the West with gratitude, and westerners trapped in the humid swamps of the Tidewater or in the increasingly crowded and immoral cities of the East complained bitterly. The fact that the Confederacy drew soldiers from all regions of the state stands as testimony that men could imagine an interest in the integrity of other sections. In this way, the service of Shenandoah Valley soldiers in the swamps around Suffolk or of Petersburg men fighting their way across the Allegheny plateau offers evidence for their embrace of a nationalism larger than themselves or their community interests. Though it could be argued that soldiers from Louisiana or Mississippi performed more demanding acts of imagination to identify themselves with the defense of Virginia, Virginians, too had to imagine themselves part of one nation.

In the face of setbacks along the North Carolina coast, along the Mississippi River, and at Forts Henry and Donelson, in Tennessee, Confederates across the South took joy in reports of Stonewall Jackson's army during the Shenandoah Valley campaign of 1862. The accomplishments of Jackson's army revealed the extent of suffering and hardship that men would accept in exchange for military success. Further, the campaign demonstrated the interdependence of civilian and soldier morale and the dual importance of home front and battlefront. The wildly enthusiastic response of Valley residents released from Union occupation added a tangible sense of accomplishment to Confederate soldiers' pride in their strategic accomplishment of driving northern forces from the region. Especially for Virginians, the liberation of Winchester and other occupied places reinforced the extent to which defense of nation was also defense of home.

The 1862 Shenandoah Valley campaign has drawn the attention of military historians because of Jackson's effective use of his smaller army to stymie several larger Union forces. The episode also provides a useful window into the patterns of experience that help explain Confederate perseverance through the war as a whole. Jackson's Valley Army recovered from an initial loss at Kernstown in March to defeat Union troops at McDowell, Front Royal, Winchester, Cross Keys, and Port Republic. Jackson's creative leadership and the incompetence of his opponents certainly helped make this outcome possible. Equally important were soldiers' visits home and their encounters with Confederate civilians who had been living under Union occupation. These meetings renewed Virginia soldiers' vision of themselves as defenders of their homes and fueled outrage over the treatment of southern noncombatants. Jackson's soldiers suffered immensely during the campaign, but his men accepted the hardships because they won battles. These successes, in turn, fueled a stronger commitment to prosecute the war. The campaign demonstrated the resolve of Virginians to win the war and set a standard for accepting personal hardship and suffering that would sustain that resolve for several more years.

Problems of discipline also plagued the Valley Army during the campaign. In one episode, Jackson displayed the temper and willingness to use force that made him both a loved and a feared commander. Watkins Kearns, a private with the 27th Infantry, which served throughout the campaign, noted in his diary, "A mutiny broke out amongst the Hibernians [Irish] 17 of whom stacked arms. They were reported to Gen Jackson who gave them their choice of taking up their arms or being instantly shot. They took arms."[11] The private's sarcastic conclusion to the episode reveals the summary nature of justice at this stage of the campaign.

Jackson earned a reputation for the high expectations he set for soldiers, but even he recognized that a flexible approach might improve the chances of the Confederacy. For instance, Jackson did not force the enlistment of confirmed members of the Valley's pacifist Mennonite community during the campaign. Accurately sensing that mandatory military service might spur antipathy among community members for the Confederacy, Jackson focused on keeping order in his army. In the meantime, the state government granted Mennonites an exemption from military duty based on their religious beliefs.[12] The result was that most Mennonites remained in the Valley; although they opposed the Confederacy's decision to wage war, their productive farms provided valuable sustenance for Confederate soldiers and civilians around the state. Benjamin Bragg's behavior in Kentucky in 1862 provides an illuminating contrast to Jackson's more politically astute handling of opposition in the Shenandoah Valley. Upon entering central Kentucky in mid-1862, Bragg immediately enforced the Draft Act. By this time, most Confederate Kentuckians of military age had already enlisted in Tennessee units so Bragg's order fell on a generally unsympathetic public. Instead of spurring enthusiasm, the draft alienated neutral supporters and generated little additional manpower for the Confederacy.

Less serious episodes, especially those outside the purview of Jackson himself, were treated with greater laxity, which helped make the campaign bearable for the men. In mid-April, Kearns and several friends fell away from the march to inspect a tunnel built the previous year. Upon returning to camp, he found his whole company under arrest but could report that he "slept very soundly none the less." The following day, Kearns was in command of the company and reluctantly had to note that he held his friend McEldowney under arrest, apparently a familiar condition for men of the 27th Infantry during the spring.[13]

The scale of the campaign impressed observers and surprised many of the soldiers. Jackson's army marched up and down the Shenandoah Valley, crossing over the Blue Ridge and Allegheny Mountains several times. The difficulty of sustaining this pace was compounded by the hard fighting all along the way. Many men in the Valley Army were new to combat and found their introduction to war a harrowing ordeal. Joseph Kauffman's report of his experience at McDowell was typical in this regard. After the Confederates had driven back the Union troops, he paused to note, "Yesterday will be a memorable day for me. I scarcely has any idea how it went in a battle until I got in it. I pray to God that I never get into another one as hot as that was. I could see the men falling in every direction. as we were going in. I cannot tell or have any idea of the number killed and wounded but it was a great deal."[14]

Many of the Valley Army soldiers, both Virginians and non-Virginians, were encountering the ridges, ravines, and rivers of the region for the first time. The movements of the Valley Army, so clearly explained in retrospect, confused men unfamiliar with the whole state or with how an army worked. Even in early 1862, the soldiers were amateurs. At this stage, many officers had little idea of how or where the army would operate, as one indicated in a letter to a friend at the close of 1861. "As to the future movements of the army you are as well if not better informed there . . . we soldiers know nothing of our movements until we receive orders, all we do is to obey orders and ask no questions."[15] Stonewall Jackson was notoriously reluctant to share his larger strategic vision with even his immediate staff, let alone the privates of his army. This was true even during the Valley campaign, when effective movements determined success on the battlefield. As the Valley Army marched east after the battle at McDowell, Sandie Pendleton admitted, "I am entirely ignorant of any plans of our Generals and cannot say what is to be done."[16]

Most soldiers reconciled themselves to following orders and trusted their commander to lead them both in their daily marches and in battles. One Virginian wrote home about their successful defense against Union forces in early May. Though he participated actively in the battle, he could not see or even sense the whole battle. "Of the particulars of the battle you have no doubt collected much more than I know," he admitted honestly.[17] Other soldiers, particularly as they gained experience, grew cautious and skeptical of the decisions their officers made. The successes of the Valley campaign compensated for the long marches made by Jackson's self-titled "foot cavalry"; in other campaigns with less productive outcomes, soldiers' morale deteriorated when the purposes behind their sacrifice remained unclear.

During the campaign, men from the Valley, who composed more than half of the Valley Army, seized whatever opportunities presented themselves to see friends and family. The practice of stopping at relatives' homes for good food, conversation, and the reassurance of family, became a hallmark of military activities in the Valley. The consequences for Valley residents were frequent updates on the progress of campaigns and battles in the area from participants, while soldiers had the opportunity to read papers and hear reports on friends in other regiments. Both soldiers and civilians took emotional succor from spending valuable time together, though each side no doubt feared it might be their last visit. On the eve of the attack on Front Royal, Philip Kauffman noted, "We left our camp at the usual hour this morning and after a short march I arrived at home and spent a few pleasant hours there." The reward of a quick trip home could be bittersweet. Kauffman spent the time at home with "the headache," not knowing that this would be his last visit with his son and wife. He was killed in the second battle at Manassas in late August.[18]

With the battle of Winchester, in late May, Jackson's men successfully pushed northern troops out of the Valley and across the Potomac River, some thirty miles to the north. This marked the emotional climax of the campaign for the men of the Valley Army. Though hard fighting still lay ahead, as two Union forces soon reentered the Shenandoah to track down and destroy Jackson's army, the victories of May welded the men of the army to each other and their idiosyncratic commander. William Peek, a cavalryman from Hampton, wrote home from Martinsburg in a state of feverish excitement: "See how near Maryland we are—how gallantly our army has cleared the valley of Yankees." Peek reported with pride, "Oh, we have completely swept them out—Jackson was everywhere—untiring and energetic—the men cheered him with the greatest enthusiasm and called back the tide of invasion like an avalanche."[19]

The confusion of natural metaphors in Peek's letter revealed more than he perhaps intended. The Valley Army did sweep down the Shenandoah like an avalanche, carrying Federal soldiers, their supplies, and the hopes of local Unionists along with them until they were dumped over the Potomac into Maryland. But the "tide" of invasion that Peek described could no more be held back than could the waters of the Potomac itself. Peek himself recognized this, noting in his letter from Martinsburg that "there are a great many union people here."[20] Recognizing that they had reached the edge of Confederate Virginia, Jackson's army pulled back to Winchester. Close behind them Union troops would return, again to occupy Winchester and parts of the upper Shenandoah Valley. Just as the battle at Manassas the previous June had failed to end the war, neither did this triumphant campaign convince the North to abandon its effort to defeat the Confederacy.

The arrival of southern soldiers brought solace and joy to Confederates in the area. As Jackson's troops pulled back to rest in Winchester, they seized valuable supplies left by the fleeing Yankees. One soldier observed, "Valuable stores have been captured at Martinsburg. Over $1,000,000 in medicines have been captured."[21] Jackson's army received a joyous welcome from the Confederate civilians of Winchester, recently under Union occupation. Laura Lee, an eager young Confederate waited for several days after Jackson's arrival in order "sufficiently to attempt to a collected account of what has occurred in the interval. Thanks be to the Lord, we are free !!!!!!!!!!!!!!!!!!"[22] The town's population maintained divided loyalties, and Unionist civilians dreaded the arrival of Confederate control as intensely as they did the threat of smallpox. The occupation of Winchester, which began when Jackson's troops retreated south after the battle at Kernstown in March, had weighed heavily on Confederate civilians in the town and surrounding area. The Union army had persecuted outspoken Confederate civilians and even luke-warm Confederates who refused to take the oath of loyalty.

Worse still was the physical toll taken on the area by Union occupation.[23] Alongside the disappearing crops, Confederates bemoaned the increasing loss of their slaves, who seized opportunities to flee to Union camps or down the Valley to the freedom of Pennsylvania.[24] The natural corridor of the Great Valley, which ran through Virginia, Maryland, and into Pennsylvania had long provided a route for slaves escaping from bondage in Virginia. The high proportion of German and Quaker residents in the Valley meant a higher-than-normal degree of ambivalence, and sometimes outright hostility, to the institution of slavery. Way stations on the Underground Railroad ran along the same lines that Confederate soldiers would march in their effort to keep slavery intact in Virginia. The chaos of war, and the decreased number of white adult men home to police slaves, meant that opportunities for escape multiplied as the conflict extended in time. Virginia Confederates bemoaned this process and worked whenever possible to reverse it.

Sandie Pendleton complained to his father about the influence of Union troops on their relatives' slaves in Strasburg. "I saw [the relatives] at Uncle Hugh's and Uncle Guerdon's—both well and their families. They lost noth-ing but their [male] Negroes. . . . The rascals [Yankees], on their retreat persuaded a number of negroes to run off by telling them that our men would kill them." Like many other Virginia Confederates, Pendleton set to work remedying this breach in the racial order and could soon report suc-cess. "We captured a number of negroes and brought them back to Winches-ter," Pendleton assured his family, "and delivered over a number to their owners and left the rest in jail." As often as the Valley served as a corridor to freedom, it could also be a route to reenslavement.[25]

In early 1862 the sole northern war goal remained preservation of the Union "as it was," but abolitionists increasingly pressed the cause of eman-cipation. On the ground, Union soldiers found that an easy way to hurt the rebels they had grown to despise was to target the most jealously guarded privilege of being a white southerner—slave ownership. At this stage in the conflict, and certainly in border areas such as Winchester, most northern soldiers did little more than chip away at slavery, yet Confederates character-ized any threat to the institution as an outright attack on the foundation of their social life. In time, immediate emancipation emerged as the central component of a harder Union war on southern society.[26]

Confirming southern fears that Republicans secretly harbored a plan to extinguish slavery in the states, the U.S. Congress enacted an increasingly harsh set of confiscation acts. This change in northern policy emerged most clearly in Lincoln's preliminary Emancipation Proclamation, issued in September after the battle at Antietam. All across Virginia, the resistance of slaves to their masters—and, more ominously, the strong efforts slaves made to seek their freedom—threatened the social order. The danger of slavery's collapse scared not just slaveholders seeking to protect their investment but all white Virginians who supported the system of slavery and received the benefits of living in a society where race determined the possibilities of one's future.[27] The addition of emancipation to the northern war goal of reunion raised the stakes of the war immensely for the South. It promised a radically different future for white southerners of the Confederacy if they lost the war and thus created a strong incentive to strive for independence.

A hard war had already developed in much of western Virginia, as Unionist and Confederates, soldiers and civilians, targeted each other and their resources for destruction.[28] The Union's shift toward hard war generated new antagonisms between Union and Confederate partisans. With the entry of Union general John Pope into the field in northern Virginia and a determined campaign by Union general Benjamin F. Kelley against Confederate guerrillas in western Virginia, northern troops adopted the tactics of an increasingly harder war. The Confederates responded in kind when and where they could. Unionists in the state came under increasing pressure to modify their beliefs. If subtle means for stemming opposition failed, Confederate officials imprisoned opponents of the administration in Richmond's Castle Thunder.[29]

This policy reached its apogee in the campaigns of William Tecumseh Sherman in Georgia and South Carolina and Philip H. Sheridan in the Shenandoah Valley in 1864 and would play a crucial role in bringing Confederate collapse in early 1865. In mid-1862, however, the halting beginnings of a policy of hard war elicited a stronger commitment from Confederate soldiers. William E. Isbell, writing to his sister from the mountains of western Virginia made the link between Union troops' behavior and the necessity of service explicit. "Every young man in Virginia," he wrote, "ought to take up arms in defence of our ancient & noble state, struggling against fearful odds of mercilefs & unprincipled foes who have already overrun a large portion of it destroying as they go & threatening destruction to the rest."[30]

The conversations between Jackson's soldiers and Valley civilians about life under Union occupation generated a deeper hatred and a stronger sense of justice among Confederates. This process was repeated across the state throughout the year, as different Union commanders adopted hard-war tactics. Soon soldiers would hear wild rumors about Union atrocities in communities from western Virginia to the Atlantic coast, and each episode exacerbated the antagonisms between North and South. Often this new motivation played a stronger and more consistent role in sustaining loyalty than did the initial enthusiasms of enlistment in early 1861. Robert Haile, serving in mid-May on the Peninsula, bemoaned the ruin of so many homes by the war. "I am heartily sick of it," he noted, revealing how war experiences themselves added a new category of motivation. "Yet am still willing to suffer any and every hardship rather than submit to the abolitionist who are now invading our soil, seeking to destroy that which our forefathers gained for us—liberty! Our battle cry should and will be victory or death."[31] Haile's language betrayed his perception of the war's cause; by labeling northerners as "abolitionist," he set the principal issue of the war as the debate over slavery.

Although Jackson's soldiers relished their reception as liberators, they had no opportunity to rest on their laurels and marched east at the conclusion of fighting to participate in the Peninsula campaign. Success in the Shenandoah Valley bound the Valley Army together internally and generated enthusiasm among civilians. Though some of Jackson's men fought in a national army for defense of their own land, Virginians and Confederates across the state celebrated the recapture of the Valley. The fight for a part of Virginia protected all of it. As the battles of 1862 drew Virginia troops away from their homes and ultimately out of the state altogether, soldiers still used the Valley campaign as a model for purposeful sacrifice. For Confederate civilians, the victories in the Valley thrilled a public desperate for good news on the military front. Although the Valley Army won relatively small engagements, compared to earlier and subsequent battles in the state, the public drew satisfaction from the seeming ease with which Jackson's men outmaneuvered Union forces. The triumph of the victories in the Valley gave succor to Confederates that larger battles might not have provided, foreshadowing one of the unusual linkages between civilian morale and battlefield events that existed in Virginia and across the South. As with the reception accorded the Valley campaign, Confederates frequently overlooked hardships and casualties if the outcome could be construed as a victory. This would be the case in the campaign on the Peninsula later in 1862 and again during the fighting in Virginia in 1864.

onfederates across the South rejoiced in the successes of Jackson's army. In lionizing him and honoring his men, they helped construct a national culture that focused on martial accomplishments and heroic imagery. Jefferson Davis and the Confederate Congress had worked through the winter to establish the trappings of a nation, devising an official seal and motto alongside the flags that flew in camps around the state.[32] Citizens all over the South joined in this effort, composing tributes to the Confederacy in prose, poem, and song. In the three decades before disunion, American nationalism had been gaining strength, as an extended international peace provided room and energy for the development of American commerce and industry. The Confederate effort built on this legacy by connecting the same imagery of Revolutionary honor and national accomplishment to Confederate instead of Federal ends.[33]

Nation building had just begun in earnest when George B. McClellan's massive Army of the Potomac landed on the southern tip of the Peninsula below Richmond in April. The Confederate capital, which had seemed so secure with Union forces stymied in northern Virginia, suddenly lay vulnerable. The capital had grown enormously since the start of the war, with refugees from northern Virginia and the Eastern Shore, garrisoned soldiers, and impressed slaves, competing with longtime residents for food and shelter. The prospect of invasion exacerbated the tension in the city and necessitated increasingly restrictive police controls on the populace. In response, Jefferson Davis imposed martial law on Richmond and the surrounding area, appointing General John H. Winder to police the increasingly turbulent city. The provost general controlled a five-mile ring around Richmond with a tight rein. Davis also suspended habeas corpus in several parts of the Confederacy. Though these moves helped maintain order, they prompted many in the city and around the Confederacy to raise questions about the growing centralization in the national government. Coming at almost the same time that the Confederacy imposed conscription, these decisions made Jefferson Davis appear to some as great a threat to state rights and individual liberties as Abraham Lincoln himself.[34]

The contrast between the widely embraced culture of nationalism and the restrictive, centralizing policies enacted in Richmond inaugurated a skeptical sense of nationhood that characterized the Confederate experiment through its brief life. The enthusiasm for independence and the accompanying celebration of the new Confederacy in 1861 may have dimmed southerners' traditional concern for central state authority, but by the following

spring that cynicism returned. As southerners settled into becoming Confederates, they revived the dubious air with which they regarded national
governments. William Ridley, a volunteer of 1861, began a letter of complaint
about the act to his sister with the sarcastic opening "You know this late
'Conscript Bill' lately passed in '*your city*.'" Ridley was angry because his
unit's official date of enrollment was several months later than when they
actually organized, but the draft required a full year's service from the date of
enrollment. Among his complaints, Ridley referred to his Confederate uniform as his "nigger cloak," a reference, no doubt, to the sense, shared by
many enlisted men, that the discipline and hierarchy of the military reduced
white men to slaves. Despite these complaints about the form and manner
with which Ridley's new nation requested his service, he showed little reluctance to participate, asserting that "in the present exigencies, all troops are in
absolute demand as it would disorganize our army too much to disband
them. I do not object to what has taken place for I would not show myself
reluctant to any demand my country may make."[35] The postwar myth of the
eternally patient and uncomplaining Confederate soldier masks a reality that
reflects a more complex and realistic engagement with nationalism. Volunteers and civilians alike willingly sacrificed for the nation but maintained a
sense of skepticism about how that nation was administered.

The residents and soldiers around Richmond felt a special responsibility
as protectors of the national capital. Virginia Confederates followed the news
in other regions carefully, and in early 1862 the string of defeats out West
increased pressure on easterners to bring victory. One Virginian remarked
wearily, "I have read news again tonight—nothing but bad news of late Fort
Henry taken—Roanoke Island taken—Fort Donelson taken Rolling mills
destroyed more prisoners captured." As for many, however, these setbacks
inspired him to imagine a better day just ahead. He wrote "To those on the
outside of Dixie the prospects of that 'paradise' look forlorn it may be this 'tis
the dark before day."[36] William Gregory, fighting in the Shenandoah Valley
that spring with Jackson's army noted that he "was very sorry to hear of the
fall of New Orleans, but dont feel at all discouraged as we may fully calculate
on their taking all of our Sea port towns." Gregory suggested a strategy that
he felt would ensure eventual success: "The place for us to track them is on
dry land and I am opposed to opposing of them any where else."[37]

The next "dry land" battle occurred on May 4 at Williamsburg, the first real
engagement of the Peninsula campaign, as outnumbered Confederates effectively resisted a mismanaged Union offensive. The violence and intensity of
the fighting—more than 1,600 Confederate and 2,200 Union casualties—

prompted many men to consider the fates of their loved ones. At this early stage in the war, few men could articulate a way to balance family and national interests. Some, like Edwin Penick simply assumed their families would be fine in the event of their deaths. After the battle at Williamsburg, Penick wrote home but offered little assurance about his role as defender of the hearth. "I shall be certain to take the best care of myself possible," he stated, "but if it be my fate to fall for my country I feel perfectly resigned. God will take care of my wife and children." Others pledged a clear defense of their homes, rather than that of the their country, as their paramount concern. Robert Bates, stationed like Penick on the Peninsula, made his feelings clear to his wife. "I suppose we have some one hundred and eighty thousand troops here waiting patiently for the Yankees," he wrote. "When they make their appearance we will give them a lively time, but if they whould whip us and, we fall back or give up Virginia you will see Bob coming home on the double quick, for I am determined not to leave you in the hands of the Yankees."[38]

The Confederates did fall back after the battle at Williamsburg, making a long and physically demanding march back into Richmond. Many arrived starving and despondent, a dramatic example of the potent combination of hardship and retreat. Refugees from the Peninsula flooded Richmond, even as Richmonders fled their city. At the same time, the central government in Richmond increased its efforts to bolster the army, issuing a special order that instructed the commanding general for the country around Richmond to arrest all absent men and return them to their regiments. "Should this arrest be disregarded," read the order, "the names of the officers and men in default will be published in the papers as deserters." As they had during period of mobilization in 1861, the Confederate government assumed that a loyal public would compel soldiers' allegiance to the demands of the army.[39]

The process of fight and retreat that characterized the first half of the Peninsula campaign revealed the desperate need among Confederate soldiers for military success to offset the hardships of army life. The withdrawals preferred by General Johnston provided insufficient compensation for what many soldiers viewed as defeat. Many of the soldiers stationed on the Peninsula had been there since late 1861 and had expended an enormous amount of energy on entrenchments and defensive preparations. William Ezell, an artilleryman from the southern Piedmont, had written home with a series of glowing reports about the progress his unit made on fortifications along the James River. He asserted with obvious pride that by early 1862 the region was now the best fortified position in the world. Ezell opposed the retreat up the Peninsula, writing, "all the Soldiers were opposed to leaving without a fight, after staying there and doing so much work as they had; it surely is the strongest fortified place in the South, without saying anything about the position, and now lost to us." Ezell did not hesitate to criticize the strategy mapped out by the commanders of the army, feeling that his personal energy had been wasted. "We have given up at the 'Tide Water' district; was there every such a piece of business done in the world?" he wrote. Though the campaign was barely half finished and the real fighting not yet begun, Ezell drew an ominous moral from the actions of the army: "The idea of giving up one hundred miles of the best country that we possess without a struggle—not until then have I ever said we were whipped but it looks very much like it now."[40]

The first phase of the Peninsula campaign ended with a battle fought around the area known as Seven Pines. During the fighting there on May 31, the Confederate general Joseph Johnston was injured, and Robert E. Lee replaced him as commander. Lee immediately reorganized the army and began preparing for the direct confrontation with the Yankees that Johnston had avoided. Lee's aggressiveness matched the mood of the soldiers, who, unlike in 1861, now eagerly sought an opportunity to expel the enemy. William Smith, who would die in the fighting on the Peninsula, noted in his diary, "I hope they [the Yankees] will fight here for I infinitely prefer fighting to the long tedious marches."[41] William Smith received his chance to fight in the week-long series of battles known as the "Seven Days." Lee's army succeeded at pushing McClellan's troops south across the Peninsula, away from Richmond, and back to the ships that had ferried them to Virginia in April. The human cost was catastrophic, with 20,000 Confederate soldiers killed, wounded, or missing. One man described the battles to his mother as "the greatest slaughter with men that I ever saw in my life."[42] Another man's account reflected the shock that volunteers felt at first witnessing violence on the scale that would come to typify the Civil War: "This fight beggars description; it has been most horrible. I have never before witnessed anything to compare to it and I pray God that I may never witness anything like it again. On the battlefield men are lying in great piles dead, mangled horribly in every way, hundreds and thousands of the Yankees lie upon every field yet unburied and many of our men and decomposition has gone on so far that it is almost if not impossible to go upon the fields."[43]

Despite the shock of violence, Confederate soldiers took considerable pride in having repulsed the most serious threat to their capital that the North would muster until late 1864. The Confederate victory in the Seven Days held enormous strategic value, as many historians have noted, because it shifted the war away from the Confederate capital, disorganized the Union high command, demoralized many Union soldiers, and provided the opportunity for Lee to initiate a more aggressive war against the North. In addition to these accomplishments, the victory also transformed men who fought their way through the Seven Days into veterans. For Virginia Confederates, this meant that soldiers fused earlier notions of defense of home with a new antagonism to Yankee depredations. Just as the soldiers gained a new and stronger sense of purpose they earned a greater confidence in their ability to achieve those goals. As one man told his wife upon the conclusion of the campaign, "I have stood so much tho' since I have been in the service that I reckon I shall do very well."[44] Indeed, the success in the Seven Days helped soldiers reconsider their experiences during the spring. The strategy under Johnston, which led to hardships in camp and retreat, had demoralized many men. By contrast, reports of the triumph under Lee, broadcast by mouth, pen, and printing press all across the South, blocked out anger over the draft and the problems of supply during the campaign itself. Soldiers and civilians immediately recast their experience in the light of victory.[45]

In addition to redeeming the hardships that soldiers experienced as a routine part of their new lives, victory in the Seven Days helped spur the conceptualization of death as a sacrifice for one's country. This idea was not new. The first Confederates to fall at Bull Run were lionized in print across the South as heroes for the cause, but the language of sacrifice remained undeveloped through much of 1861. In the early part of the war, the importance of a Christian death remained paramount.[46] As ministers and political leaders worked to make the Confederate cause synonymous with God's will, the language of Christian sacrifice blended with that of national sacrifice. Volunteers mourned the loss of comrades, and families took pride in the men who died to defend their communities. The status of these men as Christian soldiers only added to reverence in which they were held. This ability to justify soldiers' deaths across the many levels of their participation in the army remained an important element of Confederate unity throughout the war. In 1862 and beyond, however, the public would treat battlefield deaths first and foremost as expressions of support for the nation.[47]

An episode during the Peninsula campaign embodied this way of perceiving the Confederate struggle. In mid-June, Confederate cavalry commander J. E. B. Stuart executed what became known as his first "ride around McClellan," when he led 1,200 men to reconnoiter the Union line. Discovering that he could create havoc in the Union ranks at little risk to his command, Stuart circled all the way around the northern army to the James River. The most famous loss of the ride came on the first day, June 13, when Confederate Captain William Latané, of Essex County, died in what can only be called a mounted joust with the commander of the 5th U.S. Cavalry. Despite wounding the Union officer, Latané was killed in the exchange and his body brought to a nearby plantation.[48]

Robert Baylor, a Virginian who participated in the ride with Stuart, wrote home to his father, wanting to give a "true account" of their actions. Describing Latané's noble death, Baylor lamented, "I feel as if I had lost a brother, almost a sister." Latané was celebrated not as the epitome of an aggressive, martial masculinity, but rather as a whole figure, over whom men could weep openly. "It is for us to grieve for ourselves, not for him," Baylor wrote, "A nobler, braver, *better* man never lived & he has died nobly—"[49] The chivalric nature of Latané's death and his own reputation for gentlemanly conduct transformed the event into a central symbol of Confederate sacrifice. A writer, John R. Thompson, composed a poem capturing the event that appeared in the *Southern Literary Messenger*, the leading southern literary journal. The *Messenger* reported Latané's burial as a sacrifice duly recognized by those for whom it was performed. Latané's body had been carried to the home of a Mrs. Brockenbrough, but "the enemy" would not permit a clergyman to attend the service. "Then," the paper solemnized, "with a few other ladies, a fair haired little girl, her apron filled with white flowers, and a few faithful slaves, who stood reverently near, a pious Virginia matron read the solemn and beautiful service over the cold, still form of one of the noblest gentlemen and most intrepid officers in the Confederate army."[50]

William D. Washington later recreated the scene of Latané's burial in a painting that hung in the state capitol building in Richmond. The painting evoked Latané's devotion to the Confederacy and sanctified the women and slaves who gathered around his grave to lament the lost leader. Latané's death fit perfectly into both Confederate images of its heroic Cavalier past and the nobility of its present conflict.[51]

The effort to lionize Latané succeeded so well, in part, because men in the army genuinely mourned his passing. Two days after Latané's death, responding to a rumor he had died, Robert Haile rode to Latané's company's camp to verify the awful truth. "In Capt. Latané's death I have lost one of my best friends and Essex one of her worthiest sons. I have known him ever since we were children together and a more noble, brave, generous, correct man never lived." Haile found consolation for his own sense of loss in the dedication Latané displayed to his country. "He has been the first one from Essex to fall in defense of our rights and liberty. Many of us may be fated to

Burial of Latané. *This image assumed iconic status during the war, partly owing to Latané's reputation and popularity and partly because of its effectiveness as propaganda. By putting the private grief of the burial party on public display in the state capitol, Confederate leaders created a model for the national idea of sacrifice, which helped guide and inspire Virginians through the conflict. Photo courtesy of the Virginia Historical Society, Richmond.*

meet with the same end before this war shall close. But none shall be more lamented, *particularly so by me.*"[52] The effort to sanctify battle deaths as sacrifices for the nation did not spring solely from postmortem eulogizing. Soldiers' wartime adjustment to the possibility of their own death provided an unforeseen boost to Confederate success and perseverance. In turn, civilians took increasing sustenance from the actions of the army; over the course of the war, Confederates built an explicitly martial culture.[53] Haile's response to Latané's death captured how soldiers could merge the personal and the political, finding solace for emotional loss in the knowledge that death furthered their pursuit of independence. This fusion of emotion and honor served as the bedrock upon which Confederates based their pursuit of military success.

4 ★ WAR IN EARNEST
AUGUST–DECEMBER 1862

We never can keep up an army as long as men run off as they have been doing.
I think some of them will very likely be shot for desertion.
—John Neff, 33rd Virginia Infantry, August 4, 1862

The battles on the Peninsula shifted the momentum of the war away from the Federals who had initiated the campaign to the Confederates who ended it. Lee began moving his army north, first through central Virginia and then into Maryland. The battle along Antietam Creek in September, with its enormous losses and the repulse of the Confederate counteroffensive, surprised the hardened veterans, but only slightly dampened the optimism of the summer. The fighting season did not end as the leaves changed colors, but nonmilitary concerns bore down on men in uniform, as families and communities prepared for another winter. Scarcity of food and manpower threatened parts of Virginia that winter, and many soldiers struggled with how and where they could best protect their families. The year's final battle, at the town of Fredericksburg, encapsulated the contradictory trends of the year. Confederates won an overwhelming military victory, but the brief Union occupation left the town a wasteland and drove many residents to flee.

The events of the second half of 1862 contradicted the forces that motivated men earlier in the year. The reluctance of men to accept military rules and the hardships of the offensive campaign into Maryland led to a dramatic rise in the number of desertions. Soldiers' exposure to killing and bloodshed alienated them from the values of home, but the Union's hard-war tactics created a shared experience of suffering and hardship between soldiers and civilians. Although the North did not develop its full policy of destroying Confederate resources until 1864, the outlines of such a policy were already visible in central Virginia, and the result was less food to divide among hungry Confederates.

These events and the trends they produced forced Virginians to clarify still further their reasons for opposing the Union army. Their decisions to continue supporting the Confederacy were by no means certain, and not all Virginians did in any event, but the last months of the year proved to be a crucial turning point in Virginia's commitment to the Confederacy. In a variety of ways, Virginians demonstrated their continued support for the new nation. With great difficulty, soldiers accepted new stricter rules and punishments regarding absence from the army. More easily, they drew sustenance from Lincoln's decision to issue an emancipation proclamation. Although the policy would not take effect until the first day of 1863, Confederates took heart that Lincoln had inaugurated a misguided and morally treacherous plan that would redound to their benefit. The vandalism of Fredericksburg by Union soldiers in December 1862 served as one of the Confederacy's most compelling examples of national sacrifice. Though other places would suffer more, citizens around the state and the nation identified the residents of Fredericksburg as deserving of their charity and their pride. The suffering at Fredericksburg, like the death of Captain Latané in June, spurred the development of the Confederates' national culture of sacrifice. Importantly, too, Confederates had won the battles of Virginia in 1862; military victory, increasingly interpreted as God's will, served as evidence of the rightness of the Confederacy's pursuit of independence.

As Lee's army left its defenses around Richmond and began the trek north, most soldiers relished the opportunity to repel the now-infamous Union general John Pope. When Pope was given command of the Union's new Army of Virginia in late June, he had entered the state with his radical politics proudly on display. Reflecting the attitude of many Republicans in the U.S. Congress, Pope believed that the generous treatment given to disloyal citizens prolonged the conflict.[1] Most secessionists had made themselves ardent Confederates and showed no inclination to return to the protection of the United States, no matter how benevolent the treatment. In response, Pope issued several orders targeting the civilian population. The most serious orders were No. 5, which instructed soldiers to "subsist" in the area, and No. 11, which allowed the arrest and exile of "disloyal" men. Virginians viewed the former as a license to steal and plunder. Although abuse was no doubt widespread, the intentional damage done to northern Virginia farms was hard to distinguish from the unavoidable impact of either army camping on a family's farm. Order No. 11 was more pernicious in its design because it effectively made all southern white men still living in their communities susceptible to arrest. Rarely used, it nonetheless exacerbated the sense among Virginians that their foe violated the rules of civilized warfare. Virginia Confederates seethed for an opportunity to defeat Pope and his army.[2]

Pope's soldiers first felt Confederate anger on August 8, when Jackson's wing of the army repulsed a Union attack at Cedar Mountain, inflicting 2,400 casualties. For the next two weeks, the Confederates outmaneuvered Pope as he retreated north toward the old battlefield at Bull Run. Jackson directed his men around Pope's army to the northwest and by August 26 had "marched 50 miles, wrecked two trains, and captured several hundred Federals, eight cannon, and stores beyond their wildest fantasy."[3] The full Union and Confederate armies met at the end of the August in another battle on the plains of Manassas. The Confederates achieved a decisive tactical victory, but the toll on their army was severe. Jackson's wing lost 4,000 men to death and injury while Longstreet's lost 4,700, nearly 15 percent of those engaged. A young Confederate from Page County testified to the terror and tragedy of the battle. "We have been marching and countermarching all day and are now drawn up in line awaiting the enemy's advance," Joseph Kauffman recorded. "It is now sundown. They are fighting on our right. Oh, to God it would stop—" Kauffman received a mortal head wound shortly after writing his entry.[4]

Many soldiers at Second Manassas fought hand-to-hand against the Yankees, making the act of killing much more personal than many soldiers wished. James Binford wrote his sisters to describe the toll the battle took on his regiment and his psyche. His company had entered the fight with eighteen men, only six of whom left the field unhurt. Not all Confederate units experienced casualty rates this high, but survivors emerged from the battle nearly as broken down as the vanquished Federals. "We repulsed Pope & drove him from 3 miles from the field," Binford announced. "I wd not be surprised if the few who remain of Co F were allowed to go home awhile, as our Lieutenant wants it disbanded. If so," Binford wrote, "I shall come & stay with you a short while for I long to go to some quiet place, where loved ones of home are, to rest body & mind."[5] Unfortunately for Binford and his comrades, several months and hundreds of miles of marching lay between them and the possibility of rest and home.

As Pope pulled his army back toward Washington on September 1, Lee began planning his movement into the North. His army, as Binford testified, was not in shape to mount an invasion, but Lee recognized the strategic advantage that would accrue from carrying the war north. European nations were considering recognizing the Confederacy, and indeed Britain was on the cusp of doing so as the Army of Northern Virginia marched into Maryland. Another victory might propel the Confederacy into the ranks of independent nations. The *Lynchburg Daily Virginian* applauded the prospect that "our banners will soon be carried to 'the outer boundaries' of the Confederacy, and flaunted in the very face of the foe, under the walls of his beleaguered Capital."[6] Shifting the war north would also satisfy Lee's main goal of bringing relief to the farmers and families of central and northern Virginia who had suffered from the presence of Union and Confederate troops for fifteen months. Lee knew the value of further depressing morale in the North. McClellan's retreat from the Peninsula had frustrated most northerners and further divided congressman and their constituents over the merits of a harder war against the rebels. A defeat on United States soil, and perhaps the occupation of a northern city such as Harrisburg or Baltimore, might compel Union citizens to give up the war.

Before the Confederate invasion crested in Maryland, Jackson's corps captured Harpers Ferry. The 11,500 Union soldiers, 13,000 small arms, 200 wagons, and 73 pieces of artillery that Jackson's men seized when they took the town proved one of the most significant northern losses of the war and thrilled Confederates across the South.[7] Virginians especially welcomed reasserting Confederate control of sovereign soil. The main confrontation between Federals and Confederates occurred outside the small Maryland town of Sharpsburg, along Antietam Creek. The result was a catastrophic battle. In one day of fighting, the two sides inflicted nearly 23,000 casualties on each other. One Virginia soldier seemed stunned into brevity and could muster only a prayer: "We had a very hard battle in Maryland. Thank the Lord I came out safe once more."[8] The equivocal tone of this man's summary echoed through many accounts of the battle. George Coiner described the fight to his sister as "a terrible battle which closes with no considerable advantages on either side, I don't think. We had a portion of the battle ground and the Yankees a portion."[9]

Nonetheless, the Confederates' success at repulsing Union attacks and their control of the field the following day led many southerners to interpret the battle as a victory. Across the South, newspapers reported the engagement as a qualified victory and the campaign as a success. Lee's army pulled back over the Potomac on the evening of September 18, but Confederates argued over whether that move should be seen as a retreat. Few people had envisioned more than a brief invasion of the North, and McClellan's paralysis following the battle seemed to confirm soldiers' reports that the Union army had once again been trounced.

For the soldiers who participated in Jackson's offensive or, perhaps more important, reached the Union quartermaster's warehouse at Harpers Ferry while it was still full, the campaign immediately showed its value. Other soldiers, however, questioned the shift in strategy from what had been a defensive war to an offensive one. Pushing Union troops out of Virginia was good and proper but carrying the war to northern cities threatened to undo the difference between the beastly Yankees and the gentlemen soldiers of the South. Some volunteers had been reluctant to leave Richmond for this very reason. One soldier remarked at the start of the campaign, "I hope we will be kept this side of the James River for the future. I never want to cross it again. I am hoping that some event will transpire to stop this war without further bloodshed."[10] Although some complaints were undoubtedly generated by a desire to avoid more grueling marching and fighting, for many Confederates, the change in strategy contradicted the sense of purpose grounded in a policy of defense. As one man wrote regretfully when the army crossed back into Virginia, "We had to leave a great many of our wounded in the hands of the Yankees & I have no doubt they got a great many straglers. I am told that Gen. Lee said the army did not do as good fighting as they have done or he would not have had to retreat to the Va. side. This is true, I think, & that ain't the worst of it. If they drag us across the river a few more times we won't have many to fight at all. I heard a great many say they don't intend to cross again."[11]

Lee concerned himself with restoring order and morale in his dilapidated army rather than planning another offensive campaign. The scale of the battle at Antietam and the escalating problem of deserters and soldiers absent without leave threatened the ability of Confederates to resist a renewed Union campaign. Desertion, in fact, had plagued the army since the spring. In April, when McClellan's army arrived on the Peninsula, the Confederate high command decided it could not afford to defend the exposed counties of the Tidewater. Troops in the Northern Neck and the counties just north of the Peninsula fell back. Men from these counties looked upon their now defenseless families as having been abandoned by the Confederate government and responded in kind. A group of men from the 26th Virginia Infantry stayed behind to protect their families. Most of these deserters belonged to companies from Gloucester or Mathews County, which lay directly in the path of McClellan's planned offensive.[12] The same process occurred on a smaller scale in the 9th Virginia Infantry, which saw many of its men return home to the Portsmouth-Norfolk area when the Confederacy abandoned that region in early May 1862.[13] A third episode occurred among the soldiers of the 6th Infantry, which lost ninety-two men during the Confederacy's retreat from Norfolk in mid-1862. Although rare, such episodes of mass desertion indicate that the men made a simple calculation: their families demanded their immediate personal attention. As the war progressed, almost all Virginia soldiers would be faced with the same choice, but few repeated the collective response of the men from the 26th, 9th, and 6th Infantries.

In fall 1862 officers in Lee's army complained most about what they called stragglers. This word usefully blurred the distinction between actual desertion and the inability of some soldiers to maintain the army's debilitating marching schedule. Some men were temporarily separated from their units during the Shenandoah Valley and Peninsula campaigns, while others deliberately abandoned the army during the march north. No doubt exhaustion and illness held back many soldiers who wished to participate in the campaign, but the problem of desertion, with its more ominous overtones, threatened to disrupt Confederate success in 1862. As the army entered the battle at Antietam, Lee and subordinate officers down to the rank of captain could see the effects of straggling all around them. Probably every company in the Army of Northern Virginia had lost men during the marching, some falling away from exhaustion or illness, some refusing to join the invasion, and still others giving up entirely on the Confederate cause and returning home. Despite the excellent strategic position the Confederate army occupied after the battle of Second Manassas, army leaders could count almost 9,000 losses from straggling and desertions.[14] Conditions seemed to worsen on the march to Maryland. On September 13 Lee wrote to Davis, stating that "our ranks are very much diminished, I fear from a third to half of the original numbers."[15] The fighting around Sharpsburg, like the fighting along Bull Run, only exacerbated this problem. The chaos and violence of the battle broke up regiments and companies, forcing men to link up with any nearby unit and then search for their own companies once the battles concluded. Coming on the heels of the dispute over conscription, the rigors of the Maryland campaign helped make 1862 the high point for desertion from Virginia units.[16]

Almost every phase of the war brought contradictory pressures of inspiration and dejection. In late 1862 the victories at Second Manassas and Fredericksburg brought hope and confidence at the same time that the implementation of the draft and war weariness discouraged and angered Virginia Confederates. They accepted this paradox but sought ways to balance the immediate swings in their fortunes with their long-term goal of Confederate independence. Most pressing was the continuing problem of desertion, which reached its peak in late 1862 (see figure 2).[17] The solutions that Confederate leaders devised dissolved the ambiguity that had allowed

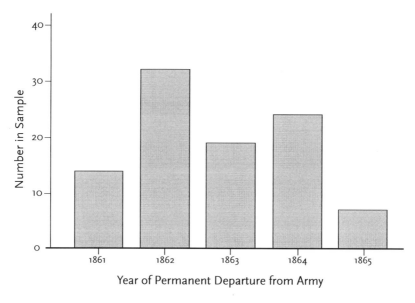

Figure 2. Permanent Absentees, 1861–1865

men to retain individual definitions of service well into the war. Lee and Jackson, in particular, enforced strict rules regarding absent soldiers. As with the debate over the Draft Act, soldiers complained about adjusting to new rules on desertion, but most accepted them. Many continued to maintain sympathy for individual men who left to be with their families, while also condemning the effect of desertion on the army's effectiveness. Men reconciled this paradox by accepting the execution of deserters because they continued to believe in Confederate victory.

As Lee's soldiers drew back from Maryland, many stragglers returned to camp on their own accord.[18] Still, the situation required more active measures. Lee launched a general reorganization, similar to the one enacted in the fall and winter of 1861, to bring units back to full strength and men back to fighting health. Officers detailed units to return men listed as absent without leave, filled up weakened units with conscripts or combined them with other depleted units, and reinstated normal army procedures that had fallen by the wayside during the campaign. William Mordecai gave his mother a summary of the recent events in the camps of the 2nd Richmond Howitzers. "Everything quiet at this time," Mordecai reported. "But the season of rest so necessary to our army does not seem, as at other times, to be given up altogether to idleness, but drilling, reorganization, & discipline seem to be the order of the day. . . . Inefficient artillery companies are being disbanded & the men taken to fill the ranks of more competent ones."[19]

Military officials implemented more forceful policies as soon as the problem of desertion presented itself. One Virginia soldier who received a plaintive note from his sick wife in July 1862 tried to explain to her why he could not return. "I would give my interest in this world to be with you," he wrote, "but alas I am doomed to fate, which is a hard one for me. . . . I do sincerely hope ere this you have entirely recovered. I would fly to you if it was in my power, but cannot leave here without running great risk of my life." Although executions remained rare in mid-1862, officers employed demeaning and painful methods of curtailing the practice. "There has so many run away from this briggade that the officers have determined to punish them to full extent of their crime," the soldier reported. "There is over fifty now in the guard house who pay will be stopt for six months. A large portion of them will have to wear a 12 pount Ball chained to the ankle and confined to hard labour for their time. Some two or three will be shot (no doubt) as they have deserted two and three times."[20]

During the summer and fall of 1862, commanders began punishing soldiers for desertion with greater severity. Stonewall Jackson represented one extreme. He was among the first officers to enforce execution as a punishment for desertion, and three soldiers from his command died as a result. During the march north from Manassas to Maryland, Jackson's corps had stopped long enough for three deserters to be executed in the type of public display that officers hoped would impress upon enlisted men the necessity of staying in the ranks. The executions occurred on August 19, 1862, as a result of the straggling and absences that plagued the Army of Northern Virginia as it moved north. Although soldiers despised the executions, and many sympathized with the reasons that drove men to leave, they accepted the new policy as necessary to preserve order in the army.[21] By forcing soldiers to stay in the army, the harsh punishments may have increased its efficiency on the march and in battle. Although Jackson's zeal to fulfill the letter of the law was unusual, the increasingly strong enforcement of desertion rules complemented the increasing formalization of rules governing military service initiated with the Draft Act earlier in the year. As with the debate over the Draft Act itself, soldiers complained about adjusting to new rules on desertion, but most accepted them.

Even with the executions of the summer, the line between loyal and disloyal continued to be fuzzy; not all men who were absent were necessarily permanent deserters. Even officers in the field wavered about the best way to classify and treat absent men. The lieutenant colonel of the 33rd Virginia Infantry, John Neff, noted the toll taken on his unit in straggling and desertions. "My Regiment is quite small now but is increasing some little," he reported. "There are still about three hundred and fifty men absent without leave." Neff did not presume the permanent disloyalty of the absent soldiers. Instead, he assumed like many that if patrols returned absent soldiers to the ranks, they would stay. "I wish men at home would send these deserters back," he wrote to his parents; "we never can keep up an army as long as men run off as they have been doing." And if the men did run off again, as undoubtedly some would, Neff admitted the consequences would be severe. "I think some of them will very likely be shot for desertion."[22] Eventually, two of Neff's soldiers would be executed, though not until 1863. In the meantime, Neff had good reason to worry; regimental rolls revealed 235 desertions in 1862, two-thirds of all the desertions experienced by his regiment over the whole war.[23]

Though Neff may not have decided on a single response to the problem of desertion, he correctly observed that the Confederacy could not "keep up an army" with the desertion problems it was experiencing. Deserters diminished commanders' options in battle and altered the political dynamic at home. By late 1862 politicians and army commanders would interpret desertion as a political act, an explicit rejection of the Confederate nation. In heavily Unionist areas, like western Virginia, eastern Tennessee, western North Carolina, and isolated counties around the Lower South, desertion could be an expression of protest against Confederate policies or against the Confederacy itself. This was not the case in Virginia in 1862, and the congressmen who denounced "stragglers" and "runaways" as cowards and traitors only added to the reasons why these men would stay away from the army. Even as politicians and editors debated the meaning of desertion and called for stricter punishments, the situation on the ground remained stubbornly complex.

The profusion of battles in Virginia in 1862 and their violent intensity, the long painful marches, and the devastation visited upon the state by traveling armies impressed upon men that the war was now in earnest. The bloody and determined charges made by northern troops at Manassas and Sharpsburg ended notions of an easy victory over effeminate Yankees. Confederates recognized that the war would be both prolonged and brutal and that defeat would mean a radically changed southern society. This last element—the high cost of defeat—encouraged Virginians to begin accepting those aspects of wartime life against which they had rebelled in 1861.[24]

Soldiers signaled their acceptance of army rules with their approval of the few executions for desertion that did occur. As one man reported, "Our Regt . . . was called out the other evening to witness one of the greatest sights that I ever want to behold again & that was the shooting of two of our soldiers who deserted last April & was a part of their time within the enemy lines." He continued, "The brigade was formed at 5 oclock Tuesday P.M. and the deserters was placed where all could seen them and 24 men with muskets in front of them all loaded, 12 with balls & 12 blank. The deserters were tied to a stake and the sentence read to the crowd & after prayer was shot dead. Poor fellows never knew what hurt them."[25] Soldiers struggled to reconcile executions with their sympathy for the victims of the policy. Writing home, another Virginia soldier noted, "there is to be two fellows shot for trying to desert to the Yankees and rebelling against their officers which is no doubt right for it is impossible to keep up dicipline unless there is severity used. . . . James Lovelass ran away again last night from the guard house and has not been heard from since. Him & Cale Mills has never been tried yet. If they catch James L. again it will go rather hard with him." Problems with discipline continued to occur, but men absorbed the things they disliked about the military in order to defeat the North.[26]

Soldiers' families, too, began to reflect the changing attitude toward desertion. Like Confederates under arms, most civilians accepted the new perspective that desertion undermined the nation, even if that was not the principal motivation for someone deserting in the first place. "It looks like my dear son Norborne will bring *my Gray Hairs* down to the grave in *sorrow* by avoiding the call of his country (as a deserter which is death by the law & to be shot)," mourned one father. He went on to reflect on his own military service and its consequences for the country at that time. "When I was 18 years old I volunteered & went in the army against the advise of my *Dear Father* & *Mother* & oh what a condition would country be in if all was to pursue the same course," he wrote. Added to the damage done to the young Confederacy was the stigma of dishonor that accompanied desertion among those who identified themselves as loyal southerners. "If I was not so infirm I would join the Army & go in his place rather to disgrace our family," he closed.[27]

Support for southern independence manifested itself in unpredictable ways, even among those men who found military service an intolerable burden. Thomas Sublett, a young Virginian, implored a friend repeatedly to find someone to take his place, but the escalating prices and the difficulty of finding the right kind of man dogged his effort. At the end of July 1862, Sublett wrote to his friend, noting that he was "glad to her from you all you say you can git me a Substitute for 6 or 7 hundred dollars well I want one & I want him as low as you can git him I dont want you to close the bargain with him until you let me know." Before Sublett would part with the money he needed assurances that the man would actually serve in his place rather than take the money and run. "I want a rite good looking man," Sublett said, "and a Sound man & one that is not subject to a draft it is mitty hard to git a Substitute in our Company write me word if he is a Virginian." Soon the asking price had reached $1,000, which Sublett thought he could pull together. "See what they will take by the month or by the year for the war If I thought the war would last long I would pay the Thousand but I will hold on a while longer & let you try & git one a little cheaper." Sublett's efforts to leave the service seem to confirm the argument that Virginia men lost faith early on in the Confederate cause, but the effort to obtain a substitute, something many men thought about and few realized, shared little with the actions of real deserters. Sublett sought a legal and proper method of leaving the service and did so in a way that would not reduce the Confederacy's manpower. Though Sublett never revealed exactly what drove him from the service, he continued to support Confederate victory and implored his friend to "git a man of a good Character & one that is true to the South."[28]

The respite from fighting also helped diminish soldiers' frustrations with the service. McClellan's refusal to move his army after the battle in Maryland gave Confederates a brief period of rest and recuperation in the lower Shenandoah Valley. Soldiers took full advantage of the first lull in many weeks. Securing food emerged as one of the most important accomplishments of the season, and soldiers indulged in all the treats they had been deprived of while on the campaign. One soldier noted how he fed his sweet tooth: "Took breakfast at Mr. Helsel's and the best breakfast I have set down to for some 18 months 10 sausers of different sorts of preserves, Big plate of Honey picher of sugar cain molasses punkin pye apple pie &c."[29]

Even more important than access to sugar, the return to Virginia allowed soldiers to reestablish mail communication. The frequent movement of the summer and fall made mail delivery unreliable, though men had continued to send and receive letters through any possible channels. All in all, the rest and opportunities of October and November provided a welcome and much-earned reward for soldiers who had accompanied Lee from Richmond to Maryland so many months before. In addition to reenergizing men for continued fighting, the organizational efforts initiated upon the return to Virginia succeeded as well in returning men to the ranks. By late December one soldier could report with pride on the progress made by the 3rd Cavalry, headquartered at Martinsburg in northwestern Virginia. "Our company has been strongly recruited by the arrival of men from home with fresh horses & will continue to be increased from time to time by the arrival of others."[30]

After their return to Virginia from Maryland, soldiers had the chance to reflect on the battles themselves. Rawleigh Downman, a sergeant in the 4th Virginia Cavalry, summarized the positive and negative aspects of the campaign. He described the battle at Antietam as "one of the terrific and obstinate battles of the whole war. The Yankees under McClellan came on us in tremendous force but by the blessing of God we withstood them and drove them back." Downman, like many noncommissioned officers charged with keeping his company in order during the battle, witnessed the carnage firsthand. Even with the satisfaction of victory, he mourned the effect of the fighting. "It is an awful thing to see men falling around you by dozens and be obliged to force them into it," Downman noted.[31] Those men who were forced into it left their own record of reluctance. As one private remarked during the campaign, "I am sick of seeing dead men & men's limbs torn from their bodies."[32]

The second half of 1862, with its increase in the level of violence, served as a crucial threshold for many Confederate soldiers. Those men who survived accepted increasingly high levels of casualties through the remainder of the war. Downman, like others, despised the process in which he was engaged but remained committed to the outcome. He continued to "force" men into battle until the war's end in 1865. Soldiers continued to wrestle with the violence that they committed and still mourned the loss of friends and relatives, but they accepted these losses as a contribution to the sacrifices they and others had already made. The violence and killing of late 1862 made possible the death and destruction of 1863 and beyond.

Following the battle of Antietam, Lincoln announced his preliminary Emancipation Proclamation and established the destruction of slavery as an official Union war goal. Henceforth, the war increased in intensity. After reading about the proclamation, J. C. Fitz condemned the policy and predicted a longer and harder war as a result. "That old fanatical President Abraham the 1st is playing his last card by officially endorsing the rank abolition policy," he wrote, "I cant see the first glimmer of peace and no man can predict the end of this cruel & bloody war."[33] Though food and supply shortages weakened the army and the Confederate civilian population, the Union policy toward emancipation epitomized the change to a hard war.

The process had begun with the gradual deterioration of slavery in Union occupied areas. On the Peninsula in April, the arrival of Union troops heralded freedom for many black Virginians who worked on Confederate fortifications. More than 1,300 slaves had been impressed from masters in the Peninsula and sent to General John Bankhead Magruder in 1862. Many of these people ran away to Union lines. Although escaped slaves were rarely treated with anything resembling equality by Union soldiers, they perceived the advantages that lay in control over their own destinies and fled by the thousands. The absence of the white men who usually imposed order in the slave system weakened slavery all across the state. By 1864 the Union counted more than 31,000 contrabands in camps in northeastern North Carolina and southeastern Virginia.[34]

Yet, instead of discouraging Confederates, the Emancipation Proclamation promoted a stronger and more public defense of slavery. The confident ignored the proclamation, asserting the inability of the North to impose its will on the South. Joseph Clay Stiles reassured his wife, "You seem to be apprehensive of some insecurity to yourself & the girls by virtue of *Lincoln's Proclamation.* I can say that I have not accounted a *word, thought, feeling,* or *act* which led me to suppose that any human being with whom I have association since its publication, considered that Proclamation anything else than a hopeless dead letter. . . . It was hardly laughed at. It lives in nobody's thoughts."[35] The *Daily Richmond Examiner* dismissed the practical implications of the policy, asserting that "it is scarcely necessary to say to anyone who know the public mind in the South that it will have absolutely no effect at all, either one way or the other." According to the paper, the importance of the proclamation was that it laid bare the northern intent to bring on a "war of extermination," and it would, the writer hoped, stimulate a stronger resolve to fight within the Confederate government.[36] By making emancipation a war aim, Lincoln compelled all Confederate soldiers to become de facto defenders of the institution.

The problems created by slavery's disintegration were, in a strange way, partially alleviated by the preliminary Emancipation Proclamation. Confederates now knew that they faced the absolute destruction of their social order if they lost. Many interpreted the proclamation as a sign of northern weakness and assumed it would split the North along party and racial lines. Virginia papers reported eagerly on the divisions created by the policy within the Union. Just two days after Lincoln issued the proclamation, the *Lynchburg Daily Virginian* thrilled to report, under the headline "First Fruit of Africanizing Ohio," that northern farmers had begun hiring black laborers to work on their farms.[37] A year later, Confederates still credited the policy with producing divisions among northern soldiers. As one man observed, it "is thought that they have lost a great manny men by desersion a great manny men men is still coming in the procklamation has bin a great for the southern confederacy."[38] Although emancipation and the use of black soldiers would ultimately be a crucial component of northern victory, in the short term, the order gave added coherence to Confederate resolve.

Virginians needed resolve in the fall and winter of 1862–63, as citizens experienced enormous difficulties in securing enough food for the winter. For many Virginia families, the coming winter would be the period of greatest need during the war. The full effects of the Union boycott spread all across the Confederacy. In Virginia, an empty state treasury meant that efforts to provide charitable or government-sponsored relief proceeded on borrowed funds or not at all.[39] In the hard-pressed winter of 1862–63, it was more often the latter. The Virginia and Confederate governments initiated their most successful relief programs in 1863 and beyond, in response to the hardships and suffering of 1862.[40] As soldiers fanned out across the lower Shenandoah Valley, and later shifted their camps east to block any northern attempt to march on Richmond, they saw firsthand the suffering of Virginia's civilian population. Most often, soldiers blamed the hardships they saw and those they experienced on the Union war strategy. Soldiers rightly recognized that northern troops had abandoned the mostly benign perspective of early 1861 and by 1862 had adopted hard-war tactics that punished civilians along with soldiers. A Valley soldier expressed this perspective in a letter to his parents just before he marched north into Maryland. "I am sorry you suffered so much from the mean scamps [Union forces]," he wrote, "and hope you may never have them near you again"—a vain hope, as it turned out. But if Union troops ever did return to the Shenandoah, he promised his men would drive them back.[41]

In assigning blame for the suffering of civilians solely to the Yankee's hard war, Confederate soldiers could relieve themselves of any guilt they might feel for the enormous toll their own movements took on the countryside. Although Confederates exercised as much caution as possible when they moved through their own state, meeting the simplest needs for food and fuel usually wrought havoc on the area around which they camped. This had been the case in the central Virginia counties of Culpeper and Orange for most of 1862 and was increasingly the situation in much of the Shenandoah Valley. The presence of armies and the resulting competition for food between civilians and soldiers drove up prices and generated shortages even as the supply across the state dwindled.[42]

Prescient soldiers recognized the difficulty facing their families and rec-

"The Effect of the Rebellion on the Homes of Virginia." This Harper's *image accurately conveyed the extent of suffering in Virginia households by the winter of 1862–63, but the downcast head and submissive posture of the woman in the central picture inaccurately characterized white Virginians' attitudes toward the war. Although civilians wished for peace, most were not willing to return to the Union in order to achieve it. Photo courtesy of the Virginia Historical Society, Richmond.*

ommended measures to help prevent suffering. One man wisely observed the dire straits many Virginians would be in with the capture of the Kanawha Valley and its saltworks. He wrote his father that he had "bought a half bushel of salt for you which cost $7 dol in discount money you might want to send you wagon to town and get a good deal of salt. it will be very scarce after while you ought to try and get enough to salt your meat this winter."[43] Preserving meat would challenge only those lucky enough to have hogs or cattle not picked up by foraging soldiers. The scarcity and hardship of the fall was nearly as difficult and important a battle for the Confederacy to win as were the fights at Manassas and Antietam. Civilian suffering held the potential to erode support for the war and undermine the solidarity of the new nation by exacerbating a localism at odds with state and national unity.

The high prices and scarcities that plagued citizens of northern, central, and western Virginia, as well as occupied districts on the Tidewater, were not yet felt by many residents of Virginia's interior. The Piedmont region, with the highest rates of slaveholding and wealth in the state, maintained its prewar productivity. Watkins Kearns recorded his observations as his regiment crossed over the Blue Ridge into Albemarle County in mid 1862. "On this march pass a beautiful place by name Whitehall. The farms in this county are in a high state of cultivation. Vegetation much more forward than the other side of the Blue Ridge. Plenty of negroes and every appearance of substantive and even luxurious living."[44] Coming out of the Shenandoah Valley after a season of Union occupation, Kearns immediately recognized the great diversity within the state in terms of war experiences. His use of the size of the slave population to measure success was a prewar habit that remained useful and appropriate in parts of the state where slavery remained intact well into the war.

The government did what it could to diminish class conflict within the state. The summer and fall of 1862 proved to be an especially trying time for Virginia civilians, as communities struggled to cope with the enormous manpower demands made by the Confederate army that spring. In the wake of conscription, towns and villages across the state took stock of their needs and began the process of petitioning for statutory exemptions for vital personnel. Citizens begged their representatives to release from military service blacksmiths, doctors, and others whose skills were needed at home. When these efforts failed, citizens would personally petition the secretary of war or the president to try and secure exemptions. Where and when it could, the War Department issued exemptions for vital occupations.[45]

Even the endorsement of appropriate exemptions could not stem criticism of the legislation. Some Confederates identified a class bias in the policies of exemption and substitution. Still, those objections did not automatically stimulate a desire to rejoin the Union. One soldier wrote home in late 1862 to complain that the "wealthy class" had left the war and taken all the substitutes, leaving no one for him to hire. Revealingly, he qualified his observation of the inequities of Confederate life with a clear articulation of his continued preference for southern independence: "I see a great deal on our side that I think is wrong not that I have become a Union man not in the least."[46] Another explained the relationship between suffering and loyalty quite plainly. "I did not volunteer for a holyday amusement," wrote one soldier, "I did not come to camp seeking ease. I came to aid a good cause in danger and while the danger continues I will be here." He then turned directly to the question asked by so many subsequent historians, "What if by the culpable neglect of unworthy officials—or the slender means possessed by the Confederate Government, my physical wants have been scantily supplied. And my hardships have thereby been increased! Do my sufferings make my country's cause less dear to me? Shall I desert a cause, for which I have suffered so many privations." To this question, he gave a clear answer, "No! No—Perish the unworthy thought!"[47]

The Confederacy contradicted its own efforts to remedy the problems facing communities in late 1862 with a second conscription act, passed in September, that increased the age limit to forty-five. Worse still, the draft exemption provisions that gave communities the right to retain the services of valuable artisans and doctors also provided relief for large slave owners. The "twenty slave" law allowed slaveholders to receive an exemption for one man of draft age for every twenty slaves. Critics of the law charged that this would allow elite slaveholders and their sons to sit out the war while the poor were forced to fight. Confederate congressmen designed the law as a way to protect slavery. They intended that some adult white males would remain on plantations with large numbers of slaves in order to ensure continued production of crops and to guard against slave rebellions. The law drew considerable criticism at the time, and it has served as a central part of the argument that the Confederacy favored the rich at the expense of the poor.[48] Virginia soldiers, however, did not spend a great deal of energy denouncing the law.[49] Some soldiers may have simply resigned themselves to policies that they considered unjust. Others may have understood and supported the law's purpose. Virginia soldiers did show, and discuss, their deep interest in retaining slavery as an institution and in keeping control over the slaves presently in the state. The law certainly must have rankled the sensibilities of nonslaveholding soldiers, but among Virginians it did not inspire a deep animosity toward the Confederacy.

Soldiers worried more about separation from their loved ones than about the legislation coming out of Richmond. The combination of separation and the hardships under which men suffered inspired soldiers to describe their relationships with their wives as transcendent unions. The letters from soldiers to their wives often contained ecstatic proclamations of their love. John Jones, with the 56th Virginia Infantry, relayed his excitement upon receiving a letter from his wife Mollie. "Before I read the first page I was so overwhelmed with Joy that I could scarcely read at all," Jones proclaimed. "It was so delightful to me to receive such a sweet affectionate and endearing letter from the one that I love with all my heart and soul. My dear Mollie, when I receive a letter from you I can scarcely every help from shedding tears when I read it because I am so filled with joy." Alongside this devotion, Jones expressed a concern that passed among many husbands and wives during the war. "You said that Lucie Putney had a baby it was one of the sweetest children you ever saw," Jones recollected. "I do not like you to be praising children too mutch. I am afraid (that is) it makes me think that you want one (do I judge)." From what Mollie told him about her recent weight gain, Jones suspected that she might be pregnant, not a situation he relished, noting, "If it is that something else [that is, a pregnancy], I am not so glad as you are." John's fears were confirmed later in the year, as it turned out Mollie was indeed pregnant. Though he never gave a reason for regretting her pregnancy, it may have been simple concern for his wife during the stresses of pregnancy and childbirth. This too was confirmed when Mollie lost the child late in her pregnancy.[50]

Attachments to family assumed a kind of protean significance among soldiers just as they did among those wives, children, and parents at home who worried about men in the service. News that a soldier was sick struck fear in those at home, who well knew the vulnerability of soldiers to illnesses of all sorts and the unpredictability of disease in the nineteenth century. Richard Arthur, a soldier stationed at Jamestown in the spring of 1862 mentioned a cold he had in a letter to his wife Phebe. She replied immediately, suspending her normal discussion of the children and local war news, to warn him to take care. "My Dear Husband," she cautioned, "I . . . was glad to hear from you but sorry to think you was so sick & hope you will take good care of your self and get well be sure and take good care and not take no more cold." Even as Phebe issued this warning to Arthur, the event she feared had already transpired. On the same day she warned her husband to take care, Arthur's captain wrote, "It becomes my melancholy duty to inform you of the death of your husband, which occurred last night about eleven O'Clock; sometime after reaching this place he was attacked with measles and before recovering from the disease was attacked with Typhoid pneumonia of what latter disease he died last night as before stated."[51]

Despite these dangers and the anxiety that accompanied every letter between parlors and camps through 1862, soldiers adopted a new set of priorities that incorporated defense of home within the organized defense of the nation in which they were participating. The rewards of an independent Confederacy, especially the protection that would afford for soldiers' families, balanced the risks that soldiers took in leaving their families. For Virginia soldiers in the Valley Army, this perspective had developed as they fought their way through their own and neighboring counties in the spring and summer of 1862 to expel Union military forces. As one of Jackson's staff officers put it, "Our men will fight desperately whenever it comes, for it is for our homes, sure enough now." Not all Virginia soldiers fought in their home regions, so their willingness to obey the rules of the army and accept the punishments meted out to those who violated them signaled their internalization of the complementary defense of home and nation. The larger cause demanded their adherence, and received it, because success promised to accomplish their goal of a secure home.[52]

The dedication of Confederate soldiers to fight until they won independence impressed itself upon Randolph Stiles. Stiles fought with Confederate forces, but his father had worked for many years before the war as a pastor in New Haven, Connecticut, and, as a result, Randolph felt like a man of neither nation. This distance gave Stiles valuable perspective on both the depth of war weariness among Confederates and the depth of their resolve. He summarized the situation after Antietam by describing the battlefield and explaining that "then you might realize why our little army, always the same front offered to their ever changing masses, is so tired of this wicked war." Stiles continued, "dont understand me to think they [Confederate soldiers] wish to give it up. they are ready for peace on any terms outside coming together with the north. they will all die before they can submit to that." Stiles observed the same transition that others had identified, as the process of fighting catalyzed a new antipathy toward the North: "At first there was not real hatred against the northern people; in the masses of our army—but now I cannot describe it—nothing can make these people one again, many many generations will have to pass ere there will be any change—and every day it grows worse."[53]

The dedication Stiles described would be tested immediately with a winter campaign in central Virginia and amply rewarded with a stunning Confederate victory. McClellan's "slows" prompted Lincoln to replace him with Ambrose E. Burnside, who moved his troops east toward Fredericksburg. Lee followed this shift and moved his own units east as well. Even with the improvements in organization made in the fall, Lee remained concerned about the stragglers and absentees. On November 27, 1862, the adjutant general issued orders instructing all absent men to return to their units. The order applied to both officers and enlisted men, evidence that straggling was not an occupation of privates alone. Officers who failed to report back to duty would be "dropped from the rolls of the Army in disgrace" and their names listed for conscription with local draft agents. Enlisted men who stayed absent would be "considered as deserters and treated accordingly," with their names given to draft agents as well.[54] The measures may have struck some men as harsh, because the season before the army had tacitly condoned or at least accepted a high rate of absence during the winter. The new orders were a measure of the maturity reached within the Confederacy military bureaucracy and a reflection that the war truly required men to serve as soldiers. For Virginia men who longed to be home with their families, especially as the holidays approached, the new discipline of the Confederate army could only be justified under absolute necessity. The battle soon fought provided incentives to spare.

The town of Fredericksburg, which housed 5,000 people in its prewar days and lay between the two armies, would soon be engulfed in an whirlwind of looting, fighting, and bombardment.[55] The devastation visited upon the city, some of it intentional and some merely the by-product of geography, shocked Confederates and stirred Virginians to new levels of hatred for the Yankee invaders. The plight of Fredericksburg residents, most of whom fled as the Union army moved into the city, reinforced for Virginians that the war had become a battle not just to build a nation but to maintain communities. Union tactics and policies seemed designed to rip apart the very fabric of Virginia's social life. Rather than cowing the Confederates, this approach broadened and reinforced the virtue of sacrifice that soldiers had begun to articulate on their own during the year. Thousands of soldiers suffered and died at Fredericksburg, but it was the suffering of civilians that helped bind personal loss to Confederate nationalism ever more tightly.

On December 11 Burnside's men successfully pushed across the Rappahannock River and entered the town. A fierce artillery battle had driven most residents from their homes and destroyed whole blocks. Now, with the town virtually vacant, starving Union soldiers enacted the hardest war Virginia had yet seen. Soldiers invaded private homes and spilled the contents out into the streets where men consumed food and alcohol, read books, and played pianos, before destroying much of what they could not eat or carry off. Confederates who watched the devastation from Marye's Heights to the west of town could only seethe in anger and await their chance for retribution.

That opportunity came on December 13, when Union forces attacked the Confederate line. The northern attacks, which, on one part of the field, required soldiers to advance over a broad open plain in range of Confederate artillery against a stone wall behind which lay well-protected Confederate troops, combined ineffective heroics with massive death and suffering. Brigade after brigade of Union troops attacked the Confederate position, and none reached the wall. Facing devastating artillery fire and the small arms of the infantry massed at the base of Marye's Heights, Union soldiers fell by the thousands. Confederate soldiers stood in awe of the ranks of blue clad troops that marched to meet them and in the evening many displayed sympathy and offered aid to their enemies, but the battle was in truth merely an extended slaughter. When Burnside at last called a halt to the attacks late in the afternoon, spent Confederates could scarcely calculate or even contemplate the scale of human loss they had seen. Unlike previous battles where the fighting was spread along fronts more than five miles long, the devastation at Fredericksburg was concentrated and the effect convinced many Confederates that they had destroyed the Union army for good. As one man wrote to his sweetheart after the battle, "This will be the last battle of this campaign I think & of the war too I hope."[56]

Burnside managed to pull the Union army back over the Rappahannock where they began the massive job of attending to their wounded. Confederates suffered 5,309 casualties, a high total but less than half the Union sum of 12,653. Although few accurately guessed these numbers at the time, everyone on both sides understood the battle as a lopsided Confederate success. Unlike previous victories, soldiers had little time to celebrate their accomplishment. The difficulties of the winter and the suffering of civilians impinged on their success almost immediately. Lee remained wary of the Union army and kept his men on alert, preventing them from building winter quarters that would have protected them from the unusually cold weather of late December. Worse still were the conditions of Fredericksburg residents who had fled as the bombardment of their town began and returned to find looted and destroyed homes and a country destitute of either fuel or food.[57]

The captain of a Confederate artillery battalion that had punished the Union troops remarked on the pitiful state of the locals. "It made me feel sad to see delicate women, beautiful girls and tender young children thus banished from their comfortable homes," he wrote, "living as it were in the woods, at this trying season of the year." His own family lived in Lexington, in the upper reaches of the Shenandoah Valley, where Union troops had not yet reached, and he realized the good fortune of the interior towns. "How thankful the people of Rockbridge should be, that the County has never been visited by the desolating tread of any army." The officer also observed the privations of his men, who endured hardships because of the incompetence of Confederate quartermaster agents and transportation officials in Richmond. "The suffering of the army is terrible. Many of our soldiers are thinly clothed and without shoes and in addition to this, very few of the infantry have tents. With this freezing weather, their sufferings are indescribable."[58]

As bad as conditions were for soldiers, many immediately organized relief efforts for Fredericksburg residents. In prewar Virginia, local elites had organized and provided relief to worthy poor neighbors during severe times on an ad hoc basis. The personal nature of charitable assistance in the antebellum Old Dominion offered elites, usually slave owners, an opportunity for exercising control over the poor whites in their communities.[59] Union artillery shells fell on rich and poor residences alike in Fredericksburg and quickly destroyed the mechanisms and the means for providing aid to the less fortunate. The city and county governments were similarly incapacitated and unable to help. Soldiers formed their own charitable entities, submitting circulars among the camps to raise money for local residents. One colonel raised more than $2,000 in an hour, a testament he felt, to the bravery and generosity of the soldiers who defended the families of Virginia on the battlefield and off.[60] The contributions were also a testament, he believed, to the relatively strong position of Virginia Confederates. By late 1862, many soldiers had the means and the desire to sustain communities to which they were bound only by ties of state and national allegiance. George S. Pickett gave $200 himself and noted that his regiment donated $500.[61]

The destruction visited upon Fredericksburg offered a vicarious lesson in Yankee cruelty for those removed from the front lines. The destruction also brought the city into the pantheon of victimized places, its citizens lauded as noble sufferers who were persecuted in the stead of all Confederates. As one Virginia paper noted, "those who are more favored—upon whom the rude touch of war has not come with its crushing weight, should spring with glad alacrity to the alleviation of the necessities of these our stricken countrymen."[62] The language—"our countrymen"—revealed the communal nature of Virginians' interpretation of the event. The generosity of southern soldiers for the victims of Fredericksburg reveals the remarkable success that Confederates had achieved in building a unified nation. Contributions came from soldiers from states all across the new nation. Louisiana and Florida men felt a common cause with the residents of this Virginia town, and their actions demonstrated the depth of Confederate nationalism at the conclusion of this awful year of war.[63]

Alongside this sense of national identity, soldiers identified other kinds of motivations that had been less apparent in the early months of 1862. While soldiers, especially those stranded without tents on cold winter nights, continued to complain about their conditions, many began to take even greater pride in a new kind of stoic bravery. This bravery was itself increasingly intertwined with a Confederate nationalism built around personal sacrifice, but for soldiers it had a tangible reward in battles won. Although few soldiers talked explicitly about bravery or cowardice in their letters, all could see the results of holding a line against a charge. With each bloody encounter, at Second Manassas, at Antietam, and at Fredericksburg, Confederate soldiers gained a stronger sense of the value of their willingness to stand in the face of almost certain death or injury.[64]

Soldiers' sense of their own mortality was reinforced more strongly than ever at Fredericksburg, where they witnessed the slaughter of so many men in such a confined space over so short a time. In the battles of the late summer and fall of 1862, Confederates left the battlefields and destruction and marched to new fights. At Fredericksburg, they camped on the bluffs above the town and contended with both their own wounded as well as the Union's dead and wounded soldiers who had not been removed. The immersion in death that soldiers experienced through fall and winter of 1862, and particularly on the harrowing night of December 13, when thousands of wounded soldiers lay dying on the field mere yards in front of the Confederate line, promoted a sense among Confederate soldiers that they possessed a unique valor and merit that even Confederate civilians lacked. That confidence spurred men to greater achievements for their cause, even as the distance between soldiers and civilians opened.

Soldiers' familiarity with death helped spur another element that promoted both solidarity and perseverance: religious revivals swept through the army in its camps along the Rappahannock. Soldiers filled the churches in Fredericksburg to capacity that winter and built their own chapels along the front. Ministers from nearby communities entered the camps to lead services and army chaplains leapt at the opportunity to perform their explicit duty rather than all the auxiliary tasks that they had assumed during the previous year. Though reliable numbers on conversions are lacking, it is reasonable to suppose that tens of thousands of Confederate soldiers participated in religious exercises, many of whom probably had spent little time in churches before the war. Intertwined with the sense of personal sacrifice that developed during the year, the new religious commitment endorsed by thousands of soldiers altered both the motivation for fighting and the purpose of the war. Men would now fight against sin in their hearts, immorality in the camps, and Yankees on the battlefield, with victories on each front lending strength to one another. A holy obligation to repel the infidel Yankees now underlay the development of more ordinary motivation issues like unit cohesion and protection of family.[65]

In early 1862, soldiers had filled their letters home with pleas for the war's end. Most saw no contradiction between a desire for victory and a desperate wish to return home. Some, like Sandie Pendleton, envisioned the war's end. In May he wrote his mother that "While [I am] determined to stay in the army and fight for our country's independence to the death if need be, I am longing for peace again."[66] Another man echoed this call in a letter to his wife: "I know one thing I never could get fond of such a life as this. I feel as if peace was declared on terms satisfactory to the South, it would be the happiest moment of my life."[67] Other soldiers contented themselves with sarcastic comments about the service itself. As one man wrote, "If all the war was to be as hard as . . . these marches in the winter, one would think quite considerably before going in for 3 years of the same work."[68]

As the conflict dragged on and men participated in more violent contests, a stronger commitment to stay in the war emerged among Confederate soldiers. The battle at Fredericksburg and particularly the looting of residents' homes by Union soldiers drained the eager anticipation of peace out of many soldiers. Mortimer Johnson, who served with a Rockbridge unit in the battle, conveyed his palpable anger after seeing the devastation in the town. "After going through Fredericksburg and seeing the results of their vandalism I felt no sympathy for their justly merited fate," Johnson reported. "Scattered books, broken [—], furniture of all kinds and every description carried into the streets and broken to pieces." The depth of his anger was measured out coldly in the length of Union dead. "All who have visited the ground concur in the opinion that the dead are thicker upon the ground than any [field] they have seen. One could walk for 400 yds. upon the dead." Despite the horror of what he had seen, no desire for peace surfaced in his reflections on the future course of the war. Instead, he vowed to bring the same hard war to the Union that they had brought to Virginia. "I can assure you," Johnson promised, "I should feel rejoice if the war could close without such another scene as we have witnessed here—but if our foes will not cease the War which it is in their power to then I hope that every conflict will result as favorable to us as this great fight at Fredericksburg."[69]

5 ⋆ THE FAMILY WAR

JANUARY—DECEMBER 1863

I had an idea of resigning some time ago, but I have come to
the conclusion that the Yankees are too close by Home to resign.
—John Peter Jones, 56th Virginia Infantry, May 27, 1863

As the Civil War entered its third year, military fortunes and home front conditions assumed a curiously inverted relationship. At the start of 1863, the Federal army was recovering from its debilitating defeat at Fredericksburg and confined to the northeastern corner of the state, while Confederates relished their recent victory. By contrast, civilian hardship and suffering in Virginia reached its wartime apogee in the winter of 1862–63.[1] In May 1863 Confederates scored a stunning victory over the Yankees at Chancellorsville, just outside Fredericksburg, and then moved north once again. Although the Confederates did not achieve the tactical or strategic success they sought in the ensuing Pennsylvania campaign, their departure brought much-needed logistical relief to the state. As military fortunes declined, then, home front conditions improved. The contrasting experiences of war in Virginia weighed heavily on soldiers, who maintained connections to both the civilian and military worlds. The challenge of the year would be how soldiers balanced the competing interests and experiences of their two worlds.

Nearly two years of war in northern and central Virginia thoroughly denuded the region of crops, livestock, and residents, many of whom had fled south to Richmond. Throughout the state, enslaved Virginians seized on the chaos of war, and the opportunity offered by the Union's increasing interest in fostering emancipation, to push against the bonds of slavery, or to break them altogether. The harder the North fought to destroy slavery, the harder the Confederacy sought to protect it. The challenge of defending slavery and controlling slaves demanded aggressive measures from individuals and government at all levels, many of which angered citizens unaccustomed to an invasive state. People across Virginia, and across the Confederacy, began to express their discontent with their national government's policies in more public ways. Ironically, citizen's objections and protests revealed the success of the national project. By 1863 most white southerners expected their new national government to defend slavery and protect them from hostile armies and hunger. The inability of the Confederate government to accomplish these goals encouraged Virginians to refine their vision of the how war should be managed. In some cases, Virginians blamed the Confederacy, with its aggressive policies of conscription and taxes for their misfortunes. In others, residents advocated a stronger hand for the government, granting it the power to defeat the despised Yankees. In both situations, they treated the Confederacy like their nation.

The ferocity of battle in 1863, the experience of capture and confinement in northern prisons, and the Confederates' own tentative use of hard-war tactics all created an increasing distance between soldiers and their homes. On the one hand, this distance threatened to alienate soldiers from one of their most important sources of motivation—defense of family. On the other, many soldiers seem to have almost appreciated the distance because it confirmed for them that the military life they despised was not the only possible world. Soldiers' idealized reminiscences of domestic life offered relief from the fear and pain that characterized the military experience.[2] But soldiers could not ignore the distress of those at home. The increasing hardships experienced by civilians forced soldiers to seek ways to understand how their military service protected their families. Most emerged from the long hiatus in the late summer and fall of 1863 with a more clearly defined belief that staying in the army would meet their families' needs. This sense of motivation inspired Virginia soldiers until the end of the war.

Many Virginians began the new year as they had those of the 1850s, by attending to the business of hiring slaves. A thirty-four-year-old Virginia soldier, named George Washington Peebles after the Revolutionary patron of liberty, noted the strong market in slave rentals just two days after Lincoln signed the Emancipation Proclamation. "January 3, 1863: Clear and moderately warm. Went to the hiring at Daniel's More negroes hired very high indeed," he reported.[3] The rise of slave hiring in the 1850s generated an annual tradition of seeking out slaves and negotiating contracts in early January. For those Confederate families now devoid of white men to labor in fields or factories, obtaining slave labor became even more crucial, but the huge numbers of slaves impressed by the Confederacy to build military fortifications around the state created an expensive renter's market. Although the continuing efforts of enslaved Virginians to escape to Union lines drove prices still higher, few Confederates suspended the old practices. The renewal of the market in "negroes" denied the impact of the

Emancipation Proclamation in a way obvious to both Abraham Lincoln and the African Americans of Virginia.

Confederate opposition to the policy of emancipation surfaced in a variety of ways throughout the year. Newspapers were filled with violent denunciations of Lincoln and his policy. A Shenandoah Valley paper proposed that Lincoln "should be declared an out law, and enemy of mankind, and a suitable reward be offered for his head. This would indicate more unmistakably than could be done in any other way, the contempt we feel for the fiat of the negro generalisimo."[4] The *Daily Richmond Examiner* described the policy as "the most startling political crime, the most stupid political blunder, yet known in American history."[5] One Virginia soldier wrote to a friend in March 1863, asking, "Don't you like that Negro Soldier Bill passed by the Federal Congress?" His sarcastic query about the recent decision by the U.S. Army to enlist black soldiers prefaced a chilling response to the North's policy. "If our Congress would only pass a bill giving each soldier all the negroes whom he could capture," he wrote, "as is suggested by some of the papers, there would be no necessity for a bounty act." He deduced that "The cavalry would become a popular branch of the service, as it would hold out so many more opportunities for speculating in 'human flesh' as the Abolitionists say." Unfortunately, he deemed his plan unrealistic because, "I expect that Seward is too cunning to give us such a chance to make our fortunes & will employ them for home garrisons mostly."[6] The Confederate army's capture of runaway slaves and free African Americans living in Pennsylvania in 1863 nearly made this soldier's dream come true.

The mercenary traffic in black people that had long symbolized the opening of a new year in Virginia reminded more than one observer of the way that the Confederacy now treated white men. The enactment of the Draft Act in April 1862 gave the government control over many white men's bodies, and the pressure of the draft on eligible men continued to increase through 1863. The War Department organized local conscription boards to evaluate whether men were eligible for service. The public nature of these hearings increased the anxiety men felt to protect both their image and their exemptions from service. Not content to wait out the arrival of men at training camps, army leaders actively sought out eligible men. A Tidewater soldier returned to his home region with the armies in mid-April to collect men. He described the process to his wife. "I was ordered with companies of infantry & two hundred cavalry to proceed into town to arrest all persons liable to conscription," he reported. The unit also arrested "all the runaway negroes to be found & to gather[ed] all stores left by the enemy. We took a few conscripts about seventy slaves and a number of loads of military stores."[7] The simultaneous capture of slaves and white men for use in the same army under similar conditions rankled even some officers, who worried about the effect on soldiers' morale.

Most soldiers applauded a recent change in army policy that had also invited comparisons between white men and slaves. Flogging had been abolished. One soldier expressed relief that two soldiers in his brigade had been executed rather than whipped, since he "knew of nothing more degrading" than flogging.[8] This soldier, like most Virginia volunteers, concerned himself exclusively with the effect of the disciplinary practices on those men already in the service. His executed comrades had obviously disgraced themselves to the point where they no longer concerned him. What did concern him was that flogging might be seen as degrading by other soldiers. By abolishing whipping as a punishment, the Confederate military command could count one more policy change that might improve the morale of the average soldier.

Virginia men adopted other strategies, some conscious and others less so, to bolster themselves through what was turning into a much larger and more deadly confrontation than any one had imagined. Ironically, one of the ways that Virginia Confederates accommodated a long war was by committing only to a short one. At almost every pause in the conflict, Virginians predicted imminent victory. The fantasy of a single-battle victory died slowly after First Manassas, and people continued to pine for the one cataclysmic contest that would end the war. Many more latched on to any piece of information that forecast Yankee defeat or Confederate victory. Martin Coiner, who served with his brother in the 52nd Infantry, anticipated the end in the early spring of 1863. "I heard that the Yanks were a fighting among themselves," he observed. "I only hope they will fight among themselves if they want to fight & let us alone but I still can't think this war will last very long."[9] Another Virginian, buoyed by the fresh recruits being brought into Confederate camps thought "the war is substantially over—tho' their armies now in the field will probably have to be beaten once more to hasten matters."[10]

In contrast to those who put their faith in a single great victory, other soldiers began to adopt a fatalistic outlook that ensured they would stay in the ranks. This outlook ensured the Confederate armies remained intact, but it could also deaden soldiers to their own fate and that of their country. One Albemarle soldier described his perspective to his cousin. He began ominously, noting, "I think it is one of the darkest days for our young Confederacy that she has ever seen. I believe that in a few months the stars and stripes will move from the frontiers to the gulf. I can almost say that it makes very little difference with me for in the first place I never expect to live to see the end of this war and if I should I have nothing to live for the future is as dark to me as night." Having just come from one of the many prayer meetings active around the Army of Northern Virginia in the winter and spring of 1863, he had a loftier goal in mind. "But for the hereafter I could face death or the cannon's mouth with as much indifference as I eat my beef and bread," he wrote.[11] Another soldier frankly admitted to his father that "like yourself I have very little faith in all this said of peace expect that it is a long way off. I think we are bound to have a long & bloody war."[12] The emotional deadening that many Virginia Confederates underwent had social ramifications as well. The early spring of 1863 was the apogee of wartime hardship for many Virginia communities, epitomized by the Richmond Bread Riot in April, and soldiers struggled with how they should respond to deteriorating conditions at home.[13]

Violence on the home front arrived in Richmond in dramatic fashion on March 13, 1863, when a mammoth explosion rocked the city. An ordnance factory on Brown's Island, in the James River, exploded, killing sixty-nine women who worked there. The physical devastation and human toll of the event terrified skittish residents.[14] It also forced a difficult confrontation with the kind of society that wartime Virginians had built. An essential industrial enterprise, and a physically dangerous one as well, located just miles from the national capital was run almost entirely by women. Over the course of the war, women filled jobs in industrial settings all over the South, and these actions prompted complaints from conservatives worried about the erosion of traditional gender roles. The Savannah, Georgia, textile mills that produced army uniforms used female labor extensively throughout the war, but this industry at least drew on prewar traditions of female labor.[15] In the Brown's Island episode, many Richmonders were surprised to learn that so many women worked in such a dangerous setting. Though Virginians could not afford to spare women from the task of factory work, the deaths on the island prompted a renewed examination of the new Confederacy.

When the city waterworks failed a few days later, it exacerbated the atmosphere of tension and concern. Following this, city women began organizing the protest that turned into a full-scale riot on April 2, 1863. The demonstration began as a way for women to express concern and anger over the prices that sellers charged for flour and the government policies that kept grain stockpiled in warehouses. Hunger and dissatisfaction overwhelmed the crowd, which began looting local stores and warehouses. The crowd was dispersed only when Confederate troops marched on the protestors. Jefferson Davis himself appeared before the mob, petitioned its dispersal, and threatened to order the massed soldiers to open fire. This last threat worked and quelled the riot. Even more than the Brown's Island disaster, the Bread Riot forced Richmonders to think seriously about the problems of their new society. The shock of a public demonstration by women in a conservative southern city has obscured the fact that city and state governments both responded with increased charity for the needy. This pattern was replicated around the state as communities built more aggressive programs to help the increasing numbers of destitute Virginians.[16]

Other towns showed the accumulated hardships of the winter as well. An Albemarle soldier who was recuperating in a Petersburg hospital in March 1863 observed "You may know it is dear living in toun I cant see what Poor people will do thet Live in town."[17] One approach that benefited many poor Virginians was appealing to the local elites for aid. In some cases this was successful. One man, posted to artillery duty at Chaffin's Bluff just south of Richmond, relayed to his wife his thoughts about a recent petition. "In regard to Mrs. Sandrum's application for meal," he wrote, "I told Mr. S I would furnish some corn for his family if I had it to spare & I suppose there some for sale."[18] This approach fit within the prewar traditions of charity which in the antebellum south remained always personal and local, not state managed. Still, the situation had become nearly desperate for almost all classes of people. One wealthy slave owner who lived just outside Richmond wrote to a friend with a plea for help. "We are on the eve of starvation," he begged, "and unless the ways are opened up very shortly we will all be laid low. I write to ask if you can't buy for me fifty bushels of wheat and have it ground for me . . . on which I may feed my servants."[19]

The Confederacy's survival depended upon two related enterprises, a condition impressed upon Jefferson Davis in dramatic fashion on April 2. Confederates armies needed to defeat, or at least stall, Union military efforts long enough for the North to give up or for foreign powers to intervene. Because of the immediate physical nature of this challenge, it received more attention from contemporaries and many subsequent historians. But the Confederacy's future also relied on the successful creation of a new nation-state. Although the apparatus of government gave the Confederacy the appearance of having achieved this, the less tangible aspects of nation building continued to bedevil Confederate and state leaders throughout the war. Paramount among the issues that leaders faced was the problem of social unity, undermined by concerns over equality of sacrifice. Antebellum southerners had long appreciated how racial unity alleviated class conflict within the white community, and racial solidarity was an important element in Confederate stability throughout the war. Unfortunately for harried Confederate leaders, like their counterparts in the North, they could not eliminate class conflict.

As a result, Confederates had to manage social strife alongside their effort to win the war. They did so awkwardly, but most recent studies indicate they did so successfully. For Culpeper County residents, all the typical frustrations of soldiering were compounded by the fact that the Confederacy could not adequately protect their loved ones at home. Union and Confederate forces fought for control of central Virginia beginning in 1862, and the result was a chaotic and dangerous life for residents. Nonetheless, most Confederate soldiers reconciled themselves to staying in the army.[20] The same dynamic prevailed in counties farther north. Loudoun and Fauquier counties both held significant numbers of Unionist civilians and were more firmly occupied by Federal forces throughout the war, but a majority of civilians in that region supported the Confederacy, often because of the repressive tactics used by northern armies.[21] The old view of the Confederacy as an entity that enjoyed universal and unstinting support from all residents has been thoroughly disproved, but it does not follow from this that the social and political tensions detailed by historians yielded a toxic combination that ultimately killed the Confederacy. Instead, the Confederacy appears to have contained the same wealth of contradictions and tensions as most societies.[22]

I n the spring of 1863, even those Confederate soldiers buckling under perceived injustices knew they had to turn their attention to the northern army. Confederates and Federals had remained in place, just across the Rappahannock River from each other, throughout the early months of the year and both knew that another major clash was in the offing. An aborted Union effort to cross the river in early January sealed the fate of Ambrose Burnside. By mid-January Lincoln relieved him of command and placed Joseph Hooker in charge of the Union army outside Fredericksburg. Hooker was well regarded by both officers and men in the Army of the Potomac, and his elevation from corps command, combined with the administrative and logistical improvements he made in February, raised the morale of northern soldiers considerably. Confederates saw Hooker as another in an already lengthy list of northern army commanders who would soon face ignominious defeat. The overwhelming Confederate victory at Fredericksburg in December 1862 had concluded the year on a triumphal note for Confederate soldiers. They entered the new year with high expectations that another victory would end the war. The much-anticipated battle finally happened in early May, at a little crossroads just west of Fredericksburg called Chancellorsville. Confederates fulfilled their expectations of victory, though not of ending the war.[23]

The cost of this victory, like those in the major battles of 1862, came in lost manpower and the crushing psychological burden on the survivors. Soldiers at Chancellorsville saw this toll intimately in the friends and relatives killed or wounded in the terrific fighting of May 2 and 3. The intense violence of combat that developed during the battles in the second half of 1862 had not been anticipated by the men who enlisted in 1861, and its persistence changed the nature of the conflict in fundamental ways. Most immediately, it demanded a psychological adjustment to death on the part of each soldier. Even those who survived the ordeal privately begged for its end.[24] After Chancellorsville, one man confined his sorrow to his diary, though even there he could muster only numerical evidence to represent the tragedy that had occurred. "5 p.m. Batalion drill 6 officers and about 80 men. Awful to think and of 430 only about 80 for drill, O this horrible war."[25] The victory could not restore the thousands of friends and neighbors lost in the battle. One skeptical soldier tallied his regiment's losses at Chancellorsville before noting grimly, "Old General Lee says he has won the largest victory ever has been since the war has been going on."[26]

Confederates derived some consolation from the fact that northern troops experienced more casualties, and that their suffering might end the war. A Shenandoah Valley soldier described the battle and its aftermath, with little regard for the Union dead around him. "That was another night spent upon the battlefield among dead and wounded," he coldly announced. "We had as yet lost but very few men and I could not have much sympathy for the Yankees." His own regiment suffered nine casualties, but this was an acceptable loss for what they inflicted on northern troops. "The loss on both sides was very heavy," he noted, "but I firmly believe the Yankees loss was two to our one if not more. Some say five to one. I never saw the likes of knapsacks, the ground was literally covered from where we started until we stopped them." In an indication how of quickly some men hardened themselves to the death and destruction they saw, this correspondent closed with a chilling observation: "The Fredericksburg fight of Dec. 13 was not a circumstance compared to this, that nothing more than play."[27]

In addition to the psychological adjustments every soldier had to make, the death toll required a strong commitment on the part of soldiers to stay in the army and participate actively in battles. They had to accept their own likely death and the promise that their death would help produce a better world. In effect, soldiers had to internalize the national culture of sacrifice that came to define the Confederacy in 1862. Though few men dwelt on this gruesome calculation, it remained a reality. As one artilleryman summarized the experience, "The victory at Fredericksburg & vicinity seems to have been a splendid one but very dearly bought. Still this we must expect, whilst we are deeply grateful for the success."[28] Just as difficult to accept as one's own death was the act of killing other men. The act of killing contradicted the sympathetic values of the domestic world and the humility and charity advocated by evangelical Christianity, both worldviews adopted by many antebellum Virginians. Soldiers accepted killing because it was the only way to end the war. To accommodate this balance, soldiers throughout the army focused on the relationship between their actions on the battlefield and the northern response.[29]

Compounding the loss of soldiers at Chancellorsville was the accidental shooting and subsequent death of Stonewall Jackson. Jackson and several of his staff officers had been scouting Union positions in advance of Confederate lines late on the evening after the main battle on May 2. When his party returned to their lines, Confederate pickets opened fire. The loss in terms of leadership was a serious one; Jackson had served as Lee's trusted lieutenant since the Peninsula campaign. More importantly, newspaper writers and ordinary people across the South had transformed him into an mythic figure even before his death. Abram Fulkerson, a twenty-nine-year-old from southwestern Virginia, observed, "the intelligence of the death of *Gen. Jackson* came upon us like a shock. We feel that his death is a national calamity. The poorest soldiers among us appreciate his worth—loved the man, and mourn his loss." News of his death generated great public rituals of grief, within and outside the army, and immediately transformed him into the noblest of Confederate martyrs. Fulkerson's evaluation was typical. "Among the many heroes of this revolution," he wrote, "none have lived so much adored, none have died so much deplored, and none have left a character as spotless as that of Stonewall Jackson."[30] Confederate defeat compounded the nostalgic view of Jackson, and his image loomed ever larger in the pantheon of Confederate heroes.[31] But it is important to recognize that the eulogizing began during the war and served immediate needs. For the remainder of the war, Jackson's image functioned as a central element of Confederate popular culture and a crucial link between civilian morale, the armies' successes, and the national government in Richmond.

The conclusion of the Chancellorsville campaign, like the conclusion of the late summer fighting in Virginia in 1862, ended with northern troops pulling back across the Rappahannock River to reorganize and reenergize their army. Also like 1862, Lee hoped to build on the success at Chancellorsville to launch another invasion of the North. Military success on northern soil seemed to hold the potential of ending the war. The usual sense that the next battle would be the last one persisted, but this time, Confederate soldiers recognized the importance of dispiriting the northern public. Salvation lay in the newspapers, where reports of unrest and disappointment in the North heralded the erosion of support for the war. If northern citizens could be made to abandon the war, Confederates could return home. The task of Confederate soldiers in the East was clear. As one Virginian phrased it, "I think we will clean the Yankees *out* this summer and whip them into secession."[32]

As always, "cleaning them out" required harder work than it seemed like it should have, given how overwhelmingly Confederates had defeated Union forces in recent major battles in Virginia. Lee's Army marched west to reach the sheltered security of the Shenandoah Valley, down which it traveled into Maryland. Throughout the war, the Valley served as a physical refuge, screening the movement and size of Confederate forces from Union observation, but equally as important was the emotional succor men drew from the region, which emerged as an iconic Confederate place. Stonewall Jackson's defense of the Valley in 1862 had immortalized the region in military history, and the southern press portrayed it as composed of stalwart Confederate supporters who lived simple and honest lives. These reports ignored the sizable Unionist presence in the lower Valley and, importantly, the resentment and concern for the already significant destruction northern armies had visited upon the whole region. Valley residents strongly supported the Confederacy, but they also loved their land and winced at the toll taken by both enemy and friendly troops.

For soldiers from the Valley, any trip through the area promised the solace of home. As Charles Lippitt marched west across the state, he reveled in the vision before him. "Came in sight of the blue outline of mountains," he noted, "a pleasant sight, reminding me of my home in the good old valley of Va." Most Valley soldiers took the opportunity on their marches to visit friends and family, and Lippitt was no exception, enjoying the "happiness of seeing my friends well & happy."[33] Although Valley soldiers spoke more frequently of these opportunities than men from other regions, Virginia men always seized the chance to visit home in between battles or during lulls in campaigns. Unlike soldiers from the Deep South, who were separated from their loved ones, Virginia men maintained throughout the war a close contact with their home communities. This proximity bolstered confidence when civilians toasted soldiers with parties and honors but discouraged them when citizens scorned or ignored their defenders.

After the war, the battle of Gettysburg assumed mythic dimensions, but for most soldiers the campaign itself and the opportunity to interact with northern civilians, provided more events of note. The confrontation between Confederate soldiers and northern civilians came on the heels of the renewed dedication to independence that had emerged in late 1862 as soldiers committed themselves to an indefinite war. The chance to interact with northerners added more clarity to the Confederate purpose in the war. Many Virginia Confederates entered Pennsylvania with a strong desire for revenge. The destruction and hardship inflicted upon their state demanded retribution in kind. Because Confederates had entered Maryland during the preceding year with the intention of drawing civilians to support the South, few soldiers had the opportunity to pursue these goals during the campaign the previous year. The more extended sojourn to Pennsylvania, and the clear recognition that this was enemy territory, opened up new possibilities for practicing a hard war. As many Virginians quickly found, the deliberate pursuit of war on civilians left them uncertain about what kind of men they were and, indeed, cast doubt on the purpose and meaning of the conflict.

As Lee's army traveled down the Great Valley and into Pennsylvania, soldiers had little sense of how northern civilians would receive them. Their families' experiences with Union soldiers had been so unpleasant that most probably anticipated an immediately hostile reception. One young Virginian expressed surprise that he and his company were well received at many places, with food and drink offered to the hungry men. Perhaps suspecting that civilians might be trying to bribe the soldiers to avoid losing everything they had, he admitted that "the people generally seemed not to know exactly what to expect and I don't think would have been at all astonished if every building had been set on fire by us, nor would a great many have been surprised if we had concluded the business by massacaring the women and children."[34]

Many Confederates, inspired by destruction of civilian property in Virginia, entertained thoughts of burning buildings. One young soldier complained to his father that "they would not allow us to pillage in Penna," although officers did allow him to impress what he needed.[35] Another objected that "Our government is pursuing a very lady like policy here—are strenuous about the preservation of property &c—just as though these scoundrels had not been the aiders & abettors of all the pillage and rapine that has made Virginia a desert wherever they have been & rendered homeless thousands of helpless women & children."[36] Filtered through the lens of war, the people of the North struck many Confederates as degraded and repulsive. One soldier described the trip with particular, though not untypical, disgust. "As a general thing they [Pennsylvania residents] are the most cringing mean-spirited people on earth. . . . The women are all gross and sinewey."[37] Another soldier described the Pennsylvanians as "a simple ignorant & degraded people, the women in the country all going barefoot."[38]

Worse still, few northerners seemed to be living in difficulty, and few seemed aware of the conditions in the South. Confederates viewed this situation with special displeasure because they had anticipated finding serious unrest based on their reading of northern newspapers. John Garibaldi wrote his wife to vent his frustration with the apparent tranquillity and productivity in the North. "They are living in a very flourishing countries' plenty of good wheat, plenty of the best meadows I ever saw in my life," he reported. "The generality of the people haven't got more than eighty acres of land and they have it in the highest state of cultivation and living like princes almost they seem to be very much unconcerned about the war very seldom do they see a soldier." In an indication that Confederates had fully grasped both the means and the purposes of hard war, Garibaldi concluded with guessing the positive impact a destructive campaign might have. "They hardly [know] what war is," Garibaldi wrote his wife, "but if the war to be carried on there as long as it was carried on in Virginia, they would learn the effects of it, and perhaps would soon be willing to make peace with us."[39]

Lee issued general orders to prohibit foraging, but he authorized the seizure of huge amounts of fodder and high numbers of animals. Soldiers in need could impress items and leave Confederate scrip in exchange.[40] A Tidewater soldier bemoaned the loss of discipline in Pennsylvania. "Our soldiers acted very disgracefully in Pennsylvania toward the citizens altho very stringent orders were issued for the protection of private property." He "did not hear of the first man that suffered for taking anything he wanted from the people which proves that the officers were as guilty as the men. I felt when I saw how our men were going on that nothing but disaster would follow and in truth I was associated with an armed mob with the broadest license and not with a disciplined army such as General Lee has had under his command."[41] In comparison with the devastation visited upon central Virginia, however, most soldiers thought Pennsylvania escaped serious harm. As one expressed it, with more than a little regret, "Our men have strict orders not to take nothing without paying, but they do just as they please, which is not a twentieth part as bad as they do in Virginia." Even with this restraint, he could report, "the fences, chickens hogs and vegetables are being consumed rapidly."[42]

When they did succumb to the temptation to hurt noncombatants, Virginia Confederates suffered remorse and concern over the type of men they were becoming. By mid-1863, most Confederates had not lost their sense of revulsion over the violence of war. George Harlow, with the 23rd Virginia Infantry, sensed this as he crossed over the old battleground at Antietam as his unit marched north into Pennsylvania. He "witnessed the most horrible sights that my eyes ever beheld. I saw dead yankees in any number just lying on top of the ground with a little dirt thrown over them and the hogs rooting them out of the ground and eating them and others lying on the top of the ground with the flesh picked off and their bones bleaching and they by many hundreds." Harlow, like many Confederates, did not thrive on bloodlust and conquest. Instead, the images before him inspired concern and sorrow: "Oh what a horrible sight for human beings to look upon in a civilized country; when will this horrid ware ever end."[43] Harlow's ability to abstract the process of war absolved him for his role in participating in the killing, but many Confederates could not obscure their participation in a hard war against Pennsylvanians so easily, and they worried that their actions as soldiers would erode their standing as men.

While on the march in Pennsylvania, Confederates seized the opportunity to advance the racial policies that developed in the wake of secession, and particularly since passage of the Emancipation Proclamation, by kidnapping runaway slaves and free blacks. As Lee's army made its way into Pennsylvania, several regiments took it upon themselves to capture African Americans, some of whom may have been recently escaped slaves and others of whom were free citizens living in the North.[44] More than 200 African Americans were captured and taken to Virginia; some of them wound up in Confederate prisons while others were returned to local jails where they were "claimed" by ostensible masters. The decision to capture and enslave northern blacks reveals the extent to which slavery and racial control permeated the actions of the Confederate army. The policy was condoned by senior military leaders and engaged in with relish by common soldiers.[45] It was the first opportunity that Confederate soldiers had since Lincoln issued the Emancipation Proclamation to make their feelings known to the North, and they eagerly seized the chance. With the North now firmly on the side of emancipation and, theoretically at least, committed to a semblance of racial equality, Confederates embraced the opposing position, as proponents of slavery and white supremacy.

The campaign through Pennsylvania gained renown less for the interactions of Confederate soldiers and northern civilians than for what happened on the battlefield, though the former had nearly as much impact on the how Confederates perceived the war as the latter. Union and Confederate troops found each other around the town of Gettysburg, in southeastern Pennsylvania, and fought there, each in the hope of destroying the opposing army. Lincoln issued clear instructions to Hooker, who yielded command of the Army of the Potomac to George Gordon Meade on the eve of the battle: "I think *Lee's* Army and not *Richmond*, is your true objective point."[46] Lee possessed a similar strategic vision; destroying the Army of the Potomac would end the war. A vague confidence in one final climactic battle and the strategic necessity of obliterating the enemy army compelled officers to pursue an impossible goal. Both armies were too well armed and too large to be utterly defeated in a single battle. Nevertheless, both officers and men held out hope that this vision could be realized. Lee's soldiers exuded special confidence. As one man described it, "Our army is in fine spirits and willing to be led everywhere or anywhere confidently expecting success under the able leadership of Genl. Lee."[47]

For those Confederates who anticipated an overwhelming victory, Gettysburg proved a disappointment. They did not sweep the Federals from the field or capture thousands in flight, but neither did the Yankees sweep them from the field. Soldiers from both sides fought in a costly sequence of battles for three days in the hills around Gettysburg. One Virginia soldier who served on a provost guard in the town, and thus avoided the worst fighting, summarized the battles in a way that most Confederates would have recognized. Gettysburg, "was the hardest fight of the ware," he asserted, "The enemy were fortified on the top of the mountain we fought them three days but they got the best of it however, both armies retreated at the same time the loss on both sides in killed wounded and prisoners was about 60 thousand."[48] Though this man overstated the losses he was remarkably close to the nearly unbelievable figure of 50,000.

Virginia soldiers performed some of the hardest service in the battle, including the now mythic "Pickett's Charge." Such intense fighting over such an extended period exposed soldiers to more death and destruction among their friends and comrades than Confederates had seen in previous battles. A soldier in the 57th Virginia Infantry sadly noted that "every field officer in our Brigade was either killed or wounded."[49] Soldiers who had begun to accommodate themselves to the role of killing other men in late 1862 found that the scale of violence at Gettysburg forced them to accept a disconcerting familiarity with death. William Peek reported back to his sister on the results of the battle. "It was a fortunate thing that Corse's Brigade was not there, for many poor Hamptonian would have measured his length on yankee soil. The slaughter was horrible."[50]

The culture of sacrifice demanded personal discipline but rewarded soldiers with a powerful sense of clarity and confidence and accomplishment. One young solider who was mortally wounded on the first day of fighting offered an eloquent demonstration of the inner peace that selfless sacrifice could bring.

> July 1, 1863
> Dear Father,
>
> I was wounded this morn in battle near Gettysburg, Pa. I may not live. There is a chance that I will not. My right leg has been amputated below the right knee. Also I have been hit by a piece of shell in my back. I lost very much blood. Please kiss mother for me. If i die, I will be buried in the field, possibly in an unmarked grave. But my number is this:
>
> Forth Virginia Infantry
> Col. Baker's Battalion
> It is a very pretty day but I feel unafraid to die.
>
> Your loving son,
> Robert L. Thompson[51]

Still, Confederates had good reason to interpret the battle as something other than a complete defeat. Most importantly, as one man noted, "both parties [held] their positions" at nightfall on the last day.[52] For Civil War soldiers, retaining position on the battlefield offered clear evidence that they had not been defeated. In this regard, the presence of Confederates in and around Gettysburg on the fourth of July repeated the pattern from Antietam in 1862. Soldiers' accounts emphasized balance and mutual destruction rather than an irreversible turning point. One man's summary echoed the feelings of many: "We lost a good many men in Pennsylvania," he reported, "but we whiped the yankys the two first days, and the third day the yankys held their position, and then we fell back, as they had such a good position. The yankys lost a good many men too in that fight. We taken a good many prisoners."[53] As this man's comments indicate, soldiers sometimes contorted logic in an effort to convince themselves that they had not been defeated.

For the previous year, Confederates had been successful in every engagement with Yankees in Virginia, and always they suffered high casualty rates. The idea that they were unable to dislodge the Yankees from their position south of Gettysburg unsettled many, but it did not constitute a full reversal of the course of the war. Further, even those soldiers who drew dire lessons from the loss admitted the necessity of staying in the army, if only because they knew they could not predict the outcome of future battles. One dissatisfied soldier talked himself into accepting the verdict of the battle over the course of a long letter home. "I was sorry when it was begun, I am glad it is over," Joseph Manson wrote. "I never expected we would have the ability to wage invasive warfare and I had enough of Maryland last year to satisfy me that we could never fight successfully upon that soil." Changing tack, he accepted his position as one soldier in a great army. "I don't trouble myself about the plans of our Generals," he noted. "If we were ordered back to the Potomac today we would have to go and we might as well take it cheerfully."[54]

Another unforeseen aspect of the campaign to the North that challenged soldiers' conceptions of war and their role in it came with the capture of Confederate soldiers. The risk of capture increased substantially with invasions of the North, as one company from the upper Shenandoah Valley learned the hard way in mid-1863. "All of our company was taken prisoner at the Fight at Aldie except 5 of us that was with the Regiment," Jacob Click reported.[55] Most men returned to service after they received a parole, but they grew increasingly wary of being captured again. As Joseph Manson explained to his wife, "I had much rather miss such a chance than fall into their hands again unless I feel there is no other choice than between capture and death. Of course I would then surrender everytime."[56] Having been captured once, Manson steeled himself for a subsequent experience. For some Confederates, a long term in prison could compel a shift in national loyalties. One Virginian wrote home from Fort Delaware, "A great many of our boys are taking the oath of allegiance and I am sorry to see it, but we can do without them. I think that is the reason they are keeping us here so long, for they get some every day."[57] More immediate was the dread with which Confederates viewed the conditions of many of the overcrowded camps. "I am in hopes that I will not have an opportunity of visiting Fort Delaware again soon," one man wrote, "for it is certainly the last place in the world."[58]

More than one-quarter of all Virginia soldiers were captured at some point during the war, and many of these served time in Federal prisoner-of-war camps.[59] The problem of prisoners of war depressed people at home as well and signaled another failure of the state. After the hard campaign in Pennsylvania, many civilians anticipated visits from their soldier relatives. Reports of capture may have relieved initial concerns about surviving the battles, but the threat of malnutrition and disease in prisons soon created intense anxiety among loved ones. The distance from home also made reports of wounding or death much more troubling. Prisoner lists slowly reached communities around the state and came well after published reports of the cataclysmic battles. After the conclusion of fighting in Pennsylvania, General Lee required his cavalry and wagon support to transport as many wounded as possible back to Virginia. Although this imposed an additional strain on Virginia hospitals already full to overflowing, the prospect of leaving wounded soldiers in the North sat poorly with him because it diminished his manpower and depressed civilian morale. The soldiers themselves bemoaned the fates of those that they had to leave behind, particularly those trapped on the battlefield itself.[60]

The fall of Vicksburg further dispirited Confederate soldiers and civilians. Virginia soldiers, like Confederates across the South, followed the news of military campaigns in other regions closely. The determination of Vicksburg's defenders to resist Ulysses S. Grant's attempts to seize it had captured the attention of Virginians in 1862. One man spoke of Vicksburg with paternal affection, calling it a "brave little city" and noting, "Her name will never be forgotten however its fate may terminate."[61] After months of false starts, Grant eventually succeeded in capturing the city, terminating its function as the last major Confederate bastion on the Mississippi River. The responses of most soldiers reflected a concerned resignation. George Thomas Rust remarked to his wife that "It seems that this is a dark and gloomy period in the history of our country. The taking of Vicksburg, Port Hudson, and our failure to carry out the program in Pennsylvania has cast a great gloom over our people." Rust did not despair, but accepted the losses as inevitable in war on the scale they were fighting. "We had no right to expect anything else," he wrote. "We must expect to meet with a great many disasters, but they have a great deal to do before they can crush the rebellion."[62]

Another Virginian with Lee's army noted that, "the fall of Vicksburg has had a very depressing effect on us all & some seem to be almost in despair." Nevertheless, he too failed to see the loss as a portent of Confederate defeat. Turning immediately to speak of the fighting in Pennsylvania, he bragged that "if the Yanks had fought us again on the other side of the river [the Potomac] where we waited for them we would have whipped the breeches off of them."[63] The reports of deadly draft riots in New York City that followed on the heels of the losses at Gettysburg and Vicksburg offered some consolation. Newspapers around the state carried reprints of northern coverage of the events.[64] John Bagby, like many soldiers, celebrated the reports in a letter to his wife. "The news from New York of the terrible riot in that city in which the citizens resisted & put down the effort at conscription makes me hope that a great change is going on in the public sentiment of the north," he noted.[65] The Confederates, it seemed, were not the only ones who had to contend with class and ethnic conflict on the home front.

The wounded and healthy men who did return to Virginia in mid-July found the state in considerably better condition than it had been when they departed from their camps along the Rappahannock in May. The destitute condition of Virginia at the close of the war leaves the impression of a continuous deterioration of the state's resources over the four years of war. In fact, conditions within the state responded to the ebb and flow of material goods, weather, and the presence of armies. One indication of the changing fortunes in Virginia during 1863 was that despite the manifest problems, the state government ran a surplus, which allowed the legislature to suspend a recently revised tax law.[66]

Still, not all of Virginia experienced relief from the demands of the previous two years. Those parts of the state that remained battlegrounds—the lower Shenandoah Valley and northern Virginia, in particular—continued to have serious problems of supply and pricing. Life in the garrison towns, those places under permanent Union occupation, remained relatively stable but, in the chaotic "no-man's-land" that typified much of the Virginia-Maryland border, people's lives bore increasingly little connection to their antebellum existence.[67] Likewise, citizens of southwest Virginia experienced increasing losses of slaves to Union troops through the year and the escalation of guerrilla warfare. Like eastern Tennessee, where Federal troops also held nominal control, Confederates in southwestern Virginia organized groups to snipe on stray Union soldiers or to attack Unionist households. The experience of occupation or persistent attack eroded support for the central government in these places, though most southwestern Virginians remained committed to Confederate victory.[68]

In fact, all over Virginia, residents struggled to accommodate the new features of their world. In late 1863 James Davidson and Samuel Reid corresponded about impressment, the new Confederate policy that allowed the government to seize needed supplies from citizens in exchange for rapidly devaluing paper money. Davidson objected to the abuses of the policy, arguing that "the system is wrong in many respects and works unjustly and unequally on the farmer." Davidson was concerned that "the system of impressments is demoralizing our best people . . . on account of the manner of its execution and the irregularity and harshness of its operation on selected cases." Still, he accepted that "some system of impressment is a necessary evil which, like all other evils, must be regulated. For it will not do, even when our own liberties are at stake, to rely on what is called patriotism. Patriotism is a pretty thing to talk about, but it seldom takes a business direction."[69] Davidson's recognition that Virginians might pursue self-interest before national interest spurred him to accept a level of federal control unimaginable before the war. He did not necessarily adopt a new ideology of centralization, but, like most residents of occupied Virginia, he adjusted his practices during wartime. He stood in good company. Confederate civilians in border areas, like Virginia, supported the more aggressive centralization measures opposed by advocates of state rights.[70]

The campaigns of the late summer and fall did not involve all the men in Lee's army. Many of the units remained in camps in the upper Shenandoah Valley or in central Virginia around Orange Courthouse and Culpeper. These men experienced a long hiatus between the battle in Pennsylvania and the beginning of active campaigning in Virginia in May 1864. The results of this rest could be seen immediately, as William Jones noted approvingly that "some men that has bin out for several months is her now."[71] Occasional skirmishes and the close presence of the Union army kept men from fully relaxing in their camps, but most spent the late summer and fall reorganizing and training. William Andrews, in the 10th Virginia Artillery, even found time to plan a new business adventure with his father. The result of this easy schedule was that most soldiers were, as one man reported in September, "generally, well pleased."[72]

For many Virginia soldiers, especially those posted around the capital, the period of rest began immediately after the army returned from Pennsylvania. John Bagby, an officer from King and Queen County, was posted to Chaffin's Bluff, a defensive post just below Richmond on the James River. In early August, he reported to his wife, "There is very little doing here in the military way we have company drill once a day & brigade drill twice a week Tuesday and Friday afternoon."[73] It was at this point in the war that differences between the branches began to emerge with the most clarity. Men in infantry and cavalry units experienced hardships of travel, food supply, and shelter, whereas many artillerymen assigned to forts or permanent defensive positions lived lives of actual comfort. Another Chaffin's Bluff assignee, William Jones, reported to his wife that he was "in hopes we will have a good time of it now." His company had been split off from his regiment, the 19th Virginia Infantry, and placed on artillery duty on the bluff. "We will have no more marching to do a tall now," Jones noted, "and I am so glad of that one thing we have splendid houses to stay in and no dout we will stay the ballance of the war we have splendid water also." The "splendid" conditions that Jones enjoyed did not go unobserved by members of his former regiment or those infantrymen who traveled through artillery posts. During late 1863 and throughout 1864, the disparity in service conditions would generate its own conflicts within the Confederacy.[74]

Shortly after Lee's army returned from Pennsylvania, a new Confederate policy helped relieve tensions within the service. On August 1 Jefferson Davis announced a general amnesty for all deserters. On August 11 the inspector general of the Confederate Armies issued General Order No. 82, which granted "a general pardon . . . to all officers and men within the Confederacy now absent without leave from the Army, who shall (within twenty days from the publication of the address of the President in the States in which the absentees may then be), return to their posts of duty." In a marked change from the 1862 effort to establish an iron-clad definition of desertion, the order included the following provision: "All men who have been accused or convicted and undergoing sentence, for absence without leave or desertion, except only those who have been twice convicted of desertion, will be returned to their respective commands for duty."[75]

This shift in the Confederate policy on desertion resembled the efforts made earlier in the year with the policy of impressment. Although that policy angered many farmers, it gave the Confederacy the ability to redistribute food to needy families.[76] In effect, the Confederate government chose to irritate one constituency in exchange for winning back some credit with another. The amnesty proclamation angered some soldiers, who believed that deserters deserved punishment, but it also revealed the sensitivity with which Confederate leaders could approach issues of loyalty and service. It seems to have worked. One soldier reported within days that the desired effect could be seen. "In our command the Army has been much increased of late by the return of deserters & sick men," he reported to his mother. "These deserters returned under Davis's Proclamation."[77]

The rise in religiosity late in the year also helped mitigate tensions within the army. As in 1862, the winter months in camp provided the opportunity for men to explore their spirituality. Joseph Manson, camped near the Rapidan River in central Virginia, was frank about the motivation for increased attention to religion among men in the camps. "When we have been near death we have a clearer and more heart piercing view of the grim monster than it is possible for us to have in health," Manson wrote. "I shall never forget the views of death I had when I came as near dying with dysentery." While some men were quick to cordon off experiences that revealed their own mortality, Manson found increased inspiration from reveling in it. "It should be our efforts to keep them fresh and in our minds in health. Nothing so quickens our spiritual life as the constant sense of our approaching dissolution in mind."[78] Manson would begin a "spiritual diary" the following year in which he pledged his devotion to God and to righteous action. Other men drew inspiration from their faith because it guaranteed them a control over the spiritual destinies that they did not have over their temporal lives.[79]

For Confederate leaders, righteous action necessitated devotion to both God and the Confederacy. They encouraged the ministers who entered the camps, or sprang up in the camps, to emphasize that theme continuously. Fast days authorized by President Davis reminded citizens of the sacred nature of the quest for independence and pious Confederates identified God's hand in their victories. Religion also served to bind men more tightly to one another. Samuel Firebaugh, with the 10th Infantry, kept special note of those men who were killed and wounded who had been members of the "Christian Society" in his regiment.[80]

At least as important was the role of religion as a moderating influence on the immorality rife in military camps across the South. More than one soldier recognized the beneficent influence that religion could have in this regard. William Jones reported to his wife, "We have a very fine protracted meeting going on at this time great many converts and is still flourishing I am so much pleased I am in hopes theare will be a greate chainges in a great manny of owr men for I now I never saw so much wickedness in all my life"[81] The revivals that began in the late fall and winter remained powerful forces well into the spring, as one man noted to his wife in April 1864, "there is a great revival among the churches in this army. There is at least three times as many more converts in this year than there was last spring."[82]

Just as the time away from fighting in the fall provided men with the opportunity for spiritual reflections, it also gave them a chance to think more clearly about why they were fighting. Soldiers had made the same effort at rethinking their purpose in the late fall of 1862, when Confederate nationalism gained focus and support. At that time, many soldiers had made resolute pledges to defend the honor of their new nation. The victories of the late summer, the stalemate at Antietam, and the growing sense that the Confederacy had earned, and would soon receive, foreign recognition generated a willingness to sacrifice for their country. The rhetoric of nationalism continued in full force during 1863. Men continued to speak in terms of the merits of the state, but they also began articulating diverse reasons for fighting, depending upon the conditions of their service and the interests that they maintained in their home communities.[83]

The repulse at Gettysburg depressed Confederates not because it signaled the loss of their struggle for independence but because it ensured that the war would continue. A soldier from the Eastern Shore county of Accomack read Lincoln's December address to the U.S. Congress in which he offered amnesty to all Confederate soldiers below the rank of colonel who would take the oath of allegiance. Although he couched his response in clichés, its directness and confidence reveal his sincerity. "I suppose by this, Mr. Lincoln thinks he has us already within his grasp and ready to submit to the most hated yoke ever attempted to be imposed upon a civilized people," the soldier recorded. "But could he know the feelings which animate the brave souls who are struggling against his hirelings . . . he would indeed be convinced that such a people are invincible and that all his efforts to subdue them are but vain delusion."[84]

Others simply insisted that the eventual outcome would be Confederate victory. As one man remarked, "I dread to hear of the coming conflict as I know an awful sacrifice of human life will be made though I am confident succefs will crown our arms."[85] Above all was the sense that independence now would be entirely the result of success on the battlefield. A deeply troubled Charles Berry wrote home in late November, after he had recently traveled through Fredericksburg where his aunt lived. "I passed through [Fredericksburg] a few days ago," he noted, "and the ravages of war are plainly visible in its almost deserted streets, and the buildings which have been shattered and torn to pieces by the enemy's artillery." Though depressed by the toll the war was taking on his state, Berry understood that the only salvation lay through more fighting: "Foreign nations seem to have forgotten us entirely and nought will save us but the God of Battles and our own strong arms."[86]

For those soldiers in the ranks in late 1863, concerns over army regulations no longer posed the most serious threat to service. Most soldiers had learned to suppress their anger at the difficulty of obtaining a furlough or obedience to a haughty officer in the interests of achieving independence. The pain of separation from home, however, could be not assuaged. The psychological toll of being away from home bore down increasingly on those men who had young children. One man posted to an artillery battery south of

Richmond worried about his pregnant wife and how she would fare during labor. "I hope you have received my letter before this time and have started one to me for I am very anxious to heare from you," he wrote. "I never was more so I dream the night that I had a sweet little daughter I hope it is true and I sincerely hope that you have an easy time of it."[87] The intense emotional attachment that men felt generated anxiety and concern for the hardships their families were suffering. "Deare I am so ankious to see my Little children," wrote William Jones of Albemarle County. "When you write to me write me word all a them and tell Georgy & Ellice I am going to Bring them somthing nice when I come home write me would wether you evver receive the heart I sent Little willie or not." In accordance with popular sentimental traditions, Jones's wife had sent him a lock of his son's hair, to serve as a reminder of the family he had left behind. "I frequently look at his little curly hare," he confessed to his wife.[88]

The lock of a son's hair, the smell of a wife's perfume on a letter, the familiar scrawl of a sister's script provided the ephemeral links that bound men back to their homes. Initial uncertainty about the course of the war had stifled questions of competing loyalties through most of 1861. By 1863, however, men saw clearly that they would be compelled to sacrifice at least their own sense of security about their family's safety, and perhaps that safety itself, as long as their presence in the army was required. For some men, this compromise was too costly to make. Reports of hardship and deprivation from family members compelled some men to leave the service. Others simply bided their time with anger, waiting for an opportunity to reach their loved ones safely. "The life of a soldier is a hard one," wrote Thomas Gordon to a friend. "I had to get up a few nights ago and the snow was over my shoes and stand guard and frequently we have to cook in the rain. I am willing to undergo all the hardships of camp life, if I can but return in safety to my quiet home again."[89]

Desertion remained an alternative, but many fewer men left the army in 1863 than in 1862. Soldiers and civilians greeted desertion with much less tolerance than they had earlier in the war. As Richard Allen, whose four brothers served in Virginia units as well, noted, "It is not worth a man's while to talk of leaving here now. They would sentence him to the penitentiary for 5 years or shoot him if he was to leave without good papers." Allen could see the effects of this new discipline all around him. "There is a man to be shot here today at 4 o'clock for deserting and going home. . . . There is some more that has ran away from that regiment. They will be shot if they catch them."[90]

Instead of leaving the army, most Virginia men sought more satisfying

John Peter and Mollie Putney Jones. John and Mollie Jones, a central Virginia
couple, wrote frank and open letters to each other during the war. Despite the
problems that Mollie faced at home, John insisted that he could better protect
her and their children from his position within the army, a perspective that
increasing numbers of Virginia soldiers adopted as the war lengthened in time.
Photos courtesy of Mary Roy Dawson Edwards.

ways to reconcile the demands of loved ones and the Confederacy.[91] The
needs of family and nation did not align perfectly, and soldiers experienced
great difficulty finding the right balance between their competing obligations, but over the first two years of the war many Virginia soldiers came to
view military service as the most effective way to protect their families. John
Jones, from Buckingham County, was in the hospital in 1863 recovering
from an illness when he explained to his wife how he had resolved the
dilemma of competing loyalties. "I had an idea of resigning some time ago,"
Jones admitted, "but I have come to the conclusion that the Yankees are too
close by Home to resign. I am afraid that they will get my Boy. Now is the
time to fight them while the Yankees are recruiting."[92]

The intense emotional and psychological demands of the war fostered
increasingly intense emotional relationships between men and their families. Emotion functioned as both a release and a catalyst to future action.
"Dear Wife," wrote John Garibaldi, from his camp in late 1863, "At this time I
have no news of any importance to tell you only that we have hard times and

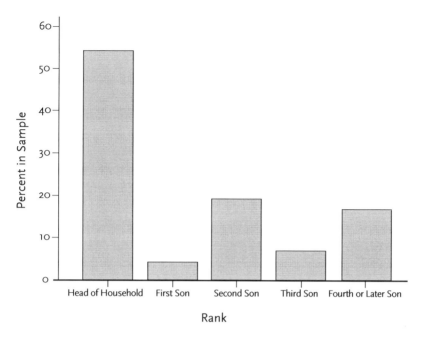

Figure 3. Soldiers' Rank in Household

wors coming. . . . I would be glad if this war was to stop so that we might all come and mind our own business at home."[93] Home was where men belonged, but most soldiers did not leave the army. The irony that men should remain away in order to defend their families did not escape the wives and young children upon whom fell the burden of maintaining farms and, in many cases, slavery. Men observed these demands as well, making the decision to remain in service all the more difficult. But the increasing confidence with which Virginia men fought the war and their increasing conviction that only Confederate military victory could protect their way of life reveal the power of this new calculus.[94]

The quantitative evidence supports this argument. A majority of the men who enlisted in Virginia forces were the heads of their households and most were in their mid-twenties (see figure 3).[95] The data on age support this argument. The average age of Virginia soldiers was twenty-six, not the eighteen-year-olds of legend. The traditional notion that Civil War armies were composed overwhelmingly of single men and younger sons does not apply in the case of Virginia. Instead, most Virginia soldiers participated with an acute sense that their absence deprived their families of their main source of income and security.

Ironically, it was that very separation that allowed some men to see more clearly the reasons for their continued participation in the war. John Welsh, a farmer from Rockbridge County in the Shenandoah Valley, served as captain of the 27th Virginia Infantry. Despite owning no slaves himself, Welsh felt the North was trying to subordinate white men's interests to blacks, and he pledged himself to resist their effort. Welsh's wife, Rebecca, who may have disagreed with his interpretation of the war or simply felt insecure in a region that attracted frequent Union invasions, pressured him to hire a substitute, which he resisted. In early 1863, he wrote, "You want me to get off if it cost half I am worth but I don't see any way of getting off honorably at any cost at present. The man who would forsake his country at a time like this when every man is needed, for any selfish purpose, deserves the contempt of every honest man." Welsh felt the only moral justification for resignation would be ill health, and his was fine. Further, he believed that the best way for him to protect his family was by staying in the army. "You must not think that I am careless about you when God knows how much I love you all and how much I would like to be with you, but I think at the present I can best serve you here for what satisfaction could I have at home with a ruthless foe trampling over me; my children it seems to me would reflect on me in the next generation and if I can do nothing else I can hand down my name untarnished to them." Rebecca had just cause for worry—as a captain, Welsh faced a higher risk for injury than many of the enlisted men whom he commanded. During the battle of Gettysburg, he was hit by a shell and died in a field hospital as Lee's army retreated back to Virginia.[96]

Men like Welsh took inspiration from the duty they performed for a family that loved and respected them, in a way their own government often failed to do. One Confederate wrote home from Petersburg, Virginia, in late summer 1863 and chronicled, in florid prose, the loved ones for whom he fought. "I am here to defend the sacred spot where repose the mortal remains of a trusting and loving wife . . . the venerated grave of a noble and cherished father whose wise counsels long since given for the last time are ever ringing in my ears, and the resting place of the fair-haired little sister who flew away on angel's wings." His duty was not merely to honor those already gone, but to provide for those still alive. "When I reflect too upon the future of my doting & pious old mother—the poor sister—and little brothers who are dependent in some degree on my strong arms a thrill of pride pervades my breast at having thrown myself in the breach for my country's defence." This man, like others, drew confidence and dedication from his actions as a son, brother, and husband. "It is for these weighty reasons that I am impressed in some degree (may I be more & more so)—with the obligations that rest upon me as a soldier. In view of this, I cheerfully consent to be a soldier—to lead a soldier's life—to bear a soldier's burdens—to die—if need be—a soldier's death."[97]

James Edmondson, the lieutenant colonel of the 27th Virginia Infantry, echoed this man's beliefs and provided an important record for how Virginia soldiers understood the relationship between their various responsibilities. "Oh, how I do wish that this cruel war was ended," he wrote his wife, "so that I might with my darling wife return to my happy home and there enjoy the comfort and pleasure which attach to such a place." Edmondson knew that his wife preferred this as well but claimed "'tis useful [-less?] to be making wishes of this sort, at this time, especially, when another fierce campaign is staring us in the face and must be made." Edmondson never felt the need to justify in detail why his absence remained necessary; he made his case by conveying information about the upcoming campaign. After further correspondence with his wife, however, he offered a more comprehensive explanation for why he stayed in the army. "'Tis for her who bears me such love," he wrote, "that I am with my life in my hands contesting the advance of the hordes of northerner Hessians who invade our soil." Importantly, Edmondson also made clear that he believed this arrangement provided her with the greatest security. "Were it however in my power I would fly to you my darling," he wrote, "and give you my personal-individual protection, which I am doing by a combined effort on the part of myself and my fellow citizens generally."[98]

Part III ★ WAR WITHOUT END

6 ★ THE COST OF INDEPENDENCE
JANUARY–JUNE 1864

There is no way to whip them but kill them all.
—John Herbert Clairborne, May 14, 1864

In 1864 a renewed battle for control of Virginia occurred. The Union army, after following Lee's army back into northern Virginia in mid-1863, camped on the north bank of the Rapidan River. The battles of 1864 all took place south of this point, subjecting Virginia citizens again to the destructive presence of both armies and battles. The Army of the Potomac subsequently pushed Lee's Confederates back to the defensive confines of Petersburg, twenty miles south of Richmond. This action, dubbed the "Overland" campaign, generated the highest number of casualties and the greatest attention from observers of any episode in the war. Often overshadowed by the bloody fighting in eastern Virginia, the 1864 campaigns in the Shenandoah Valley captured in microcosm the experiences of Virginia civilians and soldiers as the war reached its climax. Invasion, occupation, redemption, and loss characterized the unpredictable and harrowing year in the Valley. The Union campaigns, which targeted civilians and their resources all across the state and blurred the distinction between battlefront and home front, reinforced Virginians' sense that defense of family and defense of country were the same.

Arguing for Confederate optimism in 1864, in the face of rising prices, increasing scarcity of vital goods, and the continued pressure of several Union armies, seems counterintuitive. We know today that the war's end lay only a year away; surely, Virginians must have seen that as well? Few Confederates possessed such foresight, for reasons both rational and irrational. The high tide of Confederate nationalism and hope that crested in mid-summer 1864 drew on a realistic assessment of Confederates' martial capabilities and on a blind belief in the righteousness of their cause. Southerners drew confidence from the military victories won by Confederate armies and from the real interests that spurred the fight for independence. The battles of 1863 showed that Confederates could ably defend their own land, and most people expected a repeat of the events at Chancellorsville if the Union invaded again. The Confederate will to fight was also bolstered by a romantic nationalism, an increasing commitment to preserving slavery, and a clearer evocation of the sanctity and importance of family. The Confederate experience demonstrates the ability of people to willfully ignore unpleasant facts in times of crisis. After years of assurances that God favored the South, most Confederates simply could not imagine defeat. What remained clear, in the welter of motivations and inspirations, was that Confederates wanted victory over the Union and so kept fighting.

Virginians of all classes expressed confidence in Confederate victory in the early months of the year.[1] After working in the quartermaster and commissary departments for two years, George Quintis Peyton enlisted in the 13th Virginia Infantry on February 9, 1864. Peyton served the Confederacy until he was captured at the battle of Cedar Creek in late 1864 and sent to the Union prisoner-of-war camp at Point Lookout, Maryland.[2] Peyton did not leave a record of why he decided to transfer from a protected supporting role to an exposed front-line one but his decision clearly demonstrated support for the Confederate cause. Other Virginians joined him, some publicly and others privately, in avowing support for their nation at the start of 1864. "You are a most sensible woman in agreeing to adopt my opinion of the Tax Bills," Colonel Edward T. Warren wrote to his wife in February, "I consider the tax enormously high but not one cent more than is absolutely necessary," he noted. "Then the tax is levied on all alike. . . . The tax on bonds operates very hard on some people. For instance, on Mother and Grandma, but if such bonds were not taxed the richest men in the country would escape taxation—I am satisfied that the Bill is a good one because so universal in its application."[3]

George Washington Miley, serving under Warren in the 10th Virginia Infantry, gave his impressions of the unit's confidence in a letter to his future wife in late March. Although Miley desperately wanted to transfer to a cavalry regiment, he had reenlisted in October 1863. Many of his comrades seem to have done likewise. "The regiment was [re]formed a few days ago, and, after a brief address by Col. Warren, they were invited to rally 'round our flag, and the response was almost universal," he wrote. "A resolution was adopted by which all who stepped to the front avowed their determination never to lay down their arms while our soil is polluted with Lincoln's hireling crews. Those who did not come forward were old men and entitled to discharges." Miley noted that the reorganization was having the desired effect and their weakened ranks were now growing again: "Officers and men are constantly returning. Besides to see a recruit is no uncommon thing."[4]

The long period of rest after Gettysburg gave army quartermasters the time to work out supply details that were impossible to manage during a campaign, and, as a result, soldiers received adequate rations for much of the fall. This prepared them for a difficult winter. During the early spring of 1864, resources continued to be scarce and rations shrank once again. Lee worried that the inability to feed his army would reduce its effectiveness or require withdrawal to North Carolina.[5] Not everyone took such a dire view of the food supply in early 1864. John Fletcher Beale, camped along the Rapidan with Lee's troops, asserted that "the army is better fed now than it has been for some time."[6] The regimental officers under Lee struggled to meet the needs of their men, but they too had a more positive assessment of the situation. The commander of the 7th Virginia Cavalry reported, "Our men are in fine spirits and health although many of them have been entirely without tents so far. . . . We are all trying to prepare ourselves for a hard and bloody struggle in the spring and with God's help we hope to free our land of our enemies."[7] The better access to food and the experiences of soldiers and doctors contributed to another important sign of their condition: a diminished rate of death by disease. In comparison to the early phase of the war, when epidemics swept through the ranks killing thousands, 1864 was a healthy period.

Like the desertion amnesty of the previous fall, officials enacted another policy early in the new year that many families saw as long-delayed justice: the end of substitution. Although dreams of substitution promised relief from the drudgery and suffering of military service for countless soldiers, as the war progressed and the prices of substitutes rose, most Confederates saw it as a policy of privilege. In December 1862 one man argued with a cousin about the end of substitution and vaguely threatened that soldiers would abandon the fight unless the policy was modified. "I don't mean to say that I will go home," he began, "but nearly all the men saying they will if they don't call out the men that put in for substitutes and furloughs." In his missive, this soldier emphasized the issue of parity and equality of sacrifice that underlay most opposition to substitution. "I am opposed to desertion as much as any boddy can bee for I say put every one on equal footing."[8] With the price of a substitute nearing $2,000 in late 1862, few men could afford to obtain one. The revocation of this policy made all principals (those men who had secured substitutes in place of their own service) immediately eligible for the Confederate draft. This new rule promised both an influx of eligible men and a sense of greater equality among soldiers.

In this regard, the Confederacy's policies helped alleviate class tensions at a crucial point in the war. One man expressed relief at the equity of bringing men who had purchased substitutes into the war themselves. Philip Powers wrote, "It has been a dreadful spell of weather and I feel for those of our troops who are exposed to its inclemency. . . . Doesn't your heart feel for the poor destitute men and their wives?" What could have been sincere sympathy for the hardships of fellow soldiers turned quickly into sarcastic satisfaction. "The chivalry of the South as Jim calls them—how will they be able to stand the hardships of camp and the dangers of the campaign?" Powers asked. "Congress was cruel and inconsiderate with these gentlemen, and we poor devils who have volunteered to fight for them should have been allowed to die for them also." Like many other soldiers, Powers reveled in the social consequences of the policy, writing, "Congress never passed an Act more acceptable to the Army, and one passed with more joy. Perhaps it springs from a bad feeling at heart, envy, but justice has something to do with it."[9]

The *Daily Richmond Examiner* drew the parallel between the effect of the 1862 Draft Act, which held in service soldiers then enrolled for an additional two years, to the revocation of substitution. "The army yielded, in 1862, with a good grace to the canceling of their contract with the Government," the paper reminded its readers. "The volunteers saw that the salvation of the country depended upon their remaining under arms; they remained. . . . Let this example be followed by those who are innocent sufferers by what some choose to call this change of policy." Echoing the comments of Powers, the paper scolded those "who have abused the immunity which they gained by their better fortune [to] awake to a sense of their shortcomings."[10]

Still another change in policy increased the labor burden on everyone. On February 17, the Confederacy dropped the lower end of the draft age to seventeen and raised the higher end to fifty. The change in eligibility, in contrast to the revocation of substitution, struck many civilians as unreasonable. Mollie Houser, of Augusta County, derided the policy and sarcastically predicted the Confederacy would soon enlist the deceased. "They have taken almost every man & talk of calling on the men from seventeen to fifty," she reported, "& then I suppose they will search the graveyards & sware them to the length of time they have been dead." This change, and the continued battlefield stalemate, led her to a simple conclusion: "I think this Confederacy is almost gone up the spout."[11]

Although very few people applauded the change in policy, not everyone interpreted Confederate fortunes so darkly. Rawleigh Downman, a soldier with the 4th Virginia Cavalry, wrote his wife with his thoughts early in the year as well. "I think there is a great deal of useless and uncalled for despondency in the country," Downman complained. "It is very true that we have met with some serious reverses this past fall. But we should be thankful that we have been enabled to get through the year at all without being overwhelmed." Downman took heart from past successes and drew on these to predict eventual victory, arguing that "we have survived the mightiest efforts of one of the most powerful nations in the world & I can see no reason why, if we are but true to ourselves, we cannot resist them another year equally as well. All we want is nerve to stand up amid difficulties and a determination to succeed and by the help of God we shall succeed."[12] Downman's determination may have helped bolster his wife's spirits, but in the process he revealed an important strategic shift in the Confederacy's posture toward the Union. In 1864 Lee could not act on his inclination to take an offensive posture, as he had with invasions of the North in 1862 and 1863. Instead, Downman and many others, gained confidence from having resisted previous Union invasions and foresaw a strictly defensive future.

Although most soldiers seem to have accepted the desertion amnesty of 1863 with equanimity, the strong condemnation of the act of desertion that emerged in late 1862 remained intact. Very few cherished service, but they all recognized that uniform participation by eligible men would end the war faster. By 1864 most soldiers interpreted desertion for what Confederate officials called it: a shameful crime against the state and the nation. One Virginian thrilled to a report in the paper of a rare triple execution in Georgia. "The following order of Maj. Genl. Hindman directing the execution of three Confederate deserters glows with such noble sentiments and beautiful language that I think it well worth a place in these 'notes.'" "Headq'rs Hindman's Corps, Dalton, GA 1/8/64," he recorded, " 'The Major General commanding deplores the necessity of thus ordering the death of three soldiers of the Confederate States. But they themselves forced this necessity on him, and their blood is upon their own heads.' " The Virginia soldier concurred with Hindman's assessment that the men themselves brought their own deaths about and advocated repeating the procedure whenever necessary. "'Their punishment must be inflicted as often as the offence occurs."[13] Those men who deserted to join their families received sympathy from their fellow soldiers if they were truly in dire straights, but soldiers roundly condemned those men who ran to Union lines. Writing to his wife, one man observed that "several of our soldiers have deserted and gone over to the Yankees this week. How low and degraded those wretches must feel. How their conscience (if they have any) must lash them for deserting their country at such a time."[14]

Just a week earlier, Rufus Woolwine, a captain with the 51st Virginia Infantry, had noted in his diary, "Lt Col. Wolfe had me to act as Adjt the Regt being formed in Two Battalions to march out to the execution of John Jones— of 30th Batt. (of Grayson) for desertion he was executed at 2 oclock P.M."[15] The event drew the attention of soldiers and served as a clear warning about the results of abandoning one's post. John T. Cooley, a private from Wythe County serving in the 51st, was among those men whom Capt. Woolwine marched out to witness the execution. Cooley noted, in a letter to his cousin, "A man from Grayson Co by the name of John Jones was shot here last Friday. Another from the Co named Widner will be executed at the same stake tomorrow." While new recruits might have blanched at these incidents, Cooley, by this time a two-year veteran, saw no need to elaborate. Following the two sentences he allotted to the execution, Cooley reported his regiment's position and announced, "Our rations are short, but I will be content while we stay in S.W.Va."[16]

Accordingly, some men, like J. G. Smith of the 37th Cavalry Battalion, simply decided to avoid the consequences of desertion. Smith hoped the war would end soon, then admitted that his current position carried little discomfort. "I don't think I shall go home any more till peace is made," he wrote, "for I do hate to come back and after I get back I want to back home badly." "Soon after I came from home last summer," he admitted, "I wanted to go back so bad that I came very near running away and going back but this thing of deserting dont pay There is some 8 or 10 in the guard house now chained together for trying to go home."[17] Still other men sanctioned the executions but remained sickened at the personal dimensions of the killing. One unfortunate soldier had his morning religious routine shattered with the announcement—made during Bible class—that an execution would take place later in the day. After the troops had been marched to the parade grounds that afternoon, the executioners raised their rifles and fired. The volley did not finish the job, and one soldier had to march forward and kill the deserter at point blank range. "It is a horrible thing to witness an execution," the observer noted, "& especially so on God's day of rest. God grant that I may never be called upon to witness another."[18]

The act of desertion undeniably signaled a deep dissatisfaction with the Confederate war effort, and undoubtedly many deserters abandoned the army because of low morale, but it is also important to recognize the trend over time. Among Virginians, desertions declined after 1862, owing to both concrete and abstract reasons. The physical presence of the army in Virginia through 1864 deterred desertions because the army could detach units to find and return men absent without leave, unlike the previous years when an offensive campaigns had disorganized the army and increased the opportunity for desertion. More importantly, uncertain soldiers drew strength from fighting to defend their own land. The sense of hesitation that some had felt when they crossed over the Potomac in mid-1862 and again in 1863 did not trouble them in 1864.[19] The clear virtue of a defensive war emboldened soldiers. The return of fighting to Virginia had one other important advantage. It returned soldiers to an arena in which they had been indisputably the victors. The defeats and stalemates of Pennsylvania and Maryland could not diminish Confederates' certainty of victory on their own territory. One man's bragging to his sister reflected the thinking of many Virginia Confederates in early 1864: "It is now thought that yet another grand effort to take Richmond this year will be made by 'Grant' in 'Propia persona' who will doubtless follow in the foot steps of his illustrious predecessors and walk the plank into obscurity after his first engagement with Uncle Bob Lee."[20]

Another soldier reported home with an awkward mixture of confidence, expectation, and hope, "tis generally believed that we will go into the enemies country but no one knows our business but our authorities. I hope the great ruler of all things will inspire our commanders with great zeal that they may lead our armies victoriously through the coming campaigns. And if so, I think by December next we will have peace."[21] As always, "peace" meant an end to the war coupled with independence and protection of slavery. As John Garibaldi explained to his future wife, "I am pretty tired of this war by this time but there is no chance for us unless the war stops for we shall all have to keep fighting until the yankees give us up or until we shall be subjugated."[22]

Garibaldi's estimate of more fighting proved accurate. Two weeks after he wrote home, the spring campaign opened, marking the third year in which men had measured the seasons by when horses could reliably drag cannon along muddy roads. Spring was no longer the season of life and renewal but the start of death and destruction. One more measure of the distance citizens had traveled to make themselves soldiers was reflected in the ease with which men accepted the transition. In March, Andrew Long advised his sister, "we just come off picket duty day bee fore yesterday i dont think it will bee long untill we will have to march the Summer camppain will sune open."[23]

The campaign in Virginia opened in early May with little to indicate that men were inaugurating a sequence of battles that would comprise nearly six weeks of unbroken fighting and claim roughly 80,000 casualties between the two armies. The battles of the spring in eastern Virginia changed the dynamic of the war once again, returning soldiers to the intense violence and hardship of the fall of 1862. Ferocious fights at the Wilderness, Spotsylvania Courthouse, and Cold Harbor in May and June filled newspapers with casualty lists and diaries at home and on the field with mourning for lost loved ones. When men finally found time to write, their descriptions of the battles rolled events together into one extended episode of bloodshed. One man stopped in mid-May to report of the events of the previous two weeks. "Father indeed for 5 days we were so busy fighting that we could hardly get time enough to eat our meals," this soldier reported. "To-day it is 14 days since we commenced fighting and yesterday the cannon and small arms were still at work. But the fight was not really heavy all the time, the hardest fighting was on the 5, 6 & 7 and on the 9, 10 & 11 days of this month. During them six days it was awful," he noted. "There was one continual roar of thunder all the time from the artillery and small arms." Like many soldiers, this man was astounded by the scale of Union dead in the fighting at Spotsylvania, "column after column the Yankees pushed their men up to our Breastworks and our men were cutting them down as fast as flies. The dead Yankees are heaped up in piles half as high as a man, in front of our Breastworks, and all around the Battlefield the dead yanks are lying just as thick as they can be, and none of them buried, they will all rotten on top of the ground." He drew the same conclusion as many other Confederates: "All the men say that this has been the hardest fight, since the war."[24] Even when men recognized that the battles debilitated their units, they did not perceive a drop in Confederate morale. As one man summarized the effect of the fighting: "The troops are as badly worn out as I ever saw them but still in good spirits."[25]

Because journalists from both sections witnessed parts of all the battles, the reports sent back to home overflowed with dramatic accounts of the fighting. Many Virginia soldiers took steps to reassure their families whenever they could find a spare minute. These brief missives contained little information other than assurance that the writer was still alive. Philip Pendleton relayed his condition to his mother at the conclusion of the day's fighting at the Wilderness: "Knowing that you are very uneasy about me in these exciting times, I will endeavor to snatch the time to write just a line or two to say that so far we have not been in the fight." Pendleton wrote again the following day, noting "So far thanks to a merciful God, my life has been spared so far." The strain of battle impaired his usually articulate prose, though he remained impressed by the victory they seemed to be gathering. "Wherever our men have met the Yankees they have just butchered them—

they say the slaughter of Yankees is tremendous." He closed the letter with a benediction, "God preserve us all is the prayer of your Affec. son, Phil."[26] Pendleton's prayer did not protect him; he was killed in fighting the following day.

Like Pendleton, other soldiers drew upon their religious faith to help sustain them in the face of what most saw as the worst battles they had yet experienced. A man with the 4th Virginia Infantry described to his brother one source of motivation for him in the midst of the carnage. His letter was addressed from the "Battle Line near Spottsylvania C.H." and described the battle going on around him. "Knowing their tremendous numerical strength I tremble as to the possible issue of the struggle. In God is our strength. 'The battle is not to the strong' if He be on our side. It is so full of comfort to know that He rules and directs the destinies of armies & nations."[27] Religious faith bolstered a confidence that battles would conclude in Confederates' favor.

Most men were also assisted by a persistent inability to conceptualize the scale of their own losses. To be sure, Union military forces suffered higher absolute numbers of casualties and rarely succeeded in gaining any tactical advantage during the battles themselves. Nevertheless, Grant's strategy of persistent movement against and around Lee's army debilitated rebel forces and pushed the front back closer to Richmond. Though few people at the time could conceptualize the grand strategy under way, most Confederates assumed that the massive casualties in Grant's armies would sink northern morale. This hope sustained soldiers and civilians through the violence of 1864. Thomas Kelley wrote to his cousin after the battles in early May and estimated that despite being outnumbered five to one, they had whipped the Yanks: "It is generally the opinion of all the troops both officers and men that the war will not last much longer." Kelley himself was nearly exhausted, but the reason the war could not continue was that he, like many, perceived the Union army on the verge of collapse. His cousin had written with her concerns about Richmond falling into Union hands, and Kelley dismissed that prospect nearly out of hand.[28]

Despite their elation at having defeated northern troops, Confederate soldiers still had to contend with the personal dimension of the killing. The sight of so many dead almost always unnerved soldiers. As one man related, "the battle field presents one of the most horrible seens that I ever witnessed the ground is spoted over with dead bodies men that was killed ten days ago lying thare unburied and wounded men lay thare for six days. I was on picket last tuesday and I could heare them holowing for water all the time in the night, but we could not get to them."[29] On the morning of the battle of the

Wilderness, Henry Morrison described the awful contrast to his aunt: "The sun is just rising & how beautiful! It makes one feel sad to think that this beautiful spring day must be spent in slaughtering human beings." The scale of slaughter reinforced men's own mortality in a way that most had ignored for several months, and this return to violence renewed apprehensions about war in general. Morrison, after pondering the juxtaposition of natural beauty and man's ugliness, concluded, "this is likely to prove a memorable day in the history of our country I wish from the bottom of my heart if war must be fought that it will be over."[30] The intensity of the fighting alone threatened to wear men down, regardless of how they handled the psychological dimensions of combat. Richard Allen declared, "I has been in this war two years, but this is the most awful time I ever saw in my life. We has been in four hard fights. We have been in line of battle ever since the 5th of this month. We had a hard time. There hasn't been no rest night nor day," he concluded. "I never saw such hard fighting in my life as we has had down here, and I am afraid the hardest fighting hasn't come off yet."[31]

In 1861, and even 1862 to a more limited degree, Confederates had killed Federals only by suppressing their instinct against killing other men. By 1864 that gentility was beginning to wear down. Some soldiers reveled in the sight of dead Yankees, though most still needed time and space to assimilate their own role in such massive destruction of life. Frank Myers, a captain with the 35th Virginia Cavalry Battalion who had enlisted in January 1862, declared himself "badly whipped" but the army yet in good shape. "I rode over some portions of the Battle ground where the infantry fought and yankees were piled up. I doubt their no. will fall short of 30,000 killed," he reported. "Our fellows fought in brest works and the yanks charged them. They have been repulsed every-where and every time." Myers, like others, wished desperately for peace and seemed incapable of realizing why northern soldiers would fight on or why the northern public would support the war. His frustration with the war's duration led him to close by celebrating the death of so many foes. "I think our whole army thinks we are making peace," Myers hoped. "I wish they'd quit. Never have I been so tired of anything in my life as I am of this fight. I wish the whole yankee nation could see the battle ground. I think they would agree to give up the restoration scheme and let us alone." Still, if the Yankees continued to fight, Myers would continue to fight back, noting, "It does me good to the toes of my boots any time to see a dead yank and you may imagine how much good it does to look at miles of them."[32] Soldiers who gradually abandoned their natural revulsion to kill could justify their feelings as part of the culture of sacrifice.

The same creed that identified Confederate soldiers' deaths as noble sacrifices identified Union soldiers' deaths as necessary and deserved.

Many civilians developed the same lack of sensitivity to killing as soldiers.[33] Julia Whiting, a central Virginia woman, noted that "it seems doubly hard to live as Christian in times when all one's feelings of indignation, hatred and revenge are daily roused by tidings of some fresh atrocity perpetrated by the Yankees in the once happy homes of the South." Whiting's preference was simply to expel Yankees, which would then solve the problem of whether they should all be killed. "When do you expect Grant to be driven from Virginia?" she asked. "He certainly has more tenacity of purpose than any Northern general has yet exhibited. I hope nevertheless he may meet with the fate of his predecessors." Having experienced firsthand the hard war of the North, she vacillated over what response she would advocate from Confederate soldiers. "The ruffians who have ravaged our land can only be punished fitly by those who could equal them in baseness," Whiting argued. Then, shifting tack, she admitted, "I would not have our Christian soldiers sully their laurels by a single action resembling those of our enemy. I hate to think of our men destroying private property across the line, though I know that necessity compels us to retaliate." In this ambivalence, she resembled most soldiers: "Of course everything depends upon the spirit in which it is done, yet I cannot help fearing that in thus retaliating our men may lessen the high honorable feelings which they have displayed during the war. I love the honor and glory of our own army more than I hate the Yankees, much as I detest them."[34]

The sight of Union dead did Frank Myers good because it brought victory and release from war ever closer. The high casualties imposed upon Grant's army reinforced Confederates' positive assessment of the future. Even though they were retreating, most men focused on the individual battles, and this perspective only reinforced the sense of imminent victory they possessed at the start of the year. Richard Dulany gloated over Confederate victories in a letter to his daughter, whom he instructed to relay the news to her moderately Unionist grandfather: "Say to your grandpa that Genl. Lee, having now successfully repulsed every effort of what the Yanks call the greatest living General and by far the mightiest army every raised, he must now consider our cause stronger and our prospects brighter than ever."[35] Confederates like Dulany would have been surprised to find Ulysses S. Grant generally satisfied with the course of the Union efforts through mid-May, though this resulted partly from the larger strategic accomplishments of his army and others in the state.[36]

For the most part, Virginia soldiers expressed an annoyed curiosity that Grant behaved so out of character for northern generals in Virginia. As one man explained, "Grant's army has certainly been badly whipped & if any other man had command of it, it would not now be on Va. soil." A few men admitted a grudging admiration for someone who fought much more like their own commander than any previous Union general. Creed Davis happily reported the arrival in his camp of twenty Union deserters, noting that "Grant's army they report as very much demoralized." Nevertheless, Davis was forced to admit the following day in his diary, "Gen'l Grant seems to be no nearer whipped than before the battle. What an old bull-dog he is." By mid-June, with Lee's army forced south to the outskirts of Richmond, Davis pitched his tent in the same spot that McClellan's army had camped during the 1862 Peninsula campaign. Using the old post holes to erect their tent, Davis felt that "Richmond and our 'holy cause' is almost played out.'" Davis's perspective reflected exactly what Grant had hoped would occur among his adversaries, but few of his fellow soldiers shared Davis's interpretation of Confederate prospects.[37]

Most Virginia Confederates continued to devise justifications for remaining in the army. As in 1863, soldiers drew increasingly on their emotional relations with their loved ones, though this approach eventually forced soldiers to confront the contradictions between the brutality of their military lives and the peace and harmony they attributed to the domestic world. Richard Watkins gave eloquent voice to the conflicting emotions he felt after his third year in the service. "My Precious Mary," he wrote in early 1864, "I would give anything in the world to see you this evening. I am almost crazy to see you. I think of you and think of you; and I dream of you and dream of you, and wish to see you and long to see you; but the same old long miles still stretch themselves between us." Watkins envisioned his obligation in solely personal terms. He assured his wife, "the greatest, the only sacrifice which I realize at all is absence from my Mary and those whom I love." Like other Virginia Confederates, Watkins regretted his absence from home but also adapted himself to the new nature of southern masculinity. Watkins understood his duties to family and country as intertwined, for personal and national honor were closely linked. "God grant that I may so bear myself in the battle & in the camp & under all circumstances as not to bring a reproach upon them [his children]," he wrote, "for 'a good name is rather to be chosen than great riches.'"[38]

Another Virginia Confederate, Samuel Moore, accepted his situation because he had internalized the idea that his duty to his nation had absorbed his duty to protect his family in person. "I am doing what is required of me by the highest obligations of duty," he wrote to his wife Ellen. "A duty which calls upon me to risk all, and if necessary give up all even life itself, for the defence of my Country, I feel that there is no real cause for unhappiness in the fact that I have been obliged to leave you in [his father's] care."[39]

Edward Warren, in an April 5 letter to his wife Ginnie, concluded much as Richard Watkins and Samuel Moore had, that continued military service would jointly satisfy God, country, and his family. Initially, overcome by homesickness, Warren requested that "you had better have me elected commonwealth's attorney this spring in May . . . and thus keep me at home." In mid-thought, Warren reversed himself and launched a counterargument that explained why he should stay in the army in order to fulfill his wife's expectations. "To tell the truth I don't believe I ought to want to get out of it so long as the present necessity exists for my staying in it. I dont think you would have half as much respect for me as a civil officer as you have for me as a colonel." Warren resigned himself to stay in the army as an expression of love for Ginny, noting, "I could not have that you know do you see the only chance is for me to do my duty here and trust in God for success and a speedy termination of the war which everybody seems to anticipate."[40]

Other soldiers would echo this refrain in coming months. Henry Robinson Berkeley, a private with a Virginia artillery battalion, explained his motivation to a group of men after he became separated from his regiment during a fight. "They said that is they ere in my place that they would take a furlough & go home for a week or two. I told them that I did not think that this was a time for men to be going home . . . that if we did not stand to our guns, the yanks might get to our homes before we did." Berkeley's diary included scattered references to the purpose of the war throughout his notes, mostly vague references to "our future" or the fate of "our people." By the conclusion of the terrible year of fighting in 1864, he had refined his concern, focusing on the fate of his and his friends' "homes," and yet he remained convinced that the most effective way to defend those homes, and the loved ones inside them, was to stay in the army and continue fighting.[41]

Virginia soldiers reconciled family and national interests more easily than they did the erosion of slavery and their efforts to defend a nation founded on the institution. The degeneration of slavery was registered in a thousand ways. Slaves presumed loyal fled with Union troops or steered the invaders to family valuables. Of those who stayed in Virginia, many exerted their new authority to slow down work or demand more autonomy.[42] As black

Henry Robinson Berkeley. Like many Virginia soldiers, Berkeley persevered through disappointments over military defeats and dissatisfactions with service. Even after the disastrous Fall 1864 Shenandoah Valley Campaign, Berkeley insisted on Confederate independence, proclaiming that "if we [do] not stand to our guns, the yanks might get to our homes before we [do]." Photo courtesy of the Virginia Historical Society, Richmond.

Virginians pushed their preferences for freedom and autonomy, white Virginians became more embittered toward them. "I am beginning to lose confidence *in the whole race,*" noted one Virginia lady, "I see a growing inclination to the Yanks in our own servants from Peyton down it is hard to see them take a stand against us and not to believe any thing we say in regard to them."[43] James Cobb, a successful farmer in Southampton County filled his diary in late 1864 with biblical defenses of slavery. The audacity of black Virginians and their obvious lack of appreciation for the efforts whites had made to civilize them under slavery filled Cobb, and many Virginians, with disgust.[44] The *Richmond Sentinel,* an administration mouthpiece in the capital, clarified the intellectual justification for the harsher perspective white southerners brought to bear on black southerners in an article titled "The Hatred of Race." "The hatred of races . . . however slightly differing from each other, are irreconcilable and ever enduring," the paper baldly announced.[45]

In their interactions with black Virginians, soldiers paid particular attention to any suffering caused by the Union army or any indication of slaves' loyalty to the Confederacy. J. Kelly Bennette, serving in the Shenandoah Valley in mid-1864, recorded the following encounter.

I was the spectator of a scene today which tho' frequently described has but seldom fallen to the lot of any one to witness. It was a young girl pleading for rescue of her lover at hands of the bold cavaliers. She was a daughter of that region—'Where Afric's sunny fountains Roll down their golden sands' and it was quite affecting to see what sighs undulated her ebony bosom as she plead for his rescue in these pathetic accents: 'I wush massa you gemmen 'ud make dem yankees fotch back my beau, dey tucked 'im off when dey was here, I wush you gemmen ud fotch 'im back.' Ah, that was a scene worthy of the contemplation of a Stowe! It would move the heart of a stoic."[46]

Bennette's sarcasm, and his inability to sympathize with a person struggling with separation, like most soldiers' wives, revealed the depth of his antipathy toward black Virginians. Like many other white Virginians, Bennette took solace in the knowledge that former slavers, untrained and uneducated, would be unable to survive as a free people. The Union's use of former slaves and free blacks as soldiers only exacerbated this hostility. As the fruits of the Emancipation Proclamation ripened, and the northern army pulled in the 180,000 African Americans who would eventually serve in its armies, Confederates understood that the stakes in the war had escalated. Accordingly, Confederates continued to take every opportunity they could to arrest the spread of freedom among slaves. Like most Confederate chroniclers, William Corson noted the number of escaped slaves who were recaptured after they overran Union troops in Dinwiddie County. "We recovered nearly every thing they had taken and completely routed them, capturing all their ambulances, wagons, artillery, 500 prisoners, and 700 negroes," he announced.[47] The index of victory included both captured enemy soldiers and captured enemies from within.

The disaffection and violence that white Virginians expressed toward black southerners seeking their freedom comes as little surprise given white Virginians' investment in slavery. More surprising, and more dangerous in terms of the social cohesion of the Confederacy, was the increasing distance that developed between civilians and soldiers. Soldiers seethed with resentment whenever they saw or heard about healthy men who had somehow managed to avoid service. Although almost all Confederate Virginia men of military age served in the armies, soldiers believed that many men had shirked their duty and were home enjoying an easy life that soldiers defended with their lives. After the revocation of substitution, George Coiner discussed with his mother the ramifications of the new policy, which he mistakenly thought allowed the substitutes to go home. "I shall try & not envy those who may be so fortunate as to get off," he wrote, "except it be such as Bill Shirey, Tom Antrim & some more of the same stripe—all of whom should be in service, as much so as a great many others who are in."[48] The clear sense of obligation among the men Coiner knew from home colored his evaluation of both the policy and the general tenor of the war. The Confederacy's efforts to draw in every available man succeeded, but from the perspective of soldiers, especially volunteers from before conscription, a privileged group continued to dodge its responsibility.

The antagonism that developed between the parlor and the camp was partly cultural too, defined by the distinct experiences of the war on the home front and the battlefront. In some cases, the differences presented themselves for all to see. The use of churches, schools, and government buildings as hospitals or convalescence wards, which occurred throughout the state, distinguished the transformation that the war wrought on Virginia. In the case of churches, for instance, the aftermath of battles secularized sacred places, filled, as they were, with the screams of patients, the curses of porters and doctors, and pools of blood and piles of amputated limbs.[49] The war transformed soldiers' lives as well, in ways that most civilians could not understand. Many Virginia soldiers were captured or imprisoned by Union forces over the course of the war, and many of those men sent to northern prisons died of disease or malnutrition. Fear among citizens was palpable when they knew loved ones had been captured, and joy at their return provided some of the most vibrant celebrations in wartime Virginia. One man reported on the return of 1,100 prisoners from Point Lookout in Maryland in early 1864. He witnessed an "immense concourse of people—probably 10,000 on the Capitol Square to meet them in the afternoon. Large quantities of provisions distributed among them."[50] Civilians' tendency to identify their returning prisoners as heroes probably drew approval from soldiers, but civilians would never know the humiliation of capture or the terror of life in the overcrowded and undersupplied northern camps.

Soldiers' growing acceptance of a long war revealed more distance between themselves and civilians. Though the persistent belief in one cataclysmic battle that could end the war persisted, at the same time men prepared for extended service. Even before the real fighting had begun in 1864, John Garibaldi admitted to his future wife that "it seems to me that the war is going to be a long one."[51] Another soldier concurred with Garibaldi and drew out the more ominous meaning of an extended engagement. "As to peace Heaven only knows when that will come," he wrote. "I suppose however that the war can't last forever but I can see no indication of an early peace. We have gotten so used to war now that aplenty to eat is all we look for." Ominously, he noted, "We expect to make this our trade for we have become fitted for nothing else now."[52]

Though soldiers regretted that they suffered the unavoidable hardships of a military life, these difficulties helped bind soldiers together. Richard Dulany, commanding the 7th Cavalry, reported an excursion to Charlottesville made in the cold and rain of late March: "Neither myself nor men were in the most amiable humor [when they arrived], but after finding some flat rails to make a floor and fixing a 'shabang' of rails covered with our oilcloths to protect us from the rain, we were soon at the pleasant work of toasting our little pieces of bacon on the ends of forked sticks, and catching the melting fat on our hard crackers (to make them the more easy to swallow)," Dulany reported. He described his men, "As contented and happy as a set of fellows as you ever saw." Dulany's description of the episode revealed the pride that soldiers took in the new men they had become. "How comparative are all our ideas of comfort and happiness," he wrote, "and how little we really require if we can only think so. Few Princes enjoyed their breakfasts as we did and my sleep before a bright fire but on hard rails, was an unbroken as an infants."[53]

The physical hardships or service, which had drawn such condemnation and anger in 1861 and 1862, now emerged as a mark of distinction. Men related their stories of cold nights and long marches with pride and at times arrogance. In early 1864 Frank Myers casually related a story about a recent night's sleep he stole on the floor of a man's house around Strasburg in the lower Valley: "[I] slept on the floor before the fire and one of Mosby's men laid down on the hearth between me and the fire and I like to froze. I kicked him in the fire twice making out I was asleep all the time and Mr. Mosby's man got out of the way." The humor of his story masked a hardened edge that helped him refuse to share a fire with a fellow soldier. Myers continued, contrasting his savvy at protecting himself with the apparent helplessness of his family, for whom he evinced little concern. "Went to Ed Bennetts Uncles in the fork of the Shenandoah River—first rate place," he noted. Then, he casually inquired, "have the Yanks burned the barn and house yet? Write to me as soon as you can."[54] One of the many paradoxes of the war in Virginia was that the physical distance that grew between soldiers and citizens would actually inspire soldiers to fight with more energy and determination. The sense of persecution, almost living martyrdom, that many Confederate soldiers felt by 1864 imbued them with new resolve even as it isolated them from the people whom they fought to protect.

Confederate victories in the Shenandoah Valley balanced the gradual retreat of Lee's men in the East and eased the friction between home front and battlefront. The close proximity of those spaces in the Valley provided an antidote to the sense of alienation between soldiers and civilians: it encouraged all Confederates to focus their ire on the Yankees. The first Union campaign in the region began with northern troops under General Franz Sigel who made their way south into the Valley as far as New Market. There a motley collection of soldiers and youthful volunteers from the Virginia Military Institute defeated Sigel and sent him fleeing from the region. Echoing scenes of Stonewall Jackson's outnumbered troops defeating Union forces in the Valley in 1862, this type of humiliation pleased Confederates in the area and reinforced their vision of southern military superiority.

Six days after Sigel's defeat, the northern command replaced him with General David Hunter. In 1862 and 1863, while stationed along the Sea Islands of South Carolina, General Hunter had raised the first black Union regiment but earned little real military experience in a remote and relatively unimportant region. His appointment to head the Department of West Virginia undoubtedly did little to trouble Confederates in the Valley. The casual references made by civilians to the presence of an invading army revealed a confidence that bolstered their soldier relatives. Lieutenant Benjamin Lewis Blackford, who served with the 11th Virginia Infantry but was stationed temporarily in Wilmington, North Carolina, wrote home to his mother in early June 1864. After relating his anxiety over the girl he was courting and expressing relief that his soldier brothers were still well, he remarked, "By the way I wish you would tell me all about what happened at Edgewood & Dewberry during the Yankee possession."[55] The Blackford matriarch, who had five sons in Confederate military service, lived directly in the path of Hunter's troops, but all her son could muster was a "by the way" reference and a morbid curiosity about the fate of his neighbors.

Hunter initially met with more success than Sigel, defeating a Confederate force at Piedmont and capturing 1,500 Confederate prisoners.[56] Hunter continued up the Valley, occupying Staunton, where he destroyed railroads and manufacturing facilities before marching to Lexington where his troops burned the Virginia Military Institute. By mid-June, Hunter's men reached the outskirts of Lynchburg, where he hoped to destroy the East Tennessee and Virginia Railroad leading to Charlottesville and the fertile fields of the Piedmont. Lee detached Jubal A. Early and the Second Corps from the main force of the Army of Northern Virginia to stop Hunter. Eventually reorganized into the Army of the Valley, Early's corps mirrored the diverse makeup of Lee's army, with regiments from North Carolina, Georgia, Louisiana, and other Confederate states. Virginia supplied the main contingent of soldiers for the Army of the Valley, and of these, close to 30 percent were natives of the Valley themselves.[57] For Confederate soldiers from the Valley assigned to defend it from the series of Union invasions, fighting in their own region helped fuse their need to protect their homes while also serving their country.

After a brief fight at Lynchburg, Hunter retreated west over the Allegheny Mountains into Union territory. Following his expulsion, Hunter occupied Liberty, just west of Lynchburg. Frederick Anspach, a resident of the town, wrote to his brother a week after the occupation and described the destruction Hunter's troops wrought on the town. After watching Union soldiers burn the hospital, two houses, and several bridges, Anspach "left town refugeeing Tuesday night and stayed at Uncle Caleb's." Anspach probably had little use for the verb "to refugee" in his prewar lexicon, but its incorporation into his wartime vocabulary revealed that the practice had become commonplace for residents of the Valley. The disturbance only increased his anger at the North. After celebrating Hunter's eventual defeat at Lynchburg, he wrote "It is a pity we could not surround and kill, not capture or wound, every scoundrel of them, and if it shall ever be my lot to obtain revenge certainly I have more now to prompt and actuate me than ever before. I shall try to kill the last one of them." Despite Anspach's fury, his own account revealed how little lasting damage Hunter did to his area. "No mills were burnt down in this County that I know of, unless Ball's was," he reported. "In some places along the road the crops were damaged but not sufficiently to materially injure the abundance, though it will bear hard on individuals. Wheat is ripening—some few are cutting, Ad. is for one. The crop I suppose will be a good yield—corn looks well but needs rain."[58]

In fact, the drought to which Anspach refers seems to have done more long-term harm than Hunter's troops. References to the drought of the summer can be found in accounts from soldiers and civilians across Virginia. Amon Updike wrote to his sister from the east side of the state where the drought was taking its toll as well. "They see hard times this hot dry weather for we have not had any rain for a long time," Updike noted; "it looks much like starvation down hear they is a long scope of country hear that every thing is distroyed & no — a making atall I dont see what pore folks is to do if this cruel war dont end soon in fact it if was to end soon they would have to live on till they could make a crop."[59] The drought presented Virginians with a new foe against which their weapons did little good. The heat seemed at times like an agent of the North as it exacerbated the logistical strain inflicted by the Union army.

The full effect of the drought did not manifest itself until the harvest, and in the summer most Confederates celebrated the termination of Hunter's invasion. Robert Conrad, a lawyer from Winchester, traveled through the upper Valley in June and he too felt that Hunter's campaign did little lasting damage to civilian property and crops. News reports in the North and rampant rumors in the South spawned images of mass destruction, but Conrad offered a blunt assessment: "People in the Valley complaining of Yankee outrages— . . . saw nothing to compare with our inflictions." Conrad hoped that the Federals would be completely repulsed by the Valley Army, composed of "a considerable number of our best general officers, and the pick of men."[60] Conrad's enthusiasm testified to the diverse support that the young nation had drawn. A lawyer before the war, Conrad represented the citizens of Frederick County at Virginia's secession convention in 1861. A staunch Unionist at the time, Conrad had voted against secession at both opportunities during the convention but reluctantly signed the Ordinance of Secession in May 1861. Having turned fifty-five in 1860, Conrad was entitled, by both age and position, to sit out the war in Winchester. Although he did not serve in the army, Conrad refused to take an oath of allegiance to the United States and Union officials jailed him repeatedly. This treatment, along with Union occupations of his hometown, seems to have transformed Conrad's reluctance to support secession into hatred of the North. Conrad did not undergo that conversion alone; alongside his five sons, more than 60 percent of the eligible men of Frederick County joined Confederate armies.[61]

Confederate officials concurred with Conrad's sarcastic evaluation. Colonel Edward G. Lee reestablished the Confederate headquarters in Staunton after Hunter's expulsion and wrote to the War Department on June 17, 1864, to summarize the effects of Hunter's campaign. He reported the burning of several public buildings and three miles of railroad. Advance warning of Hunter's approach "enabled [him] to get off 900 sacks of salt, a large lot of leather, &c. All the ammunition was saved, all the bacon, and most of the quartermaster's stores."[62] Although he predicted that several more weeks of work would be needed to repair the railroad, the telegraph was already back in order.[63] Hunter's defeat at Lynchburg, and his subsequent expulsion from the Valley, proved both an embarrassment for the North and a boon for the Confederacy. Repeating the pattern that Lee had established in the eastern Virginia theater, Confederate troops in the Valley drove back a series of

Federal attempts and protected the rich agricultural region as a main provisioner of both civilians and soldiers.

Hunter's superior, Ulysses S. Grant, was probably more upset than Anspach. Grant explicitly urged Hunter on several occasions to make the destruction of the Virginia Central Railroad "beyond the possibility of repair for several weeks" his primary goal; Hunter failed to do this before leaving the region.[64] Worse yet, the destruction that Hunter's troops committed, including the burning of former Governor John Letcher's home and much of the Virginia Military Institute in Lexington, renewed Confederate hatred for northern troops. Although these actions had little practical effect, the wanton destruction of both public and private property added a new reason for soldiers to keep fighting. Thomas Cleveland, an artillerist with the Fluvanna battery, noted in a letter to his wife in late June, "It was truly mortifying to see the destruction at the beautiful Town of Lexington . . . I believe a great many of our soldiers are determined to avenge themselves yet, but that cannot pay us back."[65] Confederate soldiers felt they had succeeded in repulsing the enemy once again from this now-hallowed Confederate place. Isaac White, a surgeon assigned to the 62nd Virginia Mounted Infantry, expressed his perceptions succinctly. "I think our prospects are fine more so than ever."[66]

By early July, the Confederates reached Frederick County, having "swept the Valley clean of Federals."[67] The townspeople of Winchester, and the "pretty women and girls" in particular, celebrated the return of Confederate soldiers to their area. Those civilians north of Winchester, in Union territory, felt the hand of Confederate confiscation just as their neighbors to the south had experienced Union raids earlier in the year. On July 3, Early wrote to Breckinridge: "Your note of 4 p.m. is just received. You will have secured for the use of the entire army such public stores as may have been left by the enemy. All shoes in the private stores will be secured in like manner. You will seize all other goods in the stores in Martinsburg, and place them in charge of a responsible and competent quartermaster, to be confiscated for the benefit of the Government; and take the most efficient measures to prevent all plundering or private appropriation of these goods or any other captures."[68]

Aside from the need to secure valuable goods, bringing a harder war to those new *West* Virginians, who had abandoned their prewar identity as part of the Old Dominion, helped define the physical borders of the Confederacy. At the same time, commanders in the Valley helped establish the cultural dimensions of Confederate identity in their effort to bolster soldiers' allegiance to their new nation. As Early's forces pushed Hunter's troops out of Lynch-burg and proceeded down the Valley, most of the men were marched through the town of Lexington and past the grave of the late Stonewall Jackson. Henry Robinson Berkeley was one of those soldiers who marched past what was be-coming a Confederate shrine. "June 25 1864. Saturday. Passed through Lex-ington, all the Infantry filing by Stonewall Jackson's grave."[69] Many of Berke-ley's comrades made similar notes in their diaries and letters home, where the image of successful Confederate soldiers paying homage to their fallen leader could be repeated and absorbed into the emerging national culture.[70]

In July, Early's troops advanced north out of the Valley into Maryland, where they circled east, defeating a Federal force at Frederick and headed toward Washington. Early's troops drew within sight of the Capitol but did not make a serious attempt on the heavily fortified city. Nevertheless, Lin-coln called up local militia units before regular reinforcements arrived from Grant's army. Confederate papers chronicled the campaign closely, and civil-ians and soldiers gloated over the juxtaposition of Union troops stuck in the mud outside Petersburg and Early's forces nimbly cutting through northern territory to harass the Federal capital. Union commanders reluctantly recog-nized that Confederate troops had dominated northern forces in the Valley thus far in the year. Even as Grant vainly urged Hunter to "make all the Valley south of the Baltimore and Ohio Road a desert," he received a communica-tion from Assistant Secretary of War Charles A. Dana that confirmed how ineffective Union forces had been against Early's men. On July 15 Dana noted that Early's units had reentered the Valley and assessed the Confeder-ates' recent campaign through Maryland. "The enemy will doubtless escape with all his plunder and recruits, leaving us nothing But the deepest shame that yet befallen us."[71]

Alongside the plunder, Early's brief campaign through the region distin-guished itself by a decided shift in Confederate strategy toward northern noncombatants. After leaving Washington, part of Early's troops entered the mostly undefended town of Chambersburg, Pennsylvania, demanded $100,000 in gold, and, when it could not be procured, burned the town. For Achilles Tynes, who was part of the group that entered Chambersburg, the actions were regrettable. "City fired about noon. Saddest spectacle I ever witnessed to see the women and children. This inaugurates a terrible system of retaliation, and rapine."[72] Less sensitive Virginians would have argued that northerners had inaugurated the system themselves, with John Pope's 1862 orders to arrest disloyal men and confiscate property. The practices of north-ern soldiers did seem qualitatively different to most Virginians in 1864 than they had been in previous years. This experience, rather than any innate hatred, led to an endorsement of hard war from both citizens and soldiers. As one woman wrote her cousin after hearing a rumor that the Confederate army might again move into Pennsylvania, "If it was me I would be rite in for that making raids & plundering like the yankeys have been doing here."[73]

Within Virginia, the majority's opinion gradually shifted as well, toward that expressed by Isaac White. "The Lord I think is on our side," the doctor wrote, "+ I hope he will soon put a stop to the diffusion of blood; for I + all of us are tired of it + desire peace (honorable)." He then turned to the topic of Chambersburg: "I suppose you have seen an account of the burning of Chambersburg. I am opposed to burning; but I supposed they deserved it + if they desire to retaliate we can play that game with them + play it well but I do hope such warfare may cease."[74]

A participant in the raid echoed the doctor's reserved approval. "The burning of Chambersburg was generally condemned by our Regt. *at first* when all the sympathies were aroused," wrote J. Kelly Bennette, "but when reason has time to regain her seat I believe that they all thought as I thought at first; that it was Justice & Justice tempered with Mercy." Bennette elaborated his theory of hard war, noting "that *burning per se* is wrong no one can deny; and the bare idea of turning out of doors upon the cold charities of the world unprotected women and unoffending children is sufficient to cause the feelings to rebel." That said, however, he recognized that, "there may be circumstances under which it is not only justifiable but becomes a duty,— stern it is true but nevertheless binding." Bennette argued that Confederates had pursued a "conciliatory" policy toward Union civilians and property during their previous campaigns to the North, but the Yankees had not responded in kind. "Now everyone knows that the conciliatory policy has failed—utterly failed—& we are driven nolens volens to the opposite mode of procedure."[75] James Edmondson agreed. He read, "that (William) McCausland has created a considerable blaze in Chambersburg, Pa. so our government has at last accepted the rule as laid down and executed by our enemies in carrying on this war." The strategy was simple: "I hope it will continue to do so until the Yankees are willing to accept the Code of Civilized warfare— blaze for blaze is my motto, should my own dwelling be the next to blaze."[76]

I n the Shenandoah Valley and in eastern Virginia, the return to a defensive war energized the populace. John Herbert Clairborne, a young doctor, described the celebration in Richmond at the arrival of Confederate regulars in mid-May:

Then at the depot & on the streets you might have witnessed scenes which would have brot. back the first days of the war. The Ladies would rush out to cheer the soldiers as their deliverers & the workings of hand-kerchiefs & shouts of the soldiery and the marshal music stirred the blood of the coldest—Virginians—N. Carolinians—S. Carolinians—Georgians—on they came—Regiment after Regiment—Brigade after Brigade—all clamorous for the first blow at the craven foe which had been hovering around our doors.

More importantly, the doctor recognized the effect that Butler's invasion had on Virginia soldiers, who longed for the chance to expel this most hated northerner from their soil. "The Virginia troops were fairly maddened to find their homes so nearly swept away in their absence," Clairborne observed, "I have never seen so much enthusiasm amongst the troops as now. There is no way to whip them but kill them all."[77]

Hindsight complicates our ability to understand the war as Confederates saw it in mid-1864. We know that they lost the war less than a year later; how could they not have seen it coming? Without knowledge of the outcome, however, Confederate optimism seems rational given the course of the war to this point. The confidence of mid-1864, even shadowed by Lee's retreat through central Virginia, added to the psychological stake Virginians held in independence. The longer the war lasted, and the more shamefully Union soldiers behaved, the more necessary Confederate victory became. To lose at this point to so unworthy a foe would be regarded by the world, and southerners themselves, as a mark of shame. In this way, the duration and the momentum of the war itself reinforced prewar notions of masculine honor. A wealthy businessman from Richmond wrote to a friend to explain his views. Because Lincoln would not treat with either the Confederate government or the individual states, he saw little choice. The power of honor compelled a continued war. "Would it not seem that our only resort is to unite all our ability, moral physical & pecuniary to fight him to the last. Submission seems impossible either to a brave or christian people on his terms—What say you? We are into the contest & must have an honorable termination or extermination."[78]

7 ★ THE FALL OF THE CONFEDERACY
JULY 1864–MARCH 1865

Lincoln and Seward met them at Fortress Monroe and told them that
nothing but unconditional surrender would be accepted. That is we would
lay down our arms—go to our homes and submit to the laws of the
Washington government; in other words have our property confiscated, our
slaves emancipated, our leaders hung, and we become serfs in the land
of our fathers, then he (Abraham 1st) might exercise his pardoning power
with liberality. We have the alternatives of submission or war.
*   —Charles F. James, February 7, 1865*

Virginia Confederates started the second half of 1864 in their weakest military position since the war began. Although they had inflicted massive casualties on Grant's armies, they had suffered immensely. The Overland campaign cost Lee's army 33,000 casualties.[1] Worse still, they had been driven back to within twenty miles of Richmond. The summer of 1864 brought uncertainty among Confederates, unsure if they could repulse the Yankees or even hold them at bay. In the Shenandoah Valley, long a bellwether of Confederate fortunes, Confederate troops were decisively beaten and driven into disarray. By late 1864, it became clear to most soldiers that the Union would defeat the Confederacy. The pressure on supplies denied sustenance to both civilians and soldiers, divisions among Confederates flared, and Lincoln's reelection signaled the political failure of the Confederate military effort.

In response to their impending defeat, men began leaving the army in the winter of 1864–65, and this process escalated through the spring. Poorer soldiers may well have been overrepresented among those men who abandoned the army in late 1864 and early 1865.[2] Their families suffered more than wealthier families, and they may have decided that the likelihood of Union victory finally made resistance futile. Nonetheless, soldiers' decisions to leave in late 1864 and early 1865 did not necessarily convey their abandonment of the Confederacy's war goals.[3] Rather, they recognized the impending defeat of the Confederacy. As the debates over slave soldiers and the Peace Commission in early 1865 would show, many soldiers remained committed to the goals of the Confederacy even after they realized that the state could not survive. The soldiers' approach, of admitting military defeat but continuing to support the ideals for which they fought, cast doubt on northerners' accomplishment even before they attained it and predicted a dark future for a reunified America.

L ocated twenty miles south of Richmond, Petersburg protected railroads entering the Confederate capital from the southeast, southwest, and west. Grant understood that if he could take Petersburg, Richmond would fall, and he began devising and implementing plans to drive the rebel forces from the line of entrenchments that circled it. The entrenchments at Petersburg encompassed more territory than any others in the Confederacy, and Grant lead nine different offensives against the lines between mid-June 1864 and early April 1865. The defenses of Petersburg and the tenacity of Confederate soldiers manning the works ensured a long struggle to control the town; the siege at Petersburg lasted almost ten months. The stalemate produced another unpredictable shift in the nature of the war. Although Confederate soldiers contended with scarcity and hardship that reminded many of the lean days of 1862, the process of fighting at Petersburg mutated into something new and horrible. Most historians use the term "trench warfare" to characterize Petersburg, intentionally summoning images of World War I to describe the environment within which Confederate and Union soldiers fought. Contemporaries had no such example to reflect on, so they awkwardly constructed their own meaning out of the experience.

Over the course of the conflict, most veterans developed a sense of the purpose behind their movement as well as a finely tuned sense of when to expect a battle, but the novelty of the situation at Petersburg weakened this ability. In response, most infantrymen simply resigned themselves to their place. Without a doubt, men considered where they were, complained about conditions, and argued over purposes, but the initial commitment to fighting at Petersburg was fueled by general confidence in their army, supreme confidence in Lee as a leader, and a limited ability to conceptualize the direction of the war. One Virginian serving under Lee noted how much he wished he were back home in the Valley, but knew that would come soon enough. "We are all in fine spirits," he reassured a friend, "and have hope that Grant will soon be compelled to leave this country and we will get farther north."[4]

Soldiers in the Valley likewise held high hopes at the year's midpoint. They also knew the importance of sharing those hopes with family members in order to sustain morale at home. George Peyton, whose unit contended with Union soldiers in the lower Valley, noted on August 30: "During this month we have been 'on the go' near all the time. Have hardly had time to bathe or wash our clothes. Have lived very well on fresh beef, mutton, pork, all the time besides apples and roasting ears."[5] John Hoge, in the 8th Virginia Cavalry, found time to stay with friends and family in Salem for a few days late in the month and took the opportunity to trade in his worn-out horse for a new one.[6] William Corson, like many other Confederate soldiers serving the region, felt well prepared for whatever conflict might come. "The boys are all well," he noted. "My health is excellent. I can eat 14 ears of corn for supper and sleep in my saddle as soundly as a dead pig in a shuck-pen."[7] John T. Cooley of the 51st Virginia Infantry needed a little more to sustain him than Corson required, but he also anticipated hard fighting to come. "We are energized in a war which we must *fight out*, 'And the harder the storm the sooner it will be over,'" he predicted. "I can stand the storm very well if I get plenty to eat, and can enjoy good health, and be permitted to peruse the thoughts of *my highly esteemed and affectioned Cousin Julia*. Pardon me Cousin, I am candid in what I say."[8] Even residents of the Valley seemed confident; twenty-eight women of Harrisonburg sent a petition to Confederate secretary of war James A. Seddon asking for authority to create a regiment of female soldiers.[9]

Because of the relative lack of active campaigning in the state through much of 1863, Virginians found supplies of food more readily available in 1864 than they had been two years previously. The rations satisfied most soldiers at the start of the siege and foraging yielded high volumes of supplementary material for those men in other parts of the state. The connection between food and morale remained obvious to most commanders, as Charles Davidson reported to his mother in early June: "The army is in excellent spirits and all are getting a plenty to eat, they are receiving a half pound of bacon, the best bacon I have seen issued."[10] The supply of food, like the reservoir of Confederate confidence, would run low later in the year. In the middle months of 1864, however, many Virginians recommitted themselves to independence in anticipation of the victory to come.

Life for civilians in the lower Valley turned harder and more dangerous by late August, as Sheridan and his force moved into the region and began burning mills and barns.[11] On August 17, Mathella Page Harrison in Millwood recorded her memories of these experiences.

Night has closed at last on this day of horrors. Years almost seem to have rolled since I opened my eyes this morning. The first sound that greeted my ears was the rumbling of Yankee waggons. . . . At nine o'clock yankee pickets were stationed on every hill. Fires of barns, stockyards, etc. soon burst forth and by eleven, from a high elevation, fifty could be seen blazing forth. The whole country was enveloped with smoke and flame. The sky was lurid and but for the green trees one might have imagined the shades of Hades had descended suddenly. The shouts, ribald jokes, awful oaths, demoniacal laughter of the fiends added to the horrors of the day.

Harrison identified the loss of foodstuffs as the most serious effect of the raid, especially for families in the area already living on sparse resources.[12]

In this period of crisis and questioning, Confederate soldiers witnessing the destruction of the Valley's resources struggled to reorganize not just their army but also their conceptions of the changing nature of the war and of their role in it. Richard Watkins, in a letter to his wife in early October from outside Staunton, spoke first of the damage he saw, the "night sky reddened with the glare from burning barns," and then of how he understood the shift in Union tactics. "The Yankees are seriously endeavoring to starve us into submission," Watkins argued. "They are burning all the grain & all the mills within their reach." Recognizing that "the defeat of Early [which came in October] is the most serious disaster which Virginia has experienced during the war," Watkins agreed with his wife that they faced "the darkest hour of the war, but a just God still rules and controls the affairs of nations, and 'vengeance is mine I will repay saith the Lord.'" His final line of advice combined passive acceptance of events beyond their control with a deliberate choice to maintain his commitment to their new nation. "Let us not trouble ourselves too much about it," he remarked, "but go along like grown up folk and do our duty."[13]

The actions of Sheridan in the Valley and Sherman in Georgia demonstrated for many Confederates the unbridgeable gulf that existed between northerners and southerners. Southerners like Watkins, accepted, even pursued, a harder war because they felt so alienated from their former co-citizens. The *Daily Richmond Examiner* clarified the stakes in the war: "If any of our countrymen has hitherto deluded himself with the idea that this present conflict is a 'War,' in the ordinary sense of that term; an appeal to wager of battle between two nations under the conditions recognised amongst civilized people, it is time at last to awaken from that delusion and to look truth in the face. This is a war of *extirpation*;—not to subjugate and reduce us to submission, but to destroy us and our children."[14]

By fall, the strain of hosting major armies began to show on the state.

Union cavalry destroyed several communities in the lower reaches of the Valley. William V. Kie, recorded his thoughts as Jubal Early's Army of the Valley went into formation around Berryville: "The plantations in this part of Va have been turned to roads. Not a fence to be seen around a scarcely a crop. The fences have been burned and the crops trampled by the troops."[15] Those places singled out by Sheridan and his men for the hardest war experienced destruction unlike anything except the sacking of Fredericksburg in December 1862. A young woman named Lizzie cataloged the effect on a variety of family members: "The Yanks camped in Grandpa's orchard & nursery (both sides of the land) burning the fences of course and destroying the fruit, They were thick here & Grandma's all the time. Killed all of Grandpa's hogs, burnt the barn, Aunt Fannie's Cabin, new smokehouse & gernery. Took everything in the eatable line, such as bread, pies, butter, apple butter, chickens, turkey & ——."[16]

Lizzie also cursed the loss of her grandfather's slaves, who joined the Union troops. She then turned to an account of what her own family had suffered. "I believe I am through with Grandma's trials, and now for ours, which make me shudder to relate," Lizzie noted. "Took everything we had to eat, stole the beans and all the vegetables, burned the barn, waggon, carriage too and a great many things besides all the wheat & hay." She angrily reported that a "great many families here gone North. The villains tried to force us to go too, and I believe had they staid two weeks longer, they would have forced everyone to leave. I told them if they did burn us out I intended staying with my home to the last, but they said you will starve, I replied I glory in starving for my crumbs." As at Fredericksburg in 1862, the implementation of hard war by the Union pushed many civilians beyond despair to hatred of the North and celebration of the Confederacy. Lizzie was no exception. "Words are inadequate to express my joy when our dear southern Boys made their appearance," she reported happily. "I screamed, laughed & cried. The first that I spoke to was Col. Munford . . . I could have kissed the ground that their horses walked on! I was so rejoiced!"[17] The faith that civilians demonstrated in the Confederate army faltered under the strain of the Union war effort late in the year, but the Union's hard-war tactics ensured that even after the war, southerners would use their admiration for Confederate soldiers as a symbol of continued resistance to the consequences of northern victory.

Lizzie's "southern Boys," however, had their own difficulties. In the late fall, Sheridan's force targeted not just foodstuffs but also Confederate troops in the Valley for destruction. Confederate losses at Winchester and Fisher's

Hill in late September generated recriminations between units and exacerbated latent tensions between the different branches of service. John Anthony Craig wrote to his mother from Strasburg, in the lower Valley. "Since our late reverses in the valley we have had a hard time of it. The greater portion of our Cavalry is utterly worthless, that it allows our infantry to be flanked on every occasion and has come near being the ruin of the army which is composed of troops that were considered the flower of the 'Army of Northern Virginia.'"[18] William Corson of the 3rd Virginia Cavalry also blamed Confederate horsemen for the loss and in a letter to his wife called the rout at Fisher's Hill, "the most complete and disastrous cavalry stampede of the war." Brimming with anger, Corson found the time to write because he had been assigned to escort wounded men to Confederate hospitals.[19]

The politics of blame spread quickly across the state in 1864. As rumor and innuendo flowed over the Blue Ridge, soldiers and civilians in the East indicted the Valley cavalry. This tactic helped people retain their faith in the army as a whole. General Early blamed his soldiers, a tactic that neither endeared him to them nor impressed other Virginians with his competence. A soldier with the 15th Virginia Infantry, stationed in the East read "in the papers accounts of Early's defeats which are not at all pleasant or agreeable. I saw in yesterday's paper an address he made to his men he gave them particular fits he says he would have gained a complete victory if they (his troops) had not have stopted to gather plunder from what he says one might suppose that his Army was in a demoralizing condition."[20]

Infantrymen felt, by far, the most aggrieved of all men in the service. Three years of marching and increasingly ferocious fighting gave most foot soldiers the sense that they worked harder and encountered more risks than men in the other branches of service. Infantrymen singled out the artillery as the easiest branch of service, a valid charge for heavy artillery like that around Richmond and Petersburg that stayed in place. Artillery camps were usually located near sources of fresh water, and men in the units took advantage of their stability to build comfortable homes. Infantrymen who marched through these camps often left with intense jealousy for their comrades in arms. Artillerymen held their own view of the relative advantages possessed by each branch of service, and like all soldiers expressed their views forcefully to brothers who were thinking of entering the army. The jealousies and recriminations that flowed among men of different branches develop in most armies and usually cause few serious problems. Within the context of defeats and retreat in 1864, however, the conflict between branches held the potential to open damaging divisions within Lee's army as a whole.

Another split also widened during the year; veterans continued to scorn new recruits. During one battle, a veteran named L. Robert Moore singled out a recent batch of draftees who suffered the brunt of the Union attack. "The Yankees charged last night rite amongst the conscripts that came from our neighborhood I reckon that they had much rather been some where else."[21] Moore's evident enjoyment of the conscripts' predicament left little doubt that he did not consider them part of his regiment. Moore's perspective drew upon the common suspicion that conscription fell on men who had thus far shirked military service. Earlier in the war, most volunteers assumed that only poor men would accept the humiliation of being drafted, though, with the abolition of substitution, many of the 1864 conscripts may well have been wealthy men made eligible for service under the provisions of the new law. Wealthy or not, most soldiers viewed the 1864 conscripts as less worthy than volunteers, and even lower than earlier draftees, many of whom had been incorporated into regiments through the battles of 1862 and 1863. Moore's criticisms reflected a concern shared by many Confederate Virginians that the burdens of war were not being shared equally.

The circumstances of war in 1864 increased the pressure on both soldiers and civilians in Virginia, and they responded, in part, by focusing criticism on specific groups within the population. Conflict along class lines was one expression of this general tendency, but so too were complaints by soldiers about civilians and vice versa. Native southerners singled out immigrants, particularly the Germans in Richmond, who received increased scrutiny and oppression throughout the year.[22] Most especially, white Virginians cast scorn and suspicion on black Virginians, whose actions seemed increasingly disloyal as Union armies pushed deeper into the state, often with the guidance of local blacks. This last axis of conflict foreshadowed the troubled future for black Virginians in a reunited United States.

The experience of war around Petersburg also widened the fissure between civilians and soldiers. Trench warfare forced men to accept an intimacy with death that few could have imagined in the prewar years. J. J. Hill, a Virginian on the line of breastworks between the James and Appomattox Rivers remarked, "Our duty is hard, besides other duty we have to go on picket every third night, and stay 24 hours. In places, ours and the yankee pitts are in fifty steps of one another, if either one raises his head above the pitt his adversary shoots at him, in this way, almost a constant fire is kept up; though there is but little loss of life on either side." The psychological pressure of living in such an uncertain space forced most soldiers to clarify where their loyalties lay. Hill observed that "the soldiers are in as good spirits as could be expected, and do not expect anything short of another campaign, & perhaps four more years of war." Later, Hill admitted that not all soldiers shared his ability to accept the prospect of another four years of war, noting, "In this view of the matter some are deserting and going to the yankeys, but such as go were of no use while they was here, and I suppose there is as many deserters comes to us (and perhaps more) as there are of our men going to them."[23]

The two armies faced off across a narrow chasm of ground filled with obstructions and trees splintered from sniper fire. The periodic offensives launched by Grant's army kept both sides from ever fully relaxing despite the deadening boredom that filled each day. A young Tidewater soldier, recently posted to Petersburg after spending nearly a year in South Carolina, described the effect of the trench warfare to his family in late June. "I am getting to worned out with this cruel war," he noted, "fighting, working, day and night. We can't see any peace atall, no sleep. We have to stay in the trenches sometimes a week at the time. Now you may know that we are seeing a very hard time."[24] Private Bennette in the 8th Virginia Cavalry also conveyed a tone of resignation. "The last day of Summer has again come 'round. Three & a half weary years have 'like a wounded snake dragged their slow length along,'" Bennette said, quoting the poet Alexander Pope. "And now the war does not appear as near its close as at the fall of Ft. Sumter," he continued, "Verily it seems to me now that if this war continues four years longer I do not care if it lasts yet forty years more. By that time all my prospects for future life (who calls it living at all to be a soldier?) will have been blasted & what care I then?"[25]

Just as soldiers fighting in the trenches came to see themselves as suffering in a unique way, officers condemned noncombatants who were not properly appreciative of soldiers' sacrifices. Richard Dulany, the wealthy commander of the 7th Virginia Cavalry, heaped scorn on those residents who ran him ragged with requests to protect their property from the Confederate soldiers defending the farmer's livelihood. "A farmer wants a guard to protect his fences," he noted, "another wants a guard to protect his fruits and vegetables—another says that the guard reads his newspaper while some of his men steal their sweet-potatoes." As Dulany struggled to keep order in a part of Virginia continually subject to Yankee raids and occasional occupations, his patience with demanding civilians ran thin. After considering the requests, he agreed with the soldiers who worked as guards, observing, "the citizen is as mean as a Yankee [and] after guarding the fruit for days he has sold [the soldier] a little green watermelon for a dollar and a half and the only peaches he could get he paid ten dollars a basket for." When Dulany considered the costs his units had incurred in the Overland campaign that spring, he felt no sympathy for frustrated landowners, saying, "It provokes me very much to see some rich farmers make more fuss about a few hundred rails destroyed than many of my poor soldiers do at the loss of a leg or arm." Dulany's frustration mounted through the long summer, until he complained, "I am so much annoyed by farmers complaining of depredations committed by the soldiers that I almost wish that the corn and melons would become bitter to the taste. Two of my men were slightly wounded by the guard in a cornfield and one man from Chew's battery killed." Still, as a man of property Dulany believed in protecting it even in times of unusual need. "It seems cruel to kill a man for taking a few ears of corn, but we are all fighting to assert and protect individual rights, and it would not be consistent to allow our soldiers to become the oppressors of our citizens."[26]

This division between soldiers and civilians was in many ways the most serious of all the rifts that opened in the Confederacy in 1864.[27] Three and a half years of warfare had reduced the ability of many veterans to envision a life in peacetime, even as they longed for it. Both groups suffered terribly during the fall and winter of 1864, but in starkly different contexts that seem to have rendered them unable to sympathize with each other. Charles James, from the trenches outside Petersburg, condemned his sister after she described dances she had attended in Richmond early in 1865. "Dancing parties are heard of everywhere," he complained, "and the people seem to have lost sight of the fact that a war was going on and given themselves up to pleasure and dissipation." James knew one man who had returned from leave to report a dance where ladies graciously waltzed with twenty known deserters. This behavior demanded redress, he charged. "If the people at home, especially the ladies, will do their duty," he advised, "and bring such a pressure to bear upon absentees, deserters, or skulkers, as will force them from their homes or render their situation there anything but pleasant, the happiest results will follow." In short, James placed the blame for the Confederacy's manpower shortage on weak-willed civilians at home, rather than recognizing the Confederacy's eroding capacity to wage war.[28]

The tendency to shift blame onto civilians found formal expression in resolutions passed by many regiments in early 1865. These tracts contrasted soldiers' fidelity and determination to persevere with what they characterized as a weak and uncommitted civilian population. The 9th Virginia Infantry passed a typical resolution in late January 1865. The preamble began on an accusatory note: "Whereas it seems that there are some persons within the

Confederate State, who, unmindful of the blood that has been shed, and regardless of the sacrifices we have already made, are willing to accept peace upon the basis of reconstruction of the Union." The soldiers of the 9th Infantry were unwilling to accept that peace. They took special pride, as they pointed out a few lines later, in being "mostly refugees from Eastern Virginia, whose homes have been desolated, and loved ones oppressed and insulted."[29] Their appropriation of the term "refugee," which had previously referred to those civilian who had abandoned their homes to avoid the Union army, revealed the narrow world that soldiers had come to inhabit.

The resolutions themselves reinforced the isolation of the army from the civilian experience of the past year. The proclamation of the 9th Infantry opened: "1. Resolved, that the cruel vindictiveness and angry boasts of our enemy, during the past four years of strife, have but proved the justness of our cause, and should nerve a brave people to a more determined resistance. 2. Resolved, that we, in the beginning of this new year, not unmindful of our past privations and dangers, dropping a tear upon the graves of our fallen comrades, remembering with tenderest emotions our loved ones at home, weary of waiting for our return, firmly relying upon a just God, renew our pledges to liberty."[30] The notion that civilians remained comfortable at home patiently waiting for the return of their beloved soldiers ignored the alarming conditions throughout the state in the winter of 1864–65. Another resolution rejected the terms of surrender offered to the recent peace commission and eagerly accepted continued war instead, a decision that civilians might have wished to modify slightly. "The proud freemen of these States are told that they can have peace, on no other terms than abject submission?" wrote the members of Virginia's 2nd Cavalry, "Then we welcome war. War, with all its horrors, is better than life without the right to liberty & property."[31] Soldiers of the 9th Virginia Infantry and the 2nd Virginia Cavalry drafted their proclamations in an atmosphere of intense solipsism. The resolutions conveyed the belief that only soldiers made sacrifices and so were the only ones who had the authority to command the country to harder work. Their reception by noncombatants is not widely recorded, but few readers could have missed the disparaging comments directed at the home front.

Still, the spring 1865 resolutions reveal how profoundly Virginia soldiers drew upon protection of the home front as an inspiration to continue fighting. In late February, the 8th and 18th Virginia Infantries jointly drafted a resolution that reaffirmed the propriety of secession, mourned those already fallen in battle, and then articulated southerners' chief complaint against the North. "She," the resolution personified Virginia, "has seen her most fertile fields blackened by the cinders of burnt houses and granaries, help-less women and children driven from comfortable homes, and in some instances, the victims of a wrong, to which death is a mercy." "In a word," the report continued, "she has been subjected to everything . . . which could be suggested by the malice of enemies acknowledging no restrain but the limi-tations of their own ingenuity in acts of violence." The soldiers who drafted the resolution drew the necessary moral from this catalog of woes: "These wrongs make separation from those who perpetrated them, and the govern-ment which ordered and sanctioned them, a necessity from which neither regard for our honor, or safety allow escape, or alternative."[32] In the soldiers' eyes, at least, a deep unity of purpose and response demanded continued resistance.

Try as they might, Confederates knew that "determined resistance" alone would not bring victory. Instead, soldiers hoped that their actions on the battlefields would sway the northern presidential elec-tion. Virginians paid close attention to reports of discontent in the North in 1864 and anxiously awaited the results of the election that many believed would determine the fate of the war. As the Overland campaign had dragged on in the spring and casualty reports in towns around the Union mounted, northerners expressed a growing dissatisfaction with the price and course of the war. Northern Democrats, always hostile to Lincoln, saw the opportunity to regain control of the White House and nominated George B. McClellan, the former commander of the Union's Army of the Potomac. The selection pleased Confederates because it signaled a deep rift within the North over the proper goals of the war. Weary Confederates greatly preferred McClellan's conservatism, his weak support for emancipation, and, above all, the fact that his party's platform expressed a desire for the earliest possible peace to the policies adopted by the Lincoln administration.[33]

From their voracious reading of northern papers, many Confederates had taken an accurate gauge of northern temper. People in the North, though they had come to bitterly resent Confederates, had grown weary of war as well. With Richmond still defiant, many saw the Overland campaign as a gargantuan but deadly enterprise that yielded little in the way of actual ac-complishments. Confederates rightly suspected that the longer they could hold out in the summer of 1864, the more support McClellan would garner. One man went so far as to hope for Lincoln precisely because he anticipated that "his election will cause a revolution in the North West, while Maclellan, if elected, will be able to rally more men to the army than any other man can do."[34] As Democrats promoted an early end to the war, they pushed Mc-Clellan himself into an untenable position because he could not abandon the soldiers—his soldiers—who were still in the field. Still, his election looked promising until September 1, when William T. Sherman and his army captured Atlanta. The fall of the rail and industrial center dealt a major blow to the Confederacy, and northern hopes for a complete victory improved. Virginia soldiers knew that the reversal in Lincoln's fortunes stemmed from the Confederacy's military misfortunes. They also knew that the consequences would be dire. "I suppose King Abe has been reelected," one man wrote, "although we have not been able to hear yet. if so I suppose the war will continue four yrs longer."[35]

Because soldiers had long understood that their battlefield success mattered only if they inspired the right kind of political changes in the North, Sherman's capture of Atlanta and Sheridan's rout of the Valley Army convinced many that they might soon have to contemplate Confederate surrender. The defeats of September and October had left the Valley Army "much broken down and demoralized," as one soldier put it.[36] The final battle in the Valley briefly held out the promise of redemption, making ultimate Confederate defeat all the more confusing and painful. Confederate soldiers who participated in the battle of Cedar Creek on October 19 began their accounts with the glory of having surprised and routed Union forces. Victory slipped away when Sheridan rallied his troops. The Union reversed its morning losses and soundly defeated Early's troops for the third time in a month. Daniel A. Wilson, secure in New Market after the battle, felt overwhelmed by the enormity of the disaster at Cedar Creek and by the confusing reversal that had occurred. He wrote a lengthy letter to his former colonel, now working in the War Department in Richmond. As he described the battle, "Success is so blended with defeat—the shout of victory so mixed with the cry of 'all's lost' that I find myself totally unable to sift the details and place them upon paper in anything like form or method."[37] Like many soldiers, Wilson reveled in the surprise that Early's troops had sprung on the Union forces, but after describing how Confederates had stopped to loot the Union camp, Wilson was unable to account for how quickly they broke when the Union forces returned.

Confederate leaders saw that history and conviction could not defeat Grant's well-supplied army. Over the fall, Grant extended his lines farther south and west so that the Confederate defensive line thinned enough to break. Lee needed more men to keep his trenches formidable, and in October

1864 Virginia revoked all exemptions and pulled nearly 4,500 men into the army.[38] The success of this action revealed the efficiency of the Confederate conscription system, staffed by agents in localities all across the state. Further, the threat of a draft again stimulated men to volunteer lest they be stuck with the stigma of conscription. Frederick Bowen joined immediately, describing the process to his friend Charlie in glowing terms: "Since I wrote you last I have made important changes in my mode of life: you know how earnestly I have desired to enlist in the service of our beloved & suffering South, & the causes preventing my doing so." "They have at last been overcome," he announced proudly, "& I am now among that glorious army called 'Rebels,' among which you have been so long."[39]

Other men responded with more calculation and less enthusiasm than the young Fillison. Peter Guerrant, who served in the Confederate Engineer Corps, felt guilty about remaining in a soft position when other men, even relatives, risked their lives in the war. "I believe it is the duty of every citizen of the Confederacy who is capable of bearing arms, to be in the army & use every effort to assist in driving a hostile foe, who seeks our entire destruction &c. & the desolation of our homes," he stated. He wrote his uncle to seek his consent, who tried to talk him out of the decision. "If you could be satisfied," his uncle wrote, "your sister & myself think you had better stay where you are as long as you can. . . . As to your feeling an obligation to go in the army to fight you ought to reflect that you may be doing as much or more good for your country in your present position than you would at Chaffin's Bluff." After reading his uncle's harangue about the high casualty figures in a recent battle along the Petersburg-Richmond line, Guerrant divulged another motivation for changing branches of service. "The reason I spoke of going in the army is because we have all been conscripted & this is the reason we are detailed," Guerrant admitted. He "want[ed] to get rid of this conscript business, How would I feel if I should hear that every body in our neighborhood should know that I have been conscripted & sent to Camp Lee & be assigned to an Infantry Regiment of which I know nothing." Like many elite Virginians, Guerrant believed in the Confederacy but maintained a deeply rooted sense of class privilege when he considered the terms under which he would serve. Complaining about the civilians around him, who were, he believed, nearly all "submissionists," Guerrant displayed his aristocratic devotion to the Confederate cause. "How can they think of Union or Submission I can not conceive," he wrote, "They talk about union, when the blood of the best sons of the Confederacy has already tinged the land of our sunny South with human gore." This last argument succeeded, and Guerrant's uncle promised to go to Richmond to secure a place in a suitable unit, preferably in some position better than that "of a common soldier."[40]

Others, lacking the resources of the Guerrants, worried about how the poor would weather the coming winter. A Valley soldier, personally depressed over the recent death of his youngest child, agonized over how the remaining families would survive the coming winter. "We cant expect any thing but trouble in this world," he wrote, "times are hard and every thing is very scarce a great many will suffer for bread this winter Our army is moving up the vally & it is thought by some they wil give up the vally I am very tired of this war."[41] In Floyd County, in southwestern Virginia, a large group of soldiers had grown very tired as well. A sizable band of deserters roamed the mountains around Floyd, attacking Confederate troops and civilians alike. When the Confederate home guard counterattacked, the deserters organized themselves into a Unionist secret society known as the Heroes of America, which was also active in the mountains of North Carolina.[42] The pitched battles that ensued between Confederates and deserters demanded the attention of a preoccupied War Department in Richmond and symbolized, in dramatic form if limited scope, the divisions emerging within Confederate society.

As the new year of 1865 opened, more people began to see an end to the Confederate experiment. Lee's lines stretched thinly around Petersburg, and the men lived on quarter rations on good days. Federals controlled much of the Shenandoah Valley and almost all the Atlantic coastline. Farther south, Sherman's army captured Columbia, South Carolina, and moved north to close the trap around Lee. In late 1864, at Nashville and Franklin, Tennessee, John Bell Hood's Army of the Tennessee was nearly destroyed by Union general and Virginian George H. Thomas. Virginians following this news feared for their comrades in the West. William Andrews, with the 10th Virginia Artillery outside Richmond, consoled his concern over Hood's loss with the language of salvation. "It is truly a gloomy time with us but no cause for despair," Andrews wrote, "for the Bible tells us plainly that the race is not to the swift nor the battle to the strong and it is said that the darkest hour of the night is just before the dawn of day." In not uncommon language, Andrews predicted that when Confederates truly humbled themselves, victory would come. "Whenever we . . . feel our dependence on him then I believe our cause will brighten and the sunny bright days of peace will return."[43] Joseph E. Johnston rallied some of Hood's broken troops, but his army never presented a serious threat to Sherman's juggernaut. By late February 1865 the Army of Northern Virginia offered the last defense of the fledgling Confederacy. What had seemed remote as late as summer 1864 now seemed not just possible but likely: the Confederate States of America would not last.

The physical conditions for those Virginia soldiers still occupying the fetid trenches around Petersburg depressed even stouthearted veterans. In the Shenandoah Valley, where the remnants of Early's troops spent the winter, the army could no longer provision the soldiers. One man reported that he bartered his labor at woodcutting in exchange for flour with a local resident and then reflected on what this meant for the strength of his nation: "We are getting independent of the CS government for rations. Poor thing! She does the best she can for us."[44] Soldiers at Petersburg would have relished the chance to forage, but just leaving the trenches created grave risks from the snipers on either side who shot down men unlucky enough to rise above the narrow channels that ran between ditches. Periodic truces in sniping brought some relief, but the psychological damage of living under the threat of constant death had already taken its toll on many men. The reports of losses in other regions of the Confederacy only soured the atmosphere still further, as one man noted in his diary. "Our men are gloomy today over the fall of Sanannah, Ga, and we are discussing the probable death of the Confederacy at an early day."[45]

The majority of Virginia soldiers succumbed to the pressure of the Union offensive and began resigning themselves to defeat. James Bailey, in his camp in the Shenandoah Valley, admitted to his wife that if not given a furlough soon he would take one on his own accord. "We are putting up winter quarters now," Bailey reported, "and when we git in them I think we will git furlows to come home and if I dont git a furlow this winter I think I will hav to take won in the spring for I am a gitting verry tired of the war and I think the Confederacy is about gon up." Bailey did not refer to himself as a deserter and probably did not imagine himself that way. In his view, the army was collapsing, and consequently "it is no use fer me to stay when muste every boddy ses they ar a going."[46] Admitting that "the soldiers is badly whipped," Amon Updike offered a variety of causes: "We havent bin Paid in 6 Month . . . we dont git anuff to eat & from what I can learn the people at the border of starvation." In short, the strategy of logistical devastation practiced by Sherman and Grant was succeeding; the Confederate army was being driven to the point of exhaustion. "The south is badly whipped," Updike repeated as he hoped for a peaceful resolution of the war; "This war is a cruel thing and has ruined our Country." The consequences of the army's collapse showed itself all around him: "They is lots of men deserting & a good portion of them is going to the yankeys . . . they was about 23 left our Brigade one night not long since they is some leaves every night or two."[47]

Even with the steady drain of men that Updike reported, the army managed to maintain itself into March, at which point Grant began to press his numerical advantage with attacks on the Petersburg lines. Weakened by hunger and fear, the Confederates were no match for the Union troops. The exodus that Updike described became a flood. "Our men are deserting awful bad at this time," William Allen reported to his mother. "Before we moved down here our brigade deserted awfully. Three from Capt. Burks's deserted night before last. James M. Staton, Cliff Staton and Sim Staton all went to the Yankees, and there was several more went the same night. There was four more started and they were caught and brought back."[48] Allen anticipated that the men would be shot, in accordance with Confederate rules on desertion. Still, despite his continued presence in the army, he felt sympathy for the men. Updike too, managed to hang on, despite his consistent complaints and threat to leave. "It is mity hard times in the army we dont get near a nuf to eat." Like most soldiers, he was at least as worried about his family as he was about himself. "I was home in January and my wife writes to me that she has not had but two bushel and a half of corn since I was thar," he reported, "only what she has bought she is trading of her hogs for bread as to meet in our Country they dont have any than . . . I think starvation is near at hand." Updike's assessment reflected the success of Grant's strategy laid out at the beginning of the Overland campaign in May 1864: "They say we as whipped and they is no use in having any more men killed."[49]

As Grant tightened his hold on Petersburg in early 1865, more and more soldiers and civilians came to see Confederate defeat as likely. They did not, however, renounce the Confederacy's war goals. In fact, in an unintended sequence of events, the manner of Union warfare in Virginia in 1864–65 actually encouraged Confederates to pursue more aggressively their twin war aims of sectional independence and racial control. Given Virginia soldiers' experiences in the first three years of the war, their continued support through 1864 should come as no surprise. Virginia soldiers derived enormous confidence from their victories over Yankees for most of the year. They began the year not merely hoping for victory but also expecting and assuming that independence lay just ahead. Further, many Confederate soldiers in Virginia fought to protect their homes as well as their new nation. In late October, after Sheridan's defeat of Early, most Virginia Confederates grew quite concerned about their prospects, but they did not cease being Confederates.[50]

Richard Waldrop, a soldier with the 21st Virginia Infantry, embodied the transformation many Confederate Virginians experienced during the war. In the fall, he described to his wife the effectiveness of Sheridan's logistical raids in the Valley while unconsciously revealing that Sheridan failed in his larger goal of overawing pro-Confederate sentiment. He reported that "the Yankees have played sad havoc here: having burnt all the mills, barns, & workshops in their reach & night before last the country below here was illuminated by the burning houses. It is very trying to us to have to stand & look at their vandalism & not be able on account of our small numbers to punish them for their scoundrelism & relive our people from the galling trials to which they are subjected."[51] Waldrop's concern revealed the successful consolidation of Confederate identity that had occurred over the war. In 1861 he had been posted to the Northwest, where he complained bitterly about the land, the climate, and the people. Were it not that "the Yankees might get to Richmond through this way [the valley]," he had pronounced in 1861, "they are welcome to the whole country."[52] Over the course of the war, and especially in the context of what seemed to him, and others, like egregious violations of the code of civilized war, he could now speak unselfconsciously about "our people" and mean western Virginians as well. This curious and entirely unintended side effect of Sheridan's raids mirrored the reactions Virginians expressed after the battle of Fredericksburg in 1862. The dramatic suffering of one region helped mobilize support for the Confederacy as a whole.

Among soldiers and civilians, Union depredations in 1864 exacerbated already deep-seated antipathies toward the North that formed a component of their attachment to the Confederacy as their nation. Soldiers remained members of their home communities throughout the war, reflecting the same fears and hatreds as civilians. Like Henry Robinson Berkeley and the fiery civilian Mathella Page Harrison, Charles Minor Blackford reacted with anger rather than despair when he heard that Union troops were approaching his hometown of Lynchburg in June. From camp near Richmond, he wrote to his wife, "To think that my whole family, wife, child, mother, sister, are probably this very morning subjected to the insults and indignities of a band of freebooters makes my blood boil."[53] Confederate identity, like that in most fledgling nations, drew great strength from its opposition to the North, and the people who built that identity drew effectively on their rivalry with the Union to mask internal dissent and conflict. The animosity generated by the conflict left most Confederates unable to contemplate life in a reunited America, even if they had not cherished every aspect of the Confederacy. One soldier's letter to a friend in Fluvanna County captured the attitude of many: "I fear we are to be overrun & made to yield to Yankee rule. In preference to which I would rather be exterminated as a government and as a people. I have no desire to survive our defeat as a nation on such terms as we may expect from the Yankees."[54]

Very few Virginia soldiers took any satisfaction from the killing they had to perform, but as the strategy of exhaustion waged by the North increased, most advocated a more brutal response. In mid-October Henry Morrison wrote, "The Yankees have utterly desolated this & adjoining counties, burning every barn & wheat stack & in some instances burning the shocks of corn in the field. Cattle & hogs were shot down and left lying in the fields." Like Richard Waldrop, Morrison savored reports of vengeance: "A more infamous set of barbarians never yet cursed this earth with their existence. I rejoiced to hear that our cavalry caught some dozen or more of the barn burners & deliberately shot them after disarming them." At the start of the campaign season in 1864, Morrison had bemoaned his own role in bringing death into the world; he was now eager to participate. "I want to see no more yankee prisoners from Sheridan's command. Death and death alone will end their villainous conduct."[55]

An event earlier in the year outside Richmond had kindled the same sentiments among other Virginians. A small group of Yankee cavalry had been captured just outside the capital and on the body of the colonel was found a plan to take the city with brutal force. As one man reported to his wife, the paper "showed to our people the villains intentions if they could of succeeded. They had for their main object to try & release the prisoners that we hold of theirs at Richmond at the Libby prison & then they was going to murder Jeff Davis & his cabinet & all the leading men of Richmond & then plunder & take off what they could & then burn the city down regardless of the women & children or anything else."[56] Henry Robinson Berkeley, who served in a Virginia artillery battalion, dreamed of a new world even in the midst of his unit's retreat up the Valley in late September. "We are ready to measure strength again with these vile yanks. I don't see why they dont go home & leave us alone," he wrote. "But here they are with a vile mercenary army, burning our towns, destroying our crops, desolating our country and killing our people. I wish all the yanks & all the negroes were in Affrica."[57]

Although Berkeley's dream of permanent sectional and racial separation would not come to pass, two episodes in early 1865 revealed the reluctance of Virginia Confederates to accept the political consequences of military defeat. In February 1865 a peace commission sent to negotiate with northern officials briefly raised expectations that Confederates would end the war satisfactorily. One soldier reported excitedly on the procession as the commissioners passed his battery on their way north. "Our peace commissioners are here going over in front of our Battery and the soldiers are crawling to and fro to see them The top of the breastworks are full for a mile welcoming them with loud yells. You never saw such an excitement in your life I do hope they will do something this time."[58] The prospect of an end to the fighting entranced the tired soldiers.

Private John Gwyn of the 26th Virginia Infantry watched the commissioners head north more skeptically. "V Pres Stevens, Judge Campbell, Senator Hunter passed through our lines on there way to Washington to see if there were prospects of Peace," he noted, "—they go unofficially just as Blair came to Richmond—their efforts may lead to a cessation of hostilities— May be to peace—But I fear that the Yankee nation is too self confident, too arrogant and boastful of its late succefs to treat just now." Gwyn guessed correctly, as many hopeful Confederate soldiers seemed unable to do, that the North had no reason to negotiate a peace weaker than what they could achieve with military victory. Instead, Gwyn advocated continued war: "Another campaign might bring them to their senses—we in the army want peace pray for peace—but it must be a final peace one giving us Independence—no unionist or reconstructionists here—we are not willing that the blood of the thousands or our brave boys should have been poured out like water in vain—we are not willing to sacrifice one iota of the principle for which we have been contending during the past four years." Gwyn's comments revealed the powerful inertia generated by the war, a force that sustained men in the service through the hardships and defeats of late 1864. Like many soldiers, Gwyn remained committed to the goal of southern independence. "True we suffer," he concluded, "and have endured much—but we will suffer the direst extremes and endure the greatest calamities—aye extermination itself rather than be the supplicant for peace upon any terms other than these which guarantee to us and our heir forever."[59] The party sent to treat with Lincoln and Seward returned empty-handed. The conditions of peace offered by the North—the permanent emancipation of all slaves and the reunion of the states   represented exactly those elements against which Confederates had been fighting for four years.

The failure of the mission angered soldiers, surprised that the North would offer peace on such insulting terms. George Coiner relayed the temper of his unit in a short letter to his sister: "You have heard I presume of the return of the peace commissioners and their success. The movement was attended with about as much success as I predicted. It looks as though we care to fight on for the last ray of hope for our early peace seems to have vanished as quickly as it sprung." Coiner drew a distinctly Confederate lesson from the failure of the peace conference: its failure meant a longer war. "The peace movement on the part of the Yankees was a scheme to dishearten and demoralize our army," he wrote. "If so, I fear they have been partly successful. Our troops were very much elated at the idea of a negotiation for peace but since it has turned out as it has, the disappointment is truly very great. And the prospect for four years more of bloody war is very discouraging indeed."[60]

Charles James gloried in the proclamations drawn up by many Confederate units after the failure of the commissioners. He reported: "I now feel as I felt in June /61 when I first enlisted in this army—in February /62 when I reenlisted for two years or the war—and in February /64 when I again reenlisted for the war." He admitted the reverses they had experienced in 1864 but blamed desertions on newspapers spreading traitorous rumors. James had little use for Jefferson Davis. What remained of Confederate hopes for independence lay with the soldiers themselves, who had been steeled to action by the arrogant treatment of the peace commissioners. "Lincoln and Seward met them at Fortress Monroe and told them that nothing but unconditional surrender would be accepted. That is would lay down our arms—go to our homes and submit to the laws of the Washington government; in other words have our property confiscated, our slaves emancipated, our leaders hung, and we become serfs in the land of our fathers, then he (Abraham 1st) might exercise his pardoning power with liberality. We have the alternatives of submission or war."[61] James and the other remaining Confederate soldiers would soon suffer submission, but they would not accept, even in defeat, the conditions laid down by the North. The surprise and anger among Confederates who followed the peace conference revealed the lasting commitment to the ideals that brought the Confederacy together in 1861.

The second issue that catalyzed Confederates' resistance to accepting defeat was the debate over enlisting slaves in the Confederate armies. The centrality of slavery to the Confederate war effort was assumed by most though rarely articulated. Richard Watkins underscored this aspect of the Confederacy in an observation he made to his wife in the fall of 1864. In passing along his observations on the morale of Valley residents, Watkins noted, "We find the people in the Valley still loyal I am greatly surprised at this for a large majority of them are without slaves very many never having owned them and their habits & mode of living is almost Yankee." As slaves and Federals attacked slavery from inside and outside the system, the habits of all Virginians became more "Yankee." The emancipation of Virginia's

500,000 enslaved African Americans steadily proceeded from the first days of war, but Confederates clung to the idea that defeat of the North would preserve the institution.[62]

The reality came gradually to individual white Virginians, as their slaves seized opportunities to escape or aid the progress of the Union army. At that point, most fell back on the stereotype of the childish African, easily confused and tricked by the wily Yankees. The distinguished professor of law, John Minor, who taught at the University of Virginia, reported in March that "the enemy got upwards of 100 horses between Meechum's river and this place, and multitudes of servants went off with them, poor misguided creatures! Amongst them my boy Henry, hired in Staunton. I lament it more on his account that my own."[63] Minor no doubt felt genuinely sorry for Henry, because the professor imagined that his former slave would now have to contend with a far less generous set of masters. The prospect that emancipated slaves apparently might remain in Virginia apparently did not occur to Minor, though for those who lived in other parts of Virginia or the South, this was of major concern. A Maryland man who had served with a Virginia unit since the start of the war inquired at home about the progress of emancipation. "How do you get along since the darkeys were set free," he asked, "bad enough I suppose." Before most Virginians were directly confronted with this problem, he had already recognized the constraint of being so far away from what he considered a dangerous situation, and advised his family, "I would like very much to be at home since they have all been set free, for I know my services are very much needed."[64]

As Confederate officials pondered the problems of their likely defeat and the severe manpower shortage, a joint solution emerged: enlisting black men as Confederate soldiers. First offered as a serious policy by Confederate general Patrick R. Cleburne in early 1864, the Richmond leadership had buried the idea, but renewed calls began to be made in late 1864. When it was made known publicly that Robert E. Lee advocated the idea, momentum carried it through the Confederate Congress. Richard Lancelot Maury, the former colonel of the 24th Virginia Infantry, who had been injured in recent fighting and was confined to his apartment in Richmond, felt swayed by Lee's endorsement. "This Negro Soldier question is the great one of the day—and its supporters have increased very rapidly lately—it is hard for us to bring ourselves to it and I for one would rather wait a little longer before calling in their aid—but General Lee says he wants them, and so give them to him I say—What ever that great and good soldier wants give him in Heavens name." Though skeptical, Maury sensed the terrific need driving the policy.[65]

Lee derived his argument for enlisting slave soldiers solely from military necessity. In a letter to a member of the Virginia General Assembly, Lee explained his reasoning. The North wanted to turn slaves into soldiers and then into citizens. "His progress will thus add to his numbers," Lee noted, "and at the same time destroy slavery in a manner most pernicious to the welfare of our people." Paramount for Lee was designing a policy that would preserve some semblance of white control in the South. "Whatever may be the effect of our employing negro troops," he wrote, "it cannot be as mischievous as this." Lee feared the social consequences of unregulated emancipation and the military consequences of a northern army of free blacks. He closed, "I think therefore we must decide, whether slavery shall be extinguished by our enemies, and the slaves be used against us, or use them ourselves at the risk of the effects which may be produced upon our social institutions."[66] Time, and Grant's army, had distilled the debate down into a simple proposition: use slaves as soldiers to continue fighting for independence or surrender with the dignity of never having abandoned the interest that distinguished North from South. With so stark a choice, independence finally emerged as the most important single goal. As the *Marion Ensign*, a small southwestern newspaper, asserted in late 1864, "we believe we are in the right; we only ask to be left alone."[67]

Most Confederate Virginians accepted the new policy. At a public meeting in Lynchburg, in late February, citizens passed a resolution urging their representatives to approve the enlistment of black soldiers. The committee report on the matter recognized the differences among citizens over the propriety, method, and goals of such a policy, but it advocated support because it recognized "our independence to be paramount to all other considerations." Most soldiers agreed as well. William Andrews, stationed at Chaffin's Farm, below Richmond, wrote his father late in February and took heart in the idea of black soldiers. Though he lamented the fall of Columbia and Charleston, South Carolina, Andrews imagined a newly manned army under P. G. T. Bureaugard that would help protect the capital. "I think Congress will put two hundred thousand negroes in the field. I learn that Genl Lee has called for that number and Congress will be certain to give him whatever he asks for."[68]

The willingness of Confederates to accept the idea of black soldiers reveals the desperation of the Confederate cause by February 1865. As one Virginia civilian argued, "What do you all think of our having Negroes to fight for our independence; what a back down it is on the part of our Government. I really think the South must be pretty far done if she has to have Negroes for soldiers."[69] But evidence that Virginians held deep concerns about the prospects for victory in early 1865 does not support the thesis that those same people had abandoned the Confederacy. The decision to enlist black soldiers also reflects the ability of Virginians to modify their war goals and yet remain consistent on values underlying those goals. For Confederates, this meant abandoning their defense of slavery but not their commitment to racial supremacy. That Virginia Confederates would embrace such a serious challenge to the institution that had necessitated secession in the first place in order to preserve their independence seems remarkable evidence of the depth of the latter desire.[70]

The centrality of the issue of slavery to secession and the eagerness with which Lee's soldiers defended the institution during the war offer ample testimony that Alexander Stephens was right when he asserted that slavery served as the "cornerstone" of the new Confederacy. Accepting the enlistment of black soldiers was not equivalent to ending slavery, but it was a world away from Stephens's conception of the proper racial order. This shift in opinion reveals the ability of Virginians to create a new Confederate order, one that built upon and then superseded the southern order that began the war. The soldiers opposing Grant's army from the trenches of Petersburg in early 1865 were not the same people who had formed the Confederacy in 1861. During the course of the war, they had built a vibrant culture of nationalism. They had endured hardship, a hard war, and death that bound them together through shared sacrifice. Soldiers had redefined their masculine obligations to their families, finding in their private relations a source of motivation for continued involvement in the war. The collapse of slavery forced a final transformation. It spurred whites to see that their racial superiority transcended any particular historical institution and inspired them to identify a new cornerstone. The foundation of the post–Civil War South was not racial bondage but the memory of a principled and courageous pursuit of independence. It was this ability of Confederates to adapt and transform their sense of purpose that sustained the Civil War.

Epilogue ★ SWALLOWING THE
ELEPHANT TOWARD THE NEW SOUTH

We could not remain at home unless we took the oath. This we had
made up our minds to do, so in we went and swallowed the elephant.
   —*Edgar Tschiffel, July 8, 1865*

The Federals opened a coordinated attack on Petersburg from all directions in the early morning of April 2, and Lee retreated to avoid complete destruction. With the loss of Petersburg, Richmond lay undefended. Confederates frantically packaged official papers and supplies and shipped them south. With the government stored in crates on a freight train, Lee's army remained the last active presence of the Confederate state. His troops had little energy left to fight. Creed Davis recorded the retreat as the procession of an already beaten army. "Richmond is certainly evacuated and our army is in full retreat, whither no one knows, sickness, hunger, and privation of every kind has completely demoralized the army—or rather the handfull of men left Genl Lee."[1] John Walters issued a similarly solemn assessment, noting, "I fear that the last day for the Army of Northern Virginia is near at hand."[2] On April 3, the U.S. Army seized control of Richmond.[3] Abraham Lincoln arrived in person the following day, greeted by thousands of cheering African Americans. Their control of the public space in the capital of a nation devoted to maintaining slavery signaled the end of the Confederacy in a way as profound as Lee's surrender several days later.

Lee's Confederates marched west, seeking rations and escape from the Union army. They found neither. On April 6 a Union force caught a portion of Lee's army. The resulting battle at Saylor's Creek produced 7,000 Confederate casualties. The army also deteriorated from the unauthorized exit of men. Beginning with the fall of Richmond, soldiers departed at a rapid rate. Several thousand men, mostly Virginians and North Carolinians, took opportunities along the retreat to leave the army and return home. Just as they had at the war's start, these soldiers acted on their enlistment as a contract with the state; the imminent defeat of the army ended their service. As Lee's army moved west away from Richmond, soldiers abandoned it in direct proportion to the proximity of their homes. Virginians lived the closest and they left the army in the highest numbers.[4] On April 9 Union cavalry and infantry blocked the main body of Lee's army at Appomattox. Lee accepted the surrender terms offered by Grant, ending the war in Virginia.

Confederates pursued independence from the North through four years of war. Like secession, independence was not an end in itself, or even a justification for acting, but rather a means to secure for southerners the autonomy to create a society of their own design. Confederates desired political freedom, protection of slavery, and economic autonomy. The men who became soldiers remained as broadly committed to accomplishing these objectives as the civilians they left at home. Unfortunately for southerners, their pursuit of independence through the war undermined many of these goals. The cumulative impact of war policies designed by Confederate leaders eroded the reasons for which Confederates sought independence. The centralizing measures undertaken by the Richmond government, beginning with the draft and extending through impressment, the tax-in-kind, and price schedules, generated skepticism about the extent of political freedom southerners would possess under the new system. Complaints about the policies and behavior of the central government began in 1861 and continued through the war's end. The Union's hard war and the opportunities offered to enslaved southerners to emancipate themselves initiated the destruction of slavery that Confederates resisted until Appomattox and beyond. Likewise, the destruction of Virginia's physical infrastructure—its bridges, railroads, factories, and fields—generated enormous hardships for all Virginians.

From a historical perspective, the contradictions and inconsistencies of the Confederate experience seem obvious. Hindsight also makes it impossible to ignore the tremendous destructive power that the North brought to bear in its effort to win the war. This knowledge makes it difficult to understand why white southerners fought the war. Popular treatments of this topic, with their relentless focus on abstractions like courage, honor, and state rights, only serve to complicate the task. In addition, a sympathetic analysis of people who fought to perpetuate racial slavery is a tall order. Yet these challenges are precisely why we have so much to gain from investigating their experience.

The value of history lies in trying to explain situations and decisions that we cannot instinctively understand. In this study, it has meant explaining why most white Virginians supported the Confederacy. Central to this task is recognizing that Virginians' understandings of the war evolved as the war itself changed. The passions of 1861 yielded to a conception of the war as a battle for the preservation of soldiers' families. This perspective did not solve all problems. Soldiers continued to fear for their families, and some left the army because of that fear. Others left because they did not feel that the war served their interests. But a significant majority of Virginians remained committed to Confederate independence. They did so because the world promised by the Confederacy served their interests and because the Union's wartime policies targeted those interests directly. Emancipation and hard war may have weakened Confederates' ability to fight, but by threatening the racial and social order of the South they also inspired more resistance. Virginians supported the Confederacy not in spite of the hardships of war but because of them.

With defeat, the changes produced during the war assumed an ominous significance. Among the most obvious effects of four years of conflict were deep animosities between northerners and southerners. The mythology of Appomattox as a site of national reconciliation obscures the reality that it was a place of conquest and defeat. Union and Confederate commanders separated their men with armed guards because they worried violence might break out. Over the several days following Lee's surrender on April 9, activity at Appomattox remained routine and bureaucratic. The day of the official surrender, so grandly represented in later postwar accounts, elicited little emotion from the exhausted Confederates.[5] One man reported, "soon after sunrise this morning the 2d Corps . . . marched over to Appomattox C.H. and stacked arms in front of a corps of the enemy. Were then marched back to camp. Remained there until noon when I was furnished with blank paroles for the 19th Batt."[6] James Phillips was even more succinct. His full diary entry for April 12 read: "Still on Flood's Farm. Day rainy & disagreeable. We have no rations for two days. I went to see Mrs. Weeks. She gave me some bread & meat. We got our parols about 9 o'clock at night. We gave up our guns at the Court House."[7] Phillips's account reveals the attitude of many Confederates on the eve of peace; he surrendered his gun but not himself.

Virginians maintained resistance to the war's outcome for as long as they could. In July 1865 Edgar Tschiffel wrote to a friend in the upper Shenandoah Valley and captured the humiliation and difficulty of accepting defeat by extending the analogy of "seeing the elephant" that soldiers used to describe their first time in battle. Tschiffel and a friend had ridden north into Maryland, where they were stopped by Union soldiers "who informed us that we could not remain at home unless we took the oath. This we had made up our minds to do, so in we went and swallowed the elephant."[8] The impossibility of the literal image reflected the impossibility of what the Union expected in victory.

The destruction of slavery, the renunciation of secession, the political submission to Republican control, and the personal disgrace of suffering defeat by northerners layered on top of the physical destruction of large parts of the region demanded a humility that Confederates were unable and unwilling to muster. The North wished reunion with a reformed South; what it earned was an uneasy alliance with an embittered and vengeful southern nation. Tschiffel concluded his account by describing another interchange with the hated Yankees that revealed his ability to carve out some space for opposition even in defeat. "When we came out we found a guard at our horses who informed us that all government property had to be left there," he explained. "Hunter insisted that we should be allowed to ride our saddles home, but they refused they took our saddles and spurs We were then 19 miles from home, but did not mind that. We mounted our horses and in a little more than 2 hours we were home once more, as for our uniforms we were allowed to wear them, and are yet if we choose."[9] As this old soldier revealed, four years of fighting inhibited the ability of Virginia Confederates to shed their wartime identities and impeded the reintegration of the South into the nation.[10]

Edgar Tschiffel's irritable refusal to recognize the defeat of his army demonstrated the depth of the emotional commitment that most soldiers had made to their martial lives. Although these men retained close ties with their families and home communities throughout the war, the psychological experience of soldiering permanently altered how they saw the world. Active participation in battles demanded that men reconcile themselves to killing, and for many Christian soldiers in particular, this proved especially difficult.[11] The long entrenchment at Petersburg immobilized soldiers, and the result was increasing alienation from civilian practices and ways of thinking. Soldiers returned to their homes and most became productive members of society, but we still know surprisingly little about how this adjustment proceeded.[12] New studies that follow soldiers and their families into the postwar years promise to enrich our understanding of how people absorb the trauma of war and how that experience shapes their values and lives after conflict.

The most revolutionary change came with the end of slavery. As a young Confederate clerk described, "the *abolition of slavery* . . . is the most marked feature of this conquest of the South." From the crisis of secession through the debates over slave soldiers, white Virginians had made protection of the institution of slavery a central war aim. The clerk who described the impact of emancipation maintained his faith in racial supremacy after the surrender at Appomattox. "Manumission . . . will be regarded hereafter," he wrote, "as the greatest social crime ever committed on the earth."[13] The irony that emancipation succeeded only because the Confederates fought so long and so hard failed to impress most Virginians. Few white residents displayed any sense of compassion or concern for black Virginians. Instead, as the pressures of war impinged upon the privileges of slaveholding, masters focused narrowly on control. As late as January 1865, the governor received a petition from residents of Augusta County asking that he suspend a recent requisition for 100 slaves from the county to work on fortifications. Citing the large number of slaves already lost "by the invasion of the public enemy," and the difficulty this loss of labor imposed upon the county's ability to grow food, the petitioners pleaded for an exemption.[14] At the start of the war, one-quarter of Augusta households owned slaves (the southern average in 1860), and it lay within the low-slaveholding Shenandoah Valley.[15] The resistance of Augusta residents to the deterioration of the institution at this late stage in the war revealed just how deeply rooted southerners' interests in slavery ran.

The persistent and frequently successful efforts of enslaved Virginians to break free of their bondage during the war and the variety of ways that black southerners aided the Union war effort infuriated white Virginians. The shock experienced by slaveholders when they realized their slaves did not offer absolute loyalty shattered the paternalistic demeanor that had partially muted the most violent aspects of the slave system. White Virginians had imagined all African Americans, enslaved or free, as docile and submissive. During the war, enslaved Virginians had played a key role in guiding and advising Union armies to their victories in 1864 and 1865.[16] These experiences prompted ex-Confederates to view their former slaves as enemies.

The war also reinforced changes that had been occurring in the antebellum South, principally in the emphasis on men's familial connections as the most important relations they maintained.[17] Importantly, however, the war fundamentally altered the nature of those connections. In the prewar world, love and affection provided their own rewards within the world of southern families. The experience of fighting enshrined martial violence as the purest expression of love. Two related factors drove this change. Soldiers themselves grew numb to the fact of maiming and killing other men, and soldiers increasingly explained their participation in the war in terms of protection of their loved ones. The result was a new masculinity, one that required both affection and hostility, the former directed toward one's family and the latter directed toward its enemies. To a certain degree, northern soldiers participated in the same shift in values, but the relief of victory and its confirmation of prewar values muted the transforming effect of the war.

In the South, the cult of memory that diminished the sting of defeat after the war reinforced the necessity of violence as a demonstration of love. The result was a southern masculinity that differed even more sharply from the national ethos than before the war.[18]

During the conflict, men identified their interest in their families as paramount. The North's style of warfare and occupation targeted southern families and sought to pit family and national interests directly against one another. As suffering and deprivation increased on the home front, soldiers increasingly identified the army as the most effective institution for protecting their own. They did not abandon their responsibility to defend their families; rather, they believed they could accomplish that duty most effectively within the army.[19] Virginians did not abandon the Confederate nationalism they created in 1861–62. Instead, they came to express their reasons for fighting in more immediate and more personally compelling terms. Southern independence remained the object for which they contended because it promised to preserve the world that had served them so well.[20]

Virginians' tenacity on the battlefield belies the simplistic notion that they fought solely for the defense of a loving family. Their antebellum families were organized within a slave society and the two were inseparable, as Virginians recognized. The interdependence of Virginians' intimate households and the slave society that sustained them compelled Virginians to reject return to the Union. Appreciating this historical reality helps explain why Confederates fought for their independence with such determination. Understanding the perspectives of the participants themselves adds another layer of explanation to this story. Historians can see the extent to which the freedom of southern white men rested on the dependency of others, but very few white men were able to perform this act of imagination. Instead, the growing importance of intimate emotional relations within families gave men a tangible experience upon which to base a sense of motivation derived more from love and virtue than from honor and oppression.

It is here that investigating the Confederate experience generates true value. The fact that Virginia men could, and did, explain their participation in the Civil War in a diverse assortment of ways created a broader foundation for war and one easier to reconcile with moral and religious imperatives. In terms of explaining why the war was as violent as it was and lasted as long as it did, we must consider motives as well as causes because motives sustained people through the war. This study has sought to show that Virginians developed a sophisticated and compelling set of motivations, though not necessarily the ones that we would imagine or that have been emphasized in the historical literature. In the popular democracy that was the Confederacy, these values and perspectives developed out of the lived experience of individuals rather than being foisted on people by elites. The Confederate experience teaches us to evaluate skeptically the ways that we understand and explain people's motivations, particularly those that involve armed conflict. Wars are among the most complicated human endeavors and, because of this, one of the least predictable. In the Civil War, the harder the North fought, the more vigorously the Confederacy resisted. Confederate Virginians, for their part, organized a spirited defense of their society, and it produced ruin and catastrophe. The experience of Virginia should remind us that not only will perceptions of wars' causes and consequences almost certainly change as the conflicts themselves evolve, but what may appear as rational and moral at the time may not appear so in retrospect.

Appendix ✳ METHODOLOGY

My initial goal was to determine how many men from Virginia enlisted in Confederate military service and to identify the counties in which those men enlisted. Most historians use the number from the Official Records (153,876). Although this number misses the men who enlisted in 1864 (unlikely to be no more than 2 percent of total enlistments), it seems reasonable to assume that the Conscription Bureau, at a crucial point in the war, would calculate the numbers of men each state had contributed (and consequently had left to contribute) with a fair degree of accuracy. Almost all of the unit histories in the *Virginia Regimental History Series* (Lynchburg, Va.: H. E. Howard, 1982–) (hereafter *VRHS*) noted the total number of men enlisted in each regiment. Adding these numbers, however, produces an inflated total because of company transfers and regimental reorganizations that occurred throughout the war.

I created a database with county totals in order to eliminate duplication where I could. In order to identify the county origin of all companies (and to note which companies were double-counted in regimental totals), I cross-referenced Lee A. Wallace Jr.'s *A Guide to Virginia Military Organizations, 1861–1865*, 2nd. ed.(Lynchburg, Va.: H. E. Howard, 1986) with the individual unit histories from the *VRHS*. Stewart Sifakis's *Compendium of the Confederate Armies*, vol. 1: *Virginia* (New York: Facts on File, 1992) provided useful cross-reference information on the artillery batteries, which he lists by county instead of the traditional practice of identifying them by captain's name. Finally, I needed to identify company-level totals for each county. Forty of the *VRHS* unit histories included exact enlistment numbers by company. For the remaining units, I divided the regimental total evenly among the number of companies that filled each regiment. By averaging the company sizes, I maintained the accuracy of the regimental total but flattened out discrepancies in enlistment numbers from the different counties that contributed companies (on the positive side, my estimated company sizes are roughly similar to the exact company totals I pulled from the *VRHS* unit histories). My county totals offer a close degree of accuracy for each region (if we assume that few men traveled more than a county or two away to enlist) and a fair degree of accuracy for each county.

The average infantry regiment held 1,416 soldiers, yielding a total of 97,732 for the state.[1] The average cavalry unit held 1,349 soldiers, yielding a total of 45,859 for the state.[2] The average artillery unit held 185 soldiers, yielding a total of 20,986 for the state.[3] Added together, this yields a figure of 164,577 for Virginia, but this fails to consider transfers and repeat enlistments. My count by county reduces the duplication of units reassigned and drops the overall number to 155,231 (a little less than 1 percent above the official estimate cited above).

The Confederate Conscription Bureau's estimate of troop strength included a calculation of how many men each state *could have* sent, according to the 1860 census. For Virginia, it estimated 221,000 men between the ages of 18–45, but it included no notes on how it reached this number (the 1860 census included age cohorts 15–20, 20–30, 30–40, etc.) In order to calculate my base number of possible enlistees (249,805), I counted white men between the ages of 15 and 50 in 1860, figuring that this would include those men who reached the minimum of age of enlistment during the war while only omitting the small number of men older than age 55 who served in regular Confederate service. I relied upon the statistics the Conscription Bureau used to estimate the number of men who were unavailable for service because of Union occupation of parts of Virginia (49,961) and the total number of men exempted by Confederate draft officials (25,603). Thus, I calculated the percentage of *eligible* Virginia men who served in Confederate forces as follows: 155,231/(249,805 − (49,961+25,603))= 89 percent.

All of the census information in the database was obtained as a digital file through the Geospatial and Statistical Data Center at the University of Virginia.

The Virginia legislature created Bland County in 1861, so the 1860 census has no separate data for it. Confederate records credit the county with raising several companies of men for the war; I distributed these men between Giles, Wythe, and Tazewell, the counties from which Bland was formed. Following the 1860 census format, I included Petersburg in Dinwiddie County and Richmond in Henrico County, leaving Alexandria as the only independent city.

In order to gain a more detailed perspective on the patterns of enlistment, desertion, and service among Virginia soldiers, I also created a database of individual soldiers. For this group, I culled a stratified random sample of Virginia men who enlisted in Confederate armed forces. The sample is stratified by region with the weight for allocating men within the sample determined by the proportion of enlisted soldiers from each region. From a total sample size of 993 men, Tidewater had 278; Piedmont, 258; Valley, 203; Southwest, 196; and Northwest, 58. For the sampling formula, I used the enlistment rate for each region.

Using the regimental enlistment totals I drew from the *VRHS* (and imputed for those missing data), I assigned each regiment to a region. Most regiments were composed of companies from the same region. I assigned those regiments with companies from more than one region to the region within which a plurality of companies were organized (for regiments too mixed to reasonably determine a regional base, I labeled them "mixed" and pulled them from consideration for sampling purposes). I created enlistment totals for each region based on those regiments identified. I then used a random-number generator to select the appropriate number of cases for each region. I then counted through each of the units sequentially (because I had unit totals), beginning with artillery, then cavalry, then infantry. I selected individuals by counting through the rosters of each of the designated regimental histories, beginning with a different letter of the alphabet (in order) for each unit.

To find the allocations, I used the following formula:[4]

$$n = \frac{\sum_{i=1}^{5} \frac{N_i^2 p_i q_i}{w_i}}{N^2 D + \sum_{i=1}^{5} N_i p_i q_i}$$

I inserted 1 for c_i because the cost of sampling the strata does not vary. I used total enlistment as the weight because enlisted men are the population I want to sample and enlistment ratios as the proportion.

Once individual cases were identified from rosters, I entered all the service information given for each soldier in the database. This material forms the basis for the conclusions I have drawn regarding service experience, such as rates of wounding, capture, desertion, and death. The next step was to link soldiers in the sample to the census, in order to obtain individual socioeconomic and demographic information. Owing to inconsistencies in spelling and movement, this proved very difficult to do reliably. The first step was to identify the residences of men in the sample. First, I looked at county of residence and if none was available I used county of enlistment. For those residences or enlistment places, for which I had only place-names, I identified the counties using the Geostat on-line gazetteer http://fisher.lib.virginia .edu/collections/gis/vagaz/accessed on July 5, 2004.[5] In cases where the regimental history did not specify a count or place of enrollment in the roster,

I assigned a county of enlistment based on other soldiers who enlisted in the same company or using the county designations given in the narratives of the regimental histories.

If I found a name and county match for a soldier in the census, I used that record. If I could not be sure that the individual listed in the census was, in fact, the person listed in the roster, I did not include relevant census information. The result was that of the 1,000 soldiers in the sample, I was able to link only 200 men to the census. For those parts of the analysis that rely on census figures, the results should be considered illustrative but not representative in a statistical sense (as I have noted at the relevant places in the text).

I created the maps in this study using ERSI ArcView and ArcMap software. For the statistical measurements, I used the Statistical Package for the Social Sciences.

NOTES

ABBREVIATIONS

CWH *Civil War History*

DSC Duke University Special Collections, Perkins Library, Durham, North Carolina

HEH Henry Huntington Library, San Marino, California

JSH *Journal of Southern History*

MHI Military History Institute, U.S. Army War College, Carlisle, Pennsylvania

OR *The War of the Rebellion: The Official Records of the Union and Confederate Armies*

SHC Southern Historical Collection, University of North Carolina, Chapel Hill

UVa Special Collections, Alderman Library, University of Virginia, Charlottesville

VHS Virginia Historical Society, Richmond

VMHB *Virginia Magazine of History and Biography*

VMI Special Collections, Virginia Military Institute, Lexington

VoS *Valley of the Shadow*, University of Virginia, Charlottesville

VT Special Collections, Virginia Polytechnic Institute and State University, Blacksburg

INTRODUCTION

1 Among the most important recent treatments of Civil War soldiers are James M. McPherson, *For Cause and Comrades: Why Men Fought in the Civil War* (New York: Oxford University Press, 1997); Reid Mitchell, *Civil War Soldiers: Their Expectations and Their Experiences* (New York: Touchstone, 1988) and *The Vacant Chair: The Northern Soldier Leaves Home* (New York: Oxford University Press, 1993); Earl J. Hess, *The Union Soldier in Battle: Enduring the Ordeal of Combat* (Lawrence: University of Kansas Press, 1997); Joseph T. Glatthaar, *The March to the Sea and Beyond: Sherman's Troops in the Savannah and Carolinas Campaigns* (New York: New York University Press, 1985); and Randall C. Jimerson, *The Private Civil War: Popular Thought during the Sectional Conflict* (Baton Rouge: Louisiana State University Press, 1988).

2 This figure comes from a database I assembled that includes information on aggregate levels of enlistment and population by county. I also assembled a second database, drawn from a sample of Virginia soldiers. All of the quantitative evi-

dence offered in the text is drawn from these databases, unless otherwise noted. Details on the methodology of both databases can be found in the appendix.

3 I consider desertion as a major issue throughout this account. My main concern is to historicize the practice and the understanding of desertion, because a static application of the term obfuscates rather than clarifies issues of loyalty and nationalism. Important studies of desertion include Mark Wietz, *A Higher Duty: Desertion among Georgia Troops during the Civil War* (Lincoln: University of Nebraska Press, 2000); Kevin Conley Ruffner, "Civil War Desertion from a Black Belt Regiment: An Examination of the 44th Virginia Infantry," in *The Edge of the South: Life in Nineteenth-Century Virginia*, ed. Edward L. Ayers and John C. Willis (Charlottesville: University Press of Virginia, 1991), 79–109; Ella Lonn, *Desertion during the Civil War* (Gloucester, Mass.: American Historical Association, 1928); Judith Lee Halleck, "The Role of the Community in Civil War Desertion," *CWH* 29 (June 1983): 123–34; and David P. Smith, "Conscription and Conflict on the Texas Frontier, 1863–1865," *CWH* 36 (September 1990): 250–61.

4 This interpretation began in the 1930s and 1940s. See Charles H. Wesley, *The Collapse of the Confederacy* (rpt., Columbia: University of South Carolina Press, 2001); Charles Ramsdell, *Behind the Lines in the Southern Confederacy* (Baton Rouge: Louisiana University Press, 1944); and Bell I. Wiley, *The Plain People of the Confederacy* (Baton Rouge: Louisiana University Press, 1943). The more recent proponents of this argument include Paul Escott, *After Secession: Jefferson Davis and the Failure of Confederate Nationalism* (Baton Rouge: Louisiana State University Press, 1978); Richard Beringer, Herman Hattaway, Archer Jones, and William N. Still Jr., *Why the South Lost the Civil War* (Athens: University of Georgia Press, 1988); Wayne K. Durrill, *War of Another Kind: A Southern Community in the Great Rebellion* (New York: Oxford University Press, 1990); and David Williams, *Rich Man's War: Class, Caste, and Confederate Defeat in the Lower Chattahoochee Valley* (Athens: University of Georgia Press, 1998). It also appears in a variety of other sources, even those that take seriously the notion that the war's outcome was contingent and unpredictable. See, for example, Russell F. Weigley, *A Great Civil War: A Military and Political History, 1861–1865* (Bloomington: Indiana University Press, 2000), xxvii–xxviii.

5 For an excellent example of the importance of local politics to the identities of white men in one Tidewater county, see Daniel W. Crofts, *Old Southampton: Politics and Society in a Virginia County, 1834–1869* (Charlottesville: University Press of Virginia, 1992).

6 Gavin Wright, " 'Economic Democracy' and the Concentration of Agricultural Wealth in the Cotton South, 1850–1860," *Agricultural History* 44 (January 1970): 63–93; Randolph B. Campbell, "Planters and Plain Folk: Harrison County, Texas, as a Test Case, 1850–1860," *JSH* 40 (August 1974): 369–98; John T.

Schlotterbeck, "The 'Social Economy' of an Upper South Community: Orange and Greene Counties, Virginia, 1815–1860," in *Class, Conflict, and Consensus: Antebellum Southern Community Studies*, ed. Orville Vernon Burton and Robert C. McMath Jr. (Westport, Conn.: Greenwood Press, 1982): 3–28; Bradley G. Bond, "Herders, Farmers, and Markets on the Inner Frontier: The Mississippi Piney Woods, 1850–1860," in *Plain Folk of the South Revisited*, ed. Samuel C. Hyde Jr. (Baton Rouge: Louisiana State University Press, 1997), 73–99. For Virginia, see William G. Shade, *Democratizing the Old Dominion: Virginia and the Second Party System* (Charlottesville: University Press of Virginia, 1996).

7 For a study of an antebellum family in King and Queen County that provides a good example of the multiple uses to which slaves were put and of how some owners creatively integrated slavery and new technologies, see Claudia L. Bushman, *In Old Virginia: Slavery, Farming, and Society in the Journal of John Walker* (Baltimore: Johns Hopkins University Press, 2002). Other local studies emphasize this theme as well. See Lynda J. Morgan, *Emancipation in Virginia's Tobacco Belt, 1850–1870* (Athens: University of Georgia Press, 1992); David R. Goldfield, *Urban Growth in the Age of Sectionalism: Virginia, 1847–1861* (Baton Rouge: Louisiana State University Press, 1977); Gregg D. Kimball, *American City, Southern Place: A Cultural History of Antebellum Richmond* (Athens: University of Georgia Press, 2000); and Frederick F. Siegel, *The Roots of Southern Distinctiveness: Tobacco and Society in Danville, Virginia, 1780–1865* (Chapel Hill: University of North Carolina Press, 1987).

8 Several recent studies emphasize the role of love rather than anger in defining the emotional world of southern men. Peter Carmichael, in particular, draws a sophisticated picture of southern masculinity, in *The Last Generation: Young Virginians in Peace, War, and Reunion* (Chapel Hill: University of North Carolina Press, 2005), chaps. 3–4. See also Stephen W. Berry, *All That Makes a Man: Love and Ambition in the Civil War South* (New York: Oxford University Press, 2003).

9 Jacqueline Glass Campbell has found a similar reaction among South Carolinian women to the hard war waged by William T. Sherman's army in 1864–65. See Jacqueline Glass Campbell, *When Sherman Marched North from the Sea: Resistance on the Confederate Home Front* (Chapel Hill: University of North Carolina Press, 2005). See also Giselle Roberts, "'Our Cause': Southern Women and Confederate Nationalism in Mississippi and Louisiana," *Journal of Mississippi History* 62 (Summer 2000): 97–121.

10 Stephen V. Ash, *Middle Tennessee Society Transformed, 1860–1870: War and Peace in the Upper South* (Baton Rouge: Louisiana State University Press, 1988), 172.

11 For an interpretation that stresses the psychological effectiveness of the Union's hard-war campaign, see Mark Grimsley, *The Hard Hand of War: Union Military Policy toward Southern Civilians, 1861–1865* (Cambridge: Cambridge University

Press, 1995), 168. For accounts that argue that southern men enlisted as a way to defend patriarchal privilege, see Stephanie McCurry, *Masters of Small Worlds: Yeoman Households, Gender Relations and the Political Culture of the Antebellum South Carolina Low Country* (New York: Oxford University Press, 1995); and LeeAnn Whites, *The Civil War as a Crisis in Gender: Augusta, Georgia, 1860–1890* (Athens: University of Georgia Press, 1995).

12 A sizable body of literature has emerged in recent years focused on the Virginia experience, but most of these have been community studies. See, for example, William Blair, *Virginia's Private War: Feeding Body and Soul in the Confederacy, 1861–1865* (New York: Oxford University Press, 1998); Daniel E. Sutherland, *Seasons of War: The Ordeal of a Confederate Community, 1861–1865* (Baton Rouge: Louisiana State University Press, 1995); Steven Elliott Tripp, *Yankee Town, Southern City: Race and Class Relations in Civil War Lynchburg* (New York: New York University Press, 1997); and Brian Steel Wills, *The War Hits Home: The Civil War in Southeastern Virginia* (Charlottesville: University Press of Virginia, 2001). A statewide focus allows me to identify the larger patterns that emerged among the diverse localities of the Old Dominion.

13 Most studies of Civil War soldiers focus on a particular army, brigade, or regiment. Although this approach generates important insights, it emphasizes the military context at the expense of men's civilian lives. By examining all the soldiers from a single state, regardless of which units they served in, I have shifted the emphasis back to the communities to which those men belonged. This approach is based on what I see as the most important network of relationships for most soldiers—those between themselves and their families.

14 Campbell, *When Sherman Marched North from the Sea*, and Lisa Tendrich Frank, " 'To Cure Her of Her Pride and Boasting': The Gendered Implications of Sherman's March" (Ph.D. diss., University of Florida, 2001).

15 For an important study of the Civil War that adopts this tone at points, see Charles Royster, *The Destructive War: William Tecumseh Sherman, Stonewall Jackson, and the Americans* (New York: Vintage, 1991), 294–95.

16 For a lucid statement of this methodological approach, see Joseph C. Miller, "History and Africa / Africa and History" *American Historical Review* 104 (February 1999): 1–32.

17 Gerald F. Linderman's *Embattled Courage: The Experience of Combat in the American Civil War* (New York: Free Press, 1989) is an exception to this tradition.

18 See George Rable, *The Confederate Republic: A Revolution against Politics* (Chapel Hill: University of North Carolina Press, 1994); Robert E. Bonner, *Colors and Blood: Flag Passions of the Confederate South* (Princeton: Princeton University Press, 2003); and Anne Sarah Rubin, *A Shattered Nation: The Rise and Fall of the Confederacy, 1861–1868* (Chapel Hill: University of North Carolina Press, 2005).

19 Melinda Lawson, *Patriot Fires: Forging a New American Nationalism in the Civil War North* (Lawrence: University of Kansas Press, 2002); and Mary-Susan Grant, *North over South: Northern Nationalism and American Identity in the Antebellum Era* (Lawrence: University of Kansas Press, 2000). In this study, I do not intend to speak to the theoretical debate about nationalism. I do look at how and when nationalist language and beliefs helped spur Confederates to fight the Civil War.

20 I am drawing here on the work of David Potter, who argued that "national loyalty, far from being opposed to other loyalties, is in fact strengthened by incorporating them." "It is self-evident," Potter wrote, "that national loyalty flourishes not by challenging and overpowering all other loyalties, but by subsuming them all in a mutually supportive relation to one another." See David Potter, "The Historian's Use of Nationalism and Vice Versa," in *The South and Sectional Conflict* (Baton Rouge: Louisiana State University Press, 1968), 47–49.

21 Samuel J. C. Moore to Ellen Moore, October 9, 1861, Samuel Moore Papers, SHC. Throughout the text, I have retained the original spelling, phrasing, punctuation, and emphasis of the primary sources, except where additional words, marked in brackets, were necessary to clarify meaning.

CHAPTER 1

1 This figure comes from dividing the total number of enlistees by the number of men eligible for the draft. See the appendix for details on how I calculated this figure.

2 Comparative enlistment numbers can be found in Maris A. Vinovskis, "Have Social Historians Lost the Civil War? Some Preliminary Demographic Speculations," in Vinovskis, ed., *Toward a Social History of the American Civil War: Exploratory Essays* (Cambridge: Cambridge University Press, 1990), 9; Thomas R. Kemp, "Community and War: The Civil War Experience of Two New Hampshire Towns," in Vinovskis, *Toward a Social History of the American Civil War*, 59; Emily J. Harris, "Sons and Soldiers: Deerfield, Massachusetts, and the Civil War," *CWH* 30 (June 1984): 158–9; Larry M. Logue, "Who Joined the Confederate Army? Soldiers, Civilians, and Communities in Mississippi," *Journal of Social History* 26 (Spring 1993): 613; Randolph B. Campbell, "Fighting for the Confederacy: The White Male Population of Harrison County in the Civil War," *Southwestern Historical Quarterly* 104 (July 2000): 31; and David Carlson, "Civil War Enlistment Patterns in Southwest Georgia: A Reassessment of the 'Rich Man's War,'" 35 (unpublished seminar paper in author's possession).

3 Virginia's uncertain and hesitant course toward secession has been well explained and analyzed. See Daniel W. Crofts, *Reluctant Confederates: Upper South Unionists in the Secession Crisis* (Chapel Hill: University of North Carolina, 1989); Henry T. Shanks, *The Secession Movement in Virginia, 1847–1861* (Richmond:

Garrett and Massie, 1934); and Daniel W. Crofts, "Late Antebellum Virginia Reconsidered," *VMHB* 107 (Summer 1999): 253–86. In his article, Crofts explains secession as a takeover of the state by proslavery, pro-secession Democrats.

4 Martin Crawford, *Ashe County's Civil War: Community and Society in the Appalachian South* (Charlottesville: University Press of Virginia, 2001), 75.

5 Enlistment patterns in pro-Union counties support this argument. Among die-hard Unionist places, over half sent men to fight in Confederate armies and nearly a third sent more than 50 percent of their eligible men.

6 *Lynchburg Daily Virginian*, April 16, 1861. The Virginia-based *Religious Herald* echoed the secular press. In its view, "no fault of Virginia brought the calamity [of secession] upon us. She bore the olive branch, until it was stricken from her hand with the drawn sword." *Religious Herald*, April 15, 1861, quoted in Wayne Hsieh, "Stern Soldiers Weeping: Confederate Clergymen and the Civil War" (master's thesis, University of Virginia, 2002).

7 James B. Dorman to James Dorman Davidson, April 16, 1861, quoted in Bruce Greenwalt, "Unionists in Rockbridge County: The Correspondence of James Dorman Davidson concerning the Virginia Secession Convention of 1861," *VMHB* 73 (January 1965): 78–102.

8 Robert A. Granniss Diary, April 18, 1861, Robert A. Granniss Papers, VHS.

9 James D. Davidson to R. M. T. Hunter, May 2, 1861, quoted in Bruce Greenwalt, "Life behind Confederate Lines: The Correspondence of James D. Davidson," *CWH* 16 (September 1970): 205–26.

10 Alison Goodyear Freehling, *Drift toward Dissolution: The Virginia Slavery Debate of 1831–1832* (Baton Rouge: Louisiana State University Press, 1982).

11 The increase in political participation over the antebellum era is chronicled by William G. Shade, *Democratizing the Old Dominion: Virginia and the Second Party System* (Charlottesville: University Press of Virginia, 1996), chap. 3. He attributes it mostly to the growth of parties as institutions.

12 C. B. Watkins to Bettie Carrington Dinwiddie, June 12, 1861, Dinwiddie Family Papers, UVa.

13 Ironically, at the Virginia Secession Convention the delegates themselves took advantage of their position to begin considering proposals that would have disempowered common white men from politics. See Fletcher Melvin Green, ed., *Essays in Southern History Presented to Joseph Gregoire de Roulhac Hamilton, Ph.D., LL.D., by His Former Students at the University of North Carolina* (Chapel Hill: University of North Carolina Press, 1949). For a more detailed analysis of this process in another state, see Michael Johnson, *Toward a Patriarchal Republic: The Secession of Georgia* (Baton Rouge: Louisiana State University Press, 1979).

14 Werner H. Steger, "'United to Support, but Not Combined to Injure': Free

Workers and Immigrants in Richmond, Virginia, during the Era of Sectionalism, 1847–1865" (Ph.D. diss., George Washington University, 1999).

15 George M. Frederickson, *The Black Image in the White Mind: The Debate on Afro-American Character and Destiny, 1817–1914* (Middletown, Conn.: Wesleyan University Press, 1971); and U. B. Phillips, "The Central Theme of Southern History," *American Historical Review* 34 (October 1928): 30–43.

16 For instance, a study of Danville, Virginia, found a "sharply stratified society" but one that nonetheless offered a growing middle class a greater share of resources during the 1850s. See Frederick F. Siegel, *The Roots of Southern Distinctiveness: Tobacco and Society in Danville, Virginia, 1780–1865* (Chapel Hill: University of North Carolina Press, 1987), chap. 6. All of the elements elucidated in this paragraph can be seen in Augusta County, a county in the Shenandoah Valley with 25 percent slaveholding households. For a further elucidation of this argument, see Edward L. Ayers and William G. Thomas III, "Two American Communities on the Eve of Civil War: An Experiment in Form and Analysis," *American Historical Review*, December 2003, on-line edition, available at http:// www.vcdh .virginia.edu/AHR/.

17 Louis A. Wise, "Dixie's Land," no date but textual references indicate mid-1861, in Louis A. Wise Papers, UVa.

18 Michael Holt's *Political Crisis of the 1850s* (New York: Norton, 1978) provides the best analysis of this perspective.

19 See Holt, *Political Crisis*; J. Mills Thornton III, *Power and Politics in a Slave Society: Alabama, 1800–1860* (Baton Rouge: Louisiana State University Press, 1978); and William J. Cooper Jr., *Liberty and Slavery: Southern Politics to 1860* (New York: Knopf, 1983).

20 For the view that slavery in Virginia was losing its appeal and its power, see the work of William W. Freehling, whose interpretation is summarized in a 1969 article on the Virginia secession convention. "The debates reveal all the anxiety of a declining society implicated in the ironies of its former greatness and convulsed by the internal contradictions which caused the Deep South to secede." See William W. Freehling, "The Editorial Revolution, Virginia, and the Coming of the Civil War," *CWH* 16 (March 1969): 64–72, as well as *The Road to Disunion: Secessionists at Bay* (New York: Oxford University Press, 1990), 24, and *The South vs. the South: How Anti-Confederate Southerners Shaped the Course of the Civil War* (New York: Oxford University Press, 2001).

21 The best survey of agricultural reform efforts in the state is also an insightful biography of Virginia's most ardent reformer, Edmund Ruffin. See William M. Mathew, *Edmund Ruffin and the Crisis of Slavery in the Old South: The Failure of Agricultural Reform* (Athens: University of Georgia Press, 1988).

22 David R. Goldfield chronicles the efforts and evaluates the success of Virginia's urban boosters in his interpretation of antebellum urban growth in the state; see his *Urban Growth in the Age of Sectionalism*, chap. 2. No comprehensive history of Virginia's antebellum industrialization has been written, but numerous case studies provide valuable evidence on the wealth and diversity of approaches taken around the state before the Civil War. See John T. Stealey III, *The Antebellum Kanawha Salt Business and Western Markets* (Lexington: University Press of Kentucky, 1993), and Charles B. Dew, *Bond of Iron: Master and Slave at Buffalo Forge* (New York: Norton, 1994). For a view of this process in motion in Southampton County, one of the few parts of the state with soil and climate suitable for growing cotton but which also produced a variety of grains and marketable vegetables as well as the most highly prized pigs in the state, see Daniel Crofts, *Old Southampton: Politics and Society in a Virginia County, 1834–1869* (Charlottesville: University Press of Virginia, 1992). Also see Goldfield, *Urban Growth in the Age of Sectionalism*, chap. 5; John Majewski, *A House Dividing: Economic Development in Pennsylvania and Virginia Before the Civil War* (Cambridge: Cambridge University Press, 2000), 9.

23 Dean A. Arnold, "The Ultimatum of Virginia Unionists: 'Security for Slavery or Disunion,'" *Journal of Negro History* 48 (April 1963): 115–29.

24 The Virginia General Assembly, meeting concurrently with the secession convention, anticipated a possible military confrontation with the United States and began mobilization. On January 25 the state government created an Ordnance Department; four days later it appropriated $1 million for "the Defence of the Commonwealth" (and subsequently authorized the state treasury to issue bonds to raise this sum); and in late March, it made substantial revisions to the state's Militia Act. See *Acts of the General Assembly, Passed in 1861* (Richmond: William F. Ritchie, Public Printer, 1861). George H. Reese, ed., *Proceedings of the Virginia State Convention of 1861, February 13–May 1* (Richmond: Virginia State Library, 1965), 4:1149.

25 This figure comes from the paymaster general's report, cited in Governor Letcher's address to the General Assembly, December 2, 1861. The address is included as Document 1, in the *Journal of the House of Delegates of the State of Virginia for the Session of 1861–1862* (Richmond: William F. Ritchie, 1861). It is important to note that the Confederacy was forced by war circumstances to expand, both above and below, the traditional age limits on military service. This periodic redefinition of "military age" revealed the unpredictable nature of the conflict.

26 The figure of 54,950 is in the appendix to Secretary Judah P. Benjamin's letter to Confederate governors requesting troops. Benjamin to John Gill Shorter, February 2, 1862, *OR*, ser. IV, 1:903–4.

27 In early 1862, the Confederacy only anticipated receiving 64,342 troops from Virginia if full enlistment was reached. This figure is given in the preamble to the legislation passed by the Virginia General Assembly establishing the state mechanisms necessary to carry out the draft. *Acts of the General Assembly of the State of Virginia, 1861–62* (Richmond: William F. Ritchie, 1862), chap. 20, p. 41.

28 Clinton Hatcher to Mary A. Sibert, May 18, 1861, *VoS,* http://jefferson.village .virginia.edu/vshadow2/cwlettersbrowse.html.

29 Thomas L. Broun to Annie Broun, June 1861, Catherine Barbara Broun Papers, SHC. For evidence that the enlistment process demonstrated elite authority, see Steven Elliott Tripp, *Yankee Town, Southern City: Race and Class Relations in Civil War Lynchburg* (New York: New York University Press, 1997), 89; Crofts, *Old Southampton,* 194–96; Brian Steel Wills, *The War Hits Home: The Civil War in Southeastern Virginia* (Charlottesville: University Press of Virginia, 2001), 22; Daniel E. Sutherland, *Seasons of War: The Ordeal of a Confederate Community, 1861–1865* (Baton Rouge: Louisiana State University Press, 1995), 37; William Marvel, *A Place Called Appomattox* (Chapel Hill: University of North Carolina, 2000), 83–85; John V. Quarstein, *Hampton and Newport News in the Civil War: War Comes to the Peninsula* (Lynchburg, Va.: H. E. Howard, 1998), 29; and Peter Carmichael, "Paternalistic Officers: The Military Rule of Young Virginians," Douglas Southall Freeman Intellectual History Conference, Richmond, Virginia, February 2002.

30 James B. Davidson to Mary Davidson, May 16, 1861, quoted in Greenwalt, "Life behind Confederate Lines," 205–26.

31 Ted Barclay to Mary Barclay, June 10, 11, 1861, in Ted Barclay, *Liberty Hall Volunteers: Letters from the Stonewall Brigade, 1861–1864,* ed. Charles W. Turner (Natural Bridge Station, Va.: Rockbridge Publishing, 1992), 12, 13.

32 Evelyn Dupuy Ford to John Baxter Moseley, August 23, 1861, John Baxter Moseley Papers, VHS. The links formed between soldiers and their communities in ceremonies like these would help sustain volunteers during periods of isolation and hardship. In his study of Culpeper, Daniel Sutherland ably explores these connections. See Sutherland, *Seasons of War,* 37–40.

33 James Booker to Chloe Unity Blair, July 14, 1861, John and James Booker Papers, UVa.

34 See Shanks, *The Secession Movement in Virginia,* 144–17. Shanks bases his analysis of the region's preferences at this early stage on the votes for holding a convention in the state legislature and the ensuing newspaper debate.

35 I am distinguishing northwest Virginia from what becomes the state of West Virginia, because almost all of the counties in eastern and southern West Virginia sent high numbers of men to fight for the Confederacy. Richard O. Curry, *A House Divided: A Study of Statehood Politics and the Copperhead Movement in West Virginia*

(Pittsburgh: University of Pittsburgh Press, 1964), and George Ellis Moore, *A Banner in the Hills: West Virginia's Statehood* (New York: Meredith, 1963). Many counties in the Northwest did organize Confederate units, with most enrolling in excess of 25 percent of their eligible men and many in excess of 50 percent. There is no doubt that a substantial percentage of northwestern Virginians preferred to remain in the Union, and many fought in Union regiments, but neither is there any doubt that many other people in this region privileged their standing allegiance to Virginia, and its social, economic, and political order.

36 For the opposite interpretation of this process—that the breakaway of Unionist sections of the South was integral to Confederate defeat—see Freehling, *The South vs. the South.*

37 John Samuel Apperson Diary, July 7, 1861, in *Repairing the "March of Mars": The Civil War Diaries of John Samuel Apperson, Hospital Steward in the Stonewall Brigade, 1861–1865*, ed. John Herbert Roper (Macon, Ga.: Mercer University Press, 2001), 105.

38 The role of honor can be seen clearly in Craig M. Simpson's account of Henry Wise and secession: *A Good Southerner: The Life of Henry A. Wise of Virginia* (Chapel Hill: University of North Carolina Press, 1985), chap. 12. Also see Bertram Wyatt-Brown, *Southern Honor: Ethics and Behavior in the Old South* (New York: Oxford University Press, 1982). John P. Lightner to Amanda Catherine Amentrout, June 29, 1861, William Francis Brand Papers, UVa.

39 Evidence from soldiers' letters during the war reveals the centrality of being a parent to men's identity. See Stephen M. Frank, " 'Rendering Aid and Comfort': Images of Fatherhood in the Letters of Civil War Soldiers from Massachusetts and Michigan," *Journal of Social History* 26 (Fall 1992): 5–32. Samuel J. C. Moore to "My Dear Little Boy," May 16, 1861, Samuel J. C. Moore Papers, SHC. Historians who describe this shift have focused primarily on the prewar period and often on elites. The wartime correspondence of soldiers offers a remarkable avenue into this kind of social history and includes ample evidence that men sought more openly emotional relationships. One future soldier's letter yields exactly this insight. "Yes, Lucy," he wrote, "though loving me, you 'find it impossible' to talk to me in the language of love. You have been writing me such plan matter-of-fact letters so long that the habit has become as invincible as nature. All this may, and doubtless does, proceed from modesty; but, permit me to tell you without any intention of wounding you, that it is a false modesty. Is it right we, who are very dear to each other, should stand upon cold terms of courtesy and polite remarks. It would be inexpressible happiness for me to pour out my heart and love to you, if you would act as kindly. I beseech you, my darling, to overcome your diffidence, and to treat me with frankness and affection." Waddy Butler to

Lucy Wood, February 20, 1861, Fishburne Family Papers, UVa. I am grateful to Jennifer McClure for bringing this passage to my attention.

40 See *Lexington Valley Star*, May 2, 9, and 23, 1861.

41 Anne Sarah Rubin, *A Shattered Nation: The Rise and Fall of the Confederacy, 1861–1868* (Chapel Hill: University of North Carolina Press, 2005), 19–25.

42 These counties were Brooke, Clay, Doddridge, Hancock, Marshall, Mason, Morgan, Preston, Tucker, Tyler, and Wetzel. Many men from these counties undoubtedly served the Confederacy, but the fact that these places did not organize any companies indicates a lack of popular support for the Confederate cause as well as a lack of the kind of institutional support that elites in other counties directed on behalf of the Confederacy.

43 Clay County, located in the middle of the Northwest, is an important exception. It was surrounded by counties that sent high proportions of their men to fight, so it seems reasonable to assume that many Clay men did fight, in companies organized in Roane, Calhoun, Kanawha, or Fayette counties.

44 The statistics in this and the following paragraphs are drawn from the database described in the appendix.

45 Robert W. Hooke, to "Dear Father & Mother," April 20, 1861, Robert W. Hooke Papers, DSC.

46 The high enlistment rates for middle-income counties and from the mountain counties in central and southwestern Virginia support John C. Inscoe's findings on the level of economic integration and identification with the South as a whole among the residents of western North Carolina's mountain counties. See John C. Inscoe, *Mountain Masters, Slavery, and the Sectional Crisis in Western North Carolina* (Knoxville: University of Tennessee Press, 1989). Also, evidence exists to show the enthusiasm of residents from this region for slavery and market integration before the war. See Ralph Mann, "Diversity in the Antebellum Appalachian South: Four Farm Communities in Tazewell County, Virginia," in *Appalachia in the Making: The Mountain South in the Nineteenth Century*, ed. Beth Pudup, Dwight B. Billings, and Altina L. Waller (Chapel Hill: University of North Carolina Press, 1995), 132–62. Nearly 40 percent of those counties with households in the lowest income bracket sent more than 50 percent of their men to fight for the Confederacy. Analyzing the pattern of enlistment against farm value and farm size confirms this interpretation. Counties with high average farm values and sizes sent a high proportion of men, but many counties with low average farm values and sizes did as well. Wealth, in most of its forms, appears to have made little difference as an independent variable in determining rates of enlistment, and neither did farm size.

47 John Lyon Hill Diary, September 2, 1861, John Lyon Hill Papers, VHS. William

Marvel addresses this issue in *Mr. Lincoln Goes to War* (New York: Houghton Mifflin, 2006).

48 T. Lloyd Benson, the scholar upon whose research I am drawing in this paragraph, concludes that "the figures show that even after 1862, when the grim realities of the conflict had replaced early enthusiasm for rebellion in Virginia, members of propertyless households and the most wealthy families continued to enlist at similar rates. Class consciousness certainly existed in the South at this time, but it played a small role in determining the participation of ordinary soldiers in the war." T. Lloyd Benson, "The Plain Folk of Orange: Land, Work and Society on the Eve of the Civil War," in *The Edge of the South: Life in Nineteenth Century Virginia*, ed. Edward L. Ayers and John C. Willis (Charlottesville: University Press of Virginia, 1988), 73. Neither Benson, nor I, argue that poor men in the South were ignorant of their weakened position in the section's economic and social structure. Poorer whites in Orange County faced the same kinds of structural disadvantages that men of similar socioeconomic standing did in other parts of America at the time, but they enlisted nonetheless (as did poor men of the North), because they perceived the potential benefits that the southern economic system could bring.

49 As most people (then and now) would suspect, a statistically positive relationship exists between proportions of men enlisted from each county and the proportion of households with slaves from each county, but the difference in rates of slaveholding across the state explains only 27 percent of the variation in enlistment rates between counties. The contrast between these figures and Crofts's analysis of slaveholding and secession reveals how different the process of enlistment was from the political act of secession, when slavery had a statistically more significant relationship to voting on secession. Six counties with less than 5 percent slaveholding households sent 50 percent or more of their men to fight in Confederate armies.

50 The situation of southwesterners in Virginia was similar to that of westerners in North Carolina as described in John Inscoe and Gordon B. McKinney, *Confederate Appalachia: Western North Carolina in the Civil War* (Chapel Hill: University of North Carolina Press, 2000), 32: "Just as mountain residents came to think of themselves politically as westerners within their state, more momentous developments forced them to think of themselves as Southerners within the nation as well."

51 *Abingdon Democrat*, March 8, 1861.

52 Kenneth W. Noe, *Southwest Virginia's Railroad: Modernization and the Sectional Crisis* (Urbana: University of Illinois Press, 1994). This was true earlier in the antebellum era, as nascent industrialists in the area had employed slave labor extensively in the region's saltworks. See Stealey, *Antebellum Kanawha Salt Busi-*

ness, 5. *Abingdon Democrat*, March 8, 1861. For a more detailed analysis of the patterns of enlistment within the state, see Aaron Sheehan-Dean, "Everyman's War: Confederate Enlistment in Civil War Virginia," *CWH* 50 (March 2004): 5–26.

53 "The Corner-Stone of the New Republic," *Leesburg Democratic Mirror*, April 17, 1861.

54 Elizabeth Fox-Genovese has revealed the complex and insidious effect of slaveholding on the personal dynamics of households with slaves. Though she concentrates mostly on the Lower South and on large slaveholders, many of the observations she makes about the tangled relations among masters, mistresses, and slaves apply to Virginia as well. See Elizabeth Fox-Genovese, *Within the Plantation Household: Black and White Women of the Old South* (Chapel Hill: University of North Carolina Press, 1988). For Virginia, see Brenda Stevenson, *Life in Black and White: Family and Community in the Slave South* (New York: Oxford University Press, 1996). Charles B. Dew's study of the secession commissioners sent from the Lower South to the Upper South in early 1861 provides the clearest evidence that southerners recognized the centrality of slavery and race to sectional division and civil war. See Charles B. Dew, *Apostles of Disunion: Southern Secession Commissioners and the Causes of the Civil War* (Charlottesville: University Press of Virginia, 2001). Also David F. Allmendinger Jr., *Ruffin: Family and Reform in the Old South* (New York: Oxford University Press, 1990), 127. For a similar view, see Shearer Davis Bowman, "Conditional Unionism and Slavery in Virginia, 1860–1861: The Case of Dr. Richard Eppes," *VMHB* 96 (January 1988): 31–54. In his study of Southampton County, Daniel Crofts emphasizes the dependence upon slavery and fear of Republican interference with the institution as important motivators. See Crofts, *Old Southampton*, chap. 6. For another example stressing the connection between protection of slavery and the necessity of slavery, see Arnold, "The Ultimatum of Virginia Unionists."

55 "Our Position," *Winchester Republican and Daily Advertiser*, September 27, 1861.

56 Various scholars have offered compelling explanations of the many and various links that bound slaveholders and nonslaveholders in the antebellum South. See, for example, J. William Harris, *Plain Folk and Gentry in a Slave Society: White Liberty and Black Slavery in Augusta's Hinterlands* (Middletown, Conn.: Wesleyan University Press, 1985); Stephanie McCurry, *Masters of Small Worlds: Yeoman Households, Gender Relations and the Political Culture of the Antebellum South Carolina Low Country* (New York: Oxford University Press, 1995); and George Fredrickson, *Black Image in the White Mind: The Debate about Afro-American Character and Destiny, 1817–1914* (New York: Harper and Row, 1971). The relationship between the percentage of the population that was enslaved and enlistment had the greatest explanatory power out of any that I tested. This indicates

how strong a stake nonslaveholders had in slavery. Every county with more than 50 percent of its residents enslaved sent at least 25 percent of its men to fight, and most of these places sent more than 75 percent of their eligible men. Enslaved people as a percentage of the population explains 30 percent of the variation in rates of enlistment among counties.

57 Eugene D. Genovese has tracked the development of this argument carefully. See *The World the Slaveholders Made: Two Essays in Interpretation* (New York: Pantheon, 1969) and *The Slaveholders' Dilemma: Freedom and Progress in Southern Conservative Thought, 1820–1860* (Columbia: University of South Carolina Press, 1992).

58 Recent studies of Virginia recognize that class conflict occurred during the war, but stress the cohesive power of Confederate identity within the state. See Steven V. Ash, *When the Yankees Came: Conflict and Chaos in the Occupied South* (Chapel Hill: University of North Carolina Press, 1995); Tripp, *Yankee Town, Southern City*; William Blair, *Virginia's Private War: Feeding Body and Soul in the Confederacy, 1861–1865* (New York: Oxford University Press, 1998), 56, 141; Sutherland, *Seasons of War*, 355; Steger, " 'United to Support' "; Michael Stuart Mangus, " 'The Debatable Land': Loudoun and Fauquier Counties, Virginia during the Civil War Era" (Ph.D. diss., Ohio State University, 1998). Logue, "Who Joined the Confederate Army?" 616–17; Campbell, "Fighting for the Confederacy," 36–37; Carlson, "Civil War Enlistment Patterns in Southwest Georgia," 30, 37; and Blair, *Virginia's Private War*, 81. I am aware that historians' ability to verify the proportional distribution of Virginia's social classes in Confederate ranks does not change how people at the time perceived the war. Ample anecdotal evidence exists to show that at least some soldiers believed that poor men were overrepresented in the Confederate ranks, hence the common label of a "poor man's fight." Conversely, ample evidence exists to suggest that soldiers in the service recognized the socioeconomic diversity among their comrades. In the following chapters, I take account of those times when class-based disagreements surfaced within the army or at the homefront, as well as those times when other types of identities generated tension, including ethnicity, region, race, and status as a soldier or civilian. See Nimrod B. Hamner to "Dear Ma," September 15, 1861, Hamner Family Papers, VHS.

59 John Taylor Anderson to Sallie F. Anderson, May 6, 1861, in *Confederate Letters and Diaries, 1861–1865*, ed. Walbrook D. Swank (Charlottesville, Va.: Papercraft Printing and Design, 1988), 89.

CHAPTER 2

1 George K. Harlow to Thomas Harlow, May 30, 1861, June 8, Harlow Family Papers, VHS. For similar expressions of reluctance to fight at this stage in

the war, see James Henry Langhorne to "My Darling Mother," June 26, 1861, Langhorne Family Papers, VHS; John B. Fontaine to Kate F. Meade, July 8, 1861, John B. Fontaine Papers, Harrisburg Civil War Round Table Collection, MHI; and Thomas McGuffin to his son, April 22, 1861, quoted in Robert J. Driver Jr., *Lexington and Rockbridge in the Civil War* (Lynchburg, Va.: H. E. Howard, 1989), 15.

2 George Harlow to Thomas Harlow, June 20, 1861, Harlow Family Papers, VHS.

3 Clayton R. Newell, *Lee vs. McClellan: The First Campaign* (Washington, D.C.: Regnery, 1996).

4 Joseph W. Thomas, "Campaigns of Generals McClellan and Rosencrans in West Virginia, 1861–1862," *West Virginia History* 5(July 1944): 246; Herman Hattaway and Archer Jones, *How the North Won: A Military History of the Civil War* (Urbana: University of Illinois Press, 1983), 36–38; Newell, *Lee vs. McClellan*, chap. 5.

5 John A. Garnett to William Gray, September 30, 1861, William Gray Papers, VHS.

6 Tinsley Linsley Allen to Ellen Allen, November 13, 1861, in *The Allen Family of Amherst County, Virginia: Civil War Letters*, ed. Charles W. Turner, (Berryville, Va.: Rockbridge Publishing, 1995), 4. For guerrilla warfare in western Virginia, see Kenneth W. Noe, "Exterminating Savages: The Union Army and Mountain Guerrillas in Southern West Virginia, 1861–1862," in *The Civil War in Appalachia: Collected Essays*, ed. Kenneth W. Noe and Shannon H. Wilson (Knoxville: University of Tennessee Press, 1997), 104–27.

7 John Q. Winfield to Sallie Winfield, September 16, 1861, John Q. Winfield Papers, SHC.

8 William George Cabaniss to "Dear Pa," July 30, 1861, Moore Family Papers, VHS.

9 See *Daily Richmond Examiner*, September 28, 1861, for an evaluation of the crisis and potential solutions.

10 John Guerrant to Mildred Heath Massie, September 21, 1861, John Guerrant Papers, VHS. A recent study of Union soldiers indicates that "former farmers, rural residents, and natives . . . were more susceptible to disease and were more likely than, respectively, nonfarmers, urban dwellers, and nonnatives to die from the disease they contracted." This is a reliable portrait of the men who served in the West and may help explain the high rates of disease and death for this sphere of the war. See Chulhee Lee, "Socioeconomic Background, Disease, and Mortality among Union Amy Recruits: Implications for Economic and Demographic History," *Explorations in Economic History* 34 (1997), 50.

11 Tinsley L. Allen to Mary Allen, November 22, 1861, in Turner, *Allen Family of Amherst County*, 4.

12 Darrell L. Collins, *46th Virginia Infantry* (Lynchburg, Va.: H. E. Howard, 1992),

16. See also A. D. Kelly to Williamson Kelly, July 23, 1861, Williamson Kelly Papers, DSC; and Gordon Thompson to Home, July 30, 1861, quoted in J. L. Scott, *60th Virginia Infantry* (Lynchburg, Va.: H. E. Howard, 1997), 13.

13 This assessment comes from the database assembled for this study, according to which 9.2 percent of Virginia soldiers died of disease during the war and 5.7 percent were killed in action.

14 Richard Woolfolk Waldrop to Christopher Waldrop, July 27, 1861, Richard Woolfolk Waldrop Papers, SHC; Nimrod Brahaman Hamner to "Dear Ma," July 15, 1861, Hamner Family Papers, VHS.

15 Douglas Southall Freeman, *R. E. Lee*, 4 vols. (New York: Scribner's, 1934–35), 2:597.

16 My summary of the battle draws on Ethan S. Rafuse, *A Single Grand Victory: The First Campaign and Battle of Manassas* (Wilmington, Del.: Scholarly Resources, 2002); William C. Davis, *Battle at Bull Run: A History of the First Major Campaign of the Civil War* (Baton Rouge: Louisiana State University, 1981); and Hattaway and Jones, *How the North Won*, 41–49.

17 Maurice Evans to Mary Anne Evans, July 26, 1861, Maurice Evans Papers, VHS. For a similarly inflated estimate of casualties at Manassas, see William Gaines Baldwin to Margaret A. Baldwin, July 24, 1861, William Gaines Baldwin Papers, VHS. Inaccurate reports of casualties were common on both sides following the engagement at Bull Run.

18 John Q. Winfield to Sallie Winfield, July 23, 1861, John Q. Winfield Papers, SHC.

19 Philip H. Powers to "My Dearest Wife," July 23, 1861, Philip H. Powers Papers, Lewis Leigh Collection, MHI.

20 William L. Hill to "My Dear Father," July 22, 1861, box 282, Robert Alonzo Brock Papers, HEH.

21 John O. Collins to his wife, July 22, 1861, quoted in Robert J. Driver Jr., *10th Virginia Cavalry* (Lynchburg, Va.: H. E. Howard, 1992), 6.

22 William Baskerville to "My Darling Father," June 12, 1861, in William Baskerville Papers, DSC.

23 Judah P. Benjamin to Jefferson Davis, *OR*, ser. IV, 3:955–964. In his seminal study of the Confederate draft, Albert Burton Moore asserts that twelve-month men "were generally estimated at one-third of the entire force in the field." Moore includes conflicting testimony on this matter, including a reference to a report by the Confederate secretary of war to Jefferson Davis in August 1862 describing the necessity of conscription due to the high number of twelve-month men in service. It is curious that Moore never cited the Benjamin report, which clearly details the numbers and types of enlistees from all the states of the Confederacy. See Albert Burton Moore, *Conscription and Conflict in the Confederacy* (New York: Macmillan, 1924), 10, n. 14.

24 A February 1862 report by the Confederate secretary of war listed 53,950 regular soldiers from Virginia and 7,000 Virginia militia enlisted for twelve months, with only 1,500 men enrolled for the war. J. P. Benjamin to John Gill Shorter, *OR*, ser. IV, 1:902–4.

25 *Daily Richmond Examiner*, November 22, 1861.

26 The term was for three years, and all those already in would be extended for three years from the original date of enlistment. Men older or younger were to remain in service for ninety days more or less if a conscript took their place. Twelve-monthers were allowed to reorganize themselves, and a bounty and furlough system was maintained to benefit those that did reenlist. A thirty-day grace period was allowed to let companies organize themselves before enrolling began. Conscripts would be assigned to fill empty slots in volunteer units, or, if necessary, whole conscript units could be created by the secretary of war. Like other soldiers, conscripts were allowed to hire substitutes from among the pool of men above or below the draft age. Most papers supported the measure and applauded Congress's decision even as they saluted those men who had volunteered first. Moore, *Conscription and Conflict in the Confederacy*, 14–17.

27 Even the formal efforts to recruit men at the time reveal the flexibility that many officers exercised to draw men into the army without alienating them. Humphrey Marshall, who commanded Confederate forces in southwestern Virginia in early 1862, explained to War Department authorities his method for obtaining recruits. "My conscription has been mainly confined to a gentle pressure upon the young unmarried men of the country. . . . I had suggested to the people the most just classification my mind suggested for replenishing my command from the militia was to call, 1st, on the unmarried men of the country; 2d, on married men without children; 3d on men with families whose age subjected them to duty." Marshall knew that overt pressure would push men to enlist in the Union army across the border in Kentucky, so he exercised his initiative in implementing a family-sensitive approach. His efforts yielded several hundred men from several southwest counties and little backlash. Marshall's report is quoted in Jeffrey C. Weaver, *The Civil War in Buchanan and Wise Counties: Bushwhacker's Paradise* (Lynchburg, Va.: H. E. Howard, 1994), 131–32.

28 Over the next three years, the draft pulled in 13,933 men for Virginia, less than 10 percent of the total who served for the state over the course of the war. John S. Preston to John C. Breckinridge, *OR*, ser. IV, 3:1101. This figure does not include those men who enlisted to avoid the stigma of conscription, a process the Confederate Congress had anticipated. See, for instance, William Boutwell Kidd Diary, March 1, 1862, William Boutwell Kidd Papers, VHS.

29 Littleton Tazewell Robertson to "My Dear Martha," January 2, 1862, Littleton Tazewell Robertson Papers, VHS.

30 Edward Camden to "Miss Jones," February 2, 1862, William H. Jones Papers, DSC. Other men simply regarded the law as illegal on its face. See William Allen to Mary Allen, April 26, 1862, Turner, *Allen Family of Amherst County*, 9; George Rable analyzes the ideological debate over the draft most effectively. See George C. Rable, *The Confederate Republic: A Revolution against Politics* (Chapel Hill: University of North Carolina Press, 1994), 138–43.

31 Robert W. Hooke to "Dear Brother," July 12, 1861, Robert W. Hooke Papers, DSC. See also George K. Harlow to Thomas Harlow, October 4, 1862, Harlow Family Papers, VHS.

32 For example, most Southampton County soldiers reenlisted for the war in early 1862 despite the hardship they had suffered that year. See Daniel Crofts, *Old Southampton: Politics and Society in a Virginia County, 1834–1869* (Charlottesville: University Press of Virginia, 1992), chap. 7.

33 William Randolph Smith Diary, April 26, 1862, William Randolph Smith Diary, Civil War Times Illustrated Collection, MHI. See also B. L. Penick to Rawley White Martin, April 22, 1862, Rawley White Martin Papers, SHC.

34 Joseph Richard Manson to Susan Maclin Manson, July 27, 1862, Joseph Richard Manson Papers, Civil War Miscellaneous Collection, MHI.

35 "Absentees and Deserters," *Lexington Gazette*, June 26, 1862.

36 This conclusion is based upon both a close reading of the manuscript material and the quantitative data I assembled. Of the twenty-six soldiers in my sample listed as absent without leave during the period from the start of the war until passage of the Draft Act, twenty-one (or 80 percent) returned.

37 "Attention Rockbridge Greys!" *Lexington Gazette*, June 26, 1862.

38 *Daily Richmond Examiner*, July 26, 1862.

39 James W. Silver, *Confederate Morale and Church Propaganda* (New York: Norton, 1967), 75. Willard Wight's study of religion in the Confederacy also includes examples of returning deserters who are rejected by their home parishes. See Willard E. Wight, "The Churches and the Confederate Cause," *CWH* 6 (December 1960): 361–73.

40 William Boutwell Kidd Diary, March 15, 1862, William Boutwell Kidd Papers, VHS.

41 George K. Harlow to Thomas Harlow, October 4, 1862, Harlow Family Papers, VHS.

42 James W. Old to "Dearest Mother," June 20, 1861, January 9, 1862, James W. Old Papers, VHS.

43 James W. Old to "Dear Brother," February 24, 1862, James W. Old Papers, VHS; Robert T. Bell, *11th Virginia Infantry* (Lynchburg, Va.: H. E. Howard, 1985), 88.

44 Samuel B. Blymon to William Walter Christian, November 3, 1861, William Walter Christian Papers, DSC.

45 Edgar M. Ferneyhough to "Dearest Mother," September 12, 1861, Ferneyhough Family Papers, VHS. For a similarly dramatic account of a unit near the point of mutiny, see Henry Ruffner Paine Diary, September 9, 1861, Paine Family Papers, VHS.

46 James Henry Langhorne to "My Darling Mother," June 12, 1861; James Henry Langhorne to Nannie E. Kent, October 19, 1861, Langhorne Family Papers, VHS.

47 Richard Woolfolk Waldrop to John Waldrop, May 29, 1861, Richard Woolfolk Waldrop Papers, SHC. John Worsham, *One of Jackson's Foot Cavalry: His Experiences & What He Saw during the War, 1861–1865* (New York: Neale, 1912), 301.

48 Robert K. Krick, *30th Virginia Infantry* (Lynchburg, Va.: H. E. Howard, 1983), 88.

49 This was true of most Confederate soldiers. See Charles E. Brooks, "The Social and Cultural Dynamics of Soldiering in Hood's Texas Brigade," *JSH* 67 (August 2001): 535–72.

50 William Boutwell Kidd Diary, February 7, 1862, VHS; Robert K. Krick, *30th Virginia Infantry*, 4th ed. (Lynchburg, Va.: H. E. Howard, 1985).

51 William Thomas Casey to Sarah Jane Casey, March 16, 1862, William Thomas Casey Papers, VHS.

52 Steven Elliott Tripp, *Yankee Town, Southern City: Race and Class Relations in Civil War Lynchburg* (New York: New York University Press, 1997), 110; David Donald, "The Confederate Man as Fighting Man," *JSH* 25 (May 1959): 178–93.

53 Peter Carmichael reaches a similar conclusion in his recent study of the last generation of Virginia's slaveholding elite. See *The Last Generation: Young Virginians in Peace, War, and Reunion* (Chapel Hill: University of North Carolina Press, 2005), chap. 6.

54 James Jones White to Mary White, August 14, 1861, James Jones White Papers, SHC.

55 William Fleming Harrison to "Dear Maria," July 4, 1861, April 3, 1862, William Fleming Harrison Papers, DSC. Details on the service records of the men discussed here can be found in Thomas M. Rankin, *23rd Virginia Infantry* (Lynchburg, Va.: H. E. Howard, 1985).

56 David Funsten to Susan Meade Funsten, December 9, 1861, David Funsten Papers, VHS. According to one historian, this perception applied in the North as well. See Reid Mitchell, *The Vacant Chair: The Northern Soldier Leaves Home* (New York: Oxford University Press, 1993), 34.

57 Ted Ownby, *Subduing Satan: Religion, Recreation, and Manhood in the Rural South, 1865–1920* (Chapel Hill: University of North Carolina Press, 1990), 12. Ownby further argues that "women embraced [these values] more fully than men." I argue here for a more flexible notion of southern masculinity, along the lines of that described by Stephen W. Berry III, *All That Makes a Man: Love and Ambition in the Civil War South* (New York: Oxford University Press, 2003).

58 For a similar treatment of same-sex friendships among women, see Melinda S. Buza, " 'Pledges of Our Love': Friendship, Love and Marriage among the Virginia Gentry, 1800–1825," in *The Edge of the South: Life in Nineteenth-Century Virginia*, ed. Edward L. Ayers and John C. Willis (Charlottesville: University Press of Virginia, 1991), 9–36, and Anthony E. Rotundo, *American Manhood: Transformations in Masculinity from the Revolution to the Modern Era* (New York: Basic Books, 1993), chap. 4.

59 William Hope Peek to "Ma," April 29, 1862, Peek Family Papers, SHC.

60 Fletcher B. Moore to "Dear Sister," November 15, 1861, Samuel H. Moore Papers, Civil War Times Illustrated Collection, MHI.

61 William Young Mordecai to "My Dear Mother," October 19, 1862, William Young Mordecai Papers, VHA; Daniel Hileman to "Dear Brother," September 22, 1861, Hileman Family Papers, Lewis Leigh Collection, MHI. In his classic work on Confederate soldiers, Bell Wiley focuses mostly on the difficulties soldiers had in obtaining food, but he does note that men learned to cook and sometimes learned to enjoy it. See Bell I. Wiley, *The Life of Johnny Reb: Common Soldier of the Confederacy* (rpt., Baton Rouge: Louisiana State University Press, 1988), 90–107. Joseph Franklin Kauffman Diary, July 17, 1862, SHC. See also Samuel Dunbar to "Dear Home folks," May 20, 1863, Samuel Dunbar Papers, Civil War Times Illustrated Collection, MHI.

62 William Young Modecai to "My Dear Mother," October 19, 1862, William Young Modecai Papers, VHS; Daniel Hileman to Philip Hileman, September 22, 1861, Hileman Family Papers, MHI. See also William E. Isbell to "Sister Nannie," January 28, 1862, William E. Isbell Papers, Lewis Leigh Collection, MHI. Mitchell, *The Vacant Chair*, 71–87.

63 James K. Edmondson, in *My Dear Emma (War Letters of Col. James K. Edmondson, 1861–1865)*, ed. Charles W. Turner, (Verona, Va.: McClure Press, 1978), 63–4; Unknown to "My very dear Sister," June 6, 1861, box 71, James Eldridge Papers, HEH.

64 John P. Harrison to his wife, September 1, 1861, John P. Harrison Papers, Lewis Leigh Collection, MHI; John Hamilton Ervine to Ellen Ervine, June 18, 1861, John Hamilton Ervine Papers, VMI, http://new.vmi.edu/archives/Manuscripts/ms331trn.html.

65 J. A. Jones to "My Dear Mother and Father," May 12, 1861, J. A. Jones Papers, Lewis Leigh Collection, MHI.

66 Benjamin F. Wade to "Dear Bro," January 7, 1862, Benjamin F. Wade Papers, Lewis Leigh Collection, MHI.

67 John B. Snodgrass to Kate Snodgrass, February 22, 1862, John B. Snodgrass Papers, VMI.

68 James R. McCutchan to His Sister, March 19, 1862, McCutchan Papers, *VoS*, http://etext.lib.virginia.edu/etcbin/civwarlett-browse?id=A0309.

69 Richard Woolfolk Waldrop to Ellen Douglas Waldrop, February 21, 1862, Richard Woolfolk Waldrop Papers, SHC. See also William Goodwyn Ridley to Elizabeth Norfleet Neely, April 19, 1862, Ridley Family Papers, VHS.

70 Armistead Burwell to "My Dear Brother," January 25, 1862, Armistead Burwell Papers, Lewis Leigh Collection, MHI. For a similar sentiment, see William E. Isbell to "Sister Nannie," February 15, 1862, William E. Isbell Papers, Lewis Leigh Collection, MHI.

71 John Barrett Pendleton to Sallie Ann Pendleton, May 22, 1861, Pendleton Family Papers, VHS.

72 Samuel J. C. Moore to Ellen Moore, October 19, 1861, Samuel J. C. Moore Papers, SHC.

73 David Waldstreicher, *In the Midst of Perpetual Fetes: The Making of American Nationalism, 1776–1820* (Chapel Hill: University of North Carolina Press, 1997).

CHAPTER 3

1 For a typical example of high expectations, see Algernon S. Wade to Mrs. David L. Hopkins, April 27, 1862, Algernon S. Wade Papers, Lewis Leigh Collection, MHI: "They say we are to remain in service for three months longer and by that time the war will be closed."

2 Robert Nathaniel Neblett to Sterling Neblett, April 2, 1862, Neblett Family Papers, VHS. The average Virginia infantry company held 100 men, so the estimate here of 125 is probably higher than could be expected.

3 Randolph Harrison to Elizabeth Gatewood Harrison, April 30, 1862, Randolph Harrison Papers, VHS.

4 Darrell L. Collins, *46th Virginia Infantry* (Lynchburg, Va.: H. E. Howard, 1992), 36–37.

5 According to Joseph E. Johnston, the commander of Confederate forces in Virginia, "Re-elections have greatly reduced its [the army's] value." See Joseph E. Johnson to George W. Randolph, April 28, 1862, *OR*, ser. I, 11(3):470–71. For a similar sentiment, see *Daily Richmond Examiner*, November 29, 1861.

6 George Washington Peebles Diary, February 20, 1862, George Washington Peebles Papers, VHS.

7 Historians of the Valley and Peninsula campaigns both blame officers for tactical errors in their discussions of the spring battles. See Robert G. Tanner, *Stonewall in the Valley: Thomas J. "Stonewall" Jackson's Shenandoah Valley Campaign, Spring 1862* (New York: Doubleday, 1976), and Stephen W. Sears, *To the Gates of Richmond: The Peninsula Campaign* (New York: Ticknor and Fields, 1992).

8 A recent account of the Union army of the Ohio stresses regimental solidarity, often to the detriment of the larger purpose of brigade, corps, and army. See Gerald Prokopowicz, *All for the Regiment: The Army of the Ohio, 1861–62* (Chapel Hill: University of North Carolina Press, 2001). This was the opposite experience of most soldiers in the Army of Northern Virginia. The heights reached by Lost Cause oratory in praise of Lee have a created a skeptical sense about how well regarded he was during his actual tenure. All of the men whose diaries and letters I have read speak about him with tremendous confidence and affection during the war itself. See also Gary W. Gallagher, "Shaping Public Memory of the Civil War: Robert E. Lee, Jubal A. Early, and Douglas Southall Freeman," in *Lee and His Army in Confederate History* (Chapel Hill: University of North Carolina Press, 2001), 255–82.

9 Alexander Pendleton to Anzolette Page Pendleton, February 12, 1862, quoted in W. G. Bean, "The Valley Campaign of 1862 as Revealed in Letters of Sandie Pendleton," *VMHB* 78 (July 1970): 326–64.

10 Virginius Lorraine Weddell to Margaret Stanley Beckwith, December 19, 1861, Margaret Stanley Beckwith Papers, VHS.

11 Watkins Kearns Diary, April 15, 1864, Watkins Kearns Diary, VHS.

12 Alice I. Hohenberg, "Civil War Draft Problems in the Shenandoah Valley," *Journal of the Rockbridge Historical Society* 7 (Summer 1970): 26–33.

13 Watkins Kearns Diary, May 18, 1862, Watkins Kearns Diary, VHS.

14 Joseph Franklin Kauffman, May 9, 1862, Joseph Franklin Kauffman Diary, SHC. See also Tinsley Linsley Allen to Mary Allen, May 26, 1862, in *The Allen Family of Amherst County, Virginia: Civil War Letters*, ed. Charles W. Turner (Berryville, Va.: Rockbridge Publishing, 1995), 10–11.

15 H. Sidney Wallace to A. R. Blakey, August 12, 1861, H. Sidney Wallace Papers, Lewis Leigh Collection, MHI.

16 Alexander Pendleton to Anzolette Page Pendleton, May 16, 1862, in Bean, "The Valley Campaign of 1862," 326–64. This problem plagued men in all parts of the army. See, for example, Greenlee Davidson to James Dorman Davidson, August 28, 1862, in Charles W. Turner, ed., "Captain Greenlee Davidson: Letters of a Virginia Soldier," *CWH* 17 (September 1971): 197–221.

17 William Young Mordecai to "My Dear Mother," May 9, 1862, William Young Mordecai Papers, VHS. The inability to visualize strategy was not limited to those men on the ground; even Virginia's governor working in the Confederate capital of Richmond had trouble divining the purpose behind the military maneuvers in his state. See F. N. Boney, "Governor Letcher's Candid Correspondence" *CWH* 10 (June 1964): 167–80.

18 Joseph Franklin Kauffman Diary, May 22, 1862, Joseph Franklin Kauffman Diary, SHC.

19 William Hope Peek to "Ma," May 26, 1862, Peek Family Papers, SHC.

20 Ibid.

21 William Elzey Harrison to William Burr Harrison, March 20, 1862, Harrison Family Papers, VHS.

22 Laura Lee Diary, May 27, 1862, in *Winchester Divided: The Civil War Diaries of Julia Chase & Laura Lee*, ed. Michael G. Mahon (Mechanicsburg, Pa.: Stackpole, 2002), 40.

23 Julia Chase Diary, October 19, 1862, in Mahon, *Winchester Divided*, 64.

24 Laura Lee Diary, March 22, 1862, in Mahon, *Winchester Divided*, 25–26.

25 Alexander Pendleton to William Nelson Pendleton, June 1, 1862, in Bean, "The Valley Campaign of 1862," 362.

26 This is one of the central arguments advanced by Mark Grimsley in *The Hard Hand of War: Union Military Policy toward Southern Civilians, 1861–1865* (Cambridge: Cambridge University Press, 1995). Grimsley offers ample testimony from Union soldiers that they understood the punishing effect of emancipation on white southerners.

27 Lynda J. Morgan, *Emancipation in Virginia's Tobacco Belt, 1850–1870* (Athens: University of Georgia Press, 1992), especially chaps. 5 and 6.

28 See Grimsley, *The Hard Hand of War*, chap. 6. For a cogent analysis of the deterioration of slavery under Union occupation in one region of Virginia, see James Marten, " 'A Feeling of Restless Anxiety': Loyalty and Race in the Peninsula Campaign and Beyond," in *The Richmond Campaign of 1862: The Peninsula and the Seven Days*, ed. Gary W. Gallagher (Chapel Hill: University of North Carolina Press, 2000), 121–52.

29 This was the experience of Charles Chase of Winchester, who was arrested by Confederate authorities in March 1862 and eventually confined in Richmond. His daughter, Julia Chase, the famous Unionist diarist of Winchester, felt that his early death resulted from the harsh conditions of his confinement. See Julia Chase Diary, March 10, 1862, January 30, 1864, in Mahon, *Winchester Divided*, 21, 132.

30 William E. Isbell to "Sister Nannie," February 15, 1862, William E. Isbell Papers, Lewis Leigh Collection, MHI.

31 Two recent works suggest that in Georgia and the Carolinas, Sherman's actions encouraged stronger Confederate sentiment and will to fight among women. This finding is similar to the experience for many Confederate Virginians. See Jacqueline Glass Campbell, *When Sherman Marched North from the Sea: Resistance on the Confederate Home Front* (Chapel Hill: University of North Carolina Press, 2005), and Lisa Tendrich Frank, " 'To Cure Her of Her Pride and Boasting': The Gendered Implications of Sherman's March" (Ph.D. diss., University of Florida, 2001). Robert Gaines Haile Diary, June 12, 1862, Robert Gaines Haile Papers, VHS.

32 Robert Bonner's recent book on the evolution of the Confederate national flag stresses the ways that martial accomplishments helped inspire nationalist sentiment across the white South. Robert E. Bonner, *Colors and Blood: Flag Passions of the Confederate South* (Princeton: Princeton University Press, 2003), esp. chap. 4.

33 Drew Gilpin Faust, *Creation of Confederate Nationalism: Ideology and Identity in the Civil War South* (Baton Rouge: Louisiana State University Press, 1988), 9–21.

34 In his study of conscription, Albert Burton Moore argues that Virginians accepted the centralizing efforts of the Confederacy more readily than residents of other Confederate states. See Albert Burton Moore, *Conscription and Conflict in the Confederacy* (New York: Macmillan, 1924), chap. 13.

35 William Goodwyn Ridley to Elizabeth Norfleet Neely, April 19, 1862, Ridley Family Papers, VHS.

36 James Z. McChesney personal writing, undated, 1862, James Z. McChesney Papers, Lewis Leigh Collection, MHI.

37 William H. Gregory to "Dear Sister," May 6, 1862, William H. Gregory Papers, Civil War Miscellaneous Collection, MHI. For a nearly identical statement, see John Hampden Chamberlayne to Lucy Parke Chamberlayne, May 6, 1862, in *Ham Chamberlayne—Virginian: Letters and Papers of an Artillery Officer in the War for Southern Independence, 1861–1865*, ed. C. G. Chamberlayne (Richmond: Dietz, 1932), 78. Chamberlayne closes his assertion of Confederate invincibility on land with the memorable line: "Their 'Anaconda' will have a slow meal after he has swallowed the sea side & the frontier; our army will be indigestible."

38 Edwin Anderson Penick to "My fond wife," April 16, 1862, Edwin Anderson Penick Papers, VHS. See also John L. Gwyn to "Dearest Wife," July 17, 1862, John L. Gwyn Papers, Lewis Leigh Collection, MHI. Robert L. Bates to "Most Affectionate Wife," May 20, 1862, Robert L. Bates Papers, Lewis Leigh Collection, MHI.

39 Special Orders No. 107, May 9, 1862, *OR*, ser. IV, 1:1120–21.

40 William Robert Ezell to Buckner Davis Ezell, May 19, 1862, Ezell Family Papers, VHS. Ezell was not along in his observations. For another dour assessment of Confederate fortunes at this time, see Andrew Jackson Dawson to Milly B. Dawson, May 20, 1862, Andrew Jackson Dawson Papers, UVa.

41 William Randolph Smith Diary, May 12, 1862, William Randolph Smith Diary, Civil War Times Illustrated Collection, MHI.

42 Robert Henry Allen to Mary Allen, July 12, 1862, in Turner, *The Allen Family of Amherst County*, 15.

43 James K. Edmondson to Emma Edmondson, July 5, 1862, in *My Dear Emma (War Letters of Col. James K. Edmondson, 1861–1865)*, ed. Charles W. Turner (Verona, Va.: McClure Press, 1978), 99–100.

44 Joseph Richard Manson to Charlotte Manson, July 12, 1862, Joseph Richard Manson Papers, Civil War Miscellaneous Collection, MHI.

45 For a cogent summary of the arguments for interpreting the Seven Days as a turning point in the war, see Gary W. Gallagher, "A Civil War Watershed: The 1862 Richmond Campaign in Perspective," in Gallagher, *The Richmond Campaign of 1862*, 3–27.

46 Drew Gilpin Faust, "The Civil War Soldier and the Art of Dying," *JSH* 67 (February 2001): 3–38.

47 G. Ward Hubbs identifies this same shift among Alabama soldiers and civilians. He argues that "Personal letters back and forth from the front and home [in late 1862] divulge a profound reexamination of both the meaning of their ultimate sacrifice and the reasons for continuing the fight." See G. Ward Hubs, *Guarding Greensboro: A Confederate Company in the Making of a Southern Community* (Athens: University of Georgia Press, 2003), 143.

48 Sears, *To the Gates of Richmond*, 169, 173.

49 Robert Payne Baylor to "My Dear Father," June 15, 1862, Robert Payne Baylor Papers, VHS. Paul Christopher Anderson draws a similar portrait of Turner Ashby in his recent study of the Virginia cavalry leader. See Paul Christopher Anderson, *Blood Image: Turner Ashby in the Civil War and the Southern Mind* (Baton Rouge: Louisiana State University Press, 2002), chap. 1.

50 *Southern Literary Messenger*, as quoted in "A Touching Incident," *Lynchburg Daily Virginian*, October 3, 1862.

51 Drew Gilpin Faust focuses more closely on the symbolism of the painting in an insightful essay on this episode, but draws a very similar moral, arguing that "ideology could transform deprivation into sacrifice by imposing on it a meaning that gave it transcendence and purpose." See Drew Gilpin Faust, "Race, Gender, and Confederate Nationalism: William D. Washington's *Burial of Latané*," *Southern Review* 25 (April 1989): 304.

52 Robert Gaines Haile Diary, June 15, 1862, Robert Gaines Haile Papers, VHS.

53 Robert E. Bonner's recent study of Confederate flag culture makes this point. He argues that "When the Southern Cross was placed as the defining feature of a new national banner, the colors of war signaled the fundamentally military nature of collective purpose. As congressmen and other civilian leaders faltered in their effort to shape the national imagination, commanders and soldiers who had made this Cross famous nurtured national commitments and sustained national morale." Bonner, *Colors and Blood*, 97.

CHAPTER 4

1 For the prime example of the effectiveness of the "rosewater" policy, see Lawrence N. Powell and Michael S. Wayne, "Self Interest and the Decline of Confederate Nationalism," in *The Old South in the Crucible of War*, ed. Harry P. Owens and James J. Cooke (Jackson: University of Mississippi Press, 1983), 29–45.

The Union pursued a similar "soft" policy on the eastern shore of Virginia in mid-1861 where it yielded somewhat similar results. After an initial period of resistance, locals seem to have cooperated with Federal troops, though men from the region who wished to serve the Confederacy did escape. See Susie M. Ames, "Federal Policy toward the Eastern Shore of Virginia in 1861," *Virginia Magazine of History and Biography* 69 (Fall 1961): 432–59.

2   John J. Hennessy, *Return to Bull Run: The Campaign and Battle of Second Manassas* (Norman: University of Oklahoma Press, 1999), chap. 1. Daniel Sutherland follows the civilian reaction to these orders in his study of Culpeper, in the northern Piedmont. See Daniel E. Sutherland, *Seasons of War: The Ordeal of a Confederate Community, 1861–1865* (Baton Rouge: Louisiana State University Press, 1995), chap. 6.

3   Hennessy, *Return to Bull Run*, 115.

4   Joseph Franklin Kauffman Diary, August 28, 1862, Joseph Franklin Kauffman Diary, SHC.

5   James Marshall Binford to Carrie and Annie Binford, August 13, 1862, Charles Brown Gwathmey Papers, VHS.

6   "The Prospect," *Lynchburg Daily Virginian*, August 30, 1862.

7   Stephen W. Sears, *Landscape Turned Red: The Battle of Antietam* (New Haven, Conn.: Yale University Press, 1983), chap. 5.

8   Tinsley Allen to Mary Allen, September 22, 1862, in *The Allen Family of Amherst County, Virginia: Civil War Letters*, ed. Charles W. Turner (Berryville, Va.: Rockbridge Publishing, 1995), 19; Gary W. Gallagher, "The Net Result of the Campaign Was in Our Favor: Confederate Reaction to the Maryland Campaign," in *The Antietam Campaign*, ed. Gary W. Gallagher (Chapel Hill: University of North Carolina Press, 1999), 11.

9   George Marion Coiner to Kate Coiner, 10/20/62, Coiner Family Papers, VHS. See also Hodijah Lincoln Meade to "Dear Mother," September 18, 1862, Meade Family Papers, VHS.

10 Joseph Richard Manson to Charlotte Manson, July 12, 1862, Joseph Richard Manson Papers, Civil War Miscellaneous Collection, MHI.

11 George Marion Coiner to Kate Coiner, October 10, 1862, Coiner Family Papers, VHS.

12 Alex L. Wiatt, *26th Virginia Infantry* (Lynchburg, Va.: H. E. Howard, 1984), 4.

13 Benjamin Trask, *9th Virginia Infantry* (Lynchburg, Va.: H. E. Howard, 1984), 10–11.

14 Hennessy, *Return to Bull Run*, 456.

15 For Lee's estimate, see Robert E. Lee to Jefferson Davis, September 13, 1862, in *The Wartime Papers of Robert E. Lee*, ed. Clifford Dowdey (Boston: Little Brown, 1961), 307. In his study of Antietam, Stephen Sears estimates that Lee's forces

were reduced by 20 percent owing to straggling. See Sears, *Landscape Turned Red*, chap. 5.

16 One picture of the state of the army can be found in looking at the condition of the Allen family of Amherst County in late 1862. Five brothers from the clan served in Confederate military forces, most having enlisted in early 1862. By late that year, James and Thomas were noted absent without leave on the roster of the 13th Virginia Infantry, William was at home recovering from an illness, and Richard was in the Farmville hospital recuperating from an adverse reaction to a smallpox vaccine he had been given. Of the five, only Tinsley, who had enlisted in August of 1861, remained present for duty with his regiment. See Turner, *The Allen Family of Amherst County*, 22–26.

17 This conclusion is drawn from the sample of soldiers I created for this study. It contradicts the traditional argument that desertion steadily increased in severity over the course of the year, but confirms much of the anecdotal evidence coming from soldiers and civilians. In terms of absolute numbers, the permanent desertion rate for Virginia soldiers in my sample was 10.6 percent. This figure includes men listed as deserters or as absent without leave who never returned to service. Adjusted for sample size, this would yield roughly 15,000 Virginia deserters over the course of the war. Ella Lonn's 1928 study of desertion offers one of the only quantitative assessments of the problem available. Her analysis yields 13,000 deserters for Virginia, but this number fails to include men listed as AWOL who did not return to the service. See Ella Lonn, *Desertion during the Civil War* (Gloucester, Mass.: American Historical Association, 1928; Lincoln: University of Nebraska Press, 1998), 231, table 1.

18 Samuel A. Firebaugh Diary, October 4, 1862, Samuel A. Firebaugh Papers, Civil War Miscellaneous Collection, MHI. For evidence on the efforts to return men to their units, see Heath James Christian to "Dear Father," August 29, 1862, Christian Family Papers, VHS.

19 William Young Mordecai to "My Dear Mother," October 7, 1862, William Young Mordecai Papers, VHS.

20 Edwin Anderson Penick to "My Dear Wife," July 28, 1862, Edwin Anderson Penick Papers, VHS.

21 Peter S. Carmichael, "So Far from God and So Close to Stonewall Jackson. The Executions of Three Shenandoah Valley Soldiers," *VMHB* 111 (Winter 2003): 62–63, 65.

22 John F. Neff to "Dear Parents," August 4, 1862, John F. Neff Papers, Civil War Times Illustrated Collection, MHI.

23 Lowell Reidenbaugh, *33rd Virginia Infantry* (Lynchburg, Va.: H. E. Howard, 1987), 106.

24 Another indication of this shift can be seen in Confederates' acceptance of the

pass regulations for riding on the railroads. For an insightful analysis of this program see Mark E. Neely, *Southern Rights: Political Prisoners and the Myth of Confederate Constitutionalism* (Charlottesville: University Press of Virginia, 1999).

25 Martin Diller Coiner to Kate Coiner, August 21, 1862, Coiner Family Papers, VHS.

26 Edwin Anderson Penick to "My Dear Wife," August 5, 1862, Edwin Anderson Penick Papers, VHS.

27 M. M. Harris to Henry St. George Harris, March 24, 1863, Henry St. George Harris Papers, DSC.

28 Thomas C. Sublett to R. Thaxton, July 29, 1862, Thomas C. Sublett to R. Thaxton, August 2, 1862, William Walter Christian Papers, DSC. See also Henry Edward Neal to Lucy Ann Neal, September 11, 1862, Henry Edward Neal Papers, VHS.

29 Samuel A. Firebaugh Diary, October 29, 1862, Samuel A. Firebaugh Papers, Civil War Miscellaneous Collection, MHI.

30 John Bolling to Jesse Scott Armistead, December 24, 1862, Armistead Family Papers, VHS.

31 Rawleigh William Downman to Mary Magruder Downman, September 18, 1862, Downman Family Papers, VHS.

32 James Marshall Binford to Carrie and Annie Binford, August 13, 1862, Charles Brown Gwathmey Papers, VHS; Kenneth L. Stiles, *4th Virginia Cavalry* (Lynchburg, Va.: H. E. Howard, 1985), 107.

33 J. C. Fitz to "Dear Brother," October 10, 1862, box 18, James Eldridge Papers, HEH.

34 James Marten, " 'A Feeling of Restless Anxiety': Loyalty and Race in the Peninsula Campaign and Beyond," in *The Richmond Campaign of 1862: The Peninsula and the Seven Days*, ed. Gary W. Gallagher (Chapel Hill: University of North Carolina Press, 2000), 136.

35 Joseph Clay Stiles to Clifford Stiles, Richmond, December 11, 1862, box 106, Robert Alonzo Brock Papers, HEH.

36 *Daily Richmond Examiner*, September 29, 1862.

37 "First Fruit of Africanizing Ohio," *Lynchburg Daily Virginian*, September 24, 1862; see also "Natural Antipathy vs. Fanatical Fancy," *Richmond Sentinel*, March 16, 1863.

38 William H. Jones to Eliza Jones, August 20, 1863, William H. Jones Papers, DSC; Gallagher, "The Net Result of the Campaign Was in Our Favor," 3–44.

39 Harvey M. Rice, "Jonathan M. Bennett and Virginia's Wartime Finances," *West Virginia History* 4 (October 1942): 5–20.

40 Bill Blair has made a persuasive reinterpretation of the policy of impressment that reveals the ways that the impressment stabilized food supplies and benefited

the poor and hungry across the state, at the expense of wealthy farmers and speculators. See William A. Blair, *Virginia's Private War: Feeding Body and Soul in the Confederacy, 1861–1865* (New York: Oxford University Press, 1998), 70–72.

41 John F. Neff to "Dear Parents," August 4, 1862, John F. Neff Papers, Civil War Times Illustrated Collection, MHI.

42 Food shortages exacerbated by competition between soldiers and civilians occurred in Virginia's cities and in the countryside. See, for example, Marie Tyler-McGraw, *At the Falls: Richmond, Virginia and Its People* (Chapel Hill: University of North Carolina Press, 1994), 135; Steven Elliott Tripp, *Yankee Town, Southern City: Race and Class Relations in Civil War Lynchburg* (New York: New York University Press, 1997), 120; and Laura Lee Diary, April 1, 1862, in *Winchester Divided: The Civil War Diaries of Julia Chase & Laura Lee*, ed. Michael G. Mahon (Chambersburg, Pa.: Stackpole Books, 2002), 28.

43 C. R. Woolwine to "Dear Pa," December 25, 1862, C. R. Woolwine Papers, Civil War Miscellaneous Collection, MHI. For one example of a common Virginian who remained focused on local rather than national concerns throughout the war, see Claudia L. Bushman, *In Old Virginia: Slavery, Farming, and Society in the Journal of John Walker* (Baltimore: Johns Hopkins University Press, 2002), chap. 14.

44 Watkins Kearns Diary, May 3, 1862, Watkins Kearns Diary, VHS.

45 Blair, *Virginia's Private War*, 58.

46 Joseph W. Griggs to George King Griggs, December 19, 1862, Griggs Family Papers, VHS.

47 Unknown to Mattie Harrison, August 23, 1862, box 67, James Eldridge Papers, HEH.

48 For instance, for the argument that "the law defined the nature of the war for plain folk," see David Williams, *Rich Man's War: Class, Caste, and Confederate Defeat in the Lower Chattahoochee Valley* (Athens: University of Georgia Press, 1998), 130. See also Paul D. Escott, *After Secession: Jefferson Davis and the Failure of Confederate Nationalism* (Baton Rouge: Louisiana State University Press, 1978), 120–21; and Mark A. Weitz, *A Higher Duty: Desertion among Georgia Troops during the Civil War* (Lincoln: University of Nebraska Press, 2000), 2, 123. Importantly, none of these sources quote any "plain folk" directly on the impact of the law.

49 In the 400 plus manuscript collections that I consulted for this project, I found no comment on the twenty-slave law. Undoubtedly, some Virginia soldiers complained about the law in writing, but given the volume and breadth of the sources I read, I find it significant that I encountered not a single denunciation of a law that historians have asserted was central to understanding the Confederate experience.

50 John Peter Jones to Mary Elizabeth Jones, April 8, 1862, John Peter Jones Papers,

UVa. Drew Faust has compiled evidence from women's perspectives on this issue, mostly testifying to the reluctance of women to become pregnant during the war. See Drew Gilpin Faust, *Mothers of Invention: Women of the Slaveholding South in the American Civil War* (New York: Vintage, 1996), 123–24, 126–27. Richard Putney to Mary Elizabeth Jones, October 20, 1862, John Peter Jones Papers, UVa.

51 Phebe Updike Arthur to Richard Admire Arthur, April 26, 1862, J. O. Hensley to Phebe Updike Arthur, April 26, 1862, Updike and Arthur Family Papers, Civil War Miscellaneous Collection, MHI. Illness and death could facilitate stronger emotional bonds within families during peacetime. As one scholar of the antebellum family argues, "Death likewise drew families together in bereavement, creating a deep sense of affection and commitment between most members of the nuclear family." Daniel Blake Smith, *Inside the Great House: Planter Family Life in Eighteenth-Century Chesapeake Society* (Ithaca, N.Y.: Cornell University Press, 1980), chap. 7.

52 James Marten makes a similar argument in his study of Confederate fatherhood. He argues that "in the minds of southern men, the war had made being a good and loyal soldier one of the duties of being a good father." James Marten, "Fatherhood in the Confederacy: Southern Soldiers and Their Children," *JSH* 63 (May 1997): 279. Alexander Pendleton to William Nelson Pendleton, May 25, 1862, in W. G. Bean, "The Valley Campaign of 1862 as Revealed in Letters of Sandie Pendleton" *VMHB*, 78 July 1970: 349.

53 Randolph Stiles to Clifford Stiles, September 30, 1862, Joseph Clay Stiles Papers, box 106, Robert Alonzo Brock Papers, HEH.

54 *OR*, ser. IV, 2:214–15.

55 George Rable has recently written a superb history of the battle, the people, and the meaning of Fredericksburg. The account of the fighting which follows draws heavily on his work. See George C. Rable, *Fredericksburg! Fredericksburg!* (Chapel Hill: University of North Carolina Press, 2002).

56 Hodijah Lincoln Meade to "Dear Lizzie," December 17, 1862, Meade Family Papers, VHS.

57 Rable, *Fredericksburg! Fredericksburg!*, 288.

58 Greenlee Davidson to James Dorman Davidson, December 9, 1862, Charles W. Turner, ed., "Captain Greenlee Davidson: Letters of a Virginia Soldier," *CWH* 17 (September 1971): 217.

59 For examples of personal charity, see Suzanne Lebsock, *The Free Women of Petersburg: Status and Culture in a Southern Town, 1784–1860* (New York: Norton, 1984), 224; and Tripp, *Yankee Town, Southern City*, chap. 1.

60 Thomas T. Munford to "My Dear Nannie," December 22, 1862, Thomas T. Munford Papers, Lewis Leigh Collection, MHI.

61 George S. Pickett Diary, December 21, 1862, George S. Pickett Papers, Civil War Times Illustrated Collection, MHI.

62 *Lynchburg Daily Virginian*, December 16, 1862.

63 Montgomery Slaughter was the wartime mayor of Fredericksburg. The collection of his papers at the Henry E. Huntington library contains numerous contributions from individuals and organizations all over the Confederacy. Randall Jimerson reached a similar conclusion in his study of motivation among Civil War soldiers, arguing that "Invasion . . . provided an even stronger impetus toward unity." See Randall C. Jimerson, *The Private Civil War: Popular Thought during the Sectional Conflict* (Baton Rouge: Louisiana State University Press, 1988), 195–96.

64 Rable, *Fredericksburg! Fredericksburg!*, chap. 18 and 434.

65 Drew Gilpin Faust, "Christian Soldiers: The Meaning of Revivalism in the Confederate Army" *JSH* 53 (February 1987): 63–90; Herman Norton, "Revivalism in the Confederate Armies," *CWH* 6 (December 1960): 410–24; Thomas M. Gordon to Mrs. Edward Brown, February 9, 1863, Thomas M. Gordon Papers, Lewis Leigh Collection, MHI.

66 Alexander Pendleton to Anzolette Page Pendleton, May 10, 1862, Bean, "The Valley Campaign of 1862," 354.

67 Robert G. Haile to Mollie Haile, April 16, 1862, Robert G. Haile Papers, DSC.

68 Hodijah Lincoln Meade to "Dear Sister," March 9, 1862, Meade Family Papers, VHS.

69 Mortimer H. Johnson to Eliza Dulaney Kemble Johnson, December 18, 25, 1862, Johnson Family Papers, VMI, http://www.vmi.edu/archives/Manuscripts/ms 341007.html.

CHAPTER 5

1 My assertion that the winter of 1862–63 was harder on Virginians than subsequent years rests on testimony from both soldiers and civilians. The most obvious factor in this was the presence of several large armies in the state for most of the year. For most of 1863, the armies were in the far north of the state or out of it entirely, and as a result, crops recovered. In 1864 Grant's successful movement through the Tidewater effectively cut off that section of the state, but it was not until late in the year, with Sheridan's capture of the Shenandoah Valley, that hardship began to again rival the winter of 1862–63. Daniel Sutherland's account of Culpeper County during the war categorizes this period in stark terms as well. See Daniel E. Sutherland, *Seasons of War: The Ordeal of a Confederate Community, 1861–1865* (Baton Rouge: Louisiana State University Press, 1995), chap. 7.

2 In his account of gender relations in the Confederacy, Ted Ownby stresses the

idealized vision of home that men constructed during the war. See Ted Ownby, "Patriarchy in the World Where There Is No Parting?: Power Relations in the Confederate Heaven," in *Southern Families at War: Loyalty and Conflict in the Civil War South*, ed. Catherine Clinton (New York: Oxford University Press, 2000), 229–44.

3 George Washington Peebles Diary, January 3, 1863, George Washington Peebles Papers, VHS.

4 "The Monster," *Lynchburg Daily Virginian*, January 7, 1863.

5 *Daily Richmond Examiner*, January 7, 1863; similar sentiment can be found in "What We Are Fighting For," *Richmond Sentinel*, July 17, 1863, where the paper proclaims that "of all the crimes against humanity which have blackened the records of shame, that of attempting to incite a servile insurrection . . . is, by common consent, the foulest, basest, and most diabolical."

6 Hodijah Lincoln Meade to "Dear Everard," March 12, 1863, Meade Family Papers, VHS.

7 B. L. Penick to Rawley White Martin, January 16, 1863, Cephus Williams to Rawley White Martin, January 24, 1863, Rawley White Martin Papers, SHC; John Robert Bagby to Betty Pollard Bagby, April 16, 1863, Bagby Family Papers, VHS.

8 A. Baldwin to Frederick W. M. Holliday, April 12, 1863, Frederick W. M. Holliday Papers, DSC.

9 Martin Diller Coiner to Kate Coiner, March 22, 1863, Coiner Family Papers, VHS.

10 Virginius Dabney to Parke Chamberlain, January 28, 1863, Bagby Family Papers, VHS.

11 John Bowie Magruder to "My Dear Cousin," March 29, 1863, John Bowie Magruder Papers, DSC.

12 James Graham Tate to Charles Campbell Tate, March 25, 1863, Graham Family Papers, UVa.

13 Some historians have seen the Bread Riot, and others like it around the Confederacy, as the beginning of the collapse of Confederate morale on the home front. More recent scholarship has viewed the riot itself as an expression of want, not politics. See Werner Steger, "'United to Support, but Not Combined to Injure': Free Workers and Immigrants in Richmond, Virginia, during the Era of Sectionalism, 1847–1865" (Ph.D. diss., George Washington University, 1999), chap. 5.

14 Marie Tyler-McGraw, *At the Falls: Richmond, Virginia and Its People* (Chapel Hill: University of North Carolina Press, 1994), 130.

15 LeeAnn Whites, *The Civil War as a Crisis in Gender: Augusta, Georgia, 1860–1890* (Athens: University of Georgia Press, 1995), 43.

16 William A. Blair, *Virginia's Private War: Feeding Body and Soul in the Confederacy, 1861–1865* (New York: Oxford University Press, 1998), 111.

17 William H. Jones to Eliza L. Jones, March 21, 1863, in Rick Britton, ed., "Letters Home from Private William H. Jones of the Albemarle Rifles," *Magazine of Albemarle County History* 57 (1999): 65–70.

18 John Robert Bagby to Betty Pollard Bagby, April 30, 1863, Bagby Family Papers, VHS.

19 T. Bassett French to James Dorman Davidson, March 31, 1863, in Bruce Greenwalt, "Unionists in Rockbridge County: The Correspondence of James Dorman Davidson concerning the Virginia Secession Convention of 1861," *VMHB* 73 (January 1965): 102.

20 Sutherland, *Seasons of War*, chap. 8.

21 Michael Stuart Mangus, " 'The Debatable Land': Loudoun and Fauquier Counties, Virginia during the Civil War Era" (Ph.D. diss., Ohio State University, 1998), 301.

22 I explore the issue of class conflict within wartime Virginia in more detail in "Justice Has Something to Do with It: Class Relations and the Confederate Army," *VMHB* 113(December 2005): 340–77.

23 Stephen W. Sears, *Chancellorsville* (Boston: Houghton Mifflin, 1996), chap. 3.

24 Earl Hess's evaluation of Union soldiers and their ability to reconcile a dislike for war with the necessity of fighting holds equally true for Confederates. "Becoming men of war," Hess writes, "did not necessarily destroy the soldier's commitment to the issues of the conflict or his willingness to temporarily embrace the deadly game of the warrior to achieve the war's goals. . . . It was possible for the average Union soldier to recognize the folly of liking war without rejecting the need to use war as a legitimate method of settling important issues." See Earl J. Hess, *The Union Soldier in Battle: Enduring the Ordeal of Combat* (Lawrence: University of Kansas Press, 1997), 157.

25 Samuel A. Firebaugh Diary, May 13, 1863, Samuel A. Firebaugh Papers, Civil War Miscellaneous Collection, MHI.

26 William Allen to Mary Allen, May 10, 1863, in *The Allen Family of Amherst County, Virginia: Civil War Letters*, ed. Charles W. Turner (Berryville, Va.: Rockbridge Publishing, 1995), 42–43.

27 George W. Koontz to "Dear Mattie," May 10, 1863, George W. Koontz Papers, VMI, http://www.vmi.edu/archives/Manuscripts/ms102ktz.html.

28 Armistead Bolling to Jesse Scott Armistead, June 9, 1863, Armistead Family Papers, VHS.

29 See Martin Diller Coiner to Kate Coiner, May 24, 1863, Coiner Family Papers, VHS. In his recent study of the first half of the war, Edward Ayers argues that the

Union's hard war mostly alienated white southerners and helped consolidate Confederate sympathy. "Despite the brutal impact of the war on its farms and cities," he argues, "white Virginia had not lost the will to fight. In fact, the war had forged Virginia into far greater unity and identity with the Confederate cause than ever before." Edward L. Ayers, *In the Presence of Mine Enemies: War in the Heart of America, 1859–1863* (New York: Norton, 2003), 390–91.

30 Abram Fulkerson to "My Dear Wife," May 18, 1863, Fulkerson Family Papers, VMI, http://www.vmi.edu/archives/Manuscript/ms363009.html.

31 Charles Royster makes a careful analysis of the reception of Jackson's death among Confederates. See Charles P. Royster, *The Destructive War: William Tecumseh Sherman, Stonewall Jackson, and the Americans* (New York: Vintage, 1991), 193–99, 226–31.

32 Ferdinand J. Dunlap to "Dear Sister," June 22, 1863, Ferdinand J. Dunlap Papers, Civil War Miscellaneous Collection, MHI. See also J. L. Henry to "Bet," June 20, J. L. Henry Papers, DSC.

33 Charles Edward Lippitt Diary, June 20, 22, 1863, Charles Edward Lippitt Diary, SHC.

34 Halsey Wigfall to Louly Wigfall, July 12, 1863, Halsey Wigfall Papers, Brake Collection, MHI.

35 Heath James Christian to "Dear Father," July 16, 1863, Christian Family Papers, VHS.

36 Watkins Kearns Diary, June 24, 1863, Watkins Kearns Diary, VHS.

37 Florence McCarthy to Florence and Jane McCarthy, July 10, 1863, McCarthy Family Papers, VHS.

38 Hodijah Lincoln Meade to "Dear Mother," August 15, 1863, Meade Family Papers, VHS.

39 John Garibaldi to "Dear Wife," July 19, 1863, John Garibaldi Papers, Brake Collection, MHI.

40 Because Confederate scrip was not accepted in the North, such a transaction was little improvement on simple confiscation.

41 Joseph Richard Manson to Susan Maclin Manson, July 30, 1863, Joseph Richard Manson Papers, Civil War Miscellaneous Collection, MHI.

42 Florence McCarthy to Florence and Jane McCarthy, July 10, 1863, McCarthy Family Papers, VHS. For further corroboration that Confederates took only what was necessary, see also Heath James Christian to "Dear Father," July 13, 1863, Christian Family Papers, VHS.

43 George K. Harlow to Thomas Harlow, June 20, 1863, Harlow Family Papers, VHS.

44 Ted Alexander, "'A Regular Slave Hunt': The Army of Northern Virginia and

Black Civilians in the Gettysburg Campaign," *North and South* 4 (September 2001): 82–89.

45 David G. Smith, "Race and Retaliation: The Capture of African Americans during the Gettysburg Campaign," in *Virginia's Civil War*, ed. Peter Wallenstein and Bertram Wyatt-Brown (Charlottesville: University of Virginia Press, 2005), 137–51.

46 Abraham Lincoln, *The Collected Works of Abraham Lincoln*, ed. Roy P. Basler and others, 9 vols. (New Brunswick, N.J.: Rutgers University Press, 1953), 6:257.

47 Benjamin Lyons Farinholt to Lelia May Farinholt, July 1, 1863, Benjamin Lyons Farinholt Papers, VHS.

48 George K. Harlow to Thomas Harlow, July 15, 1863, Harlow Family Papers, VHS.

49 Charles Edward Lippitt Diary, July 3, 1863, Charles Edward Lippitt Diary, SHC.

50 William Hope Peek to Maria Peek, July 8, 1863, Peek Family Papers, SHC.

51 Robert L. Thompson to "Dear Father," July 1, Robert L. Thompson Papers, Brake Collection, MHI.

52 Samuel Horace Hawes to his family, July 3, 1863, Katherine Heath Hawes Papers, VHS. Also, see Gary W. Gallagher, "Lee's Army Has Not Lost Any of Its Prestige: The Impact of Gettysburg on the Army of Northern Virginia and the Confederate Home Front," in *Lee and His Army in Confederate History* (Chapel Hill: University of North Carolina Press, 2001), 83–114.

53 Ambrose M. Hite to Susan R. Hite, July 19, 1863, Ambrose M. Hite Papers, Brake Collection, MHI. For another positive assessment of the battle's results, see Samuel A. Firebaugh, July 3, 1863, Samuel A. Firebaugh Papers, Civil War Miscellaneous Collection, MHI.

54 Joseph Richard Manson to Susan Maclin Manson, July 30, 1863, Joseph Richard Manson Papers, Civil War Miscellaneous Collection, MHI.

55 Jacob B. Click to "Dear Old Friend," July 17, 1863, Jacob B. Click Papers, DSC.

56 Joseph Richard Manson to Charlotte Ashby Manson, May 17, 1863, Joseph Richard Manson Papers, Civil War Miscellaneous Collection, MHI.

57 Joseph E. Purvis Diary, July 13, 1863, Joseph E. Purvis Papers, Civil War Times Illustrated Collection, MHI.

58 Joseph T. Binford to Robert A. Lancaster, August 17, 1863, Robert Alexander Lancaster Papers, VHS.

59 Of all the soldiers in the database assembled for this study (see the appendix), 26.8 percent were captured during the war.

60 Joseph Richard Manson to Susan Maclin Manson, July 30, 1863, Joseph Richard Manson Papers, Civil War Miscellaneous Collection, MHI.

61 John L. Gwyn to "Dearest Wife," July 17, 1862, John L. Gwyn Papers, Lewis Leigh Collection, MHI.

62 George Thomas Rust to "My Darling Wife," July 18, 1863, George Thomas Rust
Papers, VHS; see also George K. Harlow to Thomas Harlow, July 15, 1863, Harlow Family Papers, VHS.

63 Richard Woolfolk Waldrop to Christopher Waldrop, July 16, 1863, Richard Wool-
folk Waldrop Papers, SHC. For a similar comment, see William J. Hatchet to
"My Dear Friends," late July, 1863, William J. Hatchett Papers, Civil War Times
Illustrated Collection, MHI.

64 See "The Outbreak in New York," *Lynchburg Daily Virginian*, July 21, 1863, and
Richmond Sentinel, July 18, 1863.

65 John Robert Bagby to Betty Pollard Bagby, July 19, 1863, Bagby Family Papers,
VHS. See also Watkins Kearns Diary, August 19, 1863, Watkins Kearns Diary,
VHS.

66 Harvey M. Rice, "Jonathan M. Bennett and Virginia's Wartime Finances," *West
Virginia History* 4 (October 1942): 5–20.

67 Steven V. Ash has created a three-part typology of occupation that reflects the
situation in Virginia. "Garrison towns" witnessed strong Union control over
trade, travel, and politics, but they helped maintain order. "Frontier" residents
led something like a normal life only because Union raids were not frequent
enough to completely disrupt the institutional life of the communities. "No-
Man's Lands" were totally unproductive. See Steven V. Ash, *When the Yankees
Came: Conflict and Chaos in the Occupied South* (Chapel Hill: University of North
Carolina Press, 1995), chap. 3.

68 For southwestern Virginia, see Kenneth W. Noe, *Southwest Virginia's Railroad:
Modernization and the Sectional Crisis* (Urbana: University of Illinois Press, 1994),
chap. 7. For eastern Tennessee, see Noel C. Fisher, *War at Every Door: Partisan
Politics and Guerrilla Violence in East Tennessee, 1860–69* (Chapel Hill: University
of North Carolina Press, 1997).

69 James Dorman Davidson to Samuel McDowell Reid, November 22, 163, in Bruce
Greenwalt, "Life behind Confederate Lines: The Correspondence of James D.
Davidson," *CWH* 16 (September 1970): 205–26.

70 Richard Bensel, *Yankee Leviathan: The Origins of Central State Authority in America, 1859–1877* (Cambridge: Cambridge University Press, 1990), 208.

71 William H. Jones to Eliza Jones, August 20, 1863, William H. Jones Papers, DSC.

72 William B. G. Andrews to "Dear Father," October 15, 1863, William B. G. Andrews Papers, DSC. See also Charles Edward Lippitt Diary, July 20, 1863, Charles
Edward Lippitt Diary, SHC; Richard Henry Allen to Mary Allen, August 31, 1863,
in Turner, *The Allen Family of Amherst County*, 55–56; Jedediah Carter to "My
Dear Wife," October 18, 1863, Jedediah Carter Papers, DSC; and John Garibaldi
to Sarah A. W. Poor, August 14, 1863, John Garibaldi Papers, VMI, http://new
.vmi.edu/archives/Manuscripts/ms284016.html.

73 John Robert Bagby to Betty Pollard Bagby, August 3, 1863, Bagby Family Papers, VHS.

74 William H. Jones to "My Deare Wife," September 23, 1863, William H. Jones Papers, DSC. The disputes and recriminations ran between and among all the branches over the last year and a half of war. Infantrymen, for example, complained about the easy life of artillery units and the liberal foraging practices of the cavalry. For an example of the latter, see James Henry Allen to Mary Allen, April 13, 1863, in Turner, *The Allen Family of Amherst County*, 38–39.

75 Jefferson Davis, August 1, 1863, *OR*, ser. IV, 2:687; General Order No. 82, August 12, 1863, box 35, James Eldridge Papers, HEH.

76 Blair, *Virginia's Private War*, 71–72.

77 Hodijah Lincoln Meade to "Dear Mother," August 15, 1863, Meade Family Papers, VHS.

78 Joseph Richard Manson to Matilda Manson Cogbill, November 13, 1863, Joseph Richard Manson Papers, Civil War Miscellaneous Collection, MHI.

79 Drew Gilpin Faust, "Christian Soldiers: The Meaning of Revivalism in the Confederate Army," *JSH* 53 (February 1987): 86.

80 Samuel A. Firebaugh Papers, Civil War Miscellaneous Collection, MHI.

81 William H. Jones to Eliza Jones, August 20, 1863, William H. Jones Papers, DSC.

82 John Garibaldi to Sarah A. W. Poor, April 22, 1864, John Garibaldi Papers, VMI, http://new.vmi.edu/archives/Manuscripts/ms284033.html.

83 See Reid Mitchell, "The Creation of Confederate Loyalties," in *New Perspectives on Race and Slavery in America: Essays in Honor of Kenneth M. Stampp*, ed. Robert H. Abzug and Stephen E. Maizlish (Lexington: University Press of Kentucky, 1986), 93–108.

84 John W. Stott Diary, December 14, 1863, John W. Stott Diary, Civil War Times Illustrated Collection, MHI.

85 William B. G. Andrews to "Dear Father," November 19, 1863, William B. G. Andrews Papers, DSC.

86 Charles Berry to "Dear Father," November 24, 1863, Charles Berry Papers, DSC. For the sense that the Confederacy had been deserted by foreign supporters at this time, see also Joseph E. Purvis Diary, July 27, 1863, Joseph E. Purvis Papers, Civil War Times Illustrated Collection, MHI.

87 Jedediah Carter to "My Dear Wife," October 18, 1863, Jedediah Carter Papers, DSC. In his study of fatherhood among Civil War soldiers, Stephen Frank found a strong commitment to the practice of parenting and a "vital" identification with fatherhood that lasted through the war. See Stephen M. Frank, " 'Rendering Aid and Comfort': Images of Fatherhood in the Letters of Civil War Soldiers from Massachusetts and Michigan," *Journal of Social History* 26 (Fall 1992): 5–32. For similar evidence that antebellum southern men were active parents, see Sally G.

McMillen, "Antebellum Southern Fathers and the Health Care of Children," *JSH* 60 (August 1994): 513–32. The sickness of a child also inspired worry. John F. Hatchett wrote to his wife on this topic in late 1864, saying "if our little dear angel continues to get worse you must send for Doct Gregory or old Doc Lacy & tell them to write to the col about your condition & perhaps he will let me come to stay a few days. I am in hopes though our dear little baby will get well soon." See John F. Hatchett to "My Dear Wife," late Oct, 1864, William J. Hatchet Papers, Civil War Times Illustrated Collection, MHI.

88 William H. Jones to Eliza Jones, March 21, 1863, in Britton, "Letters Home," 68.

89 Thomas M. Gordon to Mrs. Edward Brown, February 9, 1863, Thomas M. Gordon Papers, Lewis Leigh Collection, MHI, and Richard Harrison Allen to Mary Allen, April 10, 1863, in Turner, *The Allen Family of Amherst County*, 37–38.

90 George K. Harlow to "Dear Sister," April 14, 1863, Harlow Family Papers, VHS; Richard Harrison Allen to Mary Allen, June 1, 1863, in Turner, *The Allen Family of Amherst County*, 47–49.

91 In *A Shattered Nation: The Rise and Fall of the Confederacy, 1861–1868* (Chapel Hill: University of North Carolina Press, 2005), 111, Anne Rubin argues that "National identity, loyalty, and patriotism were ever changing during the war, and we do Confederates a disservice when we hold them to a fixed standard."

92 John Peter Jones to Mary Elizabeth Putney Jones, May 27, 1863, John Peter Jones Papers, UVa.

93 John Garibaldi to "Dear Wife," date unknown, probably late 1863, John Garibaldi Papers, Brake Collection, MHI.

94 For the argument that the increasing divide between men's patriarchal duties in protecting their families and their ability to meet those duties undermined southern masculinity, see Whites, *The Civil War as a Crisis in Gender*, chap. 3.

95 While a handful of these men lived alone and thus would have been listed by census takers as the head of household, an analysis of marriage status confirms the interpretation advanced above; 51 percent of those soldiers in the sample who could be linked to the census were married.

96 John Welsh to Rebecca Snider Welsh, January 19, 1863 in W. G. Bean, "A House Divided: The Civil War Letters of a Virginia Family," *VMHB* 59 (October 1951): 409.

97 Unknown to Mattie Harrison, August 23, 1862, box 67, James Eldridge Papers, HEH. See also James Phillips Simms to "My Dear Wife," March 30, 1865, box 55, James Eldridge Papers, HEH. In *All That Makes a Man: Love and Ambition in the Civil War South* (New York: Oxford University Press, 2003), 183–4, Stephen W. Berry III identifies love as a prime incentive for men joining Confederate armies, though he juxtaposes this with their love of country.

98 James K. Edmondson to Emma Edmondson, April 5, 15, 1863, in *My Dear Emma*

(War Letters of Col. James K. Edmondson, 1861–1865), ed. Charles W. Turner (Verona, Va.: McClure Press, 1978), 120–21, 122–23.

CHAPTER 6

1 Gary W. Gallagher's survey of Confederate attitudes just before the opening of the Overland campaign offers extensive evidence of the positive morale in Virginia. See " 'Our Hearts Are Full of Hope': The Army of Northern Virginia in the Spring of 1864," in *The Wilderness Campaign*, ed. Gary W. Gallagher (Chapel Hill: University of North Carolina, 1997), 36–65. See also John Herbert Clairborne to "My Dear Wife," April 24, 1864, John Herbert Clairborne Papers, UVa; Amon Updike to "Dear Sister," April 30, 1864, Amon W. Updike Papers, Civil War Miscellaneous Collection, MHI; Albert Davidson to Hannah Greenlee Davidson, June 1, 1864, in Charles W. Turner, ed., "Lieutenant Albert Davidson—Letters of a Virginia Soldier," *West Virginia History* 34 (October 1977): 49–71; Richard Henry Dulany to Mary Dulany, April 27, 1864, in *The Dulany's of Welbourne: A Family in Mosby's Confederacy*, ed. Margaret Ann Vogtsberger (Berryville, Va.: Rockbridge Publishing, 1995); William Wirt Gilmer, late March 1864, Gilmer Family Papers, UVa; and Edward Warren to Virginia Warren, March 9, 1864, Edward T. Warren Papers, UVa.

2 Details on Peyton's activities before he enlisted can be found in David F. Riggs, *13th Virginia Infantry* (Lynchburg, Va.: H. E. Howard, 1988).

3 Edward Warren to Virginia Warren, February 25, 1864, Edward T. Warren Papers, UVa.

4 George Washington Miley to Tirzah Amelia Baker, undated (but given the references Miley makes to previous letters, it was likely written after March 20 and before April 12), George Washington Miley Papers, VHS.

5 Gallagher, "Our Hearts Are Full of Hope," 121–22.

6 John Fletcher Beale to Edith Beale, April 17, 1864, Beale Family Papers, VHS. Also, see William A. Blair, *Virginia's Private War: Feeding Body and Soul in the Confederacy, 1861–1865* (New York: Oxford University Press, 1998), 111. See also John Garibaldi to Sarah A. W. Poor, January 9, 1864, John Garibaldi Papers, VMI, http://www.vmi.edu/archives/Manuscript/ms284029.html.

7 Richard Henry Dulany to Fanny Dulany, January 29, 1864, in Vogtsberger, *The Dulany's of Welbourne*, 128. Abram Henkel to David Kagey, January 15, 1864, Henkel Family Papers, VMI, http://new.vmi.edu/archives/Manuscripts/ms 284029.html.

8 John Booker to Chloe Unity Blair, December 22, 1863, John and James Booker Family Papers, UVa.

9 Philip H. Powers to "My Dear Wife," January 1, 1864, Philip H. Powers Papers, Lewis Leigh Collection, MHI.

10 *Daily Richmond Examiner*, January 4, 1864.

11 Mollie F. Houser to "Dear Cousin," February 28, 1864, John F. Houser Papers, DSC.

12 Rawleigh William Downman to Mary Magruder Downman, January 16, 1864, Downman Family Papers, VHS. By midyear, a sense of determined resignation replaced the buoyant optimism among many Virginia Confederates. For examples, see J. G. Smith to unknown, April 26, 1864, J. G. Smith Papers, Leigh Collection, MHI.

13 John W. Stott Diary, January 23, 1864, John W. Stott Diary, Civil War Times Illustrated Collection, MHI.

14 Overton Stegel to Cordelia Stegel, April 23, 1864, Overton Stegel Papers, Lewis Leigh Collection, MHI. For another example of a soldier who expresses sympathy for a deserter returning to his family, see Henry Robinson Berkeley Diary, January 8, 1864, Henry Robinson Berkeley Papers, VHS.

15 Rufus James Woolwine Diary, April 15, 1864, Rufus James Woolwine Papers, VHS.

16 John T. Cooley to Julia Ann (Cooley) Price, April 21, 1864, Cooley Family Papers, VHS. For another brief report on an execution at this time, see Henry Robinson Berkeley Diary, January 8, 1864, Henry Robinson Berkeley Papers, VHS.

17 J. G. Smith to unknown, April 2, 1864, J. G. Smith Papers, Leigh Collection, MHI.

18 Charles M. Walsh Diary, January 10, 1864, Charles M. Walsh Papers, Civil War Miscellaneous Papers, MHI. Similar concern about executions can be found in other sources as well. See, for example, Richard Henry Allen to Mary Allen, February 25, 1864, in *The Allen Family of Amherst County, Virginia: Civil War Letters*, ed. Charles W. Turner (Berryville, Va.: Rockbridge Publishing, 1995), 61–62.

19 At least one of the soldiers that accompanied Early on his ride into Maryland in July expressed sentiments more commonly heard the previous year. Just as they crossed the Potomac, J. Kelly Bennette recorded, "I don't much like this *invading*; I don't think it is our policy but at the present time it will doubtless doe good by drawing these troops from before Petersburg which Grant can ill afford to spare." See J. Kelly Bennette Diary, July 5, 1864, J. Kelly Bennette Papers, SHC.

20 Samuel Selden Brooke to "My dear Sister," March 27, 1864, Samuel Selden Brooke Papers, VMI, http://new.vmi.edu/archives/Manuscripts/ms022105 .html.

21 John Fletcher Beale to Edith Beale, April 17, 1864, Beale Family Papers, VHS.

22 John Garibaldi to Sarah A. W. Poor, April 22, 1864, John Garibaldi Papers, VMI, http://new.vmi.edu/archives/Manuscripts/ms284033.html.

23 Andrew Long to Cynthia Long, March 9, 1864, Eli Long Papers, DSC.

24 Michael F. Rinker to his parents, May 17, 1864, Michael F. Rinker Papers, VMI, http://new.vmi.edu/archives/Manuscripts/ms0381.html.

25 V. E. Lucas to John James Dillard, May 20, 1864, John James Dillard Papers, DSC.

26 Philip Henry Pendleton to "Dear Mother," May 5, 6, 1864, Philip Henry Pendleton Papers, UVa.

27 Henry Ruffner Morrison to "My Dear Brother," May 6, 1864, Henry Ruffner Morrison Papers, Civil War Times Illustrated Collection, MHI.

28 Thomas F. Kelley to "Martha," May 21, 1864, Thomas F. Kelley Papers, DSC.

29 Robert B. Dunlap to Margaret Dunlap, May 20, 1864, Dunlap Family Letters, VMI.

30 Henry Ruffner Morrison to "My Dear Aunt," May 5, 1864, Henry Ruffner Morrison Papers, Civil War Times Illustrated Collection, MHI.

31 Richard Henry Allen to Mary Allen, May 19, 1864, in Turner, *The Allen Family of Amherst County*, 69.

32 Frank McIntosh Myers to "Dear Home Folks," May 16, 1864, Frank McIntosh Myers, Civil War Times Illustrated Collection, MHI.

33 Two recent authors argue that civilians experienced this same conflict between violence and sentimentality. Harry Stout and Christopher Grasso demonstrate that "what Richmond's male inhabitants took from their world of print and speech must have been the sense that they had to be both Christian and Spartan, both converted and manly, both loving and violent. And it is in this tension that Confederate ideology in Richmond derived its tensile strength and upheld it citizens to the last days of defeat and beyond." Harry S. Stout and Christopher Grasso, "Civil War, Religion, and Communications: The Case of Richmond," in *Religion and the American Civil War*, ed. Randall M. Miller, Harry S. Stout, and Charles Regan Wilson (New York: Oxford University Press, 1998), 343.

34 Julia B. Whiting to Richard Henry Dulany, July 27, 1864, in Vogtsberger, *The Dulany's of Welbourne*, 188–89.

35 Richard Henry Dulany to Mary Dulany, June 8, 1864, in Vogtsberger, *The Dulany's of Welbourne*, 159–60.

36 Mark Grimsley, *And Keep Moving On: The Virginia Campaign, May–June 1864* (Lincoln: University of Nebraska Press, 2002).

37 Creed Thomas Davis Diary, May 18 and 13, June 14, 1864, Creed Thomas Davis Papers, VHS.

38 Richard Henry Watkins to Mary Purnell Watkins, Richard Henry Watkins Papers, April 12, 1864, VHS.

39 Samuel J. C. Moore to Ellen Moore, October 3, 1864, Samuel J. C. Moore Papers, SHC. For a similar sentiment, see Edward T. Warren to his wife, March 12, 1864, Edward T. Warren Papers, UVa.

40 Edward Warren to Virginia Warren, April 5, 1864, Edward T. Warren Papers, UVa.

41 Henry Robinson Berkeley, October 19, 1864, Henry Robinson Berkeley Papers, VHS. See Gary W. Gallagher, *The Confederate War* (Cambridge, Mass.: Harvard University Press, 1997), 40, for a similar petition from another soldier in Early's army in late 1864.

42 Lynda J. Morgan, *Emancipation in Virginia's Tobacco Belt, 1850–1870* (Athens: University of Georgia Press, 1992), chap. 6; and James Marten, "'A Feeling of Restless Anxiety': Loyalty and Race in the Peninsula Campaign and Beyond," in *The Richmond Campaign of 1862: The Peninsula and the Seven Days*, ed. Gary W. Gallagher (Chapel Hill: University of North Carolina Press, 2000), 140.

43 Catherine Barbara Broun, May 1, 1864, Catherine Barbara Broun Papers, SHC.

44 Daniel W. Crofts, *Old Southampton: Politics and Society in a Virginia County, 1834–1869* (Charlottesville: University Press of Virginia, 1992), chap. 7.

45 "The Hatred of Race," *Richmond Sentinel*, August 24, 1864.

46 J. Kelly Bennette Diary, June 19, 1864, J. Kelly Bennette Papers, SHC.

47 William Clark Corson to Jennie Hill Caldwell, July 6, 1864, William Clark Corson Papers, VHS.

48 George Marion Coiner to "Dear Mother," February 21, 1864, Coiner Family Papers, VHS.

49 Stephen Cushman's recent meditation on the difficulty of reconciling the violence of war with the charity and humility demanded by Christianity speaks directly to this point of distinction between civilian and military worlds. Writing about Robert E. Lee in a church in Orange, Virginia, he envisioned the burden of this juxtaposition:

> he cannot dodge the image of a farmboy,
> shot in the cheek or the groin,
> laid in that pew after Cedar Mountain
> or Chancellorsville, the house of the Lord
> become the house of chloroform and amputation

Stephen Cushman, "Except I Shall See," in *Blue Pajamas* (Baton Rouge: Louisiana State University Press, 1998), 3.

50 John Reuben Thompson Diary, March 20, 1864, John Reuben Thompson Papers, UVa. The suffering of Confederates in the North was severe but still better than that of northern soldiers taken South to regions pressed for food to feed their own citizens. A Richmonder's observation on the condition of the returning Confederate prisoners in relation to those held in Richmond reveals this gap. "I have seen a good many of our prisoners that were confined at Point Lookout They look very well a great deal better than the yankees here." See John A. Williams to his sister, March 29, 1864, John A. Williams Papers, VHS.

51 John Garibaldi to Sarah A. W. Poor, January 9, 1864, John Garibaldi Papers, VMI, http://new.vmi.edu/archives/Manuscripts/ms284029.html.

52 Samuel Selden Brooke to "My dear Sister," March 27, 1864, Samuel Selden Brooke Papers, VMI, http://new.vmi.edu/archives/Manuscripts/ms022105 .html.

53 Richard Henry Dulany to Carlyle Whiting, March 28, 1864, in Vogtsberger, *The Dulany's of Welbourne*, 136–37.

54 Frank McIntosh Myers to Washington Myers, January 6, 1864, Frank McIntosh Myers Papers, Civil War Times Illustrated Collection, MHI.

55 Benj. Lewis Blackford to Mrs. Wm. M. Blackford, June 7, 1864, Blackford Family Letters, UVa.

56 *OR*, ser. I, 70:7. Col. E. G. Lee, commanding the 33rd Virginia Infantry, wrote to General Lee with a frank assessment of their defeat at Piedmont. "We have been pretty badly whipped." See E. G. Lee to R. E. Lee, June 5, 1864, *OR*, ser. I, 70:151.

57 Of the 555 Virginia companies that composed Early's Army of the Valley, 157 (or 28.3 percent) were organized in Valley counties. Scholars have defined the Valley in a variety of ways. I have adopted the regional boundaries identified by the Virginia state auditor in response to a request from the 1861 Virginia Secession Convention. The report is document 37, table A in *Journals of the Virginia State Convention of 1861*, vol. 3: *Documents* (Richmond: Virginia State Library, 1966); an appendix provides a list of counties in the Valley.

58 Frederick Anspach to Robert Anspach, June 23, 1864, Anspach Letters, UVa.

59 Amon W. Updike to "Dear Sister," July 14, 1864, Amon W. Updike Papers, Civil War Miscellaneous Collection, MHI. See also George Quintis Peyton, Diary of George Quintis Peyton, UVa; Marcus Blakemore Buck, Marcus Blakemore Buck Diary, UVa; and Thomas Cleveland to Bettie Cleveland, July 18, 1864, in Ellen Miyagawa, ed., "The Boys Who Wore the Gray: A Collection of Letters and Articles Written by Members of the Fluvanna Artillery, 1861–1865," *Bulletin of the Fluvanna County Historical Society* 42 (October 1986): 79. Cornelius Hart Carlton's diary includes almost daily references to the heat and dryness from April through July, 1864. See Cornelius Hart Carlton Papers, VHS. Also see the Mathella Page Harrison and Gilmer Family Papers at UVa.

60 Robert Young Conrad to Elizabeth Conrad, June 21, June 28, 1864, Holmes Conrad Papers, VHS.

61 J. E. Norris, ed., *History of the Lower Shenandoah Valley* (Chicago: A. Warner and Co., 1890), 571–73. For a short account of Conrad's deliberations in the Virginia Secession Convention, where he voted against secession, see David F. Riggs, "Robert Young Conrad and the Ordeal of Secession," *VMHB* 86 (July 1978): 259–74. For a contrary interpretation of loyalty toward the Confederacy among Frederick County residents, see Michael J. Gorman, "'Our Politicians

Have Enslaved Us': Power and Politics in Frederick County, Virginia," in *After the Backcountry: Rural Life in the Great Valley of Virginia, 1800–1900*, ed. Kenneth E. Koons and Warren R. Hofstra (Knoxville: University of Tennessee Press, 2000), 274–86.

62 E. G. Lee to Gen. S. Cooper, *OR*, ser. I, 70:152–54.

63 This assessment of the impact of Siegel's and Hunter's raids on the Valley corresponds with that reached by Will Thomas in his essay on 1864 campaigns. See William G. Thomas, "Nothing Ought to Astonish Us: Confederate Civilians in the 1864 Shenandoah Valley Campaign," in *The Shenandoah Valley Campaign of 1864*, ed. Gary W. Gallagher (Chapel Hill: University of North Carolina Press, 2006).

64 Grant to Halleck, May 25, 1864, *OR*, ser. I, 70:536; see also the dispatch from Assistant Secretary of War Dana to Secretary of War Stanton, June 5, 1864, *OR*, ser. I, 67:89–90; and Grant to General George G. Meade, June 5, 1864, *OR*, ser. I, 67:90.

65 Thomas Cleveland to Bettie Cleveland, June 28, 1864, in Miyagawa, "The Boys Who Wore the Gray," 75. See also Buckner Magill Randolph, June 21, 1864, Randolph Family Papers, VHS.

66 Isaac White to Mary Virginia (Day) White, June 27, 1864, Isaac White Letters, VT, http://spec.lib.vt.edu/mss/white/white.htm.

67 Gary W. Gallagher, "The Shenandoah Valley in 1864," in *Struggle For the Shenandoah: Essays on the 1864 Valley Campaign* (Kent, Ohio: Kent State University Press, 1991), 9.

68 Early to Breckenridge, July 3, 1864, *OR*, ser. II, 71:591.

69 Henry Robinson Berkeley Diary, June 25, 1864, Henry Robinson Berkeley papers, VHS. I am drawing on the work of Drew Gilpin Faust who argues that "Nationalism is contingent; its creation is a process." Drew Gilpin Faust, *Creation of Confederate Nationalism: Ideology and Identity in the Civil War South* (Baton Rouge: Louisiana State University Press, 1988), 6. The practice of marching Confederate soldiers by Jackson's grave resembles a dynamic counterpart to the painting *The Burial of Latané*, which hung in the Richmond state capital. Faust described the effects of paintings from this heroic genre, "In their portrayal of virtue, personal sacrifice, and heroism as the essences of national greatness, these works invoke Christian iconography to extend a quasi-religious dimension to their subject matter; they are the visual counterparts to the transcendent language of the era's nationalist rhetoric." Faust, *Creation of Confederate Nationalism*, 70. The process that Berkeley, Randolph, and Peyton observe accomplished the same thing on a wider scale by offering Confederate citizens heroic martyrs whom they could cherish. For an exploration of the religious meaning of Jack-

son's death among Confederates, see Daniel W. Stowall, "Stonewall Jackson and the Providence of God," in *Religion and the American Civil War*, ed. Randall M. Miller, Harry S. Stout, and Charles Reagan Wilson (New York: Oxford University Press, 1998), 187–207. Although Stowall too sees Confederates creating a process of "corporate cultural ritual" in memories of Jackson's death, he reads these efforts as the prelude to how Confederates interpreted their eventual loss to the North. My sense is that during the war, Confederate military leaders, and soldiers as well, used Jackson's image and memory to model the selfless sacrifice they expected from soldiers. Charles Royster makes a similar point in his analysis of the meaning of Jackson's death for his fellow soldiers, arguing that "even in death [Jackson's presence would] help to win Confederate independence." See Charles Royster, *The Destructive War: William Tecumseh Sherman, Stonewall Jackson, and the Americans* (New York: Vintage, 1991), 204.

70 See Buckner Magill Randolph Diary, June 25, 1864, Randolph Family Papers, VHS, and George Quintis Peyton, June 25, 1864, Peyton Papers, UVa. J. Tracy Power quotes several soldiers from other units who noted their passes by Jackson's grave. See J. Tracy Power, *Lee's Miserables: Life in the Army of Northern Virginia from the Wilderness to Appomattox* (Chapel Hill: University of North Carolina Press, 1998), 93–94.

71 Charles A. Dana to Ulysses S. Grant, July 15, 1864, *OR*, ser. II, 71:329.

72 Achilles J. Tynes to Harriet Lousia Tynes, July 29, 1864, Achilles J. Tynes Papers, SHC.

73 Mollie F. Houser to "Dear Cousin," March 21, 1864, John F. Houser Papers, DSC.

74 Isaac White, August 9, 1864, Isaac White Letters, VT, http://spec.lib.vt.edu/mss/white/white.htm.

75 J. Kelly Bennette Diary, July 30, 1864, J. Kelly Bennette Papers, SHC. "Nolens volens" translates as "unwilling or willing."

76 James K. Edmondson to Emma Edmondson, August 7, 1864, in Turner, *My Dear Emma*, 131–32.

77 John Herbert Clairborne to "My dear wife," May 14, 1864, John Herbert Clairborne Papers, UVa.

78 Robert A. Lancaster to "Dear Bob," March 25, 1864, Robert Alexander Lancaster Papers, VHS. The persistence of Confederate support is present even in places where neither side could establish definitive control. In his study of the aptly named "Debatable Land" in the northern Piedmont, Michael Stuart Mangus finds continuing support for Confederate victory among most residents through 1864; see " 'The Debatable Land': Loudoun and Fauquier Counties, Virginia during the Civil War Era" (Ph.D. diss., Ohio State University, 1998), chap. 8.

CHAPTER 7

1   Mark Grimsley, *And Keep Moving On: The Virginia Campaign, May–June 1864*
    (Lincoln: University of Nebraska Press, 2002), 226.

2   Record keeping during the last months of the war was sporadic at best and makes
    it very difficult to offer a definitive quantitative assessment of the socioeconomic
    characteristics of those soldiers who left the army during this period.

3   Chronology remains a crucial issue in this regard. Most histories that stress the
    internal collapse of the Confederacy due to class tensions identify a falling away
    beginning either immediately after the war's outbreak or at least by mid-1863. In
    these arguments, class conflict is generated from within Confederate society and
    ripples outward to disrupt Confederate military performance. See, for example,
    David Williams, *Rich Man's War: Class, Caste, and Confederate Defeat in the Lower
    Chattahoochee Valley* (Athens: University of Georgia Press, 1998), 168–173. In
    Virginia, class conflict was present throughout the war but did not impede a
    common devotion among almost all white residents to separation from the
    Union. Class-based resentments exacerbated, and were exacerbated by, the mili-
    tary success of the northern armies late in the war.

4   Reuben E. Hammond to Ella V. Rinker, July 7, 1864, Reuben E. Hammond
    Papers, DSC.

5   George Quintis Peyton Diary, August 30, 1864, George Quintis Peyton Papers,
    UVa. Evidence of the abundance of food at this time in the Valley abounds in
    most soldiers accounts. Henry Robinson Berkeley noted on September 1 from
    Winchester, "We are getting an abundance of nice & ripe apples now. I weigh
    more now than I ever did before in my life." Henry Robinson Berkeley Diary,
    September 1, 1864, Henry Robinson Berkeley Papers, VHS. See also J. Tracy
    Power, *Lee's Miserables: Life in the Army of Northern Virginia from the Wilderness to
    Appomattox* (Chapel Hill: University of North Carolina, 1998), 105. Power also
    highlights the role that farmers in the Valley played in providing food and other
    crops to Confederate armies.

6   Journal of John Milton Hoge, late August, 1864, John Milton Hoge Papers, UVa.

7   William Clark Corson to Jennie Hill Caldwell, September 10, 1864, William
    Clark Corson Papers, VHS.

8   John T. Cooley to Julia Ann (Cooley) Price; September 17, 1864, Cooley Family
    Papers, VHS.

9   Gary W. Gallagher, *The Confederate War* (Cambridge, Mass.: Harvard University
    Press, 1997), 77.

10 Charles A. Davidson to Hannah Greenlee Davidson, June 1, 1864, in Charles W.
    Turner, ed., "Major Charles A. Davidson: Letters of a Virginia Soldier," *CWH* 22
    (March 1970): 16–40.

11 See Gary W. Gallagher, "The Shenandoah Valley in 1864," in *Struggle For the*

Shenandoah: Essays on the 1864 Valley Campaign (Kent, Ohio: Kent State University Press, 1991), 13–18, for more detail on Grant's decision to send Sheridan to the Valley and a summary of the fall campaign between Sheridan and Early.

12 Mathella Page Harrison Diary, August 17, 1864, Mathella Page Harrison Diary, UVa.

13 Richard Henry Watkins, October 3, 1864, Richard Henry Watkins Papers, VHS.

14 *Daily Richmond Examiner*, October 12, 1864.

15 William V. Kie Diary, September 3, 1864, William V. Kie Papers, UVa.

16 Lizzie to G. Julian Pratt, October 12, 1864, G. Julian Pratt Papers, Lewis Leigh Collection, MHI.

17 Ibid. This same transformation even occurred among Unionists civilians in Culpeper who lived through the destruction of their county in late 1863 and early 1864 by Federal troops. See Daniel E. Sutherland, "The Absence of Violence: Confederates and Unionists in Culpeper County," in *Guerrillas, Unionists, and Violence on the Confederate Home Front*, ed. G. Julian (Fayetteville: University of Arkansas Press, 1999), 75–87. Hatred and anger was also the response of Carolina women to the invasion of William T. Sherman and his forces in early 1865. See Jacqueline Glass Campbell, *When Sherman Marched North from the Sea: Resistance on the Confederate Home Front* (Chapel Hill: University of North Carolina Press, 2005).

18 John Anthony Craig to Ann Parke (Jones), October 15, 1864, John Anthony Craig Papers, VHS.

19 William Clark Corson, October 13, 1864, William Clark Corson Papers, VHS.

20 Robert Ryland Horne to Mollie Horne, October 29, 1864, Horne Family Papers, VHS.

21 L. Robert Moore to "Dear Ma," October 28, 1864, L. Robert Moore Papers, VHS.

22 Werner H. Steger, " 'United to Support, but Not Combined to Injure': Free Workers and Immigrants in Richmond, Virginia, during the Era of Sectionalism, 1847–1865" (Ph.D. diss., George Washington University, 1999), chap. 6.

23 J. J. Hill to Phebe Howson Bailey, December 16, 1864, Bailey Family Papers, VHS.

24 William Thomas Casey to "My Dear Brother," June 30, 1864, William Thomas Casey Papers, VHS.

25 J. Kelly Bennette Diary, August 31, 1864, J. Kelly Bennette Papers, SHC. Reid Mitchell has identified this aspect of Confederate service as well, arguing that "suffering proved his patriotism and thus raised his self-esteem." See Reid Mitchell, "The Creation of Confederate Loyalties," in *New Perspectives on Race and Slavery in America: Essays in Honor of Kenneth M. Stampp*, ed. Robert H. Abzug and Stephen E. Maizlish (Lexington: University Press of Kentucky, 1986), 99.

26 Richard Henry Dulany to James Peyton Dulany, August 9, 1864, in Margaret

Ann Vogtsberger, ed., *The Dulany's of Welbourne: A Family in Mosby's Confederacy* (Berryville, Va.: Rockbridge Publishing, 1995), 196, 206.

27 Lisa Laskin explores this issue in more detail in "The Army Is Not Near So Much Demoralized as the Country Is," in *The View from the Ground: Experiences of Civil War Soldiers*, ed. Aaron Sheehan-Dean (Lexington: University Press of Kentucky, 2007), 91–120.

28 Charles Fenton James to Emma Fenton, February 13, 1865, Charles Fenton James Papers, SHC. For a similar division opening between soldiers and their home community in Lynchburg, Virginia, see Steven Tripp, *Yankee Town, Southern City: Race and Class Relations in Civil War Lynchburg* (New York: New York University Press, 1997), 120. Some soldiers could equate their suffering with their own family's experience but rarely could they identify anyone else who had suffered as they did. A typically self-centered evaluation can be found in Robert Brooke Jones to Elizabeth Hill Jones, August 24, 1864, Jones Family Papers, VHS.

29 Confederate Pamphlets #252, 9th Virginia Infantry, January, 1865, DSC. These resolutions can be found reprinted in the Virginia General Assembly, to which they were submitted, and in local newspapers, throughout January and February 1865.

30 Ibid.

31 2nd Virginia Cavalry, February 28, 1865, box 141, Robert Alonzo Brock Papers, HEH.

32 "The Spirit of the Army," *Richmond Whig and Public Advertiser*, February 24, 1865.

33 See, for example, Creed Thomas Davis Diary, September 6, 1864, Creed Thomas Davis Papers, VHS.

34 Richard Henry Dulany to James Peyton Dulany, September 5, 1864, in Vogtsberger, *The Dulany's of Welbourne*, 217–20.

35 Willis Michael Parker to Peter Guerrant, September 10, 1864, Guerrant Family Papers, VHS. See also, Peter Guerrant to William Waddy Anderson, October 9, 1864, Guerrant Family Papers, VHS. Joseph H. Trundle to "My Dear Mother," November 15, 1864, Joseph H. Trundle Papers, Lewis Leigh Collection, MHI.

36 Buckner Magill Randolph, September 25, 1864, Randolph Family Papers, VHS.

37 Daniel A. Wilson to "Col.," October 21, 1864, Daniel A. Wilson Papers, VHS.

38 William A. Blair, *Virginia's Private War: Feeding Body and Soul in the Confederacy* (New York: Oxford University Press, 1997), 127.

39 Frederick Fillison Bowen to "Dear Charlie," October 15, 1864, Frederick Fillison Bowen Papers, VHS.

40 Peter Guerrant to William Waddy Anderson, October 2, 1864, William Waddy

Anderson to Peter Guerrant, October 7, 1864; Peter Guerrant to William Waddy Anderson, October 9, 1864, Guerrant Family Papers, VHS.

41 Unknown to James A. Sutherland, December 3, 1864, James A. Sutherland Papers, DSC.

42 Rand Dotson, " 'The Grave and Scandalous Evil Infected to Your People': The Erosion of Confederate Loyalty in Floyd County, Virginia," *VMHB* 108 (2000): 430–31. Dotson provides a compelling account of the escalation of conflict in Floyd County, as deserter bands, the Confederate home guard, and the Confederate military collided with increasing violence in late 1863 and 1864. He identifies concern over families as the initial incentive for men to desert from the army but offers little evidence to support this aspect of his argument. Another study of this region emphasizes civilian despair and social chaos in later 1864, along the lines of that detailed by Paul Escott for North Carolina; see Kenneth W. Noe, *Southwest Virginia's Railroad: Modernization and the Sectional Crisis* (Urbana: University of Illinois Press, 1994), chaps. 6–7. This situation had a specific regional context. For a nearly identical problems of control and violence in eastern Tennessee, see Noel C. Fisher, *War at Every Door: Partisan Politics and Guerrilla Violence in East Tennessee, 1860–1869* (Chapel Hill: University of North Carolina Press, 1997), 153.

43 William B. G. Andrews to "Dear Father," December 26, 1864, William B. G. Andrews Papers, DSC.

44 Creed Thomas Davis Diary, January 2, 1865, December 24, 1864, Creed Thomas Davis Papers, VHS.

45 John L. Gwyn to "My Dear Sister," February 3, 1865, John L. Gwyn Papers, Lewis Leigh Collection, MHI; Green William Penn to "Dear Ma," October 27, 1864, Green William Penn Papers, DSC.

46 James Bailey to Polly Bailey, January 1, 1865, Bailey Family Papers, VHS.

47 Amon W. Updike to "My Dear Sister," January 17, 1865, Amon W. Updike Papers, Civil War Miscellaneous Collection, MHI.

48 William T. Allen to Mary Allen, March 17, 1865, in *The Allen Family of Amherst County, Virginia: Civil War Letters*, ed. Charles W. Turner (Berryville, Va.: Rockbridge Publishing, 1995), 81.

49 Amon W. Updike to "My Dear Sister," March 20, 1865, Amon W. Updike Papers, Civil War Miscellaneous Collection, MHI.

50 Kurt O. Berends has recently offered another explanation for why Confederate soldiers may have remained optimistic about the likelihood of victory until the very end of the war. The religious military press (RMP) of the Confederacy, which provided voluminous reading material to soldiers, adopted relentlessly positive interpretations of all battles, even those that the Confederacy lost, and continued

to predict imminent victory until the last weeks of the war. More substantively, Berends shows that by articulating the religious dimensions of the conflict, RMP editors gave soldiers a way to understand military defeats as transient temporal setbacks that provided opportunities for atonement and repentance, which God would reward with ultimate victory. See Kurt O. Berends, " 'Wholesome Reading Purifies and Elevates the Man': The Religious Military Press in the Confederacy," in *Religion and the American Civil War*, ed. Randall M. Miller, Harry S. Stout, and Charles Reagan Wilson (New York: Oxford University Press, 1998), 148.

51 Richard Woolfolk Waldrop to Ellen Douglas Waldrop, October 8, 1864, Richard Woolfolk Waldrop Papers, SHC.

52 Richard Woolfolk Waldrop to Ellen Douglas Waldrop, July 27, 1861, Richard Woolfolk Waldrop Papers, SHC.

53 Charles Minor Blackford to Susan Leigh Blackford, June 13, 1864, in *Letters from Lee's Army*, ed. Charles Minor Blackford III (New York: Charles Schribner's, 1947; rpt., Lincoln: University of Nebraska Press, 1998), 255. The cliché of "boiling blood" and the theme of unbridled anger against the North surfaces frequently in soldiers' writings at the time. See materials in the collections of William Wilson, William Corson, Frederick Anspach, and Lewis M. Blackford.

54 R. H. Field to George Hamilton, February 28, 1865, Downman Family Papers, VHS. See also Robert Ryland Horne to "Dear Sister Eddie," February 25, 1865, Horne Family Papers, VHS.

55 Henry Ruffner Morrison to "My Dear Brother," October 11, 1864, Henry Ruffner Morrison Papers, Civil War Times Illustrated Collection, MHI. See also Horace M. Wade to "My Dear Sister," June 22, 1864, Horace M. Wade Papers, Lewis Leigh Collection, MHI.

56 William M. Willson to J. Francis Willson, October 15, 1864, Elizabeth Ann Willson Papers, UVa. Andrew Jackson McCoy to Martha E. McCoy, March 11, 1864, Andrew Jackson McCoy Papers, VMI, http://new.vmi.edu/archives/Manu scripts/ms039303.html.

57 Henry Robinson Berkeley Diary, September 23, 1864, Henry Robinson Berkeley Papers, VHS.

58 Robert L. Moore to "Dear Ma," January 30, 1865, Robert L. Moore Papers, VHS.

59 John L. Gwyn to "Dearest Wife," February 3, 1865, John L. Gwyn Papers, Lewis Leigh Collection, MHI. See also John L. Gwyn to "My Dear Sister," February 3, 1865.

60 George Marion Coiner to Kate Coiner, February 6, 1865, Coiner Family Papers, VHS.

61 Charles Fenton James to Emma Fenton, February 7, 1865, Charles Fenton James Papers, SHC.

62 Richard Henry Watkins to Mary Purnell Watkins, September 13, 1864, Richard

Henry Watkins Papers, VHS. Watkins was correct that "a large majority have never owned slaves," and in comparison to Virginia's Piedmont region, Valley families held far fewer numbers of slaves, but the percentage of Valley households owning slaves was nonetheless reasonably high in comparison to other southern places. Seventeen percent of Valley households owned slaves; see 1860 U.S. Census Population and Agricultural Schedules. For an example of the prominence of slavery in one Valley county, see J. Susanne Simmons and Nancy T. Sorrells, "Slave Hire and the Development of Slavery in Augusta County, Virginia," in *After the Backcountry: Rural Life in the Great Valley of Virginia, 1800–1900*, ed. Kenneth E. Koons and Warren R. Hofstra (Knoxville: University of Tennessee Press, 2000), 169–85.

63 Anne Freudenberg and John Casteen, eds., "John B. Minor's Civil War Diary," *Magazine of Albermarle County History* 22 (1963–64): 45–55.

64 Joseph H. Trundle to "My Dear Mother," November 15, 1864, Joseph H. Trundle Papers, Lewis Leigh Collection, MHI.

65 Richard Lancelot Maury Diary, February 21, 1865, Richard Lancelot Maury Diary, VHS. For a more extensive treatment, see Philip D. Dillard, "Independence or Slavery: The Confederate Debate over Arming the Slaves" (Ph.D. diss., Rice University, 1999), and Robert F. Durden, *The Gray and the Black: The Confederate Debate on Emancipation* (Baton Rouge: Louisiana State University Press, 1972).

66 Robert E. Lee to Andrew Hunter, January 11, 1865, box 35, James Eldridge Papers, HEH.

67 "Will We Succeed?" *Marion Ensign*, October 14, 1864.

68 Dillard traces the debate over this issue carefully, showing the deep reluctance with which many Virginians eventually accepted the policy. Dillard, "Independence or Slavery," 85–87, and Durden, *Gray and the Black*, 196–99. William B. G. Andrews to "Dear Father," February 21, 1865, William B. G. Andrews Papers, DSC.

69 Nina Whiting to Alice Whiting, November, 1864, January 1, 1865, in Vogtsberger, *The Dulany's of Welbourne*, 239, 252. See also B. H. Anthony to Callie Anthony, February 20, 1865, Anthony Family Papers, UVa.

70 Dillard also reaches the latter conclusion in his study of the Confederate debate over arming slaves. See Dillard, "Independence or Slavery," 283–84. Giselle Roberts, in her study of attitudes among white southern women in Mississippi and Louisiana reaches a similar conclusion as well, arguing that "by separating the Cause and the honorable actions of southern people from the military outcome of the war, the women of Mississippi and Louisiana were able to preserve the very ideals upon which their lives rested. See Giselle Roberts, " 'Our Cause': Southern Women and Confederate Nationalism in Mississippi and Louisiana," *Journal of Mississippi History* 62 (Summer 2000): 121.

1 Creed Thomas Davis Diary, April 4, 1865, Creed Thomas Davis Papers, VHS. For a similar description, see Cornelius Hart Carlton Diary, April 4, 1865, Cornelius Hart Carlton Diary, VHS. Unlike almost every other aspect of the war, Confederate soldiers did not keep good personal records of the events after the fall of Petersburg. Very few wrote letters (as demonstrated in the predominance of diaries in the citations that follow) and of those that did few reached their intended recipients.

2 Evidence that soldiers foresaw the final defeat of the Confederacy from the fall of Richmond can be seen in the diaries and letters of soldiers from this period. See, for example, John H. Walters Diary, April 4, 1865, in *Norfolk Blues: The Civil War Diary of the Norfolk Light Artillery Blues*, ed. Kenneth Wiley (Shippensburg, Pa.: Burd Street Press, 1997), 219.

3 Nelson Lankford's recent history of the fall of Richmond offers the best narrative of this period. See Nelson Lankford, *Richmond Burning: The Last Days of the Confederate Capital* (New York: Penguin, 2002).

4 Russell F. Weigley, *A Great Civil War: A Military and Political History, 1861–1865* (Bloomington: Indiana University Press, 2000), chap. 13. The number of men still in Lee's army during the retreat and the number of men who surrendered at Appomattox has remained a point of contention since the war's end. William Marvel offers the fullest and most convincing analysis of the numbers in his recent book on the Appomattox Campaign. He counts as many as 77,400 men with Lee prior to the attack at Fort Steadman on March 25. The subsequent two weeks of fighting imposed 26,000 casualties, and 28,000 men surrendered at Appomattox. Thus, in addition to the 3,000 known deserters, Marvel estimates that at least 14,400 and as many as 20,400 Confederate soldiers abandoned Lee's army along the retreat to Appomattox. Virginia units suffered the highest rates of desertion during the march, losing 75 percent of their strength in the last month of fighting. Marvel identifies a pattern in men's abandonment of the army during this period: the closer soldiers were to their homes, the more likely they were to leave. See William Marvel, *Lee's Last Retreat: The Flight to Appomattox* (Chapel Hill: University of North Carolina Press, 2002), 205–6.

5 Marvel, *A Place Called Appomattox*, 250.

6 Kena King Chapman Diary, April 12, 1865, Kena King Chapman Papers, SHC.

7 James Eldred Phillips Diary, April 12 1865, James Eldred Phillips Papers, VHS. Outside of Appomattox, few men seem to have taken the oath. Of the records collected in the database for this study, only 15.9 percent were officially paroled and only 10.5 percent were noted as having taken the oath. Because these oaths and paroles were usually given out after the end of the active hostilities, many men could have received Federal absolution in private. Nonetheless, it is striking

that as many as two-thirds (adding in the 15 percent who died during the conflict) of the men who served in Virginia forces may have simply walked away from the conflict without ever being asked to officially renounce their actions.

8 Edgar Tschiffel to Mrs. Francis Harnsberger, July 8, 1865, Edgar Tschiffel Papers, Lewis Leigh Collection, MHI.

9 Ibid.

10 Confederates' demonization of their enemy promoted cohesion during the conflict but left a broken foundation for postwar reconciliation. For a more thorough treatment of this issue, see Jason Phillips, "A Brother's War? Exploring Confederate Perceptions of the Enemy," in *The View from the Ground: Experiences of Civil War Soldiers*, ed. Aaron Sheehan-Dean (Lexington: University Press of Kentucky, 2007), 67–90.

11 For an analysis of how northern soldiers managed this problem, see David W. Rolfs, "No Nearer Heaven but Rather Farther Off," in Sheehan-Dean, *The View From the Ground*, 121–14.

12 Eric T. Dean's comparative analysis of post-traumatic stress disorder among Civil War and Vietnam War veterans explores the experiences of those who did not make such an easy shift back into civilian life. See Eric T. Dean, *Shook All over Hell: Post-Traumatic Stress, Vietnam, and the Civil War* (Cambridge, Mass.: Harvard University Press, 1997).

13 Robert Garlick Hill Kean, June 1, 1865, in *Inside the Confederate Government: The Diary of Robert Garlick Hill Kean*, ed. Edward Younger (New York: Oxford University Press, 1957), 208–10.

14 Augusta County Court Petition, January 16, 1865, box 219, Robert Alonzo Brock Papers, HEH.

15 United States Bureau of the Census, *Eighth Census of the United States, 1860*, 4 vols. (Washington, D.C.: Government Printing Office, 1865).

16 Gordon Rhea's excellent volumes on the Overland campaign of 1864 show this process in detail. See, for examples, Gordon Rhea, *To the North Anna River: Grant and Lee, May 13–25, 1864* (Baton Rouge: Louisiana State University Press, 2000), 271, 319.

17 The interdependence of men and women in the postwar world was as much physical as it was emotional. My interpretation resonates with a recent study of Virginia planter families after the Civil War, which found that "former masters and mistresses . . . renegotiated the terms of their relationships away from antebellum patriarchal norms and toward mutuality." Amy Feely Morsman, "The Big House after Slavery: Virginia's Plantation Elite and Their Postbellum Domestic Experiment" (Ph.D. diss., University of Virginia, 2004), 10.

18 The major histories of masculinity in nineteenth-century America tend to focus on the northern, urban, white middle class. See Anthony E. Rotundo, *American*

Manhood: Transformations in Masculinity from the Revolution to the Modern Era
(New York: Basic Books, 1993); Stephen M. Frank, *Life with Father: Parenthood
and Masculinity in the Nineteenth-Century American North* (Baltimore: Johns Hopkins University Press, 1998); and Shawn Johansen, *Family Men: Middle Class
Fatherhood in Early Industrializing America* (New York: Routledge, 2001). Our
awareness of the war's impact makes the need for new studies of southern
masculinity, both before and after the Civil War, all the more pressing.

19 My assessment of the Virginia experience contrasts with that reached by Mark
Weitz in his study of Georgia soldiers, where he argues that family obligations
inspired men to desert the Confederate armies. See *A Higher Duty: Desertion
among Georgia Troops during the Civil War* (Lincoln: University of Nebraska Press,
2000).

20 James Marten draws a similar message from his study of Confederate fatherhood. See James Marten, "Fatherhood in the Confederacy: Southern Soldiers and
Their Children," *JSH* 63 (May 1997): 292. Likewise, a recent essay by Amy
Murrell identifies the success Confederates had in blending family and national
interests. "Over the course of the war, soldiers' families and government leaders
actually appear to have grown closer to an agreement about how to reconcile the
interests of families and the greater nation." See Amy Murrell, " 'Of Necessity
and Public Benefit': Southern Families and Their Appeals for Protection," in
Southern Families at War: Loyalty and Conflict in the Civil War South, ed. Catherine
Clinton (New York: Oxford University Press, 2000), 79.

APPENDIX

1 Exact totals were available for all units except the 14th Infantry.

2 Exact totals were available for all units except the 6th and 10th Cavalry.

3 Exact totals were not available for six artillery regiments and nine batteries.
I used the company average of 127 soldiers for artillery units to estimate the size
of these units.

4 Richard L. Sheaffer, William Mendenhall, and Lyman Ott, *Elementary Survey
Sampling* (Boston: PWS-Kent, 1990), 119.

5 I identified West Virginia place-names using the *West Virginia Atlas and Gazetteer*
(Yarmouth, Maine: DeLorme, 2001).

BIBLIOGRAPHY

PRIMARY SOURCES

Manuscript Sources

Duke University Special Collections Department, Perkins Library,
Durham, North Carolina

William B. G. Andrews Papers

Fletcher Harris Archer Papers

William Baskerville Papers

George S. Bernard Papers

Charles Berry Papers

Alexander Brown Papers

Isaac Howell Carrington Papers

Jedediah Carter Papers

John Joseph Chadick Papers

William Walter Christian Papers

Jacob B. Click Papers

Confederate Pamphlets #252

Henry Copenhaver Papers

John James Dillard Papers

Thomas J. Elliott Papers

James C. Franklin Papers

Robert G. Haile Papers

Reuben E. Hammond Papers

Orsin V. Hancock Papers

Henry St. George Harris Papers

William Fleming Harrison Papers

J. L. Henry Papers

Frederick W. M. Holliday Papers

Robert W. Hooke Papers

John F. Houser Papers

William H. Jones Papers

Thomas F. Kelley Papers

Williamson Kelly Papers

Eli Long Papers

John Howie Magruder Papers

William Miller McAllister Papers

John Monroe Papers

Pankey Family Papers

Green William Penn Papers

Hugh N. Ponton Papers

Staunton Artillery Collection

James A. Sutherland Papers

Robert C. Trigg Papers

James M. Willcox Papers

George Newton Wise Papers

Henry E. Huntington Library, San Marino, California

William E. Arnold Papers

Robert Alonzo Brock Papers

John V. Clendenen Papers

Jubal Early Papers

James Eldridge Papers

Lamar Fontaine Papers

Michael G. Harman Papers

Robert E. Lee Papers

Francis Lieber Papers

James Longstreet Papers

Montgomery Slaughter Papers

James Ewell Brown Stuart Papers

John Baker Tapscott Papers

Ansel Whedan Papers

Military History Institute, U.S. Army War College, Carlisle, Pennsylvania

Brake Collection

John Garibaldi Papers

Ambrose M. Hite Papers

Robert L. Thompson Papers

Halsey Wigfall Papers

Civil War Miscellaneous Collection

B. H. Coffman Papers

Ferdinand J. Dunlap Papers

Samuel A. Firebaugh Papers

William H. Gregory Papers

Hart Brothers Papers

Joseph Richard Manson Papers

Amon W. Updike Papers

Updike and Arthur Family Papers

Charles M. Walsh Diary

C. R. Woolwine Papers

H. D. Yancy Papers

Civil War Times Illustrated Collection

William A. Barger Papers

William G. Caboniss Papers

Samuel Dunbar Papers

George Greer Diary

William J. Hatchet Papers

William S. Keller Papers

Sue E. Litchford Papers

Samuel H. Moore Papers

Henry Ruffner Morrison Papers

Frank McIntosh Myers Papers

John F. Neff Papers

George S. Pickett Diary

Joseph E. Purvis Papers

James L. Sharp Papers

William Randolph Smith Diary

John W. Stott Diary

Charles M. Watts Papers

Harrisburg Civil War Round Table Collection

John B. Fontaine Papers

Alfred T. Forbes Papers

R. D. Funkhouser

Janney Family Papers

Musick Collection

Lewis Leigh Collection

Philip Airhart Papers

Robert L. Bates Papers

Armistead Burwell Papers

M. H. Easery Papers

George W. Finley Papers

Thomas M. Gordon Papers

A. W. Graves Papers

Thomas H. Grayson Papers

John L. Gwyn Papers

John P. Harrison Papers

Hileman Family Papers

G. W. Imboden Papers

Robert B. Isbell Papers

William E. Isbell Papers

Edmund J. Jarvis Papers

J. A. Jones Papers

James Z. McChesney Papers

Thomas T. Munford Papers

Hugh Nelson Papers

Washington Nelson Papers

J. B. Philips Papers

Philip H. Powers Papers

G. Julian Pratt Papers

J. G. Smith Papers

Richard T. Spotwood Papers

Staunton General Hospital (unidentified author)

Overton Stegel Papers

Samuel M. Tisdell Papers

Joseph H. Trundle Papers

Edgar Tschiffel Papers

Unknown Author Papers

Algernon S. Wade Papers

Benjamin F. Wade Papers

Horace M. Wade Papers

H. Sidney Wallace Papers

S. H. Wise Papers

Southern Historical Collection, University of North Carolina, Chapel Hill

J. Kelly Bennette Papers

Thomas F. Boatwright Papers

Catherine Barbara Broun Papers

Irving A. Buck Papers

Kena King Chapman Diary

Robert A. Jackson Papers

Charles Fenton James Papers

Joseph Franklin Kauffman Diary

Joseph Mason Kern Diary

Charles Edward Lippitt Diary

Rawley White Martin Papers

Samuel J. C. Moore Papers

Peek Family Papers

Achilles J. Tynes Papers

Richard Woolfolk Waldrop Papers

James Jones White Papers

John Q. Winfield Papers

University of Virginia Special Collections Department, Alderman Library,
Charlottesville

Alexander Family Papers

Anspach Family Letters

Anthony Family Papers

Blackford Family Letters

John and James Booker Papers

William Francis Brand Papers

Brown Family Papers

Marcus Blakemore Buck Diary

William D. Cabell Papers

John Herbert Clairborne Papers

Giles Buckner Cooke Papers

Eugene M. Cox Papers

Andrew Jackson Dawson Papers

Dinwiddie Family Papers

Nancy Emerson Papers

Fishburne Family Papers

Gilmer Family Papers

Graham Family Papers

Wesley A. Hammond Papers

Mathella Page Harrison Diary

John Milton Hoge Diary

Walter Quarles Hullihen Papers

John Peter Jones Papers

William V. Kie Papers

Leftwich Family Papers

Lewis Family Papers

Marcey family papers

Hugh Thomas Nelson Diary

Joseph W. Parrish Papers

Philip Henry Pendleton Papers

George Quintis Peyton Diary

Levi Pitman Papers

Richard Wingfield Quarles Papers

Stoddard Family Papers

John Reuben Thompson Diary

Twyman Family Papers

Joseph Addison Waddell Diary

Wallace Family Papers

Edward T. Warren Papers

B. K. Whittle, Whittle Family Papers

Willson Family Papers

Louis A. Wise Papers

Charles Yancey Papers

University of Virginia, *Valley of the Shadow*, World Wide Web Manuscript Resource

William Smith Hangor Baylor Papers

Brooks Family Papers

A. H. Byars Papers

A. M. Chacky Papers

Cochran Family Papers

Henry H. Dedrick Papers

William B. Gallaher Papers

Garber Family Papers

Michael G. Harman Papers

Clinton Hatcher Papers

Jedediah Hotchkiss Papers

John N. Hull Papers

Adam Wise Kersh Papers

Jacob Kent Langhorne Papers

McCutchan Family Papers

Wilson Family Papers

John Wise Papers

Virginia Historical Society, Richmond, Virginia

Armistead Family Papers

Bagby Family Papers

Bailey Family Papers

William Gaines Baldwin Papers

Robert Payne Baylor Papers

Beale Family Papers

Margaret Stanley Beckwith Papers

Henry Robinson Berkeley Papers

William Barrett Blair Papers

Frederick Fillison Bowen Papers

Armistead Burwell Papers

James Thomas Butler Papers

John William Campbell Papers

Cornelius Hart Carlton Diary

William Thomas Casey Papers

Chisolm Family Papers

Christian Family Papers

Coiner Family Papers

Holmes Conrad Papers

Cooley Family Papers

William Clark Corson Papers

John Anthony Craig Papers

Daniel G. Cushwa Papers

Creed Thomas Davis Papers

Charles Achilles Douglas Papers

Downman Family Papers

Edward Samuel Duffey Papers

Maurice Evans Papers

Ezell Family Papers

Benjamin Lyons Farinholt Diary

Benjamin Lyons Farinholt Papers

Ferneyhough Family Papers

Philip H. Franklin Papers

David Funsten Papers

Mary Boykin Gatewood Papers

Godwin Family Papers

Robert A. Granniss Papers

Gray Family Papers

William Gray Papers

Griggs Family Papers

Guerrant Family Papers

John Guerrant Papers

Charles Brown Gwathmey Papers

Robert Gaines Haile Papers

Hamner Family Papers

Harlow Family Papers

Harrison Family Papers

Randolph Harrison Papers

Richardson Wallace Haw Papers

Katherine Heath Hawes Papers

Charles August Henninghausen Papers

John Lyon Hill Papers

Achilles Whitlocke Hoge Papers

Horne Family Papers

Jones Family Papers

Watkins Kearns Diary

William Boutwell Kidd Diary

Robert Alexander Lancaster Papers

Langhorne Family Papers

Manson Family Papers

Mason Family Papers

Richard Lancelot Maury Diary

McCarthy Family Papers

Meade Family Papers

John Lawrence Meems Papers

George Washington Miley Papers

Moore Family Papers

L. Robert Moore Papers

Samuel Johnson Cramer Moore Papers

William Young Mordecai Papers

William Goodridge Morton Papers

John Baxter Moseley Papers

Oscar Ogelsby Mull Diary

Henry Edward Neal Papers

Neblett Family Papers

James W. Old Papers

Paine Family Papers

George Washington Peebles Diary

Pendleton Family Papers

Edwin Anderson Penick Papers

Aquila Johnson Peyton Diary

James Eldred Phillips Papers

Randolph Family Papers

Ridley Family Papers

Littleton Tazewell Robertson Papers

Addison Brown Roler Papers

George Thomas Rust Papers

Richard Henry Watkins Papers

John A. Williams Papers

Daniel A. Wilson Papers

Virginia Military Institute Special Collections, Preston Library, Lexington

Samuel H. Craun Papers

Dunlap Family Papers

Henkel Family Papers

John B. Snodgrass Papers

Virginia Military Institute, *Civil War Resources*, World Wide Web Manuscript
Resource

Julie Pendleton Allen Papers

William Weldon Bentley Papers

William Johnson Black Papers

Samuel Selden Brooke Papers

Campbell/Varner Family Papers

Clayton Glanville Coleman Papers

Henry H. Dedrick Papers

John Hamilton Ervine Papers

Fulkerson Family Papers

John Garibaldi Papers

Andrew C. L. Gatewood Papers

Sutton I. Harris Papers

Johnson Family Papers

George W. Koontz Papers

Andrew Jackson McCoy Papers

Michael F. Rinker Papers

Virginia Polytechnic Institute and State University Library, World Wide Web
Manuscript Resource

Henry C. Carpenter Papers

Isaac White Papers

Published Narratives

Bean, W. G. "A House Divided: The Civil War Letters of a Virginia Family." *Virginia
Magazine of History and Biography* 59 (October 1951): 397–422.

———. "The Valley Campaign of 1862 as Revealed in Letters of Sandie Pendleton."
Virginia Magazine of History and Biography 78 (July 1970): 326–64.

Blackford, Charles Minor, III, ed. *Letters from Lee's Army; or, Memoirs of Life in and out
of the Army in Virginia during the War between the States.* New York: Charles
Scribner's, 1947; reprint, Lincoln: University of Nebraska, 1998.

Britton, Rick, ed. "Letters Home from Private William H. Jones of the Albemarle
Rifles." *Magazine of Albemarle County History* 57 (1999): 65–70.

Chamberlayne, C. G., ed. *Ham Chamberlayne—Virginian: Letters and Papers of an
Artillery Officer in the War for Southern Independence, 1861–1865.* Richmond: Dietz,
1932.

Childers, William C. "A Virginian's Dilemma." *West Virginia History* 27 (April 1966): 173–200.

Crofts, Daniel W., ed. *Cobb's Ordeal: The Diaries of a Virginia Farmer, 1842–1872.* Athens: University of Georgia Press, 1997.

Durkin, Joseph T., ed. *John Dooley, Confederate Soldier: His War Journal.* Washington, D.C.: Georgetown University Press, 1945.

Freudenberg, Anne. "Sheridan's Raid: An Account by Sarah A. G. Strickler." *Magazine of Albermarle County History* 22 (1963–4): 56–65.

Freudenberg, Anne, and John Casteen, eds. "John B. Minor's Civil War Diary," *Magazine of Albermarle County History* 22 (1963–64): 45–55.

Greenwalt, Bruce, ed. "Unionists in Rockbridge County: The Correspondence of James Dorman Davidson concerning the Virginia Secession Convention of 1861." *Virginia Magazine of History and Biography* 73 (January 1965): 78–102.

Hilldrup, Robert Leroy. "The Romance of a Man in Gray Including the Love Letters of Captain James S. Peery, Forty-fifth Virginia Infantry, C.S.A." *West Virginia History* 22 (January 1961): 83–116.

Hotchkiss, Jedediah. *Make Me a Map of the Valley: The Civil War Journal of Stonewall Jackson's Cartographer.* Edited by Archie P. McDonald. Dallas, Tx.: Southern Methodist University Press, 1973.

Jones, John B. *A Rebel War Clerk's Diary.* New York: Sagamore Press, 1958.

Kean, Robert Garlick Hill. *Inside the Confederate Government: The Diary of Robert Garlick Hill Kean.* Edited by Edward Younger. New York: Oxford University Press, 1957.

Mahon, Michael G., ed. *Winchester Divided: The Civil War Diaries of Julia Chase & Laura Lee.* Mechanicsburg, Pa.: Stackpole Books, 2002.

McGuire, Judith. *Diary of a Southern Refugee during the War, Written by a Lady of Virginia.* 1867; reprint, Lincoln: University of Nebraska, 1995.

McMullen, Glenn L., ed. *The Civil War Letters of Dr. Harvey Black.* Baltimore: Butternut and Blue.

Miyagawa, Ellen, ed. "The Boys Who Wore the Gray: A Collection of Letters and Articles Written by Members of the Fluvanna Artillery, 1861–1865." *Bulletin of the Fluvanna County Historical Society* 41 (April 1986): 9–41.

——. "The Boys Who Wore the Gray: A Collection of Letters and Articles Written by Members of the Fluvanna Artillery, 1861–1865." *Bulletin of the Fluvanna County Historical Society* 42 (October 1986): 51–85.

Oram, Richard W., ed. "Harpers Ferry to the Fall of Richmond: Letters of Colonel John De Hart Ross, C.S.A., 1861–1865." *West Virginia History* 45 (1984): 159–74.

Rachal, William M. E., ed. " 'Secession Is Nothing But Revolution': A Letter of R. E. Lee to His Son 'Rooney.' " *Virginia Magazine of History and Biography* 69 (January 1961): 3–6.

Robertson, Mary, ed. *Lucy Breckenridge of Grove Hill: The Journal of a Virginia Girl, 1862–1864.* 2nd ed. Columbia: University of South Carolina Press, 1994.

Roper, Jason Herbert, ed. *Repairing the 'March of Mars': The Civil War Diaries of John Samuel Apperson, Hospital Steward in the Stonewall Brigade, 1861–1865.* Macon, Ga.: Mercer University Press, 2001.

Shephard, Walker F. "Diary and Letters of Walker F. Shephard." *Bulletin of the Fluvanna County Historical Society* 38 (October 1984): 5–39.

Swank, Walbrook D., ed. *Confederate Letters and Diaries, 1861–1865.* Charlottesville, Va.: Papercraft Printing and Design, 1988.

Tompkins, Ellen Wilkins. "The Colonel's Lady: Some Letters of Ellen Wilkins Tompkins, July–December 1861." *Virginia Magazine of History and Biography* 69 (October 1961): 387–419.

Turner, Charles W., ed. *The Allen Family of Amherst County, Virginia: Civil War Letters.* Berryville, Va.: Rockbridge Publishing, 1995.

——, ed. *My Dear Emma (War Letters of Col. James K. Edmondson, 1861–1865.* Verona, Va.: McClure Press, 1978.

——, ed. "Lieutenant Albert Davidson—Letters of a Virginia Soldier." *West Virginia History* 34 (October 1977): 49–71.

——, ed. "Major Charles A. Davidson: Letters of a Virginia Soldier." *Civil War History* 22 (March 1970): 16–40.

——, ed. "Captain Greenlee Davidson: Letters of a Virginia Soldier." *Civil War History* 17 (September 1971): 197–221.

——, ed. "James B. Dorman's Civil War Letters." *Civil War History* 25 (September 1979): 262–78.

Vogtsberger, Margaret Ann, ed. *The Dulany's of Welbourne: A Family in Mosby's Confederacy.* Berryville, Va.: Rockbridge Publishing, 1995.

Wiatt, Alex L., ed. *Confederate Chaplain William Edward Wiatt: An Annotated Diary.* Lynchburg, Va.: H. E. Howard, 1994.

Wiley, Kenneth, ed. *Norfolk Blues: The Civil War Diary of the Norfolk Light Artillery Blues.* Shippensburg, Pa.: Burd Street Press, 1997.

Worsham, John. *One of Jackson's Foot Cavalry: His Experiences & What He Saw during the War, 1861–1865.* New York: Neale, 1912.

Newspapers
Abingdon Democrat
Daily Richmond Examiner
Leesburg Democratic Mirror
Lexington Gazette
Lexington Valley Star
Lynchburg Daily Virginian

Marion Ensign
Richmond Daily Dispatch
Richmond Daily Whig
Richmond Sentinel
Richmond Whig and Public Advertiser
Scottsville Register
Winchester Republican and Daily Advertiser

Government Documents

Army Regulations, Adopted for Use by the Confederate Army. Richmond: West and
   Johnson, 1861.

Gaines, William H. *Biographical Register of Members of the Virginia State Convention of
   1861, 1st Session.* Richmond: Virginia State Library, 1969.

*General Orders from the Adjutant and Inspector-General's Office, Confederate States
   Army, from January, 1862, to December, 1863 (both inclusive). In two series. Prepared
   from the Files of Head-Quarters, Department of S.C., GA., and FLA.* Columbia, Ga.:
   Evans and Cogswell, 1864.

Journal of the House of Delegates of the State of Virginia for the Session of 1861–1862.
   Richmond: William F. Ritchie, 1864.

Journals of the Virginia State Convention of 1861. 3 vols. Richmond: Virginia State
   Library, 1966.

Reese, George H., ed. *Proceedings of the Virginia State Convention of 1861.* 4 vols.
   Richmond: Virginia State Library, 1965.

United States Bureau of the Census. *Eighth Census of the United States, 1860.* 4 vols.
   Washington, D.C.: Government Printing Office, 1865.

United States War Department. *The War of Rebellion: A Compilation of the Official
   Records of the Union and Confederate Armies.* 127 vols., index, and atlas.
   Washington, D.C.: Government Printing Office, 1880–1901.

Reference Sources

Sifakis, Stewart, ed. *Compendium of the Confederate Armies.* Vol. 1: *Virginia.* New York:
   Facts on File, 1992.

Virginia Regimental History Series. Lynchburg, Va.: H. E. Howard, 1982–.

Wallace, Lee A., Jr., ed. *A Guide to Virginia Military Organizations, 1861–1865.* 2nd. ed.
   Lynchburg, Va.: H. E. Howard, 1986–.

Wise, Jennings C. *Long Arm of Lee; or, The History of the Artillery of the Army of
   Northern Virginia, with a Brief Account of the Confederate Bureau of Ordnance.*
   Lynchburg, Va.: J. P. Bell, 1915.

SECONDARY SOURCES

Books

Allmendinger, David F., Jr. *Ruffin: Family and Reform in the Old South.* New York: Oxford University Press, 1990.

Anderson, Paul Christopher. *Blood Image: Turner Ashby in the Civil War and the Southern Mind.* Baton Rouge: Louisiana State University Press, 2002.

Archdeacon, Thomas J. *Correlation and Regression Analysis: A Historian's Guide.* Madison: University of Wisconsin Press, 1994.

Ash, Stephen V. *Middle Tennessee Society Transformed, 1860–1870: War and Peace in the Upper South.* Baton Rouge: Louisiana State University Press, 1988.

——. *When the Yankees Came: Conflict and Chaos in the Occupied South.* Chapel Hill: University of North Carolina Press, 1995.

Ayers, Edward L. *In the Presence of Mine Enemies: War in the Heart of America, 1859–1863.* New York: Norton, 2003.

——. *Vengeance and Justice: Crime and Punishment in the 19th-Century American South.* New York: Oxford University Press, 1984.

Baptist, Edward. *Creating an Old South: Middle Florida's Plantation Frontier before the Civil War.* Chapel Hill: University of North Carolina Press, 2002.

Bardaglio, Peter W. *Reconstructing the Household: Families, Sex, & the Law in the Nineteenth-Century South.* Chapel Hill: University of North Carolina Press, 1995.

Bensel, Richard. *Yankee Leviathan: The Origins of Central State Authority in America, 1859–1877.* Cambridge: Cambridge University Press, 1990.

Beringer, Richard E., Herman Hattaway, Archer Jones, and William N. Still Jr. *Why the South Lost the Civil War.* Athens: University of Georgia Press, 1986.

Berry, Stephen W. *All That Makes a Man: Love and Ambition in the Civil War South.* New York: Oxford University Press, 2003.

Blair, William A. *Virginia's Private War: Feeding Body and Soul in the Confederacy, 1861–1865.* New York: Oxford University Press, 1998.

Bleser, Carol K., and Lesley J. Gordon, eds. *Intimate Strategies of the Civil War: Military Commanders and Their Wives.* New York: Oxford University Press, 2001.

Bolton, Charles C. *Poor Whites of the Antebellum South: Tenants and Laborers in Central North Carolina and Northeast Mississippi.* Durham: Duke University Press, 1994.

Bonner, Robert E. *Colors and Blood: Flag Passions of the Confederate South.* Princeton: Princeton University Press, 2003.

Bryant, Jonathan M. *How Curious a Land: Conflict and Change in Greene County, Georgia, 1850–1885.* Chapel Hill: University of North Carolina Press, 1996.

Bushman, Claudia L. *In Old Virginia: Slavery, Farming, and Society in the Journal of John Walker.* Baltimore: Johns Hopkins University Press, 2002.

Burton, Orville Vernon. *In My Father's House Are Many Mansions: Family and Community in Edgefield, South Carolina.* Chapel Hill: University of North Carolina Press, 1985.

Bynum, Victoria. *The Free State of Jones: Mississippi's Longest Civil War.* Chapel Hill: University of North Carolina Press, 2001.

Campbell, Jacqueline Glass. *When Sherman Marched North from the Sea: Resistance on the Confederate Home Front.* Chapel Hill: University of North Carolina Press, 2005.

Campbell, Randolph B. *A Southern Community in Crisis: Harrison County, Texas, 1850–1880.* Austin: University of Texas Press, 1983.

Carmichael, Peter S. *The Last Generation: Young Virginians in Peace, War, and Reunion.* Chapel Hill: University of North Carolina Press, 2005.

———. *Lee's Young Artillerist: William J. Pegram.* Charlottesville: University Press of Virginia, 1995.

Cecil-Fronsman, Bill. *Common Whites: Class and Culture in Antebellum North Carolina.* Lexington: University Press of Kentucky, 1992.

Censer, Jane Turner. *North Carolina Planters and Their Children, 1800–1860.* Baton Rouge: Louisiana State University Press, 1984.

Clinton, Catherine, and Nina Silber, eds. *Divided Houses: Gender and the Civil War.* New York: Oxford University Press, 1992.

Chesson, Michael B. *Richmond after the War, 1865–1890.* Richmond: Virginia State Library, 1981.

Coddington, Edwin B. *The Gettysburg Campaign: A Study in Command.* New York: Scribner's, 1968.

Connelly, Thomas Lawrence. *Army of the Heartland: The Army of Tennessee, 1861–1862.* Baton Rouge: Louisiana State University Press, 1867.

———. *Autumn of Glory: The Army of Tennessee, 1862–1865.* Baton Rouge: Louisiana State University Press, 1971.

Coontz, Stephanie. *The Social Origins of Private Life: A History of American Families, 1600–1900.* London: Verso, 1988.

Cott, Nancy F. *The Bonds of Womanhood: "Woman's Sphere" in New England, 1780–1835.* New Haven: Yale University Press, 1977.

Crawford, Martin. *Ashe County's Civil War: Community and Society in the Appalachian South.* Charlottesville: University Press of Virginia, 2001.

Crofts, Daniel W. *Old Southampton: Politics and Society in a Virginia County, 1834–1869.* Charlottesville: University Press of Virginia, 1992.

———. *Reluctant Confederates: Upper South Unionists in the Secession Crisis.* Chapel Hill: University of North Carolina Press, 1989.

Current, Richard Nelson. *Lincoln's Loyalists: Union Soldiers from the Confederacy.* Boston: Northeastern University Press, 1992.

Dailey, Jane E. *Before Jim Crow: The Politics of Race in Postemancipation Virginia.* Chapel Hill: University of North Carolina Press, 2000.

Davis, William C. *Battle at Bull Run: A History of the First Major Campaign of the Civil War.* Baton Rouge: Louisiana State University Press, 1981.

Dew, Charles B. *Apostles of Disunion: Southern Secession Commissioners and the Causes of the Civil War.* Charlottesville: University Press of Virginia, 2001.

———. *Bond of Iron: Master and Slave at Buffalo Forge.* New York: Norton, 1994.

———. *Ironmaker to the Confederacy: Joseph R. Anderson and the Tredegar Iron Works.* New Haven: Yale University Press, 1966.

Dickinson, Jack L. *Tattered Uniforms and Bright Bayonets: West Virginia's Confederate Soldiers.* Huntington, W.V.: Marshall University Library Associates, 1995.

Durden, Robert F. *The Gray and the Black: The Confederate Debate on Emancipation.* Baton Rouge: Louisiana State University Press, 1972.

Durrill, Wayne K. *War of Another Kind: A Southern Community in the Great Rebellion.* New York: Oxford University Press, 1990.

Escott, Paul D. *After Secession: Jefferson Davis and the Failure of Confederate Nationalism.* Baton Rouge: Louisiana State University Press, 1978.

———. *Many Excellent People: Power and Privilege in North Carolina, 1850–1900.* Chapel Hill: University of North Carolina Press, 1985.

Faust, Drew Gilpin. *Creation of Confederate Nationalism: Ideology and Identity in the Civil War South.* Baton Rouge: Louisiana State University Press, 1988.

———. *Mothers of Invention: Women of the Slaveholding South in the American Civil War.* New York: Vintage, 1996.

Feinstein, Charles H., and Mark Thomas. *Making History Count: A Primer in Quantitative Methods for Historians.* Cambridge: Cambridge University Press, 2002.

Fischer, David Hackett, and James C. Kelly. *Away, I'm Bound Away: Virginia and the Westward Movement.* Charlottesville: University Press of Virginia, 2000.

Fisher, Noel C. *War at Every Door: Partisan Politics and Guerrilla Violence in East Tennessee, 1860–1869.* Chapel Hill: University of North Carolina Press, 1997.

Floud, Roderick. *An Introduction to Quantitative Methods for Historians.* 2nd ed. London: Methuen, 1979.

Fox, William F. *Regimental Losses in the American Civil War, 1861–1865.* Albany, N.Y.: Albany Publishing, 1889.

Fox-Genovese, Elizabeth. *Within the Plantation Household: Black and White Women of the Old South.* Chapel Hill: University of North Carolina Press, 1988.

Frank, Joseph Allen. *With Ballot and Bayonet: The Political Socialization of American Civil War Soldiers.* Athens: University of Georgia Press, 1998.

Freehling, Alison Goodyear. *Drift toward Dissolution: The Virginia Slavery Debate of 1831–1832.* Baton Rouge: Louisiana State University Press, 1982.

Freehling, William W. *The Road to Disunion: Secessionists at Bay.* New York: Oxford University Press, 1990.

———. *The South vs. the South: How Anti-Confederate Southerners Shaped the Course of the Civil War.* New York: Oxford University Press, 2001.

Gallagher, Gary W. *The Confederate War.* Cambridge, Mass.: Harvard University Press, 1997.

———. *Lee and His Army in Confederate History.* Chapel Hill: University of North Carolina Press, 2001.

Genovese, Eugene D. *The Political Economy of Slavery: Studies in the Economy and Society of the Slave South.* New York: Random House, 1967.

Glatthaar, Joseph T. *The March to the Sea and Beyond: Sherman's Troops in the Savannah and Carolinas Campaigns.* New York: New York University Press, 1985.

Goen, C. C. *Broken Churches, Broken Nation: Denominational Schisms and the Coming of the American Civil War.* Macon, Ga.: Mercer University Press, 1985.

Goldfield, David R. *Urban Growth in the Age of Sectionalism: Virginia, 1847–1861.* Baton Rouge: Louisiana State University Press, 1977.

Goldin, Claudia Dale. *Urban Slavery in the American South, 1820–1860: A Quantitative History.* Chicago: University of Chicago Press, 1976.

Greven, Philip J. *The Protestant Temperament: Patterns of Child-Rearing, Religious Experience, and the Self in Early America.* New York: Knopf, 1977.

Grimsley, Mark. *And Keep Moving On: The Virginia Campaign, May–June 1864.* Lincoln: University of Nebraska Press, 2002.

———. *The Hard Hand of War: Union Military Policy toward Southern Civilians, 1861–1865.* Cambridge: Cambridge University Press, 1995.

Groce, W. Todd. *Mountain Rebels: East Tennessee Confederates and the Civil War, 1860–1870.* Knoxville: University of Tennessee Press, 1999.

Hattaway, Herman, and Archer Jones. *How the North Won: A Military History of the Civil War.* Urbana: University of Illinois Press, 1983.

Hennessy, John J. *Return to Bull Run: The Battle and Campaign of Second Manassas.* Norman: University of Oklahoma Press, 1999.

Hess, Earl J. *Liberty, Virtue, and Progress: Northerners and Their War for the Union.* New York: New York University Press, 1988.

———. *The Union Soldier in Battle: Enduring the Ordeal of Combat.* Lawrence: University of Kansas Press, 1997.

Heyrman, Christine Leigh. *Southern Cross: The Beginnings of the Bible Belt.* Chapel Hill: University of North Carolina Press, 1997.

Hoganson, Kristin L. *Fighting for American Manhood: How Gender Politics Provoked the Spanish-American and Philippine-American Wars.* New Haven: Yale University Press, 1998.

Holt, Michael F. *The Political Crisis of the 1850s.* New York: Norton, 1978.

———. *The Rise and Fall of the American Whig Party: Jacksonian Politics and the Onset of the Civil War.* New York: Oxford University Press, 1999.

Hubbs, G. Ward. *Guarding Greensboro: A Confederate Company in the Making of a Southern Community.* Athens: University of Georgia Press, 2003.

Inscoe, John C. *Mountain Masters, Slavery, and the Sectional Crisis in Western North Carolina.* Knoxville: University of Tennessee Press, 1989.

Inscoe, John C., and Gordon B. McKinney. *Confederate Appalachia: Western North Carolina in the Civil War.* Chapel Hill: University of North Carolina Press, 2000.

Jabour, Anya. *Marriage in the Early Republic: Elizabeth and William Wirt and the Companionate Ideal.* Baltimore: Johns Hopkins University Press, 1998.

Jimerson, Randall C. *The Private Civil War: Popular Thought during the Sectional Conflict.* Baton Rouge: Louisiana State University Press, 1988.

Kenzer, Robert C. *Kinship and Neighborhood in a Southern Community: Orange County, North Carolina, 1849–1881.* Knoxville: University of Tennessee Press, 1987.

Kimball, Gregg D. *American City, Southern Place: A Cultural History of Antebellum Richmond.* Athens: University of Georgia Press, 2000.

Koons, Kenneth E., and Warren R. Hofstra, eds. *After the Backcountry: Rural Life in the Great Valley of Virginia, 1800–1900.* Knoxville: University of Tennessee Press, 2000.

Lankford, Nelson. *Richmond Burning: The Last Days of the Confederate Capital.* New York: Penguin, 2002.

Lebsock, Suzanne. *The Free Women of Petersburg: Status and Culture in a Southern Town, 1784–1860.* New York: Norton, 1984.

Lewis, Jan Ellen. *The Pursuit of Happiness: Family and Values in Jefferson's Virginia.* Cambridge: Cambridge University Press, 1983.

Linderman, Gerald F. *Embattled Courage: The Experience of Combat in the American Civil War.* New York: Free Press, 1989.

Link, William A. *Roots of Secession: Slavery and Politics in Antebellum Virginia.* Chapel Hill: University of North Carolina Press, 2003.

Livermore, Thomas L. *Numbers & Losses in the Civil War in America: 1861–65.* Bloomington: Indiana University Press, 1957.

Lonn, Ella. *Desertion during the Civil War.* Gloucester, Mass.: American Historical Association, 1928; Lincoln: University of Nebraska Press, 1998.

Loveland, Anne C. *Southern Evangelicals and the Social Order, 1800–1860.* Baton Rouge: Louisiana State University Press, 1980.

Majewski, John. *A House Dividing: Economic Development in Pennsylvania and Virginia before the Civil War.* Cambridge: Cambridge University Press, 2000.

Marten, James A. *Texas Divided: Loyalty and Dissent in the Lone Star State, 1856–1874.* Lexington: University Press of Kentucky, 1990.

Marvel, William. *Lee's Last Retreat: The Flight to Appomattox*. Chapel Hill: University of North Carolina Press, 2002.

———. *A Place Called Appomattox*. Chapel Hill: University of North Carolina Press, 2000.

Mathew, William M. *Edmund Ruffin and the Crisis of Slavery in the Old South: The Failure of Agricultural Reform*. Athens: University of Georgia Press, 1988.

Mathews, Donald G. *Religion in the Old South*. Chicago: University of Chicago Press, 1977.

McCardell, John. *The Idea of a Southern Nation: Southern Nationalists and Southern Nationalism, 1830–1860*. New York: Norton, 1979.

McCurry, Stephanie. *Masters of Small Worlds: Yeoman Households, Gender Relations and the Political Culture of the Antebellum South Carolina Low Country*. New York: Oxford University Press, 1995.

McPherson, James. *For Cause and Comrades: Why Men Fought in the Civil War*. New York: Oxford University Press, 1997.

Mintz, Steven, and Susan Kellogg. *Domestic Revolutions: A Social History of American Family Life*. New York: Free Press, 1988.

Mitchell, Reid. *Civil War Soldiers: Their Expectations and Their Experiences*. New York: Touchstone, 1988.

———. *The Vacant Chair: The Northern Soldier Leaves Home*. New York: Oxford University Press, 1993.

Mohr, Clarence L. *On the Threshold of Freedom: Masters and Slaves in Civil War Georgia*. Reprint, Baton Rouge: Louisiana State University Press, 2001.

Moore, Albert Burton. *Conscription and Conflict in the Confederacy*. New York: Macmillan, 1924.

Moore, George Ellis. *A Banner in the Hills: West Virginia's Statehood*. New York: Meredith, 1963.

Morgan, Lynda J. *Emancipation in Virginia's Tobacco Belt, 1850–1870*. Athens: University of Georgia Press, 1992.

Neely, Mark E., Jr. *Southern Rights: Political Prisoners and the Myth of Confederate Constitutionalism*. Charlottesville: University Press of Virginia, 1999.

Newell, Clayton R. *Lee vs. McClellan: The First Campaign*. Washington, D.C.: Regnery, 1996.

Noe, Kenneth W. *Southwest Virginia's Railroad: Modernization and the Sectional Crisis*. Urbana: University of Illinois Press, 1994.

Olsen, Christopher. *Political Culture and Secession in Mississippi: Masculinity, Honor, and the Antiparty Tradition, 1830–1860*. New York: Oxford University Press, 2000.

Owens, Harry P., and James J. Cooke, eds. *The Old South in the Crucible of War*. Jackson: University Press of Mississippi, 1983.

Ownby, Ted. *Subduing Satan: Religion, Recreation, and Manhood in the Rural South, 1865–1920.* Chapel Hill: University of North Carolina Press, 1990.

Phillips, Edward H. Phillips. *The Lower Shenandoah Valley in the Civil War: The Impact of War upon the Civilian Population and upon Civil Institutions.* Lynchburg, Va.: H. E. Howard, 1993.

Power, J. Tracy. *Lee's Miserables: Life in the Army of Northern Virginia from the Wilderness to Appomattox.* Chapel Hill: University of North Carolina, 1998.

Prokopowicz, Gerald J. *All for the Regiment: The Army of the Ohio, 1861–62.* Chapel Hill: University of North Carolina Press, 2001.

Rable, George C. *Civil Wars: Women and the Crisis of Southern Nationalism.* Urbana: University of Illinois Press, 1989.

———. *The Confederate Republic: A Revolution against Politics.* Chapel Hill: University of North Carolina Press, 1994.

———. *Fredericksburg! Fredericksburg!* Chapel Hill: University of North Carolina Press, 2002.

Rafuse, Ethan S. *A Single Grand Victory: The First Campaign and Battle of Manassas.* Wilmington, Del.: Scholarly Resources, 2002.

Rhea, Gordon C. *The Battle of the Wilderness: May 5–6, 1864.* Baton Rouge: Louisiana State University Press, 1994.

———. *The Battles for Spotsylvania Courthouse and the Road to Yellow Tavern: May 7–12, 1864.* Baton Rouge: Louisiana State University Press, 1997.

———. *To the North Anna River: Grant and Lee, May 13–25, 1864.* Baton Rouge: Louisiana State University Press, 2000.

Robertson, James I. *Soldiers Blue and Gray.* Columbia: University of South Carolina Press, 1998.

Robertson, William Glenn. *Back Door to Richmond: The Bermuda Hundred Campaign, April–June 1864.* Newark: University of Delaware Press, 1987.

Rotundo, E. Anthony. *American Manhood: Transformations in Masculinity from the Revolution to the Modern Era.* New York: Basic Books, 1993.

Rosyter, Charles. *The Destructive War: William Tecumseh Sherman, Stonewall Jackson, and the Americans.* New York: Vintage, 1991.

Rubin, Anne Sarah. *A Shattered Nation: The Rise and Fall of the Confederacy, 1861–1868.* Chapel Hill: University of North Carolina Press, 2005.

Schwarz, Philip J. *Twice Condemned: Slaves and the Criminal Laws of Virginia, 1705–1865.* Baton Rouge: Louisiana State University Press, 1988.

Schweiger, Beth Barton. *The Gospel Working Up: Progress and the Pulpit in Nineteenth-Century Virginia.* New York: Oxford University Press, 2000.

Scott, Anne Frior. *The Southern Lady: From Pedestal to Politics, 1830–1930.* Chicago: University of Chicago Press, 1970.

Sears, Stephen W. *Chancellorsville*. Boston: Houghton Mifflin, 1996.

———. *Landscape Turned Red: The Battle of Antietam*. New Haven, Conn.: Yale University Press, 1983.

———. *To the Gates of Richmond: The Peninsula Campaign*. New York: Ticknor and Fields, 1992.

Shade, William G. *Democratizing the Old Dominion: Virginia and the Second Party System*. Charlottesville: University Press of Virginia, 1996.

Shanks, Henry T. *The Secession Movement in Virginia, 1847–1861*. Richmond: Garrett and Massie, 1934.

Shattuck, Gardiner H., Jr. *A Shield and a Hiding Place: The Religious Life of Civil War Armies*. Macon, Ga.: Mercer University Press, 1987.

Shifflett, Crandall A. *Patronage and Poverty in the Tobacco South: Louisa County, Virginia, 1860–1900*. Knoxville: University of Tennessee Press, 1982.

Shorter, Edward. *The Making of the Modern Family*. New York: Basic Books, 1975.

Siegel, Frederick F. *The Roots of Southern Distinctiveness: Tobacco and Society in Danville, Virginia, 1780–1865*. Chapel Hill: University of North Carolina Press, 1987.

Silver, James W. *Confederate Morale and Church Propaganda*. New York: Norton, 1967.

Simpson, Craig M. *A Good Southerner: The Life of Henry A. Wise of Virginia*. Chapel Hill: University of North Carolina Press, 1985.

Sinha, Manisha. *The Counter-Revolution of Slavery: Politics and Ideology in Antebellum South Carolina*. Chapel Hill: University of North Carolina Press, 2000.

Smith, Daniel Blake. *Inside the Great House: Planter Family Life in Eighteenth-Century Chesapeake Society*. Ithaca, N.Y.: Cornell University Press, 1980.

Snay, Mitchell. *Gospel of Disunion: Religion and Separatism in the Antebellum South*. New York: Cambridge University Press, 1993.

Sommers, Richard J. *Richmond Redeemed: The Siege at Petersburg*. Garden City, N.J.: Doubleday, 1981.

Stealey, John E. *The Antebellum Kanawha Salt Business and Western Markets*. Lexington: University Press of Kentucky, 1993.

Stearns, Peter N. *Be A Man! Males in Modern Society*. New York: Holmes and Meier, 1979.

Stevenson, Brenda E. *Life in Black and White: Family and Community in the Slave South*. New York: Oxford University Press, 1996.

Stone, Lawrence. *The Family, Sex and Marriage in England, 1500–1800*. New York: Harper and Row, 1977.

Stowell, Daniel W. *Rebuilding Zion: The Religious Reconstruction of the South, 1863–1877*. New York: Oxford University Press, 1998.

Sutherland, Daniel E. *Seasons of War: The Ordeal of a Confederate Community, 1861–1865*. Baton Rouge: Louisiana State University Press, 1995.

Tadman, Michael. *Speculators and Slaves: Masters, Traders, and Slaves in the Old South.* Madison: University of Wisconsin Press, 1989.

Tanner, Robert G. *Stonewall in the Valley: Thomas J. "Stonewall" Jackson's Shenandoah Valley Campaign, Spring 1862.* New York: Doubleday, 1976.

Thomas, Emory M. *The Confederate Nation: 1861–1865.* New York: Harper and Row, 1979.

Tripp, Steven Elliott. *Yankee Town, Southern City: Race and Class Relations in Civil War Lynchburg.* New York: New York University Press, 1997.

Trudeau, Noah Andre. *Bloody Roads South: The Wilderness to Cold Harbor: May–June, 1864.* Boston: Little Brown, 1989.

——. *Gettysburg: A Testing of Courage.* New York: HarperCollins, 2002.

——. *The Last Citadel: Petersburg, Virginia, June 1846–April 1865.* Baton Rouge: Louisiana State University, 1991.

Tyler-McGraw, Marie. *At the Falls: Richmond, Virginia and Its People.* Chapel Hill: University of North Carolina Press, 1994.

Varon, Elizabeth R. *We Mean to Be Counted: White Women and Politics in Antebellum Virginia.* Chapel Hill: University of North Carolina Press, 1998.

Vinovskis, Maris A., ed. *Toward a Social History of the American Civil War: Exploratory Essays.* Cambridge: Cambridge University Press, 1990.

Wallenstein, Peter, and Bertram Wyatt-Brown, eds. *Virginia's Civil War.* Charlottesville: University of Virginia Press, 2005.

Weigley, Russell F. *A Great Civil War: A Military and Political History, 1861–1865.* Bloomington: Indiana University Press, 2000.

Weitz, Mark A. *A Higher Duty: Desertion among Georgia Troops during the Civil War.* Lincoln: University of Nebraska Press, 2000.

Wert, Jeffery D. *From Winchester to Cedar Creek: The Shenandoah Valley Campaign of 1864.* Carlisle, Pa.: South Mountain Press, 1987.

Whites, LeeAnn. *The Civil War as a Crisis in Gender: Augusta, Georgia, 1860–1890.* Athens: University of Georgia Press, 1995.

Wiley, Bell I. *The Life of Billy Yank: Common Soldier of the Union.* Reprint, Baton Rouge: Louisiana State University Press, 1988.

——. *The Life of Johnny Reb: Common Soldier of the Confederacy.* Reprint, Baton Rouge: Louisiana State University Press, 1988.

Williams, David. *Rich Man's War: Class, Caste, and Confederate Defeat in the Lower Chattahoochee Valley.* Athens: University of Georgia Press, 1998.

Williams, David, Teresa Crisp Williams, and David Carlson. *Plain Folk in a Rich Man's War: Class and Dissent in Confederate Georgia.* Gainesville: University Press of Florida, 2002.

Wills, Brian Steel. *The War Hits Home: The Civil War in Southeastern Virginia.* Charlottesville: University Press of Virginia, 2001.

Woodworth, Steven E. *While God Is Marching On: The Religious World of Civil War Soldiers.* Lawrence: University Press of Kansas, 2001.

Wyatt-Brown, Bertram. *Southern Honor: Ethics and Behavior in the Old South.* New York: Oxford University Press, 1982.

Articles and Chapters

Alexander, Ted. " 'A Regular Slave Hunt': The Army of Northern Virginia and Black Civilians in the Gettysburg Campaign." *North and South* 4 (September 2001): 82–89.

Allardice, Bruce. "West Points of the Confederacy: Southern Military Schools and the Confederate Army." *Civil War History* 43 (December 1997): 310–31.

Ames, Susie M. "Federal Policy toward the Eastern Shore of Virginia in 1861." *Virginia Magazine of History and Biography* 69 (Fall 1961): 432–59.

Anderson, Fred. "A People's Army: Provincial Military Service in Massachusetts during the Seven Years' War." *William and Mary Quarterly* 40 (October 1983): 499–527.

Arnold, Dean A. "The Ultimatum of Virginia Unionists: 'Security for Slavery or Disunion.' " *Journal of Negro History* 48 (April 1963): 115–29.

Athey, Lou. "Loyalty and Civil Liberty in Fayette County during the Civil War." *West Virginia History* 55 (1996): 1–24.

Ayers, Edward L. "Worrying about the Civil War." In *Moral Problems in American Life: New Perspectives on Cultural History*, edited by Karen Halttunen and Lewis Perry, 145–65. Ithaca, N.Y.: Cornell University Press, 1998.

Barber, E. Susan. " 'The White Wings of Eros': Courtship and Marriage in Confederate Richmond." In *Southern Families at War: Loyalty and Conflict in the Civil War South*, edited by Catherine Clinton, 119–32. New York: Oxford University Press, 2000.

Battan, Jesse F. "The 'Rights' of Husbands and the 'Duties' of Wives: Power and Desire in the American Bedroom, 1850–1910." *Journal of Family History* 24 (April 1999): 165–86.

Bohannon, Keith S. "Dirty, Ragged, and Ill-Provided For: Confederate Logistical Problems in the 1862 Maryland Campaign and Their Solutions." In *The Antietam Campaign*, edited by Gary W. Gallagher, 101–42. Chapel Hill: University of North Carolina Press, 1999.

Boney, F. N. "Governor Letcher's Candid Correspondence." *Civil War History* 10 (June 1964): 167–80.

Bowman, Shearer Davis. "Conditional Unionism and Slavery in Virginia, 1860–61: The Case of Dr. Richard Eppes." *Virginia Magazine of History and Biography* 96 (Winter 1988): 31–54.

Brooks, Charles E. "The Social and Cultural Dynamics of Soldiering in Hood's Texas Brigade." *Journal of Southern History* 67 (August 2001): 535–72.

Brundage, Fitzhugh. "Shifting Attitudes towards Slavery in Antebellum Rockbridge County." In *Proceedings of the Rockbridge County Historical Society*, vol. 10: *1980–1989*, edited by Larry I. Bland, 333–44. Lexington, Va.: Rockbridge Historical Society.

Buckley, Thomas E. "Unfixing Race: Class, Power, and Identity in and Interracial Family." *Virginia Magazine of History and Biography* 102 (Fall 1994): 349–80.

Burstein, Andrew. "The Political Character of Sympathy." *Journal of the Early Republic* 21 (Winter 2001): 601–32.

Buza, Melinda S. " 'Pledges of Our Love': Friendship, Love, and Marriage among the Virginia Gentry, 1800–1825." In *The Edge of the South: Life in Nineteenth-Century Virginia*, edited by Edward L. Ayers and John C. Willis, 9–36. Charlottesville: University Press of Virginia, 1991.

Cain, Marvin R. "A 'Face of Battle' Needed: An Assessment of Motives and Men in Civil War Historiography." *Civil War History* 28 (January 1982): 5–27.

Carmichael, Peter S. "So Far from God and So Close to Stonewall Jackson: The Executions of Three Shenandoah Valley Soldiers." *Virginia Magazine of History and Biography* 111 (Winter 2003): 33–66.

Crofts, Daniel. "Late Antebellum Virginia Reconsidered." *Virginia Magazine of History and Biography* 107 (Summer 1999): 253–86.

Crowther, Edward R. "Holy Honor: Sacred and Secular in the Old South." *Journal of Southern History* 58 (November 1992): 619–36.

Curry, Leonard P. "Urbanization and Urbanism in the Old South: A Comparative View." *Journal of Southern History* 40 (February 1974): 43–60.

Curry, Richard O., and F. Gerald Ham. "The Bushwhackers' War: Insurgency and Counter-Insurgency in West Virginia." *Civil War History* 10 (December 1964): 416–33.

Dill, Alonzo Thomas. "Sectional Conflict in Colonial Virginia." *Virginia Magazine of History and Biography* 87 (1979): 300–315.

Donald, David. "The Confederate Man as Fighting Man." *Journal of Southern History* 25 (May 1959): 178–93.

Dotson, Rand. " 'The Grave and Scandalous Evil Infected to Your People': The Erosion of Confederate Loyalty in Floyd County, Virginia." *Virginia Magazine of History and Biography* 108 (Fall 2000): 393–434.

Escott, Paul D. "The Failure of Confederate Nationalism: The Old South's Class System in the Crucible of War." In *The Old South in the Crucible of War*, edited by Harry P. Owens and James J. Cooke, 15–28. Jackson: University Press of Mississippi, 1983.

———. "Yeoman Independence and the Market: Social Status and Economic Development in Antebellum North Carolina." *North Carolina Historical Review* 66 (1989): 275–300.

Faust, Drew Gilpin. "Christian Soldiers: The Meaning of Revivalism in the Confederate Army" *Journal of Southern History* 53 (February 1987): 63–90.

———. "Evangelicalism and the Meaning of the Proslavery Argument: The Reverend Thornton Stringfellow of Virginia." *Virginia Magazine of History and Biography* 85 (Winter 1977): 3–17.

———. "Race, Gender, and Confederate Nationalism: William D. Washington's *Burial of Latané.*" *Southern Review* 25 (April 1989): 304.

Foster, Gaines M. "Guilt over Slavery: A Historiographical Analysis." *Journal of Southern History* 56 (November 1990): 665–94.

Frank, Stephen M. " 'Rendering Aid and Comfort': Images of Fatherhood in the Letters of Civil War Soldiers from Massachusetts and Michigan." *Journal of Social History* 26 (Fall 1992): 5–32.

Freehling, William W. "The Editorial Revolution, Virginia, and the Coming of the Civil War." *Civil War History* 16 (March 1969): 64–72.

Gallagher, Gary W. "A Civil War Watershed: The 1862 Richmond Campaign in Perspective." In *The Richmond Campaign of 1862: The Peninsula and the Seven Days*, edited by Gary W. Gallagher, 3–27. Chapel Hill: University of North Carolina Press, 2000.

———. "Home Front and Battlefield: Some Recent Literature Relating to Virginia and the Confederacy." *Virginia Magazine of History and Biography* 98 (Spring 1990): 134–68.

———. "The Net Result of the Campaign Was in Our Favor: Confederate Reaction to the Maryland Campaign." In *The Antietam Campaign*, edited by Gary W. Gallagher, 3–44. Chapel Hill: University of North Carolina Press, 1999.

———. " 'Our Hearts Are Full of Hope': The Army of Northern Virginia in the Spring of 1864." In *The Wilderness Campaign*, edited by Gary W. Gallagher, 36–65. Chapel Hill: University of North Carolina Press, 1997.

Genovese, Eugene. "Yeoman Farmers in a Slaveholders' Democracy." *Agricultural History* 49 (April, 1974): 331–42.

Goldfield, David R. "Communities and Regions: The Diverse Cultures of Virginia." *Virginia Magazine of History and Biography* 95 (Fall 1987): 429–52.

Griffen, Clyde. "Reconstructing Masculinity from the Evangelical Revival to the Waning of Progressivism: A Speculative Synthesis." In *Meanings for Manhood: Constructions of Masculinity in Victorian America*, edited by Mark C. Marnes and Clyde Griffen, 183–204. Chicago: University of Chicago Press, 1990.

Halleck, Judith Lee. "The Role of the Community in Civil War Desertion." *Civil War History* 29 (June 1983): 123–34.

Harris, Emily J. "Sons and Soldiers: Deerfield, Massachusetts and the Civil War." *Civil War History* 30 (June 1984): 157–71.

Harrison, Noel G. "Atop an Anvil: The Civilians' War in Fairfax and Alexandria Counties, April 1861–April 1862." *Virginia Magazine of History and Biography* 106 (Spring 1998): 133–64.

Herlihy, David. "Family." *American Historical Review* 96 (February 1991): 1–16.

Higginbotham, R. Don. "The Martial Spirit in the Antebellum South: Some Further Speculations in a National Context." *Journal of Southern History* 58 (February 1992): 3–26.

Hohenberg, Alice I. "Civil War Draft Problems in the Shenandoah Valley." *Journal of the Rockbridge Historical Society* 7 (Summer 1970): 26–33.

Horton, Paul. "Submitting to the 'Shadow of Slavery': The Secession Crisis and Civil War in Alabama's Lawrence County." *Civil War History* 44 (June 1998): 111–36.

Huston, James L. "Property Rights in Slavery and the Coming of the Civil War." *Journal of Southern History* 65 (May 1999): 249–86.

Jabour, Anya. "Male Friendship and Masculinity in the Early National South: William Wirt and His Friends." *Journal of the Early Republic* 20 (Spring 2000): 83–112.

Karsten, Peter. "The 'New' American Military History: A Map of the Territory Explored and Unexplored." *American Quarterly* 36 (Spring 1984): 389–418.

Kerber, Linda. "Separate Spheres, Female Worlds, Woman's Place: The Rhetoric of Women's History." In *Toward an Intellectual History of Women*, 159–99. Chapel Hill: University of North Carolina Press, 1997.

Kierner, Cynthia A. "Women's Piety within Patriarchy: The Religious Life of Martha Hancock Wheat of Bedford County." *Virginia Magazine of History and Biography* 100 (Winter 1992): 79–98.

Kincaid, Mary Elizabeth. "Fayetteville, West Virginia, during the Civil War." *West Virginia History* 14 (July 1953): 339–65.

Klement, Frank. "General John B. Floyd and the West Virginia Campaigns of 1861." *West Virginia History* 8 (April, 1947): 319–33.

Kruman, Marc W. "Dissent in the Confederacy: The North Carolina Experience." *Civil War History* 27 (December 1981): 293–313.

Link, William A. "The Jordan Hatcher Case: Politics and 'A Spirit of Insubordination' in Antebellum Virginia." *Journal of Southern History* 64 (1998): 615 48.

Mann, Ralph. "Diversity in the Antebellum Appalachian South: Four Farm Communities in Tazewell County, Virginia." In *Appalachia in the Making: The Mountain South in the Nineteenth Century*, edited by Mary Beth Pudup, Dwight B. Billings, and Altina L. Waller, 132–62. Chapel Hill: University of North Carolina Press, 1995.

Marten, James. "Fatherhood in the Confederacy: Southern Soldiers and Their Children." *Journal of Southern History* 63 (May 1997): 269–92.

———. " 'A Feeling of Restless Anxiety': Loyalty and Race in the Peninsula Campaign and Beyond." In *The Richmond Campaign of 1862: The Peninsula and the Seven Days*, edited by Gary W. Gallagher, 121–52. Chapel Hill: University of North Carolina Press, 2000.

Maslowski, Pete. "A Study of Morale in Civil War Soldiers." *Military Affairs* 34 (December 1970): 122–26.

McMillen, Sally G. "Antebellum Southern Fathers and the Health Care of Children." *Journal of Southern History* 60 (August 1994): 513–32.

Mering, John V. "The Slave-State Constitutional Unionists and the Politics of Consensus." *Journal of Southern History* 43 (August 1977): 395–410.

Mitchell, Reid. "Christian Soldiers? Perfecting the Confederacy." In *Religion and the American Civil War*, edited by Randall M. Miller, Harry S. Stout, and Charles Reagan Wilson, 297–312. New York: Oxford University Press, 1998.

———. "The Creation of Confederate Loyalties." In *New Perspectives on Race and Slavery in America: Essays in Honor of Kenneth M. Stampp*, Robert H. Abzug and Stephen E. Maizlish, 93–108. Lexington: University Press of Kentucky, 1986.

Moore, George Ellis. "Slavery as a Factor in the Formation of West Virginia." *West Virginia History* 18 (October 1956): 5–90.

Moore, John Hammond. "Appomattox: Profile of a Mid-Nineteenth-Century Community." *Virginia Magazine of History and Biography* 88 (1980): 478–91.

Murrell, Amy E. " 'Of Necessity and Public Benefit': Southern Families and Their Appeals for Protection." In *Southern Families at War: Loyalty and Conflict in the Civil War South*, edited by Catherine Clinton, 77–99. New York: Oxford University Press, 2000.

Noe, Kenneth. " 'Appalachia's' Civil War Genesis: Southwest Virginia as Depicted by Northern and European Writers, 1825–1865." *West Virginia History* 50 (1991): 91–108.

———. " 'Deadened Color and Colder Horror': Rebecca Harding Davis and the Myth of Unionist Appalachia." In *Confronting Appalachian Stereotypes: Back Talk from an American Region*, edited by Dwight B. Billings, Gurney Norman, and Katherine Ledford, 67–84. Lexington: University Press of Kentucky, 1999.

———. "Exterminating Savages: The Union Army and Mountain Guerrillas in Southern West Virginia, 1861–1862." In *The Civil War in Appalachia: Collected Essays*, edited by Kenneth W. Noe and Shannon H. Wilson, 104–27. Knoxville: University of Tennessee Press, 1997.

Norton, Herman. "Revivalism in the Confederate Armies." *Civil War History* 6 (December 1960): 410–24.

Norton, Mary Beth. "Eighteenth-Century American Women in Peace and War: The Case of the Loyalists." *William and Mary Quarterly* 33 (1976): 386–409.

Ownby, Ted. "Patriarchy in the World Where There Is No Parting?: Power Relations in the Confederate Heaven." In *Southern Families at War: Loyalty and Conflict in the Civil War South*, edited by Catherine Clinton, 229–50. New York: Oxford University Press, 2000.

Pierson, Michael D. " 'Guard the Foundation Well': Antebellum New York Democrats and the Defense of Patriarchy." *Gender and History* 7 (April 1995): 25–40.

Potter, David M. "The Historians' Use of Nationalism and Vice Versa." In *The South and the Sectional Conflict*, 34–84. Baton Rouge: Louisiana State University Press, 1968.

Preisser, Thomas M. "The Virginia Decision to Use Negro Soldiers in the Civil War, 1864–1865." *Virginia Magazine of History and Biography* 83 (January 1975): 98–113.

Rice, Harvey M. "Jonathan M. Bennett and Virginia's Wartime Finances." *West Virginia History* 4 (October 1942), 5–20.

Riggs, David F. "Robert Young Conrad and the Ordeal of Secession." *Virginia Magazine of History and Biography* 86 (July 1978): 259–74.

Roberts, Giselle. " 'Our Cause': Southern Women and Confederate Nationalism in Mississippi and Louisiana." *Journal of Mississippi History* 62 (Summer 2000): 97–121.

Robinson, Armstead L. "In the Shadow of John Brown: Insurrection Anxiety and Confederate Mobilization, 1861–1863." *Journal of Negro History* 65 (Autumn 1980): 279–97.

Rosenwein, Barbara H. "Worrying about Emotions in History." *American Historical Review* 107 (June 2002): 821–45.

Rubin, Anne. "Between Union and Chaos: The Political Life of John Janney." *Virginia Magazine of History and Biography* 102 (Summer 1994): 381–416.

Scheiber, Harry N. "The Pay of Confederate Troops and Problems of Demoralization." *Civil War History* 15 (September 1969): 226–36.

Schlotterbeck, John T. "The 'Social Economy' of an Upper South Community: Orange and Greene Counties, Virginia, 1815–1860." In *Class, Conflict and Consensus: Antebellum Southern Community Studies*, edited by Orville Vernon Burton and Robert C. McMath Jr., 3–28. Westport, Conn.: Greenwood Press, 1982.

Scott, Joan Wallach. "Gender: A Useful Category of Historical Analysis." *American Historical Review* 91 (December 1986): 1053–75.

Sevy, Roland Lee. "John Letcher and West Virginia." *West Virginia History* 27 (October 1965): 10–55.

Shaffer, John W. "Loyalties in Conflict: Union and Confederate Sentiment in Barbour County." *West Virginia History* 50 (1991): 109–28.

Simmons, J. Susanne, and Nancy T. Sorrells. "Slave Hire and the Development of Slavery in Augusta County, Virginia." In *After the Backcountry: Rural Life in the*

Great Valley of Virginia, 1800–1900, edited by Kenneth E. Koons and Warren R. Hofstra, 169–85. Knoxville: University of Tennessee Press, 2000.

Smith, David G. "Race and Retaliation: The Capture of African Americans during the Gettysburg Campaign." In *Virginia's Civil War*, edited by Peter Wallenstein and Bertram Wyatt-Brown, 137–51. Charlottesville: University of Virginia Press, 2005.

Smith, David P. "Conscription and Conflict on the Texas Frontier, 1863–1865." *Civil War History* 36 (September 1990), 250–61.

Stout, Harry S., and Christopher Grasso. "Civil War, Religion, and Communications: The Case of Richmond." In *Religion and the American Civil War*, edited by Randall M. Miller, Harry S. Stout, Charles Regan Wilson, 313–59. New York: Oxford University Press, 1998.

Stowe, Steven. "Private Emotions and a Public Man in Early Nineteenth-Century Virginia." *History of Education Quarterly* 27 (Spring 1989): 323–33.

Sutherland, Daniel E. "The Absence of Violence: Confederates and Unionists in Culpeper County." In *Guerrillas, Unionists, and Violence on the Confederate Home Front*, 75–87. Fayetteville: University of Arkansas Press, 1999.

Talbott, Forrest. "Some Legislative and Legal Aspects of the Negro Question in West Virginia during the Civil War and Reconstruction." *West Virginia History* 24 (October 1962): 1–32.

Watson, Harry L. "Conflict and Collaboration: Yeoman, Slaveholders and Politics in the Antebellum South." *Social History* 10 (Fall 1985): 273–98.

Watson, Samuel J. "Flexible Gender Roles during the Market Revolution: Family, Friendship, Marriage, and Masculinity among U.S. Army Officers, 1815–1846." *Journal of Social History* 29 (Fall 1995): 81–106.

——. "Religion and Combat Motivation in the Confederate Armies." *Journal of Military History* 58 (January 1994): 29–55.

Wight, Willard E. "The Churches and the Confederate Cause." *Civil War History* 6 (December 1960): 361–73.

Williams, John Alexander. "Class, Section, and Culture in Nineteenth-Century West Virginia Politics." In *Appalachia in the Making: The Mountain South in the Nineteenth Century*, edited by Mary Beth Pudup, Dwight B. Billings, and Altina L. Waller, 210–32. Chapel Hill: University of North Carolina, 1995.

Wyatt-Brown, Bertram. "God and Honor in the Old South." *Southern Review* 25 (April 1989): 283–98.

——. "Honor and Secession." In *Yankee Saints and Southern Sinners*, 183–213. Baton Rouge: Louisiana State University Press, 1985.

Yacovone, Donald. "Abolitionists and the 'Language of Fraternal Love.'" In *Meanings for Manhood: Constructions of Masculinity in Victorian America*, edited by Mark C. Marnes and Clyde Griffen, 85–95. Chicago: University of Chicago Press, 1990.

Theses, Dissertations, and Unpublished Papers

Blake, Russell Lindley. "Ties of Intimacy: Social Values and Personal Relationships of Antebellum Slaveholders." Ph.D. diss., University of Michigan, 1978.

Dillard, Philip D. "Independence or Slavery: The Confederate Debate over Arming the Slaves." Ph.D. diss., Rice University, 1999.

Frank, Lisa Tendrich. " 'To Cure Her of Her Pride and Boasting': The Gendered Implications of Sherman's March." Ph.D. diss., University of Florida, 2001.

Greenwood, Neil Voss. "Opponents in the Valley: A Study of the Attitudes and Views of Union and Confederate Soldiers Who Participated in the 1864 Shenandoah Valley Campaign." Ph.D. diss., University of California, Los Angeles, 1992.

Hsieh, Wayne. "Stern Soldiers Weeping: Confederate Clergymen and the Civil War." Master's thesis, University of Virginia, 2002.

Mangus, Michael Stuart. " 'The Debatable Land': Loudoun and Fauquier Counties, Virginia during the Civil War Era." Ph.D. diss., Ohio State University, 1998.

Manning, Chandra Miller. "What This Cruel War Was Over: Union and Confederate Soldiers on the Meaning of the Civil War." Ph.D. diss., Harvard University, 2002.

Morsman, Amy Feely. "The Big House after Slavery: Virginia's Plantation Elites and Their Postbellum Domestic Experiment." Ph.D. diss., University of Virginia, 2004.

Ruffner, Kevin. " 'A Dreadful Affect upon Good Soldiers': A Study of Desertion in a Confederate Regiment." Master's thesis, University of Virginia, 1987.

Schlotterbeck, John T. "Plantation and Farm: Social and Economic Change in Orange and Greene Counties, Virginia, 1716–1860." Ph.D. diss., Johns Hopkins University, 1980.

Steger, Werner H. " 'United to Support, but Not Combined to Injure': Free Workers and Immigrants in Richmond, Virginia, during the Era of Sectionalism, 1847–1865." Ph.D. diss., George Washington University, 1999.

Troutman, Phillip Davis. "Slave Trade and Sentiment in Antebellum Virginia." Ph.D. diss., University of Virginia, 2000.

INDEX

Confederate States of America: boundaries with the Union, 41–42, 44; centralizing policies of, 79, 128, 190; collapse of, 178–79, 189–90; foreign recognition of, 65, 89; manpower issues and, 47, 73, 118; nationalism, 9–10, 60–62, 70–71, 79–80, 108–9, 111–12, 116–17, 132, 141, 244 (n. 69); patterns of support and opposition for, within Virginia, 2–7, 13, 21–37 passim; Virginia troops join, 20–21. *See also* Class; Draft; Family; Habeas corpus; Impressment; Soldiers, Virginia: motivation

Conrad, Robert, 160

Conscription. *See* Draft

Conscripts, 171

Contraband, 99. *See also* Slaves, runaway

Cooley, John T., 146, 167

Corson, William, 155, 167, 170

Craig, John Anthony, 170

Culpeper County, 100, 117

Daily Richmond Examiner, 47, 99, 113, 144, 168

Dana, Charles, 162

Davidson, Charles, 16

Davidson, James, 128–29, 167

Davis, Creed, 152, 189

Davis, Jefferson, 40, 92, 115–16, 130–31

Democratic Party, 2, 20, 176

Deserter bands, 178

Desertion, 81, 91–96, 102–3, 105–6, 133, 145–47, 178–80; amnesty for, 130; establishing definitions of, 48, 50–41; quantitative data on, 3, 227 (n. 17). *See also* Draft; Soldiers, Virginia: morale; Soldiers, Virginia: motivation

Disease, 43–44, 104, 143

Dorman, James, 15–16

Downman, Raleigh, 98, 144–45

Draft, 6, 40, 65–68, 73, 94, 103, 144, 217 (nn. 26, 28); exemptions from, 102, 177; implementation of, 47–53, 113–14, 176–77, 217 (n. 27); soldiers' responses to, 48–50, 62, 80. *See also* Desertion; Soldiers, Virginia: social pressure to serve

Draft riots (New York City), 127–28

Dulany, Richard, 151, 157, 172–73

Early, Jubal A., 158, 161–63, 168–70, 176. *See also* Shenandoah Valley: 1864 invasion of

Edmondson, James, 137, 163

Emancipation, 2, 5, 113, 123, 155, 184–85, 192–93. *See also* Slavery; Soldiers, Virginia: motivation; Soldiers, Virginia: and slavery

Emancipation Proclamation, 5, 77, 88, 98–100. *See also* Emancipation

Engineer Corps, Confederate, 177

Enlistment, Confederate, 1, 3, 13, 68–69; of nonslaveholders, 1, 18. *See also* Desertion; Soldiers, Virginia: motivation

Evans, Maurice, 45

Executions, 96, 145–46

Ezell, William, 81–82

Family, 2, 7, 9, 27, 58–60, 62, 132–37, 153; and desertion, 91–92, 94, 103–5, 112; effect of the war upon, 193–95. *See also* Soldiers, Virginia: and families; Soldiers, Virginia: motivation

Fauquier County, 117

Fisher's Hill, battle of, 170

Fitz, J. C., 98

Floyd, John B. 44

Peek, William, 75, 125

Pendleton, Alexander "Sandie," 70, 74, 76, 110

Pendleton, John Barrett, 62

Pendleton, Philip, 148

Pennsylvania, 122–25

Petersburg, 71, 166, 171–73, 177–81, 189

Peyton, George Quintis, 142, 166–67

Philippi, battle of, 41

Phillips, James, 191

Pickett, George S., 108

Piedmont, battle of, 16

Pocahontas County, 44

Pope, John, 77, 88–89, 162

Powers, Philip, 46, 144

Prisoners, 126–27, 156

Quakers, 76

Race, 17, 18, 123–24, 153–55, 171, 185, 193. *See also* Emancipation; Slavery; Soldiers, Virginia: and slavery

Rapidan River, 53, 143

Rappahannock County, 117

Reenlistment, 49, 52, 66–67, 142

Religion, 4, 21, 46–47, 51, 83, 119, 149; revivals, 109–15, 130–31

Republican Party, 14, 17, 19, 20, 30, 61, 77, 88

Rich Mountain, battle of, 44

Richmond, 15, 19, 44, 48, 65, 71, 79, 81, 147, 149, 189

Richmond Bread Riot, 115–16. *See also* Civilians, Virginia: and hardship; Civilians, Virginia: morale

Richmond Enquirer, 33, 50–51

Richmond Sentinel, 154

Ridley, William, 80

Roane City, 31

Robertson, Littleton, 48

Rockbridge County, 15, 16, 21, 52, 107

Rockingham County, 24

Rosecrans, William, 44

Ruffin, Edmund, 29, 34

Sacrifice, 5, 83–85, 108–10, 187. *See also* Confederate States of America: nationalism; Soldiers, Virginia

Saylor's Creek, battle of, 189

Secession, 15–16, 19, 20, 23

Seddon, John A., 167

Seven Days, battles of, 82–83

Seward, William, 41

Sharpsburg. *See* Antietam, battle of

Shenandoah Valley, 43, 53, 60, 65, 71, 100, 107, 120, 126, 129, 158; enlistment within, 23, 25; secession of, 15; trade within, 19; 1862 invasion of, 71–78; 1864 invasion of, 163, 166–70

Sheridan, Philip H., 77, 168–69, 182. *See also* Shenandoah Valley: 1864 invasion of

Sherman, William T., 77, 176, 178

Sigel, Franz, 158

Slaveholders, 16, 31, 34–35

Slavery, 1, 4, 5, 13, 17, 18, 19, 77, 103, 184, 250 (n. 62); condition of, during war, 102, 112–23, 116, 153–55, 169, 193; effect of, on Confederate enlistment, 31–35. *See also* Emancipation; Race; Soldiers, Virginia: and slavery

Slaves, runaway, 76, 98–99; enlistment as Confederate soldiers, 184–87

Smith, J. G., 146

Smith, William Randolph, 49

Soldiers, Virginia: alienation from civilians, 156–57, 171–73, 192, 242 (n. 49); assessments of battle, 45–46, 73, 81–83, 90, 98, 118–19, 124–25, 129–30,

148, 170–72; average age, 135; campaigning, 74, 97, 157, 166–67; and camp life, 53, 143, 179; and defense of state, 77–78; and discipline, 54–58, 72–73, 93–94, 132, 146; and disputes between branches, 170; and domesticity, 58–59; effect of hard war on, 106–10; and families, 62, 132–37, 190–91; and ideology, 29, 61–62; and invasion of the North, 91, 121–24, 240 (n. 19); morale, 40–41, 53–54, 70–71, 74, 80, 81–82, 102–3, 105, 110, 114–15, 122, 124, 126, 129, 132, 142, 144–45, 147, 149–52, 161, 166–67, 169–83 passim, 191–92; motivation, 1–3, 6, 13, 17, 20–21 37, 66, 71, 87–88, 174–75, 187, 190–91; and officer elections, 55–56, 67–68, 221 (n. 5); and political rights, 2, 3, 16; and punishments, 73, 94, 114; and slavery, 31–35, 98–100, 184; and social pressure to serve, 23, 28; and violence of war, 82, 89, 98, 118, 123, 149–51, 182, 193. *See also* Class; Confederate States of America: nationalism; Desertion; Emancipation; Family; Hard War; Religion; Slavery; Virginia Troops
Southern Literary Messenger, 84
Southwestern Virginia, 23, 33
Spotsylvania, battle of, 148
State rights, 29–30
Staunton, 23, 158
Stephens, Alexander, 33, 157
Stiles, Joseph Clay, 99
Stiles, Randolph, 105
Stuart, J. E. B., 83
Sublett, Thomas, 96
Substitution, 51, 97, 143–44, 155–56
Suffolk, 71
Surrender, 191–92

Tax policy, 142
Tennessee, 8
Thompson, John R., 84
Thompson, Robert L., 125
Tidewater Virginia, 71, 82
Troop strength, 252 (n. 4)
Tschiffel, Edgar, 191–92
Twenty-slave law, 103, 229 (n. 49)
Tynes, Achilles, 162

Unionists, 41–44; and secession, 14, 15, 24, 27, 120, 151
Unit resolutions, 173–75
Updike, Amon, 159, 179–80

Vicksburg, Miss., fall of, 127
Virginia: agricultural reform in, 19; conditions in, 75–76, 101–2, 106, 115–17, 128; distribution of wealth within, 35–36; drought, of 1864, 159–60; economic development in, 19–20; enlistment patterns in, 3, 13, 25, 28–38, 206 (n. 5), 211 (nn. 42, 46), 212 (n. 49); military fortunes within, in 1861, 4, 5, 39; military fortunes within, in 1862, 78, 87, 92, 95, 107; military fortunes within, in 1863, 111–12, 117–18, 125–26; military fortunes within, in 1864, 141, 148, 161–62, 165–66, 169–70; military fortunes within, in 1865, 175–77; politics in, 16; regional tensions within, 16, 43, 71; relief programs of, 100; secession of, 14–16, 25–27; as subject of study, 7, 8. *See also* Central Virginia; Civilians, Virginia; Hard War; Northwest Virginia; Shenandoah Valley; Soldiers, Virginia; Southwestern Virginia; Tidewater Virginia; Western Virginia
Virginia Military Institute, 61, 158, 161

Virginia troops
—Artillery: 1st, 54; 10th, 129; 19th Battalion, 191; Fluvanna Battery, 161; Richmond Howitzers, 18
—Cavalry: 1st, 29; 2nd, 174; 3rd, 97–98, 170; 4th, 98, 144; 5th, 84–85; 7th, 43, 143, 157; 8th, 167, 172; 35th Battalion, 150; 37th Battalion, 146
—Infantry: 1st, 54; 1st Brigade, 27; 4th, 56, 125; 6th, 91–92; 8th, 174; 9th, 66–67, 91–92, 173–74; 10th, 142; 11th, 57, 158; 13th, 142; 18th, 48, 174; 21st, 180–81; 23rd, 57, 123; 24th, 185; 26th, 91–92, 183; 27th, 72–73, 136–37; 30th, 55–56; 38th, 23; 41st, 70–71; 46th, 43, 67; 51st, 146; 52nd, 114; 56th, 103–4
Volunteers, 2, 68. *See also* Enlistment

Wade, Benjamin F., 61
Waldrop, Richard, 55, 61–62, 180–82

Walters, John, 189
Warren, Edward T., 122, 152
Washington, D.C., 45; Confederate attack on, 162
Washington, William, 84
Watkins, C. B., 17
Watkins, Richard, 152, 168, 184
Welsh, John, 136–37
Welsh, Rebecca, 136–37
Western Virginia, 41–44, 161
Whig Party, 2, 16
White, James Jones, 56
Whiting, Julia, 151
Wilderness, battle of, 148
Williamsburg, battle of, 80–81
Wilson, Daniel A., 176
Winchester, 43, 53, 175–76, 160, 169
Winchester Republican, 34
Winfield, John, 43, 45
Wise, Henry, 44
Woolwine, Rufus, 146